2013

NEW PLAYWRIGHTS: THE BEST PLAYS

# 2013
## NEW PLAYWRIGHTS: THE BEST PLAYS

Edited and with a Foreword
by Lawrence Harbison

Smith and Kraus Publishers

ISSN: 978-1-57525-867-6
ISBN: 1-57525-867-6


Typesetting and layout by Elizabeth E. Monteleone
Cover by Borderlands Press

Photo Credit:
Lisa D'Amour photo by: Zach Smith
Colman Domingo photo by: Paul Gregory
Greg Kalleres photo by: Stuart Jennings
Hamish Linklater photo by: Larry Busacca/Getty Images North America
Laura Marks photo by: Nasilele Photography
Anne García-Romero photo by: Barbara Johnston/University of Notre Dame
C. Denby Swanson photo by: Brett Brookshire

A Smith and Kraus book
177 Lyme Road, Hanover, NH 03755
editorial 603-643-6431 To Order 1-877-668-8680
www.smithandkraus.com

# TABLE OF CONTENTS

# Foreword

I am often asked, "Who do you consider a 'New Playwright?'" For the purposes of this annual anthology, which I have edited for Smith and Kraus since 2000, I consider a "New Playwright" to be one I've never heard of, or who I may have heard of but have never seen a play of his/hers. Then, I choose the plays which I think represent the best in contemporary American playwriting. I try to include plays written in a wide variety of styles. I always try to include some comedies if I can, though it's usually hard to find these as comedies are usually only desirable to American theatres if they are "dark comedies." Fun is out—angst is in. This year, though, I found three wonderful comedies, though none are what you could remotely call "fluff."

Six of the seven plays in this volume played in New York, though none on Broadway. I read a lot of fine plays produced outside of New York, and seriously considered them all, but ultimately I had to go with the New York plays. Why? Because I just thought they were the best.

Among these is Julia Marks' *Bethany*, produced by the exemplary Women's Project, about a woman who has lost everything—her home, her job, even her 5 year-old daughter. When we meet her, she's living as a squatter in a foreclosed house which has another month's worth of electricity, and has gotten a job at a Saturn auto dealership. If she manages to make a sale, she can demonstrate to the Child Welfare Agency that she is capable of caring for her daughter, Bethany. The first name of the actress who played Our Heroine was particularly appropriate— she was America Ferrera, of "Ugly Betty" fame—because this play is truly about what has happened to this country, in which the "American Dream" seems a relic of the distant past.

Lisa D'Amour's *Detroit*, at Playwrights Horizons, is about two couples, neighbors whose economic prospects are bleak.

Like *Bethany*, it tapped into the *zeitgeist* of dread we are all feeling these days, as we watch helplessly as the American middle class goes down the tubes. *Detroit* was a finalist for the Pulitzer Prize.

Greg Kalleres' *Honky*, produced at Urban Stages, is a comedy about a sneaker manufacturer determined to break into the "urban market"—i.e., black teenagers—because if they do, suburban white kids will want their shoes, too. Who would have thought that the subject of race could be so funny?

C. Denby Swanson's *The Norwegians*, produced by the Drilling Company, was also a hilarious comedy about a distraught Minnesota woman who wants to hire two Norwegian hit men to whack her ex. Will Tor and Gus take her on as a client? And, if they do, will she go through with it?

Anne García-Romero's *Paloma*, the sole play in this book not produced in New York, is a powerful drama about a pair of star-crossed lovers. She's a Catholic—he's a Muslim. It was produced in Albuquerque, NM by Camino Real Productions.

Hamish Linklater's *The Vandal*, produced by the Flea Theatre, was a haunting drama about three lost souls—a lonely middle-aged woman, a teenaged boy and the boy's father, a bar owner. The boy strikes up a conversation with the woman at a bus stop. He's a garrulous kid, but more than what he seems. This touching play marked the playwriting debut of one of NYC's finest actors.

Speaking of plays by actors, *Wild with Happy*, produced by the Public Theater, is another one. Colman Domingo, the playwright, wrote a terrific role for himself, a gay actor named Gil whose mother passes away. Gil goes on an epic journey to Disney World, accompanied by a flamboyant friend named Mo, there to scatter Mom's ashes. Hot on his trail is his eccentric aunt, who's determined to thwart his plan. *Wild with Happy* is wonderfully funny.

Well, there you have it—he best damn plays by "New Playwrights" I could find this season. I hope you like them as much as I do.

*Lawrence Harbison*
New York, New York

# INTRODUCTION

Why is it that when I started writing no one was available to take me aside and tell me frankly that writing plays can be the worst thing on earth?

It's lonely, it's undervalued, you're not well paid for it—you're lucky if you're paid at all—and the lifetime attendance of even a wildly successful play will never equal one viewing of the worst-rated television show. And when someone asks what you do—no matter how much you try to puff out your chest and say with pride, *I'm a writer*, you're always met with the horrible question, *What kind of writer*. When you say *Playwright* you're either met with a glassy stare or the same sort of amused pitying look a child is given when they announce they're off the join the circus.

Another thing nobody told me when I started writing was that it would take me thirteen years of doing it before I landed my first professional production. Some people get lucky and have a production after two or three years. Many playwrights never have a production. As for me, no matter how I say it I still can't believe it: Thirteen years. One three. Ten plus three. Six long hard years . . . and then *seven more of them.* —That's how long it took. Not to make a living, mind you, this was just to get produced.

No, after that first professional run of mine, at the Humana Festival of New American Plays in 2006, I realized making a living was pretty much off the table when an envelope came for me about five weeks after the play closed, and inside was a check for $2300. Two thousand three hundred dollars. I almost committed suicide. *And I was one of the lucky few.* What's sad—or is it amusing?—is that I guarantee there's a playwright reading this right now who's laughing, saying *Oh ho ho, that's not going to happen to me!* Well let me tell you something, Mr.

or Ms. Laughing Playwright: I hope not being able to make a living *does* happen to you. Because that would mean *you're one of the lucky few.*

If you're a playwright, you've got a box somewhere with hundreds of rejections in it (OK, perhaps fewer in Hamish Linklater or Colman Domingo's box, both of whom are represented in this collection—but it takes a special brand of balls for a well-known performer to put himself out there the way Linklater has done with *The Vandal*, and it takes a rarer-still dose of courage to act in your own work, like Domingo has . . . and oh yeah, they both happen to be wonderful plays). Most of these rejections are form letters ; some typewritten, a few handwritten . . . stock replies from a hidden handful of overworked, underpaid dramaturges (all right, there *is* one thing harder than being a playwright) who work for mostly regional theatres, most of which are one ill-attended play away from closing their doors and shutting off their lights forever.

Many of us, in desperate moments, have embarrassed ourselves to these desperately underfunded theatres who can't afford to take a chance on us. I sent a letter to one theatre, a long letter—this was in 1997, only four years into my long journey—begging. Pleading. Just give me a reply. Give me a break. Give me anything (I'm glad there was no reply). To another very prominent New York theatre who *did* give me a hand-written no-thank-you I sent a vitriolic broadside. Some phrase had offended me, and I was still that "*Oh ho ho!*" playwright I mentioned above, though perhaps one who was on the verge of feeling the edges of the cage in which I had trapped myself. —Even in 1997 I was beginning to feel the impossibility of what I had embarked on. Little did I know that in 1997 I was barely halfway through the beginning of what I had begun.

Needless to say, I spent many, many days coming up with reasons why I couldn't seem to get a play read by a theatre. This is something I now call *The Tyranny of Because*, which is an especially potent affliction among the ranks of playwrights. I told myself I wasn't getting produced because I didn't go to Brown. Or NYU, or Yale, or Julliard. I can't get a break, I insisted, because none of the breaks go to white males (yes, holy crap, I *actually* said that to myself!). It is easy to let The Tyranny of

Because lead you into the deep woods, and my brand of tyranny led me deeper and deeper: because, because, because.

It goes without saying that when we're unproduced we also love to invert The Tyranny of Because. We love to say "That writer's being produced because they're . . ." fill in the blank. Because they're white. Black. Male. Female. Famous, son or daughter of famous, daughter of artist, son of director, in bed with someone, in bed with everyone.

What The Tyranny of Because does, though, is allow you to hide from the one and only truth that matters as a writer. It's pretty much the only truth there is, and it's an ugly one. Here it is: If you're a playwright and you haven't been produced, it's not because—OK, and I'm going to catch flak for this—it's not because you're white. It's not because you're a man. It's not because you're black. And it's not because you're a woman. It's not because life is hard for you, your checking account is overdrawn, you haven't been to the gym, you lost your wallet, your eyes are set minutely too far apart, you've got that damned hangnail, or you're potassium-deficient. It's not because some faceless "them", or "the dramaturges", or "the theatre world" are excluding you: It's you.

Why The Tyranny of Because is so dangerous is that it keeps us from pushing ourselves back from our desks, having a long hard look at ourselves in the mirror, and admitting to ourselves "I'm not being produced because I'm not a good enough writer yet."

Sorry, young me in 1997: you weren't a good enough writer yet. Sorry, older me in 2004: you weren't a good enough writer yet. Maybe I'm still not and I've fooled a few people. Certainly on certain projects I'm absolutely not good enough. There are so many things I don't yet know how to accomplish. Every day I get myself into the deep woods and aren't yet good enough to find my way out.

But to me, there's a crucial word here. It's the word "yet". In the word *yet* is great promise, but also great demand. You could say it's also a threat and a portent. *Yet* demands hundreds, even thousands of hours of work. *Yet* demands an alarm set for five, a big pot of coffee and a sharp slap on the cheek—every day. *Yet* demands humility, and self-reflection, and the willingness to actively search for the flaws in your work. But only when you feed its demands are you allowed its promise. The threat and the portent inherent in *yet* are the simple fact that if you do not feed it, that promise will never come.

What I love about the Smith & Kraus *New Playwrights Best Plays* series is that it acts like a lone sentry, scanning the terrain for survivors. Every year battalions of writers march into the woods, and every year, a few hungry stragglers make their way out. These survivors are the *Yets* of American playwrighting. They're good enough yet. And they'll be even better yet.

Certainly not every new playwright of worth is represented in these volumes. In fact, most of them are not. And gladly, neither are the best-reviewed writers. During the year I was published, in 2006, the New York Times pretty much peed on my play *Six Years*. And the good lads at The Grey Lady ripped my fellow publishee, John Cariani, from balls to crown that year. (The irony of course is that one survives the wilderness only to face a machine-gunning from the critics—but hey, you wanted to be produced, right? So get ready to duck.)

It's a delicious turn of events and vindication for everyone who believes in him that John's play *Almost Maine* has gone on to be the most produced play in America. Young actors and actresses everywhere are being introduced to theatre through his play. And my play that year . . . Well all right. So *other* plays of mine have done well enough to excuse Smith & Kraus's including me. But the point is, editor Larry Harbison, who reads everything, sees everything, considers everything, chooses writers not based on popularity, or reviews, or success, but whom he feels demand attention from us.

And the fact is, attention must be paid to any volume that would place Lisa D'Amour's juggernaut *Detroit* in the same collection as C. Denby Swenson's *The Norwegians*—this season's mouse that roared. Or Laura Mark's *Bethany*—the rare piece that can comment on the financial events of *now* on people's lives without crossing the line into preachy—along with Greg Kelleres' *Honky*, the rare play about race (and by a white guy) that manages to tackle truths without failing to be hilarious; or Anne García-Romero's modern *Romeo and Juliet* tale *Paloma*, which yearns earnestly for a world in which love is paramount.

These are bold choices plucked from an exceptionally strong season of playwrighting debuts. Read them, love them, don't love them, argue about their inclusion here . . . the one thing you can't do is ignore them. These playwrights have each, one way or another, had their descent into their own dark forest. They have kept going in the face of the perennial warnings about the lives of playwrights, the death of theatre, the wide-eyed tales of riches to be made in other mediums, and the thousands of other reasons we all have every day to stop what we're doing—or worse, to not even begin.

Like the old saw that it takes years of work to become an overnight success, these are writers who are being called new only because, this season, they became new to us.

*Sharr White*
Cold Spring, New York

**SHARR WHITE'S** SIX YEARS premiered at the Humana Festival in 2006 and is included in *New Playwrights: The Best Plays of 2006*. His THE OTHER PLACE premiered Off Broadway in 2011 at the Lucille Lortel Theatre, produced by MCC Theatre, and was presented in 2012 on Broadway by Manhattan Theatre Club at the Samuel J. Friedman Theatre. Both productions starred Laurie Metcalf. His latest play, THE SNOW GEESE, opened on Broadway (also by Manhattan Theatre Club, at the Friedman Theatre) in October of 2013, starring Mary Louise Parker.

# BETHANY

*Laura Marks*

The World Premiere of BETHANY was in New York City by

WOMEN'S PROJECT THEATER

Julie Crosby, Producing Artistic Director

Opening Night: January 20, 2013
City Center Stage II, New York City

Cast in Alphabetical Order:
        SHANNON: Emily Ackerman
        CRYSTAL: America Ferrera
        PATRICIA: Kristin Griffith
        CHARLIE: Ken Marks
        GARY: Tobias Segal
        TONI: Myra Lucretia Taylor

Directed by Gaye Taylor Upchurch

Scenic Design by Lauren Helpern
Costume Design by Sarah J. Holden
Lighting Design by Mark Barton
Sound Design by Leon Rothenberg

**LAURA MARKS** is a resident playwright at New Dramatists and an alumna of the Juilliard School and the Public Theater's Emerging Writers Group. Her play Bethany received a 2013 World Premiere in New York by the Women's Project, directed by Gaye Taylor Upchurch, starring America Ferrera. Bethany received Lucille Lortel nominations for Outstanding Play and Outstanding Lead Actress, won the Leah Ryan Prize for Emerging Women Writers, was a Susan Smith Blackburn finalist and runner-up for the Yale prize, and will have its West Coast premiere at the Old Globe in early 2014. Ms. Marks is also the recipient of a Lilly Award, a Helen Merrill Award a commission from South Coast Repertory and an award from the Fellowship of Southern Writers. Other plays include Mine (produced by the Gift Theatre, Chicago) and Gather at the River (workshopped at TheatreWorks, Palo Alto). Her work has been developed at the Public Theater, Juilliard, the Lark, the Black Dahlia, Manhattan Theatre Club, the Royal Exchange Theatre (UK), HighTide Festival Theatre (UK), the Wilma Theater, Steppenwolf, Partial Comfort, Prospect Theater, Naked Angels, Synchronicity, Reverie Productions et al. She's a native of Kentucky, now living in New York.

CHARACTERS (in order of appearance):

CHARLIE
CRYSTAL
GARY
SHANNON
TONI
PATRICIA

TIME: Early 2009.

PLACE: The exurbs of a small city in America.

> *"Do you know the definition of charisma?*
> *Believing in your own bullshit!"*
>
> —Lukas Foss

# PROLOGUE.

*(A middle-aged man stands facing out, giving a speech. His style is presentational, yet intimate and folksy—think Rick Warren at Saddleback.*

CHARLIE: There's a reason you're here today.

You might not believe that, but I do.

You see, there's a higher power that guides our destiny.

I don't care if you call it God or Yahweh or Uncle Fred, doesn't matter.

And I'll tell you one thing about this higher power:

He wants you to be rich.

Rich beyond your wildest dreams.

He doesn't want you to lie awake all night, wondering how you're gonna make that mortgage payment when your kid's college tuition is due, and your credit cards are already maxed to the limit.

You know, last year, in the town where I live, over thirty-five thousand people lost their homes to foreclosure. Thirty-five thousand!

There are some neighborhoods where you can go for a walk and you won't hardly see *anyone*.

And do you know what's the saddest part about all that?

Those people could have saved their homes . . . if they'd known the secrets that I'm about to share with you today.

These secrets are as old as the hills, and more powerful than a thunderstorm.

They're the reason that I live in a beautiful five-bedroom home with a hot tub, and a flat-screen TV, and everything else a man could ever want.

If you've been living a life based on hard work, and anxiety, or even fear,

your life is about to change forever.

So if you haven't already, open up your notebooks;

and while you're at it, open up your minds.

*(He pauses for a moment and peers strait ahead—straightens his tie, picks food out of his teeth. It's clear now that he's actually been giving this speech to himself, in a mirror.)*

CHARLIE: *(to himself)* That's when I should do that thing with the kazoos.

---

*Laura Marks*

## Scene One.

*(Night. The empty, eat-in kitchen of a small house in the suburbs. Built-in cabinets but no furniture. The counters are bare except for a pile of mail. After some lengthy fumbling with the sliding-glass door, a woman enters from outside. She has a small wheeled suitcase, purse and garment bag. She's conservatively dressed, in a suit jacket, skirt and heels, and attractive.*

*She puts down her things. She's cautious, listening. Turns on the small light over the stove. Quickly looks through the pile of mail. She opens the refrigerator and realizes it's not running. As she kneels down to check the plug, she suddenly stops.)*

CRYSTAL: Hello?

*(No answer. She plugs in the fridge. There's an audible hum as it starts to run. She opens the refrigerator again, and this time the light comes on. It takes a few seconds for her to notice the man who has silently entered the room.)*

| CRYSTAL: | GARY: |
|---|---|
| Oh my God— | It's okay— |

| CRYSTAL: | GARY: |
|---|---|
| Oh, I'm so sorry— | Shh. It's okay, I'm going— |

CRYSTAL: You know? I think—I, I, I must have just wandered into the wrong house by mistake, I'm so terribly sorry, I'll just be on my—

*(A long moment while they stare at each other.)*

CRYSTAL: *(Grabbing something from her purse.)*
I have pepper spray.

GARY: I won't hurt you.

CRYSTAL: I'll just get my things here—

GARY: You don't have to go. I'm leaving right now.

CRYSTAL: What are you saying?

GARY: It's okay. You don't have to call the police.

CRYSTAL: I'm sorry, what's the deal? Do you live here?

GARY: No. Do you?

CRYSTAL: . . .Yes. I mean—
Not exactly, but my friend. It belongs to my friend.

GARY: What's his name?

CRYSTAL: Joe. Parker.

*(Pause. He laughs.)*

CRYSTAL: What?

GARY: You got that from looking at the mail.

CRYSTAL: It's true. Joe is my boyfriend.

GARY: Joe is eighty.

*(pause)*

CRYSTAL: What are you doing here?

GARY: I just need a place to lay my head.

I won't bother you.

You won't need your "pepper spray".

*(pause)*

CRYSTAL: It's really just breath spray.

*(She sprays some in her mouth.)*

CRYSTAL: Fresh breath is important in my line of work.

GARY: What do you do?

CRYSTAL: Sales. You?

*(He laughs. From the looks of him, he hasn't held a job in quite a while. She laughs too, nervously.)*

GARY: What?

*(She shuts the refrigerator door.)*

CRYSTAL: It's good that the electric still works. He's only been gone a few days, right?

GARY: More like a week.

CRYSTAL: That makes sense. Who wants to wait around for the marshals?

GARY: Do you know how much he owed?

CRYSTAL: No.

GARY: Two hundred and fifty-four thousand.

CRYSTAL: Unbelievable. Did he have a line of credit?

GARY: How can people be so dumb?

CRYSTAL: He might have been sick.

GARY: He might have been stupid.

CRYSTAL: Well, why don't you go buy a house someday and show us all how it works.

*(Pause. She backs away slightly.)*

GARY: Do I smell bad?

CRYSTAL: No— not really, I can't really tell—

GARY: I haven't been showering.

CRYSTAL: Is the water shut off already?

GARY: No. Sometimes I just forget.

*(A pause while she looks at him, weighing her options.)*

CRYSTAL: Where are you sleeping?

GARY: Upstairs. So I guess you could have the downstairs if you want. The living room carpet is pretty soft.

CRYSTAL: How long do you think— I mean—

GARY: Water should stay on until the end of the month. Electric, who knows. Eventually the bank'll put it up for auction, but at this point it might not be worth the trouble.

*(She's silent, considering.)*

CRYSTAL: What's your name?

GARY: Gary.

CRYSTAL: Hi Gary. I'm Crystal.

*(She initiates a handshake. Pause. She reaches into her purse, gets out a packet of nuts and opens it.)*

CRYSTAL: Are you hungry? Here:

*(She hands him the packet. He pours some into his hand and wolfs them down.)*

GARY: Thanks.

*(He offers the packet back to her.)*

CRYSTAL: Go ahead, have the rest. I already had Quizno's.

*(pause)*

CRYSTAL: Oh Christ. I can't do this. Fuck, fuck fuck fuck fuck.

*(She starts frantically gathering her things. A contradictory impulse stops her. She leans on the counter, trying to think.)*

GARY: You don't have to go. I'm pretty harmless.

But if you have another option, by all means . . .

There's always the park, but people can come and fuck with you in the park.

I mean, literally.

If I were you, I'd go with the devil you know, so to

speak.

*(pause)*

Think it over. I'm going upstairs.

CRYSTAL: Are you going to sleep?

GARY: No, probably just a little meditation.

Maybe jerk off if I need to. But I don't think I do.

*(pause)*

If I do, I'll shut the door.

CRYSTAL: Okay.

GARY: Good night.

*(He leaves. After a moment she slides her purse off her shoulder and sets it down. She digs in the purse and gets out a photograph: it's wallet-sized, like a school picture. She looks at it as the lights dim.)*

## Scene Two.

*(The next day. Crystal stands on the sales floor of a Saturn dealership. Light background music. Charlie stands next to her, holding a couple of glossy spec sheets.)*

CRYSTAL: . . .The two-door XE has a hundred and thirty-eight horsepower engine, five-speed manual transmission, cruise control; it's virtually the same as the XR except that it doesn't have the sixteen-inch alloy wheels or the advanced audio system, or the sport bucket seats with driver-side lumbar, which I'm thinking you might actually need since you say you do a lot of driving. If you want to save fifteen hundred dollars, hey, in this economic climate, I completely understand. But I see that iPod in your pocket so I know you're a man who likes his music, and I gotta say, having all those audio controls right on the steering wheel is an amazing feeling: it's like, you're heading down the highway and you've got the whole world right there . . .

CHARLIE: How did you learn so much about cars? Did your boyfriend teach you?

CRYSTAL: I don't have a boyfriend.

CHARLIE: You really know your stuff.
I was here about a month ago, but I didn't see you then. Are you new?

*(Her smile abruptly vanishes.)*

CRYSTAL: Did you work with a salesperson the last time you were here?

CHARLIE: A girl named Tammy.

CRYSTAL: Oh no.
I should . . . I should probably get Tammy for you then.

CHARLIE: You trying to get rid of me?

CRYSTAL: Oh, God no! I would love to work with you—it's just that we're really not allowed to take each other's customers. It's really complicated, but basically, you see, we work on straight commission—

CHARLIE: How about we just pretend I never told you?

*(She looks around.)*

CHARLIE: I don't want to work with her anyway. I'd rather

work with you.

*(pause)*

CHARLIE: Come on. "The customer is always right."

CRYSTAL: I know, but—

CHARLIE: Shhh, I love this song:

*(A new song surges forward on the dealership soundtrack: "Sea of Love," or something equally lush and romantic. They listen to it together for a while.)*

CHARLIE: I swear I've seen you somewhere before.

CRYSTAL: I used to work at the Ford dealership.

CHARLIE: No, that's not it.

CRYSTAL: Well, I just have one of those faces; people always think they went to high school with me.

CHARLIE: You were in diapers when I was in high school.

*(pause)*

CHARLIE: Anyway, I filled out the form.

*(He hands her a thin Lucite clipboard.)*

And here's my card.

*(She looks at it.)*

CRYSTAL: . . ."Transformative Motivational Speaker"— wait a minute. I know you! I went to that free talk you gave at the Holiday Inn.

CHARLIE: See, there you go.

CRYSTAL: I still have my notebook. And I remember when I got home, I made a list of all my bills and put it out to the universe, just like you said.

CHARLIE: And look at you now. You're doing great.

CRYSTAL: Well . . .

You know, that same week, I did have a couple of parking tickets and when I went to pay them, they couldn't find one in the computer, so it was free.

CHARLIE: We call that "synchronicity". The more you use the tools, the more it starts to happen.

CRYSTAL: I don't know. I probably wasn't doing it right.

CHARLIE: That lecture was just the tip of the iceberg. You should have signed up for my boot camp. That's where we really get into challenging your assumptions.

CRYSTAL: You know, I just didn't have the money—

CHARLIE: People always say that. It's an investment. But it ends up paying for itself, a hundred times over.

*(pause)*

CHARLIE: Well, speaking of investments . . .
Aren't you gonna offer me a test drive?

CRYSTAL: Would you like to go for a test drive?

*(He gestures for her to go first, and they start off.)*

## Scene Three.

*(Evening of the same day. Crystal comes into the kitchen
again through the sliding glass door. This time it's appar-
ent that she's using a thin, plastic ID card to jimmy the
lock. She does it more easily now. She has her luggage as
before, along with a couple of stuffed, no-label shopping
bags and a greasy bag of takeout.)*

CRYSTAL: Gary?

Are you still here?

*(He pops up from behind the counter. He's holding a
two-by-four.)*

CRYSTAL: —Oh Jesus—

GARY: Sorry.

CRYSTAL: What the hell is that for?

GARY: Just . . . protection.

CRYSTAL: Protection from what?

*(He thinks for a moment. He gently lays the two-by-four
on the counter.)*

CRYSTAL: I brought hamburgers. Are you hungry?

*(She starts unpacking the bag.)*

GARY: I was just going to fix some C-rations.

CRYSTAL: What are those?

*(He shows her a small cardboard box.)*

GARY: From the Army-Navy store.

They keep forever.

CRYSTAL: Well, great, keep it for another night. I'm buying.

GARY: Do you always wear a suit?

CRYSTAL: It's . . . you know. I have to.

But I can't afford to get anything dry cleaned. Pretty soon
I'm gonna smell like a . . .

*(Embarrassed silence.)*

GARY: I took a shower.

CRYSTAL: That's great!

*(They start eating picnic-style on the floor.)*

CRYSTAL: So tell me about your day. Did you go anywhere?

*(Gary shakes his head.)*

CRYSTAL: It was really nice out.

GARY: I didn't have anywhere to go.

CRYSTAL: Well, I hear you, but you could go hang out at the library, or . . . I don't know . . .

GARY: I mean I didn't *need* to go anywhere.

CRYSTAL: So you don't go anywhere unless you need to?

GARY: Pretty much.

CRYSTAL: Do you have . . . like, a phobia, or something?

*(No answer.)*

. . .I'm sorry, I'm usually not this rude . . .

*(pause)*

GARY: I don't like crowds. Crowding is unnatural; it causes stress and aggression. They've proved it with animals.

CRYSTAL: Okay.

*(pause)*

CRYSTAL: Anyway, I had a good day at work. I think, maybe, I've finally met someone who wants to buy a goddamned car.

GARY: Hooray for fossil fuels.

CRYSTAL: Hooray for seven percent commission.

GARY: Is it new, or used?

CRYSTAL: Do I look like the used car type?
This guy is strictly top-of-the-line. He's looking at a Sky RedLine, fully loaded.

GARY: I only know cars from the seventies and eighties. Nowadays they make them out of plastic.

CRYSTAL: It's polymer.

GARY: That's because the government is saving the metal. They're hoarding it.

CRYSTAL: What for?

GARY: Think about it. Metal is going to be one of the key substances in the new barter economy. As long as your fire is hot enough, you can make metal do whatever you want. Plastic just melts and turns into poison.

CRYSTAL: Okay.

GARY: You should take your seven percent commission and invest in a scrap-metal yard.

*(She laughs.)*

CRYSTAL: You know . . . investing is not really my top prior-
ity right now.

> *(She starts unpacking the shopping bags, stocking the
> kitchen with various things: paper towels, china plates
> and cutlery from Goodwill.)*

GARY: Don't tell me you're gonna go rent some apartment.
That's just throwing money away.

CRYSTAL: So how does it work: you just stay someplace until
the water gets turned off, and then you go and try to find
some other house?

GARY: There's always another house; the hard part is finding
one with lights and water. Take a look outside. You see any
lights in those houses? It's a ghost town.

> *(She looks out the glass door for a long while, realizing
> how alone they are.)*

CRYSTAL: That street light's not on.

> *(pause)*

CRYSTAL: Well, at least it's quiet.
You can see the stars.
Did you ever do any camping?
I mean . . . voluntarily?
I went once. I couldn't believe the sky. Like it was just
dusted with white.

GARY: Plenty more where that came from. The days of trying
to get "back to nature"— that's all over. Nature's coming
back to us.

CRYSTAL: What do you mean?

GARY: These cheap-ass houses— they're just scrap now. We're
sitting in a drywall junkyard. Pretty soon you're gonna see
squirrels nesting in these cabinets. Vines crawling over
the floor.

CRYSTAL: That's insane.

GARY: You'll see people start to change too. Fighting to survive.
It doesn't bring out the best in a person.

> *(pause)*

CRYSTAL: Listen:
I need to ask a couple of favors of you.

GARY: This oughta be good.

CRYSTAL: Will you be home during the day tomorrow?

*(He nods.)*

CRYSTAL: Okay, good. I'm having some stuff delivered. Just a table and chair set, from Goodwill.

I just need someone here to open the door.

And the other thing is even easier.

The day after tomorrow, I have this appointment. This person needs to come over and see where I live. So I was wondering if you could maybe just . . .not be here.

GARY: That's a problem.

CRYSTAL: Just for a couple of hours. You could go for a walk, or run some errands . . .It's not like you'd run into crowds or anything.

GARY: What time?

CRYSTAL: Afternoon.

GARY: No way.

CRYSTAL: Come on. You must go out all the time to get your C-rations or whatever.

GARY: Only when I need to.

CRYSTAL: Please, Gary, I can't— I can't even begin to tell you how important this is.

GARY: Do you seriously expect me to go out and wander around the neighborhood for two hours?

CRYSTAL: So go to the library.

GARY: You and that fucking library!

No. No way. I see your M. O.

You buy me a hamburger like I'm your buddy, and now you want to kick me out and change the locks on me.

I was here first, lady.

CRYSTAL: I'm really hurt that you would think that, Gary.

I've never been anything but nice to you.

And you've been so kind to me, letting me stay here.

I don't know if I could do this if I didn't have you here to help me.

I appreciate it so much.

*(pause)*

GARY: What if I just stay upstairs?

CRYSTAL: They need to see the whole house.

GARY: Who does?

CRYSTAL: It's complicated.

GARY: Why can't you just say, "This is my friend, Gary?" I'll take a shower.

CRYSTAL: Because they'll assume that I'm involved with you.

GARY: And that would be deeply embarrassing to you; I get it. Because I'm such a disgusting specimen—

CRYSTAL: No, I swear, you could be Brad Pitt—I mean, you're perfectly attractive, as far as I can tell, but I absolutely cannot look like I'm involved with anyone or living with anyone. At all.

GARY: Okay.

So, I got it.

I'll be the plumber.

CRYSTAL: What?

GARY: Like they say in the porno films: "I'm just here to fix the sink."

CRYSTAL: . . . Do you . . . do you have any tools, or anything?

GARY: One or two. I can improvise.

CRYSTAL: I don't know.

GARY: It's a good cover. And you know, if you're having the place worked on, it helps it look like you really live here. Because a table and chair set isn't gonna cut it.

CRYSTAL: I bought other things too, like toilet paper and some sheets to put on the bed, I mean, *your* bed.

I'll say that I just moved in.

GARY: That's true enough.

CRYSTAL: Gary: don't take this the wrong way, but I need to know that you're not gonna screw this up. If we do this, you have to be completely quiet. Let me do all the talking.

GARY: I know what I'm doing.

I've been living under the radar for a long time.

CRYSTAL: Okay! We're a team, right?

*(Gary starts sliding his pants down.)*

CRYSTAL: What the hell are you doing?

GARY: Just . . . that's how the plumbers wear their jeans . . . 'Cause when they bend over—

CRYSTAL: Okay, that's too far.

GARY: Just trying to look realistic . . .

CRYSTAL: You should go to bed now.

GARY: You're not the boss of me.

CRYSTAL: I didn't mean—oh God, that's such a mom thing. I'm—I'm sorry.

*(Crystal quickly turns away and busies herself in the kitchen. Gary watches her, then gathers up his remaining food and his two-by-four.)*

GARY: Hey.

It's all fine.

I'm not gonna screw anything up.

I don't want you to worry.

*(She tries to smile.)*

CRYSTAL: Good night.

GARY: Good night.

*(He exits.)*

## Scene Four.

*(Charlie stands alone, practicing a speech in his mirror.)*

CHARLIE: What do you want?

*(He points to an imaginary person as if calling on someone, and holds for their response, which he repeats.)*

CHARLIE: "More money." Okay.
Come here a minute:

*(To himself)*

I have to make sure I have a nickel.
Here's a nickel.
Now you're richer than when you came in.
Seriously, though:
Anyone have a more specific answer?

*(Calling on people, as before.)*

"More sales." "More commissions."
Ah. "I want to be rich." Okay, let's hold for a minute.
This is my favorite answer: "I Want To Be Rich."
Let me ask you this:
Why do you want to be rich? Why?
"So you don't have to worry anymore. "
More answers, come on:
"So you won't lose your house. "
"Medical expenses."
"So your wife will respect you."
"So you can buy things."
Okay, stop.
Let me ask you this:
What things?
—uh uh, don't tell me:
Close your eyes.
Now visualize the first thing that comes to mind.
How big is it? What color is it?
Is the light hitting it in a special way?
Now stretch out your hand—can you see your hand?
—and run your fingers over it.
How does it feel?
Now come right up next to it, and see if you can press your

face against it,
What does it smell like?
What does *she* smell like?  Ha, just kidding.
Now: I want you to say something to yourself.
Don't say, "I want this."
Say: "This Is Mine."

## Scene Five.

*(Sounds of rain and thunder. Lights rise on SHANNON, a woman in her thirties, who stands on the sales floor of the dealership reviewing a checklist on a clipboard. Crystal rushes in. She's soaked.)*

CRYSTAL: Sorry I'm late, I took the—

SHANNON: Did you punch in?

CRYSTAL: No, I'll go do it right now.

SHANNON: Do it later. You have a customer.

CRYSTAL: No way.

SHANNON: He's in the men's room. Are you . . .?

CRYSTAL: What?

SHANNON: Is something up?

CRYSTAL: I'm fine. Do I look all right?

SHANNON: We need to talk when you have a second.

CRYSTAL: Sure.

*(Shannon moves away as Charlie walks in with a newspaper.)*

CHARLIE: . . . There's my girl.

CRYSTAL: Wow, you're a real early bird.

CHARLIE: Do I need to buy you an umbrella?

CRYSTAL: It's weird, I can never manage to keep one.

*(He takes off his raincoat and puts it around her shoulders.)*

CHARLIE: Here you go.

CRYSTAL: Thank you.

CHARLIE: I was getting cold just looking at you.

*(pause)*

CRYSTAL: So . . . are we doing your contract today?

CHARLIE: I was thinking I'd like to see how that car handles in the rain.

CRYSTAL: You're a smart shopper. I like that.

CHARLIE: Well, it's a big investment.

CRYSTAL: Absolutely. A car is like your second skin.
Well, I'll get you the keys and you can go spend the whole day out there if you want.

CHARLIE: You free to ride shotgun?

CRYSTAL: Oh gee, I'd love to, but I, uh, I have this meeting with my supervisor.

CHARLIE: I don't mind waiting. You all have free coffee in the lounge.

CRYSTAL: . . .Okay then. Great. I'll come find you.

*(He exits.)*

SHANNON: What's his deal?

CRYSTAL: He's pre-qualified.

SHANNON: A twelve-year-old can get pre-qualified.

CRYSTAL: What did you want to talk about?

SHANNON: We're closing.

CRYSTAL: Closing early?

SHANNON: No, closing forever. The service center's hanging on for a little while, but the sales floor is toast.

CRYSTAL: Oh my God.

SHANNON: So if you're working on any deals you need to close 'em by the end of the week.

CRYSTAL: Why didn't you tell me before?

SHANNON: Crystal: get a grip, okay? We've been operating in the red for two straight quarters; half the associates are gone; what did you think was gonna happen?

CRYSTAL: But that's not what you do in a change cycle; you have to— you have to hang in there, you know? Because times like these are all about thinning the herd, and that's good for us, but we have to ride it out, we have to; it's all just—it's just part of the cycle.

SHANNON: You sound like my 401K guy.

CRYSTAL: Did you talk to headquarters? Because all they have to do is find someone else to buy out the franchise, this is crazy—

SHANNON: H.Q. doesn't give two shits about it. They're busy trying to sell the whole company.

CRYSTAL: What? Who could they sell it to?

SHANNON: I don't know. Japanese.

*(pause)*

CRYSTAL: Shannon: I just want to say . . .

If we get any more walk-ins . . . I know today, with the rain—but tomorrow morning, I'm here, or Thursday or Friday . . .Shannon, please: I was salesperson of the month twice in a row when I was at Ford.

If anyone else walks through that door, you give that person to me and I will close them.

You know I will.

I will absolutely close them, and I will give you, personally, twenty-five percent of my commission.

*(pause)*

SHANNON: Did you steal a customer from Tammy?

CRYSTAL: No, I—

SHANNON: Because she told me you did.

CRYSTAL: It's not . . . no, it wasn't like that, this guy just—

SHANNON: Whatever, I don't wanna hear excuses, but you know what?

Tammy's husband is on disability. And she may not be as pretty as you, but she's been here a heck of a lot longer and worked her butt off.

So if we get any walk-ins, which at this point is about as likely as Pluto crash-landing into the parking lot, I think I'm gonna give them to Tammy.

Because you know what?

There's a special place in hell for women who don't help other women.

*(Shannon exits. After a moment, Crystal slips the borrowed coat off her shoulders and looks at it. It's an expensive raincoat. She reads the designer label in the collar, folds the coat over her arm, and exits to go find Charlie.)*

## Scene Six.

*(The next day. The kitchen. The table and chair set has arrived. Gary kneels in front of the open sink cabinet, wrench in hand. He starts futzing convincingly with the pipes when he hears Crystal coming down from upstairs along with TONI, an alert, fortyish woman in a muted pants set.)*

TONI: *(making notes in a folder)*
  . . .So the living room, we saw.

CRYSTAL: I wanted to get a couch, but they said it takes eight weeks.

TONI: Not a problem. I'd rather see you wait eight weeks than go to one of those rental places. I had a client get bedbugs.

CRYSTAL: Oh my God.

TONI: You mind if I look in your fridge?

  *(Crystal nods, and she does.)*

TONI: All right, I'd like to see more fresh vegetables in here, but I know you just moved in. Cleaning products?

CRYSTAL: Oh sure, I have . . . let's see . . . Joy, and 409 . . .

TONI: Where do you store your cleaning products?

CRYSTAL: I . . .

TONI: Under the sink?

CRYSTAL: No.

TONI: Never under the sink. Not even if you have one of those little door latches.

CRYSTAL: Absolutely—

TONI: Because kids are smart, they figure out how to open those things up in about two minutes.

CRYSTAL: I keep everything up high.

  *(Toni goes to the sliding glass door and looks closely at the handle. She sits down at the table.)*

TONI: *(writing)* Let me just catch up on my notes.

CRYSTAL: Take your time.

  *(Crystal sits and waits.)*

TONI: Okay.

  Here's what I still need to see:

  *(Crystal's face falls.)*

TONI: Don't get upset on me. You're getting there. You have a pen?

CRYSTAL: *(not moving)*

Sure.

*(Toni hands her a pen and paper.)*

TONI: Number one: window guards. On every second floor window. Write that down.

You get them at the hardware store, about twenty bucks a pop. Your handyman here probably knows how to put them in. Number two: another bed.

CRYSTAL: I thought she could just share with me for a while.

TONI: You know, she could, but we discourage it. You just don't want to know the stories I've heard. Mostly having to do with the fathers, but still.

CRYSTAL: So, I'm sorry, I don't get it. She's not supposed to be old enough to know not to drink Drano or climb out a second floor window, but she's too old to sleep in her mommy's bed?

TONI: I don't write the standards, I'm just trying to tell you, I know what my supervisor is going to say—

CRYSTAL: All right—

TONI: If you were in a motel that would be one thing, but you have plenty of room so I don't see what the problem—

CRYSTAL: Fine, I'll get a bed.

TONI: Let's say you have a gentleman who wants to spend the night—

CRYSTAL: That's not going to happen.

Let's move on.

TONI: That's about it.

I'll just need a copy of your lease, for the file.

CRYSTAL: . . .Great.

TONI: Or if you just have the original, I can take it with me and run it off at the office.

CRYSTAL: You know, the landlord still has my copy, so I can just make a copy at work and fax it to you, would that work?

TONI: Everything all right at the Saturn dealership?

CRYSTAL: Yep, it's a great team over there.

---

*(Toni looks over at Gary, who by now has run out of things to do to the pipes. He's just sitting there.)*

TONI: I'd like to ask you about something a little more sensitive.

CRYSTAL: Gary, while you're here, could you also take a look at the upstairs bathroom? The faucet is a little drippy.

GARY: Sure.

*(He exits.)*

TONI: I should get his number from you. Is he reasonable?

CRYSTAL: You know, the landlord is paying so I'm not really sure.

TONI: Crystal, I just need to ask you:

Do you have any other issues that we should know about?

Any addiction problems?

CRYSTAL: No.

TONI: Drugs? Gambling? QVC?

CRYSTAL: No.

TONI: Mental health issues?

CRYSTAL: I went over all this with the other guy—

TONI: I don't care if you did. I'm asking you now.

CRYSTAL: There's nothing wrong with me.

TONI: But you see, when I go back to my supervisor and say, "She's a nice-looking, clean woman who finished school and has a job," he's going to say, "So what exactly is her problem?"

CRYSTAL: My only problem is I lost my house. And when I went to the shelter, you people said, "Sorry, the shelter's full, but why don't we take that little girl off your hands?"

TONI: You can't have a small child sleeping in a car.

CRYSTAL: We only did that for a few nights.

TONI: It's not safe. And it's not right.

*(pause)*

I understand you stopped by the school yesterday.

CRYSTAL: I had something I wanted to give her—

*(She goes to get a letter from her purse.)*

TONI: If you don't have custody, you can't just show up at school.

CRYSTAL: I know, I just thought—I mean, they *know* me at her school—

TONI: I thought we were very clear on that.

CRYSTAL: I'm sorry, but—the thing is, I went to the park on Sunday, just like you said, and the family never showed up with her—I ended up sitting there for three hours—

TONI: I know. I've talked to the family. It won't happen again.

CRYSTAL: Can you at least give her this letter? And make sure those people read it to her?

TONI: *(taking the letter)*

I'll see what I can do.

CRYSTAL: Is she okay, or does she seem like . . .

TONI: She acts out a little at school, but at home they say she's fine.

CRYSTAL: Oh shit, I forgot the stickers.

> *(She gets a sheet of Hello Kitty stickers out of her purse, takes the letter back and starts feverishly decorating the envelope.)*

TONI: Just bear in mind that we're going to need to open that letter.

CRYSTAL: Why?

TONI: It's just policy, like everything else. And just one piece of advice: I know you'd never say anything intentionally to hurt her, believe me; but we try to discourage parents from making promises they can't keep.

> *(Crystal clutches the letter for a moment, but she gives it back to Toni.)*

CRYSTAL: I'm just telling her I've found us a house. And I'm coming to get her soon.

TONI: All right. I'll stop by again on Monday, same time. If everything looks good, then I'll make a recommendation to my supervisor.

CRYSTAL: Great. That's great. Thank you.

> *(Toni gets up.)*

CRYSTAL: I'll walk you out.

TONI: Don't bother, my car is out this way.

> *(She heads for the sliding glass door.)*

But when you get a chance . . .you need to get a better lock over here.

Anybody can bust this thing open with a credit card.

*(Toni exits. We hear her car starting as Gary comes downstairs.)*

GARY: You're in some deep shit.

CRYSTAL: No I'm not— what are you talking about? All I have to do is forge a lease; that's the easiest thing in the world.

*(pause)*

CRYSTAL: You were perfect. Thank you.

GARY: I told you you didn't have to worry about me.

See, I'm the kind of guy you want in your foxhole.

. . . Um, that's a war reference.

*(pause)*

GARY: You have a kid.

CRYSTAL: I do.

GARY: Interesting.

CRYSTAL: Why?

GARY: I don't know. I guess I didn't think you'd ever done anything worthwhile with your life.

CRYSTAL: Are you serious?

GARY: How old is she?

CRYSTAL: Five. She's in kindergarten.

GARY: Is she moving in?

CRYSTAL: I don't know.

GARY: For a long time I thought having kids was a bad idea, because of overpopulation; but now I think the people who know what's going on should have as many kids as they can, because the revolution won't be over in one person's lifetime.

CRYSTAL: What revolution?

GARY: But you have to choose the right genes. You're a good specimen; I can see why someone wanted to mate with you. You have to be a pretty tough animal to keep your genetic material alive. There's so much that can happen, like you were saying, drinking Drano or—

CRYSTAL: That lady is unbelievable. My kid is five; she knows not to drink the goddamned Drano.

And where the hell am I supposed to find two hundred bucks for window guards? And a bed?

*(pause)*

Where did you find that bed you have?

GARY: You don't want to know.

CRYSTAL: I just have to make this sale. I have to.

*(She gets out the wallet-sized photograph from before and looks at it. Gary comes and looks over her shoulder.)*

GARY: What's her name?

CRYSTAL: Bethany.

*(He takes the picture for a closer look.)*

GARY: What are they teaching her in school?

CRYSTAL: . . .Um, the usual stuff. Two plus two.

GARY: That's what you think.

CRYSTAL: What are you talking about?

GARY: They're socializing her.

They're teaching her not to hit other kids, and to keep her skirt down, and raise her hand when she has to go to the bathroom.

Every single thing her body wants to do is getting smashed down by the military-industrial complex, and the worst part is that it happens all day, every day, to everyone, and everyone just lets it happen.

Look at you: you go around all day with that big, fake smile pasted across your face, selling people a bunch of crap they don't need so you can go buy crap you don't need. "I just have to make this sale."

You completely bought the government messages:

But what happens now? Are you gonna just curl up and die? Or are you gonna fight back?

Because when you have to struggle for food and shelter, just like we did millions of years ago, boom! You start getting your mind back.

And we have to take advantage of this time and fight the system until we obliterate it.

You and me, we'll never recover a hundred percent; but your daughter's young; she might still have a chance . . .

You see, it won't be a collective society anymore where technology controls the masses. It'll just be individuals and small groups.

And when the centers of technology and finance go down, we need to be ready to survive.

Small, nomadic groups have the best shot at it. I know how to trap food and I know all the edible plants.

CRYSTAL: That's great.

GARY: You said, "I don't know." How come?

CRYSTAL: I didn't say that.

GARY: No, before when I said, "Is your daughter moving in," you said, "I don't know." How come?

CRYSTAL: I— I haven't decided what to do yet.

GARY: I'll tell you what you should do.

You pick her up from school.

You say, "Don't worry, honey, we're never going back there again."

Then the three of us get in your car and we start driving.

We drive until we hit wilderness. Someplace without all this EMF radiation.

We build a shelter. Or find one.

And we've got the seeds of a new society.

XX . . . XX . . . XY.

CRYSTAL: That's really sweet, Gary.

GARY: I'm not being sweet.

CRYSTAL: I have to think about it.

GARY: Yeah, see, that's not a good answer because your mind is full of all that system bullshit. But I'm thinking about your daughter; and if you were thinking about what's best for her long-term survival you'd be down on your knees thanking me right now.

CRYSTAL: I'm very grateful, I promise, I just—

Could I have that picture back?

GARY: God, women always act like there's something wrong with me. But every time I go into a public bathroom, some guy tries to blow me. Why is that?

CRYSTAL: Gary, right now we need to focus on getting her back.

GARY: Right.

CRYSTAL: I need your help. I really need it.

You were so great today.

We just have to stay here for five more days.

*(Gary stiffens and stares out the window at the street light, which has started to sputter on uncertainly.)*

CRYSTAL: What is it? Is someone out there?

GARY: It's happening.

CRYSTAL: What is?

GARY: They know.

CRYSTAL: Who does?

GARY: The government.

CRYSTAL: . . . It's just the street light. I think it's broken.

GARY: Don't say that! I know what I'm talking about! Do you
    want to end up dead?

CRYSTAL: I'm sorry.

> *(He turns off the light over the stove.)*

GARY: No lights tonight.

CRYSTAL: I won't. I promise.

GARY: I'll go upstairs and keep a lookout.
    Think about what I said.

> *(He grabs her hand and holds it between his hands for
> a minute like it's a precious object, then lets go and runs
> upstairs. Lights fade.)*

## Scene Seven.

*(Charlie's alone at his mirror again. He's carefully tying his tie.)*

CHARLIE: Are you busy after work? Because . . .

*(He revises his approach.)*

Do you like Mexican? Because . . .
You look like you could use a good meal.
I'll drive.
No, don't bother. Save your gas . . .
This car's been good to me, but it's time to trade up, you know?
. . . No, I didn't even bring my checkbook today. This is just a social visit.

*(Revising.)*

No, I forgot my checkbook. But I'll be sure and bring it tomorrow.
I just felt like saying hello.

*(Revising again.)*

Oh, hell, I forgot it. I'll have to come back tomorrow.

*(He slips off his jackets, trying a casual pose.)*

CHARLIE: Did you get enough to eat?
Another margarita?
. . . In that case, why don't I just take you home?

*(Revising.)*

You know, instead of going to get your car, why don't I just drive you straight home?
A lot of bored cops on the road these days, waiting to pull someone over.
. . .I don't know. Let's do a little drunk test.
Hold out your arms like this.
Now, close your eyes.
Now see if you can touch your nose.
. . .That does it. I'm driving you home.

*(Blackout.)*

## Scene Eight.

*(Outside the house. Night. Charlie walks up to the sliding glass door with Crystal, holding her elbow as if he's helping an old lady across the street.)*

CRYSTAL: Okay, I'm good now. Thanks.

CHARLIE: It's so dark out here.

CRYSTAL: That stupid bulb must have burned out.

CHARLIE: Nice house.

CRYSTAL: Thanks. I really like it here.

*(Pause. She holds out her hand for a handshake.)*

CRYSTAL: Well . . . thanks again for dinner. It's a pleasure working with you.

*(He laughs at this and she joins in, lightly.)*

CHARLIE: Would you mind if I just came in and used your restroom?

CRYSTAL: . . . Oh. Sure.

CHARLIE: I'll be careful not to wake up your daughter.

CRYSTAL: Oh, she's not here . . . she's at a sleepover.

*(She starts automatically to reach for her ID card, but stops herself. At a loss, she feigns digging through her purse for an imaginary key.)*

CRYSTAL: Oh shit. I don't have my house key.

CHARLIE: That's a setback.

CRYSTAL: I must have left it in my car.

CHARLIE: Do you need me to break in?

CRYSTAL: No, I . . . , you know what? My roommate's probably here, he can let me in.

*(She starts knocking.)*

Gary! . . . Gary!

CHARLIE: *(to himself)*

Roommate.

*(Gary comes down from upstairs looking worse than ever, disheveled and confused. He's holding the two-by-four.)*

CRYSTAL: Gary, it's me! Open the door!

*(Gary comes through the kitchen, stares at Charlie, and after an eternity, opens the door. Charlie offers Gary his hand.)*

CHARLIE: Sorry to wake you. Crystal forgot her key.

CRYSTAL: Gary, this is Charlie. He's a client from work.

*(Gary doesn't take Charlie's hand.)*

CHARLIE: So. Bathroom?

CRYSTAL: Straight ahead on your left.

*(Charlie exits.)*

CRYSTAL: Gary, I need you to be my helper again, okay? You're my roommate, and you're a nice guy, not hostile; and— you know what? Just go back to bed. Go.

GARY: What's he doing here?

CRYSTAL: He gave me a ride. It's complicated. It's really good that he knows you're here, but now I need you to clear out, let me handle him.

GARY: Which of his parts do you plan to "handle"?

CRYSTAL: That's disgusting, please, just go—

GARY: I'll be listening.

CRYSTAL: Gary—

*(He goes upstairs and Crystal composes herself as Charlie returns. Charlie takes the scenic route, peering into the living room and looking around.)*

CRYSTAL: I just moved in.

CHARLIE: That guy a friend of yours?

CRYSTAL: You know . . . he's more of a family friend. He's new in town. So I agreed to let him stay with us for a little while.

CHARLIE: He's a little strange.

CRYSTAL: Oh, he's only like that when you wake him up.

CHARLIE: I don't know if you really want him around your daughter, you know what I mean?

CRYSTAL: *(softly)*
I know.

*(pause)*

CHARLIE: You mind if I sit down for a minute? I have a long ride home.

CRYSTAL: I'm sorry you went out of your way.

CHARLIE: No trouble. My back just locks up if I drive too much.

CRYSTAL: That's why you need that adjustable lumbar seat.

CHARLIE: I don't know. I might have blown my car budget tonight on all those margaritas.

*(pause)*

CRYSTAL: Can I get you a glass of water or anything?

CHARLIE: Sure.

CRYSTAL: I hope you don't have an early day tomorrow.

CHARLIE: No, just prep work for that keynote address I have on Monday.

CRYSTAL: Who is it for again?

CHARLIE: United Federation of Soybean Suppliers. It's a tristate organization.

CRYSTAL: Wow.

CHARLIE: It's their quarterly meeting, and the theme is "Keeping Optimistic in Hard Times."

CRYSTAL: And you're the keynote speaker. That's amazing.

CHARLIE: It's a nice gig. I'm hoping they'll have me back sometime, because I also do a speech on relating sports trivia to your life.

CRYSTAL: What's your speech about? Is it like the Holiday Inn one?

CHARLIE: Kind of. It's called "Getting the Wealth of Your Dreams."

CRYSTAL: Can you do some of it for me?

CHARLIE: Sure, if you want to pay my speaker's fee—

CRYSTAL: *(laughing)*
Oh, great—

CHARLIE: I'm serious. I do private sessions.
See, the secret laws that allow you to create prosperity are simple to use.
Anyone can do it; you just have to be ready to receive the transmission.
But one of the laws is the "Law of Compensation."
So in other words, I can't just give it away.
You have to commit—emotionally, mentally, spiritually and financially—or the laws won't work.
You should think about doing some sessions with me, though.
I could triple your commissions, overnight.

CRYSTAL: I'll think about it.

CHARLIE: I have powerful intuition about people, and I keep having this feeling like I was meant to meet you . . . like there's something I have to teach you . . . or maybe something you have to teach me.

CRYSTAL: Well, I don't have much of a budget for extras right now.

CHARLIE: Maybe we should work out a trade. Say, a dozen sessions for a new car?

CRYSTAL: If it was my car, instead of the dealer's, I'd be all over that.

CHARLIE: All over it, huh?

*(pause)*

CRYSTAL: More water?

CHARLIE: Sure. Unless you have something stronger.

Your buddy upstairs looks like he might know where to score some weed.

CRYSTAL: You have a long ride home, so that's probably a bad idea.

CHARLIE: I actually drive better with a little something on board, you know what I mean?

CRYSTAL: Well, driving your new Sky RedLine is gonna be the best high you've ever had.

CHARLIE: This is starting to seem like kind of a hard sell, you know?

I'm sick of hearing about the goddamned car.

CRYSTAL: Okay.

CHARLIE: Let me ask you this:

If I had come in today and said, "Look, I've decided to go with a Honda instead," would you have still gone out to dinner with me?

*(pause)*

CRYSTAL: But it's so important right now to buy American.

CHARLIE: Is that your answer?

CRYSTAL: What's the question?

CHARLIE: I get it.

*(pause)*

CHARLIE: The thing about the Honda dealership is, they're willing to negotiate.

CRYSTAL: What our customers have found is that the places that say they negotiate are really just jacking up the price to begin with, so that's the great thing about Saturn: total price transparency. We put it all right there on a sheet of paper.

CHARLIE: So in other words, you're not willing to negotiate.

CRYSTAL: . . . I might be able to throw in some free Saturn merchandise.

CHARLIE: Like what? A travel mug?

CRYSTAL: But if buying American is something that doesn't matter to you then I don't know what else I can say. If you want to buy something that came from a factory in Oki-saka-whatever, then go right ahead. But when you buy a Saturn you're buying American ingenuity and American jobs; from the person who hands you the keys all the way back to the guys on the line in Spring Hill, Tennessee; it's like a family. And when you buy a Saturn, you can feel yourself becoming a part of that family; we even do a little sort of 'thing' when you buy a car, everyone on the floor stands around and does this . . .

CHARLIE: What?

CRYSTAL: Well, it's supposed to be a surprise.

CHARLIE: Tell me.

CRYSTAL: We just sing a little song.

CHARLIE: How does it go?

CRYSTAL: You need a lot of people to do it, and I'm a bad singer.

CHARLIE: Do you want me to buy this car?

CRYSTAL: . . .Yes.

CHARLIE: Then sing me a song.

*(Hesitantly, she stands in front of him and sings the following, to the tune of "La Cucaracha." There's some humiliating choreography involving hand-clapping.)*

CRYSTAL: You bought a Saturn, you bought a Saturn,
Put our service to the test.
You bought a Saturn, you bought a Saturn,
Saturn owners are the best!
Go-o-o-o-o, Saturn!
Yay!

*(pause)*

CHARLIE: Not bad.
Can you do that last part again?

CRYSTAL: Charlie, I don't think you're really undecided.

I think you know exactly what you want to do.

I've told you about the features of this car until I'm blue in the face—

CHARLIE: Stop right there.

You see, I'm not really interested in the features. I'm interested in the benefits.

CRYSTAL: So you want to know how this car is going to change your life.

CHARLIE: Exactly.

CRYSTAL: Oh, Charlie.

You've hit on the exact reason why I love selling cars.

Because other than a house, I think a car is the single most life-enhancing purchase a person can make.

Your car is like a second skin. You're in it every day.

You live in it, you escape in it, you can even sleep in it . . . I've done that.

If you have a family, it can change your relationship with your kids.

If you're a single guy, it can be the thing that gets you laid.

It's the face you show the world. It's you.

CHARLIE: Can you be more specific?

How exactly is this car going to get me laid?

CRYSTAL: It's a really hot car. Women are going to love it.

CHARLIE: Like you, for example.

CRYSTAL: Obviously I think it's a great car.

CHARLIE: So if I buy this car, you'll be all over me like a cheap suit.

CRYSTAL: . . . I'm not really in the market these days for any kind of . . . romantic entanglements . . .

CHARLIE: Why? Because of that guy upstairs?

CRYSTAL: Oh, God no.

CHARLIE: So what's the problem?

I took you out for a nice dinner and drove you home, but no, that's not enough for you.

You want me to buy a car first.

CRYSTAL: It's not like that, I was just trying to help you make your decision—

CHARLIE: Just as a charity thing, out of the goodness of your heart. Because it's not like this sale is going to make your month or anything, oh no . . . I mean, that dealership is just *teeming* with customers . . .

CRYSTAL: Of course I want to make the sale, but I like you, Charlie, I'm just not—

CHARLIE: How much do you like me? Because I like you about thirty-two thousand, five hundred and ninety four dollars plus tax.

Do you want me to sign?

CRYSTAL: Yes I do.

CHARLIE: So where do we go?

My place is no good.

*(indicating the living room)*

In there?

*(She doesn't move. Gary comes in with his two-by-four.)*

GARY: *(to Charlie)*

Get out.

CHARLIE: Easy there.

GARY: Get out before I hurt you.

CRYSTAL: Gary, don't be stupid; put that thing down—

CHARLIE: (to Crystal)

Let's go.

CRYSTAL: Gary, I wasn't—it wasn't what you think—

GARY: *(to Crystal)*

I heard what you said.

CRYSTAL: What am I supposed to do?

CHARLIE: I'm out of here.

Are you coming?

*(She looks bewildered.)*

CHARLIE: Last call.

GARY: Get the fuck out of here!

*(Gary lifts up the two-by-four, but Crystal grabs his arm. She holds him for a moment in a sort of restraining embrace, looking into his face, keeping his arms at his sides.)*

CRYSTAL: Shhh. It's all going to be okay. I promise.

*(She lets go of him, grabs her purse, and leaves with Charlie. The sliding glass door closes. Gary flings the two-by-four after them. The glass cracks into a suspended bull's eye. He starts opening the cabinets and flinging the contents around the room, creating as much destruction as he can. Blackout.)*

## Scene Nine.

*(The dealership. The next morning. Shannon's on the sales floor. Crystal enters, looking haggard.)*

SHANNON: Long night?

CRYSTAL: Kind of, why?

SHANNON: I just wondered, since you're wearing the exact same outfit you had on yesterday.

*(Crystal looks at her with unveiled hostility.)*

CRYSTAL: Has anyone come by to drop off a check?

SHANNON: Today? No.

But someone's here to see you.

CRYSTAL: Thank God.

*(Shannon points out a middle-aged woman who's been standing some distance away, watching them and listening.)*

SHANNON: She was asking about you.

*(Crystal approaches the woman with her hand out.)*

CRYSTAL: Hi, I'm Crystal. Is there a specific model you'd like to hear more about?

PATRICIA: Are you a friend of Charlie's?

*(pause)*

CRYSTAL: Did he send you here?

PATRICIA: No.

CRYSTAL: Are you—

PATRICIA: I'm his wife.

CRYSTAL: . . . Shannon, if you have a minute—

SHANNON: *(standing very close)*

I do.

CRYSTAL: Great. Could you get me the keys for the RedLine XR?

SHANNON: Okay.

*(Shannon exits.)*

CRYSTAL: What's your name?

PATRICIA: . . . Patricia.

CRYSTAL: Patricia. It's so nice to meet you.

I know Charlie's been shopping for himself, but I think it's a great idea if you take the car for a test drive too—

PATRICIA: I'm not here about a car.

I checked his GPS. I know he's been spending all this time here but when I ask him about his day he just tells me he's been at the library or the Y.

He likes to have his secrets. I go easy on him.

He got laid off eighteen months ago, and that's so hard on a man's ego.

Now he wants to go around giving these "speeches," but honestly, no one will even give him the time of day; companies don't have money for that kind of silliness right now.

We're okay, thank God; my investment advisor is a genius; but I know it hurts when he has to ask me for money just so he can pick up the dry cleaning.

Let's not tell him I came here. I just . . . got nervous, I guess.

CRYSTAL: Sure.

PATRICIA: He didn't come home until two o'clock last night.

He said he had a few drinks with an old friend and then his friend's car got towed . . . but I just had this feeling that his friend was not a man. I think he tells little lies sometimes, just so I won't get jealous.

And I couldn't help hearing that you're wearing the same clothes you had on yesterday, so I think maybe you're the friend he was helping, is that right?

*(Shannon returns with the keys.)*

SHANNON: Here you go.

CRYSTAL: Thank you.

PATRICIA: I had my car towed once, so I know what a pain it is, you have to get someone to drive you all the way across town . . .

But he's that kind of guy. He makes friends wherever he goes.

And I think for a man his age to spend time talking with pretty young women, maybe even flirting a little bit . . . if it makes him feel better about himself, there's nothing wrong with it.

CRYSTAL: Of course not.

PATRICIA: But now . . .

*(Shannon's still there, listening.)*

PATRICIA: I'm sorry, could you give us a minute please?

SHANNON: . . . Sure.

>*(Shannon exits.)*

PATRICIA: You might think this is really out of line, but I looked up his GPS addresses from last night and one of them is a motel. So I'm thinking it all makes sense, because maybe you couldn't get home for some reason because of the car situation, and he's a gentleman, he wouldn't go home until he was sure that you at least had a safe place to spend the night.

>The only thing that doesn't make sense is why he started coming here in the first place.

CRYSTAL: He's been looking at a Sky RedLine—

PATRICIA: That man. He's certainly not in the market for a new car; if anything, *I'm* the one who needs an upgrade; but my birthday is coming up next month, so for all I know, maybe he was planning some kind of surprise.

CRYSTAL: Well, it would be a shame if you—

PATRICIA: No, no, it doesn't matter, because we can't be buying that car. Whatever he had going on, I'm putting a stop to it right now.

CRYSTAL: You're making a big mistake.

PATRICIA: I don't think I am.

>I'm glad we had this talk. I feel so much better now.

>You see, the thing about Charlie is: he may be going through a rough patch right now, but at the end of the day: we've been through twenty-six years together, and I don't need him to buy me a car to show me how much he loves me.

>*(Patricia starts to go. Crystal watches as she heads for the door.)*

CRYSTAL: Patricia, I'm sorry, I can't let you walk out that door. It wouldn't be fair to you.

PATRICIA: No. We're done here.

CRYSTAL: I think you should know the truth.

PATRICIA: No, thank you—

CRYSTAL: I love him. With all my heart. And he loves me. We've been planning to run away together.

PATRICIA: —no—

CRYSTAL: We've been planning it for months now.

PATRICIA: . . . no . . . that's not true—

CRYSTAL: I'm so sorry.

  I didn't know he was married, at least—not at first.

  We met at one of his speeches.

  We both tried to resist it, but he said he—he had this feeling like he was supposed to meet me.

  Like there was something we were supposed to teach each other.

  You know how he is . . .

  And he said— he said  he couldn't bring himself to tell you.

  He was just going to leave a note.

  *(Patricia is overcome.)*

CRYSTAL: But I have to tell you, Patricia, that until today, I would have thought that nothing in the world could keep us apart.

  It's just . . . so powerful.

  Only now that you're here, I can see how much you love him.

  And it makes me angry that he would do this to you.

PATRICIA:  . . . It's not his fault; he's not himself right now—

CRYSTAL: No, you're right, it's not his fault. It's *my* fault.

  Because men—we know how they are, right?

  They're like children.

  And it's up to us to keep them on track, isn't it?

PATRICIA: I'm afraid so.

CRYSTAL: So what are we going to do?

  *(pause)*

  Patricia, this might sound crazy, but there's only one thing I can do. I see that now . . .

  I need to leave town. Just disappear and never see him again.

  Because if I stay, eventually we'll run into each other and the whole thing will start all over again.

PATRICIA: Where would you go?

CRYSTAL: Well, you see, that's the problem. I don't know.

  You see . . . I'm sorry—

  I'm just thinking out loud here . . .

  We've been planning to leave town *together* . . .

So I sold my house at a huge loss, and I've given my notice here at work;

I don't have any savings at all; but he said not to worry, he'd take care of everything.

PATRICIA: How did he think he was going to do that?

CRYSTAL: I don't know, but the point is: because of him, I have *nothing*.

 *(pause)*

PATRICIA: Do you need me to buy you a bus ticket or . . .

CRYSTAL: Patricia, how would you manage if you took a bus to someplace where you didn't know anyone, and then got out and stood there with no money?

No, it's not going to work. I'll just have to stay here and try my best to break it off with him.

Promise me you won't worry, Patricia, because I hate to think of you sitting at home and worrying every time he's fifteen minutes late, worrying that he's with me. I would hate to think that I'm haunting you like that, maybe for years, maybe even for the rest of your life.

PATRICIA: How much do you need?

CRYSTAL: Well, let's see . . . first month's rent, food . . . and the job market is so terrible; I'm sure I'll be out of work for a long time . . .

PATRICIA: Five thousand?

CRYSTAL: That would be gone in a heartbeat. Plus there's childcare; I have a daughter.

PATRICIA: Just say a number.

CRYSTAL: I don't see how I can do it for less than ten.

*(Patricia shakes her head.)*

CRYSTAL: You see?  It's impossible. Excuse me. I'd better go beg for my job back.

PATRICIA: Assuming I could get it—and I have no idea if that's true—how soon would you be gone?

CRYSTAL: A few weeks.

*(Patricia makes a move to leave.)*

CRYSTAL: But If I had the money, let's say . . . tomorrow, I could do it a lot faster.

PATRICIA: I have to think.

CRYSTAL: Don't think too much about it, Patricia, or you'll

start to hate me.

I can tell you're a smart woman.

If you really listen to yourself, I know you'll make the right choice.

*(Patricia exits.)*

## Scene Ten.

*(Evening of the same day. CRYSTAL comes home. She sees the bulls eye of broken glass in the sliding glass door. She pushes the door open. The kitchen is trashed. The word "WHORE" has been written in huge letters on the cabinets, daubed in some dark substance. She comes closer, trying to figure out what the substance is, and then quickly recoils. She's shaking. She finds paper towels and spray cleaner and starts cleaning off the cabinets. GARY comes in and watches her.)*

CRYSTAL: Why did you do this?

GARY: I don't know.

Ifying I thought about a few other words but they had too many letters.

*(She keeps cleaning. He watches.)*

CRYSTAL: I thought I could trust you.

GARY: Yeah . . .

Welcome home.

Tough day at work?

*(She flings everything she can reach at him—the spray bottle and paper towels—missing him by a mile. For a moment, no one moves. She goes and picks up the things again, and goes on cleaning.)*

GARY: You're lucky. I could have done so much more.

CRYSTAL: I've never been anything but kind to you.

GARY: *(mimicking Charlie and Crystal)*

"I don't know if he's the kind of guy you want around your daughter." "I know!"

CRYSTAL: I was just saying what he wanted to hear.

GARY: He was never gonna buy that car.

CRYSTAL: I didn't know that.

GARY: You're a terrible prostitute.

Here's a tip: get the money up front next time.

CRYSTAL: Look: we've all done things we're not proud of.

You need to get over it, or get out of this house.

GARY: No. You get out.

*(pause)*

CRYSTAL: Gary: let's both take a minute and count to ten.

I don't want this to ruin our friendship.

GARY: Friendship. You crack me up.

CRYSTAL: It's true. Nothing's changed; I made a mistake, that's all.

GARY: Helen of Troy, Tokyo Rose.

Fucking women. It's always the same thing:

If I had a kid with you, I'd never know if it was mine.

CRYSTAL: Gary, please, I can't think about the future; I just need to focus on right now.

We just have three more days until that lady comes back.

You were so great before; can you please just help me a little while longer, and then I'll do anything you want, I promise—

GARY: Why are you always calling me Gary? That's not my name.

CRYSTAL: It's not?

GARY: That's just what it says in my underwear.

CRYSTAL: What's your real name?

GARY: I don't know.

*(pause)*

CRYSTAL: I think you need to eat something.

Can I fix you some dinner?—

*(She opens the refrigerator door, and a big mess of something flops and oozes out onto the floor.)*

GARY: Surprise.

*(She slams the door. She doesn't speak for a moment.)*

CRYSTAL: Why don't we go out and I'll buy you something to eat?

GARY: Negative.

CRYSTAL: Come on. I'll drive you. You won't even have to get out of the car.

GARY: You think I'm so stupid.

You had me going for a while there.

You're sick, you make me sick, you're a sickness.

She needs a piece of the teacher, the greens are too much,

But she can't eat, can't eat, she can't help it,

She's gonna turn out just like you . . .

Someone needs to help that little girl . . .

CRYSTAL: She needs your help, Gary, so why don't we go help her. We can go right now.

GARY: No way, no, no way, Mata Hari.

Why do you want her so badly?

What are you gonna do to her?

CRYSTAL: She needs me.

GARY: Nobody needs anyone, least of all you, fucking white-
bread government whore.

CRYSTAL: That's not true.

GARY: We're done. Get out of my house.

*(She doesn't move.)*

GARY: Get out.

CRYSTAL: Please, Gary—

*(He suddenly runs at her, trying to push her out by force.
She resists and pushes him off. He stares at her for a moment, shocked. He lunges at her again, trying to choke
her. They grapple and struggle for a while, slipping on
the detritus that still litters the floor. She manages to push
him backward and he falls, hitting his head against the
edge of the counter. He lands on the ground. She grabs
Gary's two-by-four off the counter and watches him. For
a moment he doesn't move.*

*Then he recovers and lunges at her again. Crystal hits
him with the two-by-four until he falls, cringing. She goes
over to him, lifts the two-by-four, and brings it down as
hard as she can, bludgeoning him over and over until the
end of the wood is tipped with blood. She staggers away
and begins to clean up the kitchen.)*

CRYSTAL: Oh God.

*(She goes on cleaning. She looks back at Gary. She goes
to him and looks at him closely.)*

CRYSTAL: Oh God oh God oh God—

*(She goes on cleaning. She stops, finds a blanket, and
wraps Gary's dead body in it. Outside, the street light
flicks on. She stares at it for a moment, then starts to drag
the body, with great difficulty, out of the kitchen. Else-
where lights also rise on Charlie, alone at his mirror.)*

CHARLIE: Let me tell you something:

The hardest part of making your dreams come true is simply
believing that you deserve it.

The first time someone offered me these secrets, I was resistant.

I couldn't accept what they had to offer, because deep down, I was afraid of my own personal potential.

Now, that was stupid, wasn't it?

We all have the power to manifest our own reality.

Harness that power, and you'll find that the things you need appear in your life in ways you never could have imagined.

And don't be afraid when this starts to happen.

When a gift is offered to you, you should accept it.

*(Crystal still goes on cleaning.)*

CHARLIE: And you tell yourself: this is the Universe taking care of me, giving me everything I deserve.

## Scene Eleven.

*(Lights change. The Saturn dealership. Shannon is alone, wearing a party hat and holding a drink and a balloon. She sings the Saturn song to herself, making up her own choreography, which is slightly more lascivious than Crystal's. While she sings, Crystal enters.)*

SHANNON: You bought a Saturn, you bought a Saturn,
Put our service to the test,
You bought a Saturn . . . you bought a Saturn,
Saturn owners are the best.
Saturn . . .
Working here is such a gas . . . .

*(She sucks helium from the balloon.)*

'Til they fuck you in the ass.

*(She sees Crystal.)*

SHANNON: Crystal!  Hey . . .
Happy Last Day.
Drinks are in the lounge.

*(Crystal gives her a dazed stare and keeps going, back toward the offices.)*

SHANNON: Oh! Check your box.
That lady dropped off an envelope for you.

*(pause)*

CRYSTAL: Thank you.

*(Crystal exits.)*

SHANNON: Anytime.

## Scene Twelve.

*(The kitchen. Early evening, just before dusk. Toni and Crystal sit at the kitchen table. Toni makes notes in a folder. Crystal tries to sneak a glance at what she's writing, but Toni is casually positioned to prevent this. Finally she stops writing and closes the folder.)*

TONI: Everything looks good.

And this is your lease?

*(Crystal nods and slides some papers across the table to her.)*

TONI: "Joe Parker." Huh.

I used to know a fellow by that name.

*(She shrugs and tucks the lease into the file. They look at each other for a moment.)*

CRYSTAL: So what's next?

TONI: We're done.

CRYSTAL: Done?

TONI: I'll tell my supervisor you've remediated all the problems we discussed.

And I'll recommend reinstatement of custody.

CRYSTAL: So I can go get her?

TONI: The judge needs to sign off first, and then we'll schedule a time. It'll take about a day or two.

*(pause)*

Crystal?

Are you all right?

I know it's hard, dealing with all this.

It probably seems like it's been going on forever.

*(Crystal can't speak. Toni pats her on the hand.)*

TONI: Look at everything you've done. You've turned your whole life around.

CRYSTAL: I'd do anything for her.

TONI: I know you would.

*(pause)*

TONI: Well. I'd better get on the road. Three more stops on my way home. Goddamned budget cuts.

*(They get up and move to the sliding glass door. Toni sees the splintered bull's eye in the glass.)*

CRYSTAL: Oh . . . I forgot to tell you . . .

I'm getting this fixed. They're coming tomorrow.

TONI: Bird?

CRYSTAL: Pardon?

TONI: Did a bird fly into it?

CRYSTAL: Yes.

It was so sad.

*(Toni steps outside.)*

TONI: Take care now.

*(Crystal manages a polite half-smile but doesn't answer. She stands framed in the doorway, watching Toni leave. She waves as Toni drives away. It's darker out now. For a long moment, Crystal seems frozen, almost catatonic, rooted in the doorway. The street light blinks on. She stares at it. She slides the door closed and locks it. Blackout.)*


End Of Play.

# Detroit

*Lisa D'Amour*

DETROIT received its World Premiere at the
Steppenwolf Theatre Company in Chicago
from September 9 – November 7, 2010.

Directed by: Austin Pendleton
KENNY: Kevin Anderson
SHARON: Kate Arrington
BEN: Ian Barford
FRANK: Robert Breuler
MARY: Laurie Metcalf

Scenic Design: Kevin Depinet_
Costume Design: Rachel Anne Healy
Lighting Design: Kevin Rigdon
Original Music: Josh Schmidt
Sound Design: Josh Schmidt
Stage Manager: Michelle Medvin
Assistant Stage Manager: Rose Marie Packer
Dramaturg: Polly Carl
Choreographer: Tommy Rapley
Fight Choreographer: Matt Hawkins

DETROIT received its NYC Premiere at
Playwrights Horizons in New York City
August 24 – October 28, 2012.

Directed by Anne Kauffman
FRANK: John Cullum
KENNY: Darren Pettie
MARY: Amy Ryan
BEN: David Schwimmer
SHARON: Sarah Sokolovic

Scenic Design  Louisa Thompson
Costume Design  Kaye Voyce
Lighting Design  Mark Barton
Sound Design  Matt Tierney
Production Stage Manager  Lisa Ann Chernoff

LISA D'AMOUR is a playwright and one half of Pearl-Damour, an OBIE-award winning interdisciplinary performance company she runs with Katie Pearl. Lisa's plays have been produced by theaters across the U.S., including The Women's Project, Clubbed Thumb, Theatre of a Two-Headed Calf, New Georges (all in NYC), Salvage Vanguard Theater (Austin, TX), Catastrophic Theatre (Houston, TX), ArtSpot Productions (New Orleans, LA) and Children's Theater Company (Minneapolis, MN). Lisa collaborates on site-specific performances. In 2008, Lisa created a performance for visual artist SWOON's Swimming Cities of Switchback Sea, a flotilla of six boats created from salvaged materials that navigated the Hudson River. performing in riverfront parks from Troy, NY to New York City. Detroit, originally produced by Steppenwolf Theater Company, was a finalist for the 2011 Pulitizer Prize for Drama and a finalist for the Susan Smith Blackburn Prize. In 2008, D'Amour was awarded the Alpert Award for the Arts in theater and 2011, she received the Steinberg Playwright Award. Lisa received her M.F.A. in playwriting from the University of Texas at Austin and is a New Dramatists alumni. She lives with her husband, composer Brendan Connelly, in Brooklyn and New Orleans.
lisadamour.com
peraldamour.com

# CHARACTERS

BEN: Raised in the United States, somewhere inland: Kansas City, maybe Denver. He worked at one bank for 5 years and another bank for 6 years. Recently laid off from his job.

MARY: Raised in the United States, somewhere inland: Kansas City, maybe Denver. Met Ben after college, when they were both working, at a happy hour. She works as a paralegal at a small to mid-sized law firm.

KENNY: Raised in several cities in California until he was 12 or 13 and his parents finally split up and he moved to Omaha with his mom. Now he works as a warehouse manager. Fresh out of major substance abuse rehab.

SHARON: Raised in Tucson, AZ until she was 9, then she and her mother moved to Columbus, Ohio for 2 years and then to Indianapolis, where she went to high school. In her junior year her mother moved back to Arizona with her boyfriend, and Sharon lived with her best friend to finish school. Now, Sharon works at a phone bank, answering customer service calls. Fresh out of major substance abuse rehab.

FRANK: Two generations older than the other characters. Maybe he's in his late 70's early 80's? But he's spry, the kind of man whose been fixing his roof and rewiring the electricity on his house and taking care of his impeccable lawn for many years. He's happy.

PLACE:

Not necessarily Detroit. However, we are in a "first ring" suburb outside of a mid-sized American city. There are the suburbs that comprise the first "ring" of houses outside the city proper. They were built perhaps in the late 50's, smaller houses, perhaps of outdated design. The kind of house many people today would consider a "starter house" or a house you would want to purchase, live in, and keep your eye on the lot next door so you could buy that, knock both houses down, and build a double-lot house.

TIME: Now.

*Casting Note:* When I wrote the play, I imagined Mary, Ben, Sharon and Kenny to be around 34 years old. I've since realized that there is some flexibility in terms of the ages of the characters. For example, the show can be cast with Mary and Ben a little older, in their 40's, and Sharon and Kenny younger, in their late 20's early 30's. It's also possible that Kenny is quite a bit older than Sharon. I just ask that directors consider how the age of the characters reverberates through the whole script: the focus of the story can shift quite a bit depending on how old they are.

*Set Note:* This play is set in the front and back yards of the characters houses. There is a way to produce the play by setting it only in the back yards by cutting certain lines and adding a few lines. The author will provide the line cuts and changes if the play is to be produced that way.

*"Plywood has a lifespan of 40 years. Over time, the glue that holds plywood together dries up. Then, walls buckle, split and peel. Panels pop loose. Rooms, doors and windows morph into trick-or-treat versions of themselves."*
—Herbert Muschamp,
New York Times, October 19, 1997

*"Dogs, by this same logic,
bark what they cannot understand."*
—Heraclitus

*Lisa D'Amour*

*Lights Up.*

*Sharon and Kenny are in Mary and Ben's backyard. They sit in newish looking lawn chairs—part of a set from maybe Home Depot. Mary struggles to get a patio umbrella to go up as she speaks – it's in the middle of the table and it's heavy. There is a grill nearby*

MARY: And the man with the birthmark looked up and slid a handwritten receipt across the table to me. He said "Is there anything else I can help you with" and I said no thank you and I turned and walked out onto the wooden pier and I saw a very old seagull swoop down into the water and eat a fish.

SHARON: How did you know it was old?

MARY: I just knew.

KENNY: And the bank was an old card table on the edge of an abandoned boardwalk?

MARY: And all the deposits went into an Adidas shoe box the banker kept under the table.

SHARON: They make those shoes in Germany. I went there for a week on this high school trip and everyone wanted to buy them. We all thought they were cheaper over there. I didn't buy any.

MARY: *(Under her breath.)* Shit. Shit shit shit.

KENNY: Can I help you with that?

MARY: No I'll be right back.

*Mary goes inside. Kenny and Sharon sit in the chairs in silence. They look hardly even look at each other. The sounds we hear: birds. A lawnmower in the distance. A clanging sound, like someone fixing something. A siren that we hear and quickly fades. Mary comes out with Ben following her. Ben has a pan full of meat, some kind of steaks. Mary is kind of in a tizzy.*

MARY: I hold it up and I press the button but nothing works sometimes it stays for like 2 seconds but then it falls down again.

*Ben fools with the umbrella. They all watch. He pulls his hands away. The umbrella stays up. Pause.*

BEN: Wa-lah.

*Sharon laughs just a couple laughs. No one else laughs.*

MARY: It's funny when you first moved in we didn't know if anyone was actually living next door. Ben swore he saw someone coming and going. But at weird times. And the sheets stayed up for so long it still looked empty. It was driving him crazy! So when I saw you yesterday morning I knew I had to grab you. And tell you that we didn't know you were there, that's why we didn't stop by to say hello.

SHARON: We're still not totally moved in. The house belongs to his aunt.

KENNY: Belonged to my aunt. She passed away.

MARY: Oh, that was your aunt?

KENNY: We're renting it for a while before they sell.

SHARON: We'll probably buy it, though.

BEN: That's the way to do it, from a friend or family member. You can avoid a lot of closing costs.

KENNY: That's what they say.

SHARON: So yes, it's a new start! I mean we don't have any furniture even!

MARY: Oh everybody says that "We don't have any furniture."

KENNY: Well—

BEN: There are some good outlet stores over on 265. That's where I got my TV chair.

MARY: Oh wait I've got something!

*Mary goes inside. She has a little trouble with the sliding glass door. She is just inside the house, so she can call back to the group.*

SHARON: Such a great backyard.

MARY: *(Calling from inside)* Isn't it great?

BEN: Thanks, we love it. It sold us on the neighborhood.

SHARON: Hey who is the woman who jogs around the neighborhood in the hot pink jogging outfit?

MARY: What?

SHARON: Who is the woman who jogs around the neighborhood in the hot pink jogging outfit?

MARY: I don't know. I've never seen her. Ben, have you seen this woman? Jogging?

BEN: No, I don't think so. There are a lot of people jogging in the morning.

SHARON: This one wears a hot pink jogging suit.

*Mary is back at the door, carrying a coffee table, trying to get it through the door.*

MARY: I don't know. I don't know who that is.

KENNY: Wait, wait let me help.

MARY: Oh God this door!

KENNY: Hold on, I've got it. I've got it.

*Kenny brings the coffee table through the door. It is an older model, kind of heavy and clunky, maybe with a glass top.*

*Mary puts the coffee table down in front of Sharon.*

MARY: This is for you.

SHARON: What?

MARY: You said you didn't have any furniture. So this is for you.

BEN: Honey that's our coffee table.

MARY: I hate this coffee table. Do you like it?

KENNY: Uh yeah its nice. Do you like it?

MARY: I mean it's a good coffee table, its very sturdy I think it will be good for you I just—

SHARON: I love it.

*Pause.*

Thank you.

MARY: It's for you.

SHARON: I know. It's amazing.

*Sharon half-touches the coffee table.*

MARY: Now Ben has to buy me a new table! Ha Ha!

BEN: Ha—Ha.

*Sharon sits and indicates the coffee table to Kenny, like "nice table right?" Ben speaks kind of loud.*

BEN: Alright everybody I'm going to throw these puppies on the grill!

KENNY: *(To Sharon. If Mary hears her, she pretends not to hear it.)*

Can you imagine if they really were puppies?

*Sharon and Kenny giggle at their private joke. Mary speaks to Ben.*

MARY: Did you do the marinade?

*She takes a step and something hurts in her foot.*

OW!

*Sharon half gets up from her chair.*

SHARON: Are you OK?

MARY: Yes, no, ow, its fine, I just have this well I have this oh god planters wart in the bottom of my foot god so embarrassing but do you know what that is? This is a really nasty yes wart that grows upward, INTO your foot, slowly so it takes you a while to notice it, and when you finally do it hurts hurts hurts and you try to put that drugstore wart remover stuff on it and it won't work, and so you go to the doctor—I went to the doctor, I went to the doctor today—and he said he could cut it out but he would have to inject anesthesia into my foot and then do minor surgery—I know—and since I knew you all were coming over I thought it would be best to wait so I'm having it done next Thursday and just making due until then. It is only when I step a certain way…it must hit a nerve or something.

KENNY: Like when you have a cavity?

SHARON: Oh right and you bite down on ice or something soft like an apple that goes way up?

KENNY: Or like a caramel candy.

MARY: And start chewing everything super cautiously, like half-chewing because you're afraid of that zap and then one day you forget and you bite regular—

*Everybody kinds of groans and cringes.*

BEN: OK OK let's not—eew—now you've given me the creeps.

KENNY: Let's talk about something else.

MARY: Yes, let's. Sorry, let's.

BEN: So where do you guys work?

KENNY: I work in a warehouse over off of 694.

SHARON: I work in a phone bank. Is that what you call it? It's like customer service. I sit in one of the booths take the calls and either give people answers or send them on to the supervisor.

MARY: Oh that sounds interesting.

SHARON: Really?

MARY: I work as a paralegal at Furley, Clark and Lamb.

KENNY: What do you do Ben?

BEN: Ha ha I'm a deadbeat. No but really I got laid off my job at this bank, I was a loan officer and they like laid everybody off like literally I don't know who is doing the work anymore and so they gave me this like halfway decent severance pay and also I could get unemployment so I am using it as an opportunity to set up my own business.

MARY: He's home all day.

BEN: It's a financial planning business. Helping people with their credit scores, that sort of thing.

SHARON: Ha we could use that help!

BEN: You and a lot of people, it can slip so fast.

SHARON: And then you can't get it back up again.

BEN: Well, there are strategies, but it takes a lot of patience. We can have a session sometime.

SHARON: That would be great.

BEN: I need to practice on people. You all can be my test case. And then when you're hanging out on your private yacht I can use a quote from you on my website.

SHARON: Sounds good to me!

MARY: He's designing a website. The whole business is going to be run right inside of it.

BEN: I'm building it myself to save money.

MARY: He's got this great book and it talks a lot about breathing deep and taking your time.

SHARON: Uh huh

BEN: And how important it is to spend a lot of time doing things you're passionate about. If you follow your passions, you're halfway there.

MARY: If you panic and start to cut corners, then forget it, it's like building a house on quicksand.

BEN: It's really all about envisioning your life as financially sound.

MARY: It's scary but I really think it's true. It's a great book.

KENNY: Oh so maybe that's why you had that dream?

MARY: Dream?

KENNY: The one about the bank being a card table at the edge of an abandoned whatchamacalit. With the deposits in the shoebox.

MARY: Oh right.

BEN: Alright, we gonna eat some meat!

*Ben gets up to check the meat.*

SHARON: *(To Ben.)* Are you British?

BEN: What?

SHARON: Are you from England?

BEN: No, why?

SHARON: I don't know. Something about the way you talk. "Now you've given me the creeps."

BEN: "Now you've given me the creeps" I didn't even realize I said it like that. Huh.

SHARON: Maybe you're British.

BEN: *(Kind of laughs but he doesn't really know what she means.)*

Yeah, maybe.

*We hear the meat sizzling on the grill.*

SHARON: Wow steak.

*We hear the grill and some surrounding sounds.*

BEN: Does anyone want a beer?

*Kenny and Sharon overlap in their reply.*

KENNY AND SHARON: We don't drink.

*Mary speaks under her breath.*

MARY: I told you that Ben.

*Short pause.*

BEN: Oh well does anyone need anything? What are you drinking seltzer?

KENNY: I'm OK.

SHARON: I'd love a little more ice.

MARY: Oh I'll bring out a bucket.

BEN: Mary these are just going to be a couple more minutes if you want to check the potatoes.

MARY: Oh right.

*Mary goes inside*

KENNY: So this is a nice patio. Was it here when you moved in?

BEN: Yes it was, yeah it's great.

KENNY: I thought maybe you laid it yourself.

BEN: No, no I work in a bank.

KENNY: The edges, the way the cement is pulling up from the edges, it looks like a do it yourself job.

BEN: Really? Is that a problem? I don't / think I noticed—

KENNY: No, no its totally fine, its just cosmetic, I only noticed because for a little while I was laying concrete, helping a friend with his business and we did a lot of patios so I learned a lot about it. But it's fine.

BEN: Yeah I never noticed.

KENNY: You have to buy this sealant and put it on at just the right time or the concrete wants to pull away like that. Really though you're fine.

BEN: Maybe you know why our sliding glass door slides so funny.

KENNY: Oh well I—

BEN: See you have to jiggle it like this to get it over the "hump" see? So you start to open it and you have to go—

*He jiggles the door, it opens.*

And then it opens. It isn't a big deal but—

*Kenny checks out the door.*

KENNY: Oh yeah right look it's the track, I think you might just need a whole new track but later on let me bang on it a bit with a—do you have a rubber mallet?

BEN: No I don't think so.

KENNY: I'll get one. I'll get one and I'll bring it over here and I'll bang on it and we'll see I think I can fix it.

*Mary slides through the door with the ice bucket.*

MARY: Excuse me.

KENNY: Excuse me.

MARY: The potatoes are perfect!

BEN: Ditto on the steaks!

*Sharon takes some ice and puts it in her glass and smiles at Mary.*

SHARON: This is awesome. It is so awesome. I mean who invites their neighbors over for dinner anymore?

BEN: Ha we don't have any friends.

MARY: Ben!

BEN: Well.

SHARON: Really though I mean we've lived in a bunch of

neighborhoods now—apartments, houses, condos even a hotel for a little while—

KENNY: The house we were renting had a sewer leak—

MARY: Eew—

SHARON: So the landlord had to put us in a hotel—we've lived in a lot of places and never, never did the neighbors give us the time of day. Neighbors. I mean why is that word still in the dictionary its archaic am I saying the right word? Because you don't need to talk to your neighbors anymore I mean does anyone borrow a cup of sugar anymore? No you drive to the 24-hour grocery.

Because you don't want to bother your neighbors.

And so if you come home from work and you do see your neighbor like, getting out of their car or calling their kid inside—wait, what am I saying, kids don't play outside anymore, they might get seduced by some homicidal drug addicts ahhhh! Anyway if you get home and your neighbor is out setting the timer off on their watering system then you look at the ground or maybe give a quick wave and run inside. Because maybe you had a bad day or maybe you have pink eye or something and you don't want to get too close to them. Always an excuse. And when you get inside, behind your closed door, quiet in your house, you make a pact with yourself to talk to them next time but then things get … fucked up … oh sorry I didn't mean to say that I apologize—

KENNY: She has a sailor mouth.

SHARON: I do, I'm working on it, but I just think there is no real communication anymore, real communication about real things, about that steak or that sliding glass door or yes I would love some more ice but here we are, having that sort of communication and its just so…its so beautiful—

> *Sharon starts to cry. Head in hands. A moment or two of just Sharon crying, like, deep, private weeping. Ben and Mary look for a moment then Ben busies himself at the grill. Kenny gets up.*

KENNY: It's OK sweetie, just—

*Ken leans over to comfort Sharon and WHAM the patio umbrella comes crashing down hitting him on the head.*

KENNY: OW!

BEN: Oh shit.

*Kenny is holding the back of his head.*

SHARON: Baby are you OK?

KENNY: Yeah, yeah its just hold on I gotta sit down. Whoo I'm seeing stars.

MARY: Oh wait you're bleeding you're bleeding let me get a towel.

*Mary races inside, she can't get the sliding door open.*

BEN: You have to jiggle it jiggle it jiggle it no like this—

*Ben runs over and jiggles the door or does Kenny get up and jiggle it with his hand still on his head?*

KENNY: No its OK really I'm sure its just I just need a second—

*He takes his hand away—he really is bleeding.*

KENNY: Oh wait yeah, maybe a towel.

SHARON: Shit, baby, just keep the pressure on—

*Mary runs back out with a towel.*

MARY: I can't believe this. Ben, that

*Quickly, almost under her breath—*

God damned

*Back to normal voice—*

MARY: umbrella!

BEN: I know, I know.

KENNY: It's OK its gonna be fine—

SHARON: He's got a hard head right baby?

KENNY: Heh-heh. Maybe a little ice?

SHARON: The ice is right here.

*Sharon gets a handful of ice out of the bucket and puts it in the towel.*

MARY: Ben let's just take the umbrella out, OK? Like I suggested yesterday. Because this keeps happening and I didn't want anyone to get hurt. So let's just take the 30 seconds—

*Ben slips the umbrella out from the hole and leans it against the house.*

Yes the 30 seconds it takes to take the umbrella out so no one gets hurt, and we can consider a new umbrella, that isn't from the fucking—excuse me—bargain basement—

BEN: Mary—

MARY: So that our guests aren't required to get stitches just for daring to come into our back yard.

SHARON: It's OK really—

KENNY: I don't need stitches. I've had stitches before.

BEN: Where's the tag. I'm calling the manufacturer. In fact I should call them right now—

Maybe Sharon and Kenny are like no no no no don't worry, really—

Kenny we can take you to the hospital.

Sharon and Kenny are even more like no no no really.

BEN: Where is that tag—

*Ben realizes something about the situation. He slips outside of his tizzy and returns to calm host mode.*

OK. OK look at us. Look at us. Kenny you're fine?

KENNY: Totally. I'm just going to keep the pressure on for a bit.

BEN: Alright, then.

SHARON: *(In a bad British accent)* "Alrighty, then, Ben"

BEN: What?

SHARON: I said "Alrighty ole chap, cup a tea!" You're British! Admit it! Admit it!

KENNY: Sharon—

BEN: So. How bout some steak?

SHARON: Let's do it!

*Ben starts taking steaks off the grill.*

BEN: Kenny you get the first one in honor of your concussion.

KENNY: Ha Ha.

MARY: Potatoes.

SHARON: Do you all ever have "twice baked" potatoes.

BEN: Oh yeah with all that cream in them.

SHARON: Yes!

MARY: Sometimes but they are so much work.

---

SHARON: My mom used to make those all the time.

*A few moments of sitting down and settling in. Ben is sitting down and they are all taking their first bites.*

KENNY: Aw yeah.

*Kenny gives Ben the thumbs up.*

MARY: Delicious honey.

Does one of them get a piece of gristle and do that weird chewing thing where you have to get it out of your mouth and spit it in your napkin? Ben glances over into Kenny and Sharon's yard.

SHARON: I can't believe I cried.

MARY: Oh, now—

BEN: Cried?

SHARON: A few minutes ago. When I was talking about neighbors.

BEN: God did I miss that? Did I forget?

SHARON: They say its part of the process, feeling things, letting your emotions just happen, in real time, rather then running away from them on that glossy motorcade of substances.

MARY: Process?

KENNY: *(Under his breath)* Baby we were going to keep that / to ourselves—

SHARON: Kenny and I met in Eldridge Smith Tomforde.

MARY: *(Gets it)* Oh.

*Ben is eating.*

BEN: *(Chipper, Oblivious)* What's Eldridge Smith Tomforde?

*Pause for a moment.*

MARY: It's a rehab facility, honey. For substance abuse.

BEN: *(Still Chipper)* Oh so that's why you don't drink.

KENNY: Yes and that's why we don't smoke crack or shoot meth or snort big fat lines of cocaine at 4 in the morning for the third day in a row.

*Quick pause then Sharon starts to laugh. Then Kenny laughs and Mary sort of smiles. Mary stays really quiet during this next section.*

BEN: Well, more power to you. And so you met in this…. this….

SHARON: Facility. Yes we were both in for three months—we

arrived the same week.

KENNY: And we resisted the attraction for at least a month.

SHARON: Because you're supposed to. You're actually supposed to resist it for a year but—

KENNY: *(Re: Hot Sharon)* But who can resist this right?

*Ben and Kenny laugh knowingly but it is a little weird.*

SHARON: And it's so strange "getting out". Those doors part
and you walk outside into the hot air, thinking about your
apartment that's waiting for you, still sealed shut, filled
with all your crappy stuff, dishes molding in the sink, coun-
tertops piled with old beer cans and underwear and pipes
and stuffed animals covered in puke. And you're standing
outside the hospital, clutching each other's sweaty hands
for dear life—

And then there was this house.

KENNY: My aunt died.

SHARON: There was this house, and—this is not a lie—we went
to TJ Maxx, and I bought a dress with flowers on it, and a
pair of "flats". "Flats" and Kenny bought a suit—

KENNY: It was $250 marked down to $34.99.

SHARON: And he bought shoes also, and an undershirt and
socks...

KENNY: And we went to see my great-uncle, who was very
close to my aunt—she left the house to him—

SHARON: And we asked if we could live here. We asked him
to give us a chance.

*BLACKOUT*

*The sounds of the neighborhood moving into night:*

*The hum of air conditioning units, and air conditioning units starting up and shutting off, a couple cars driving by, a car or two parking, doors opening and closing. Perhaps an automatic garage door opening? The faint sound of a few joggers jogging, and a few kids riding their bikes.*

*The car and people sounds begin to fade and are replaced by crickets and maybe a few frogs, still mixed in with the air conditioning sounds.*

*And someone is having a fight behind closed doors. Then the sound of "No, No, No, No, NO" as a door opens and the No's become louder. The same door slams.*

*Loud knocking on another door. A knocking and then the sound of Mary yelling "Sharon! Sharon open up! Shaaaaron!" And more knocking.*

*Lights up, middle-of-the-night outdoor light. We are in Kenny and Sharon's front yard. Theirs is a very basic brick suburban house. Or maybe siding. Some shrubs but no flowers. Really bare bones. There is one taller potted plant on the porch, a plant that is like a small tree, with some blossoms on it. Other than that, nada.*

*Mary is in her bathrobe, banging on the front door. She is near tears.*

*Sharon opens the door in her T-shirt and underwear.*

SHARON: Mary what's—

*Mary falls into her arms. She weeps outright for maybe 5 seconds—*

Mary can you just—

*Another wave of weeping. Eventually Mary half composes herself. Anytime Mary curses she says that word kind of under her breath.*

MARY: Its just I don't know how to help him. I'm at the frayed edge of my wits. He gets to be home all day and I don't get home until 6:45 because of the *fucking* traffic on 694 and he's been home all day and I get home and he's already on his first drink. He says it's his first drink anyway. And he's cooked dinner which is of course very sweet but then I say something about how his green beans taste different my green beans you know like "oh these taste different" just like that, not saying anything bad but he drops his fork and I know he's offended and then it starts. And I hate "NASCAR Unmasked and Personal" and he knows I hate it I mean he's not a NASCAR kind of guy he doesn't like NASCAR he just likes that show, and he turns it on anyway while I'm finishing my dinner, while I'm washing the dishes and he watches the TV so fucking loud even the commercials and he laughs at commercials, at *dumbfuck* commercials like the one with the cartoon chicken getting rubbed down with chicken magic.

*Mary imitates the commercial. It is a Latino Chicken*

"Ieeee! It tickles!" I mean Sharon its so *fucking crackass* dumb.

He says it helps him decompress, he's at the computer all day long. And I'm like "doing what? Looking at one of those titty websites? Live chatting with some stripper lying on her crappy couch somewhere? How long can a making a WEBSITE possibly take?"

No. No I don't say that. I just think it.

What I say is: "So how was your day? Did you bring the files to Kinkos" And he's like "No I forgot oh well I'll do it tomorrow" and I say "You know you can do it on their website through the file uploader, its super easy" And he says "Yes YES I know" and I say "well you know that book you bought for $65.00 said you've got to be hard on yourself about keeping to a schedule. Because Joe Blow down the street is also probably laid off, and also probably about to set up his dream business where you get to sit home all day and tell other people how to clean up the fucking financial wasteland of their day to day existence. And if Joe Blow gets his portfolio together before you do then Joe Blow gets the clients, not you." And he's says "Joe Blow can suck my *nutsack*"

*Pause for a moment, that word is like a bad taste in her mouth.*

*Lisa D'Amour*

And I say "Oh that's a winning attitude." And then that's it—we're fighting and he's all "I'm trying to be proactive" and I'm all "Today sucked, I barely got to eat lunch" and he's all "I'm afraid" and I'm like "Don't say it like that" and he's like "Look I have to put my beer on the floor! The photo album too!" And I'm like "That coffee table didn't GO in this ROOM—

SHARON: You can have it / back—

MARY: I don't want it back.

I want to live in a tent in the woods. With one pot and one pan. And an old fashioned aluminum mess kit with its own mesh bag. I want my hair to smell like the smoke from yesterday's fire, when I cooked my fish and my little white potatoes. I want to dry out my underwear on a warm rock. And feel the cold water rushing around my ankles, my feet pressing into the tiny stone bed that holds up the stream. Silver guppies nosing their heads into my calves…

*Quiet for a moment. We hear suburban wind, maybe a car passing on another street. Maybe some teenagers laughing, maybe some kid in the house across the street listen to music in their room.*

SHARON: Were you a girl scout?

MARY: Yes.

SHARON: I thought so.

Mary leans over into the bushes, she doesn't get up, she just leans over, and pukes. And pukes. And sits back up.

MARY: Oh god, my head. I think I need some water.

SHARON: Mary, have you ever thought about getting some help?

MARY: Some help with what?

SHARON: With your drinking problem.

*Mary looks at Sharon like she is an alien from another planet.*

MARY: I thought I could just come to you and talk.

SHARON: You can, you did.

MARY:  Because you cried at          SHARON: I know.
          my house and

MARY: *(CONT)* I thought that was awesome.
          that you felt comfortable

enough to do that it made me feel like
a good host that you felt OK letting go
In that way—

SHARON: You are a good host.

But you can be a great host and still have a drinking problem.

*Mary gets loud. Too loud for this neighborhood. She no longer quiets her curse words.*

MARY: You know what FUCK YOU.

*She stands up and stumbles a little.*

I come over here asking for HELP and what is the FIRST THING YOU FUCKING DO? Accuse me of being a fucking DRUNK? I MEAN IF THAT IS NOT THE BLACK CALLING THE KETTLE POT. God. My husband is offering the two of you his services FOR FREE. He wouldn't even blink to ask for payment. Wouldn't even BLINK. And look at you. This fucking yard.

*Ben walks up, he is obviously not drunk he is stone cold sober and it takes Mary a little while to see him.*

MARY: There's not even a single FERN. You've made no effort.

SHARON: Well we just moved in—

*Maybe Mary grabs on to Sharon?*

MARY: I was hiding behind our bushes. I snuck out the door to get some air. I JUST NEEDED SOME AIR, I needed to get out of the house. And he wouldn't let me. He kept locking the door on me. And so when the commercial came on I snuck out the back and climbed over the fence and just squatted there behind the bushes. He called and called. My toes were in the mulch, I was breathing, I was not answering. Because he doesn't like me, nobody likes me, and I just wanted to breathe.

And then I thought Sharon likes me.

She cried in my yard.

*Mary pukes over Sharon's shoulder, she has to kind of brush it off her back and the back of her arm. Ben catches Mary. Kenny opens the door, half asleep, in his boxers. Mary notices its Ben.*

GET AWAY FROM ME GET HIM AWAY!

*Lisa D'Amour*

*Ben pulls Mary too him and speaks to her softly in her ear. She's listening. She's saying these words as he whispers in her ear.*

Uh huh. Uh huh. My head is pounding. It's like there's cats inside. I know. I know I'm a good person. I know tootsie too. Yes. Yes. I want to go home. I want to get in the tub. Ow, my foot.

*Mary is quiet in Ben's arms. Ben looks at Sharon and Kenny.*

*Everyone except Mary sees someone approaching. Ben tries to hold Mary up a little better. We hear the sound of footsteps jogging by. All at once Ben, Sharon and Kenny give a quick wave, like they are waving back to someone.*

BEN: That's her?

SHARON: That's her. How dumb is that, jogging at 11 at night.

KENNY: And she'll be back at it at 6:30.

SHARON: Showoff.

KENNY: I really need to start exercising again.

*Pause for a quick moment as they watch her go.*

BEN: I'm really—

SHARON AND KENNY: No, really, it's ok really.

BEN: We'll buy you a new shirt—

KENNY: Don't worry, please—

SHARON: We've been through this—

KENNY: Remember?

BEN: I'll see you tomorrow Kenny.

KENNY: 1:30!

*Ben starts to walk Mary home.*

BEN: Please don't worry about your yard –

*Mary's foot hurts as she walks.*

MARY: Ow. OW.

BEN: It's going to be a nice yard. I like that new plant.

*Ben and Mary are almost to their house. Sharon says softly.*

SHARON: The funny thing is it's fake.

*Sharon and Kenny watch them go for a few seconds. A quick kiss then they head back inside. Before the door closes—*

*BLACKOUT*

*Daytime sounds. Lawnmowers, kids on bikes, a plane overhead, hum of air conditioner compressors in people's back yards, a couple of birds.*

*Lights up on Mary and Ben's back yard. Ben is at the grill, cleaning it off with a wire brush, turning on the gas.*

*Mary comes out of the house with a lacey table cloth.*

*We see her foot is bandaged and she is wearing a funny orthopedic sandal on that foot that doesn't let you put pressure on the front of your foot.*

*Ben crosses around the table into the house – he's on a mission.*

*She unfolds the table cloth, snaps it out and lets it settle into place on the table. Perfect.*

*Mary heads inside and she and Ben cross as he comes out with a tray of chicken covered in saran wrap.*

BEN: Excuse me.
MARY: Excuse me.

> *Ben puts the chicken on the tray next to the grill. Mary comes out with a bouquet of fresh flowers, and a candle. Ben checks one last thing, then watches Mary arrange the flowers. Mary lights the candle, and looks at Ben.*
>
> *Are Mary and Ben about to say something nice and / or real to each other?*
>
> *Kenny and Sharon call from inside Ben and Mary's house.*

SHARON: Hello-oo! Anybody home?
BEN: Come on in, we're in      MARY: Eek! Just a second!
   the back!

> *Mary rushes in the house. Perhaps we hear her say something like "Go ahead out, go, go…" Kenny appears, carrying a two liter of Dr. Pepper, followed by Sharon.*

BEN: Hi!
SHARON: Oh my god this looks amazing!
MARY: *(From inside)* It's a lawn party! Hold on!
KENNY: We brought this.

*Kenny hands Ben the Dr. Pepper. Sharon admires the flowers.*

BEN: Thanks—

*Ben puts the Dr. Pepper on the table or whatever.*

SHARON: Oh my god are these real?

*Ben points towards Kenny and Sharon's back yard.*

BEN: Hey Kenny are you building a deck?

KENNY: Yeah I'm getting started. That's the foundation you see right there, and the boards for the decking. I can't decide if I want to put up a railing or not.

BEN: Well its nice for leaning—

KENNY: Yeah but then you have to really reinforce it.

BEN: Or for kids, if you want to put kids on the deck—

KENNY: Yeah, well, we're just taking things one step at a time.

BEN: Oh, yeah, sure, of course, I mean really, yeah, us too, right? I mean, I don't know what I'm talking about, I don't even know what end of the hammer to hold.

SHARON: Yeah but you've got smarts Ben. Kenny could never start his own business.

BEN: Who knows! Kenny's got big plans right Kenny?

*Kenny makes some awkward "you got it, Ben" Kind of gesture.*

SHARON: You look like a smart person, Ben.

BEN: Ha, really?

SHARON: Yes, like you should be wearing skinny little suspenders.

MARY: *(Offstage in the house.)* Honey, will you get the door?

*Ben slides the sliding door open for Mary.*

MARY: Look how that sliding door just zips open!

BEN: Your husband's a genius, Sharon.

*Kenny smiles. Mary enters with an enormous tray of hors d'eourves, beautifully presented. It is a little intimidating how beautifully presented they are.*

MARY: Alright, everybody so we've got some dates wrapped in bacon drizzled with some chili oil and this is a Danish Havarti that I mashed with some basil and it is really great with this special olive oil—you just need a little. These are slices of "heirloom tomatoes" do you know what that is? I drove all the way to Whole Foods to get them. They've been grown from the same seed for hundreds of years, meaning the plants grow and drop their seeds and those seeds are used for the next plants. Try that with the olive oil and a little bit of this special pink salt—

KENNY: Special salt?

MARY: I know, I know, you think "salt" "salt is salt" right? But here taste it with a tomato—

KENNY: Oh I don't like tomatoes—

SHARON: *(as in: be polite)* Kenny—

MARY: Oh well taste it with the Havarti then. Go ahead taste it—

> *She hands him a cracker with havarti and a bit of salt.*
> *They watch him taste it. He chews.*

KENNY: Oh yeah.

MARY: See? I was right, right?

KENNY: Yeah it takes a second but then—wow! Taste this.

SHARON: I wish I could cook.

> *He feeds a bite to Sharon.*

MARY: Oh you can cook! It's special pink salt from the bottom of a special river. Ben, what's the name of that river? Ben? And this—

> *She holds up a little bowl.*

Is caviar.

BEN: Caviar?

MARY: Caviar that came all the way from Norway.

SHARON: Wow. Kenny won't even let me buy Dijon mustard.

> *Mary hands Sharon some caviar on a cracker.*

BEN: Where did you buy Caviar?

MARY: It doesn't matter Ben.

SHARON: Oh it's good!

MARY: Right?

> *Ben claps his hands.*

BEN: OK let's throw these puppies on the grill!

MARY: Oh Ben let's wait just a few minutes. I just brought out the appetizers.

BEN: Yes but chicken takes longer.

MARY: Let's sit a minute—

Mary pulls a patio chair so it is side by side with hers.

BEN: But I—

MARY: I know but let's just relax a minute.

KENNY: Come sit, Ben.

SHARON: Rest.

> *Tiny pause.*

BEN: OK, alright.

> *Ben sits next to Mary. Mary grabs his hand and holds it. Smile. Pause. Sharon sings to them, getting the words a bit wrong.*

SHARON: "Don't Stop. Believin'. Hold on to that Feeeever…"

BEN: Oh I love that song.

KENNY: Remember MTV?

SHARON: It's still on, dummy.

BEN: *(Singing the next line with wrong words)* "Streetlight, fever…"

MARY: What about you Sharon how's work?

SHARON: Oh, you know -

MARY: Sure and you Kenny?

KENNY: You know it's a job.

BEN: You've just got to reach the one-year mark.

KENNY: One solid year with the same job and same address. Then everything starts to open up –

MARY: Like a good bottle of wine.

BEN: *(To Sharon)* We had a great session.

SHARON: He told me. So Ben is it true you're a NASCAR man?

> *Ben laughs.*

BEN: No, no. I just like the show, that behind-the-scenes show. It's just brain drain you know. The drivers and their trophies. And their trophy wives. A good way to decompress. I barely have to pay attention.

MARY: One time I watched a whole episode of "Fit to Be Tied" and when it got to the end, I realized that I hadn't really seen any of it.

SHARON: Yes!

MARY: I was stewing about something else the whole time… to Ben it looked like I was watching the show, but really I was on another planet….a really angry planet.

KENNY: That sounds like the last 5 years of my life.

SHARON: Up until now, right?

KENNY: Sure thing, hotpants.

BEN: *(Laughing a little)* Hotpants—

SHARON: I'm going to try meditation

BEN: Really.

> *Kenny is kind of cracking up. Sharon hits his leg while she speaks.*

SHARON: So I can stay in the moment. I'm going to start with ten minutes a day, just breathing in and out through my nose, facing the wall.

KENNY: You can't sit still for 10 seconds!

BEN: Sometimes I look up from my computer and 3 hours have passed, like THAT.

> *Ben snaps.*

SHARON: See! If you meditated, you could have those 3 hours back.

KENNY: It doesn't work that way, baby.

MARY: Oh my god he gets so zoned into that computer you would swear he was looking at porn.

BEN: Mary—

MARY: Don't worry I checked your search history once. It was all mortgage rates and motivational websites – and one random site about mining rocks and minerals!

> *Mary makes a face like "Wha? What is that about!" Mary and Sharon laugh. Does Ben sort of half-laugh and shrug?*

BEN: I was just curious…

KENNY: *(To Ben, but everyone can hear, regarding his search history)* Dude you can clear that shit. Then you can go anywhere you want.


BEN: I think I'll put the meat on.

> *Ben gets up to tend to the meat.*

KENNY: Hey Mary how's your foot?

MARY: Oh it's good. The thing took like 20 minutes. The worst part was the shot. The doctor stuck the needle into the arch of my foot and I could feel it shoot all the way up, through my stomach and heart and throat and into my eyeball.

BEN: I've never heard her yell like that.

MARY: But then everything went dead and the doctor could just dig right in.

KENNY: Eew. It didn't hurt?

MARY: This shoe hurts more than the operation, actually, but they say I have to wear it.

KENNY: *(To Mary)* I'm glad you're feeling better.

SHARON: See Mary went to the doctor it was fine.

*Kenny's afraid of the doctor.*

KENNY: I'm working on it.

BEN: All I want in the whole world is a meat thermometer. Mary can we get a meat thermometer?

MARY: Kenny do you want to try some caviar?

KENNY: The funny thing is I'm allergic.

MARY: To caviar?

SHARON: He puffs up instantly. We were in the VIP section in this club in Atlanta, and they had all this fancy shit. Excuse me this fancy food. And we were well we were high as kites and just eating and eating and all of a sudden he was on the floor, his eyes turning black, his whole face getting puffier and puffier.

KENNY: I couldn't breathe.

SHARON: They called an ambulance.

KENNY: Which sucked because I didn't have insurance.

SHARON: Three days in the hospital. I slept there. He woke up with night sweats. The doctor said if I ever eat caviar I should brush my teeth because if I kiss him, especially if I tongue kiss him, he could just blow up again. Like a blowfish. He's that allergic.

KENNY: It was crazy. That was like 8 years ago. I've avoided caviar ever since.

MARY: But wait I thought you met in rehab?

KENNY: Oh that's a funny story.

MARY: What do you mean?

SHARON: We * did * meet in rehab but we just realized a couple weeks ago that we had met before. In Hotlanta. And we had that adventure together. I actually snuck out of the hospital while he was asleep and got on a bus to Chi-town. Chicago. I mean I hardly knew him then. I mean we were a mess.

KENNY: I think we both just erased Hotlanta from our minds. What was the name of that club?

SHARON: Who knows. Razoo. Numbers. Buzz Buzz.

KENNY: The Compound. Third Base.

SHARON: Ampersand.

KENNY: Pirate Dan's.

> *Sharon kind of chuckles a bit. Kenny does too. It's a private moment. Hotlanta was fucked up, yo. Mary picks up a pitcher.*

MARY: Lemon Ginger Iced Tea?

SHARON: Why thank you, I would love some Lemon Ginger Iced Tea.

BEN: *(Trying his best to focus on the meat)* OK. I think this will be about 15 more minutes. Do you two like asparagus?

SHARON: I adore asparagus.

KENNY: *(Like, what you crazy bitch?)* What?

SHARON: *(At Kenny, perturbed)* You don't eat vegetables.

BEN: Neither does Mary.

MARY: I eat potatoes.

BEN AND KENNY: That doesn't count.

> *They all kind of chuckle that they said that together.*

KENNY: Because that would make French fries count, right Mary? I love me some French fries.

MARY: Me too.

> *Mary kind of blushes as she eats a date wrapped in bacon.*

SHARON: You guys have to come over. Soon. I mean look at that, the yard is right there. I could spit and hit it. Watch I'm going to spit.

> *Sharon spits and hits the yard.*

KENNY: Yes let's make that happen. As soon as the deck is finished.

SHARON: Fuck the deck! Oh, sorry. I mean fart on the deck! These are our neighbors, Kenny. We've lived here almost 5 weeks. We've got to have our neighbors over. We've got to fight against the anonimater…anonyminimous…

MARY and BEN: *(Staggered, trying to help her with the word)* Anonymity?

SHARON: Yes! We've got to fight that. I mean everywhere else we lived we hid from our neighbors and they hid from us because nobody wanted to interact with us EVER, I mean they knew, they could see. And they could just ignore us la la la la la – that's your space, this is mine, no I don't hear the screams and moans of a drug addict no I don't see those junkie friends with blood caked in their hair la la that's your space. Dust your hands, shoot the rooster in the foot and be done with it.

But things are different now. We can have company. We can have a nice time.

MARY: Of course you can.

SHARON: Tomorrow. Come over tomorrow.

KENNY: Sharon there's nowhere to sit!

SHARON: We'll figure it out. Mary and Ben, would you like to come to our house for dinner tomorrow?

KENNY: It's not our house.

SHARON: Shut up. Will you? Come over? Will you let us make you dinner at our place? Tomorrow?

BEN: *(Singing)* "Streetlight, Fever…"

MARY: Ben. I mean Ben do we have plans?

BEN: Sure, I mean no. No plans.

MARY: That would be lovely.

*Sharon is excited but also kind of freaked out, as she really does not have the skills or money to pull this sort of thing off.*

SHARON: Awesome. Great. Fun. Alright. Dinner at our place. Fantastic.

*Sharon spins around in one circle.*

Really, super fun!

*BLACKOUT*

*Outdoor sounds again, the next day.*

*When the lights come up, we are in Kenny and Sharon's backyard. The deck Kenny has started building is half finished: the floor is only 3/4 put down and most of the boards are loose. Ben and Mary sit in super crappy folding chairs that really look second hand – maybe Sharon and Kenny got them out of the basement. There is also an old-fashioned card table with one joint taped up with duct tape. Sharon is sitting on a plastic milk crate, upturned. Maybe Kenny will sit on a couple bags of charcoal? Oh or maybe a suitcase? The grill is from the dollar general. There is a plastic pot of plastic flowers on the card table.*

*Kenny is working the grill. Sharon relates a dream.*

SHARON: And I was wandering around inside this strange house. But I knew the house was inside of another house. A house inside a house. I could feel the two houses. And there were these rubber walls, you could press your hand right into them. And I was walking through the house and thinking "I've got to get this caviar to Mary"

*Mary laughs.*

But I knew that Kenny was allergic to caviar and so I didn't want to touch it, so I built this contraption out of chopsticks? To carry the caviar and I hooked it around my waist right—

*She indicates her abdomen.*

MARY: Oh my god do you think you're pregnant?

SHARON: NO. Definitely no. God no. So I opened this door in the hallway and inside on this fancy bed was the lady in the pink jogging suit getting the shit fucked out of her / by some guy –

KENNY: Sharon!

*Sharon lifts her hand to her mouth quickly.*

SHARON: Oh god. Shit I didn't mean that.

BEN: Well, that's what was happening. In the dream.

SHARON: Can I finish it? The dream?

*Ben and Mary are like "sure, sure"*

So I closed the door on her and then I was in the supermarket, the one I used to go to when I was a kid. And I was with Ben but Ben wasn't Ben. He was this short guy, maybe 5 feet tall, with this really bad brown dye job on his hair and his beard, and he may have been a leprechaun, but I knew it was Ben and I knew he was STARVING and I had to buy him food. And I would put food in the cart and check my purse for money but the amount of money I had kept changing, so I would put back the tomatoes and put in maybe green beans because they were cheaper and I would check my purse and not have enough money and put stuff back, and so on and so on—And I knew I had to feed Ben, he was shriveling, getting smaller, he was sitting in the child's seat of the shopping cart by then.

And then we were at the butcher counter and I picked Ben up and went behind the counter into the meat locker back there. I sat Ben down on an icy side of beef and he smiled at me and the butcher came by, looked in, and closed the door right on us. It was cold and I could feel the frost on my face. I tried to form words – I tried to say "Ben, Ben get the door open, we're going to die!" But it just came out like—"Buuuh—Buuuh" and then Ben scratched his little beard and put his hand on my hand and I got this intense wave of peace. Radiating through me, like when a tab of ecstasy hits, and I thought "Oh, I'm dying" but it was so amazing, this feeling of sadness and happiness coming from inside and radiating out, like what bleeding to death must feel like, and then Ben said, in a British accent:

*Ben speaks in a British accent. It's a pretty good one. Does he touch Sharon's hand as well?*

BEN: When I look at you, I see nothing but becoming.

*Mary kind of freezes.*

MARY: Wha—

*Sharon smiles. Mary is a little freaked*

MARY: I—I—I think I'm—

BEN: *(Still in a British accent?)* Well, I was in the dream wasn't I?

*Short pause. Then Ben and Sharon start laughing.*

SHARON: No, no I already told him the dream –

MARY: Oh.

BEN: She told me before you came over.

KENNY: That was a good accent, Ben!

BEN: *(In a British accent)* Not bad there chap, eh?

SHARON: See? It's in there somewhere…

> *Does Sharon kind of tickle Ben like the Pillsbury dough-boy?*

MARY: That was…weird…

SHARON: That was my dream. And I think it was my closure dream. I think I'm better now. Kenny, I'm completely healed.

MARY: I'm going inside. Sharon did you put the vodka inside?

SHARON: It's on the counter.

MARY: And may I use your bathroom?

SHARON: Sure, you'll see it. Right there in the hallway.

> *Mary goes inside Kenny and Sharon's house. Kenny claps his hands together.*

KENNY: Alright let's throw these puppies on the grill!

SHARON: Hey Ben I figured out the other day that all the streets around here are named for different kinds of light. We're on "Sunshine Way" and then there's "Ultraviolet Lane", "Fluorescent Avenue".

KENNY: Also Rainbow Road.

BEN: Yes, AND did you also notice "Feather Way" … "Weight-less Avenue" …

KENNY: *(Getting it)* Oooh, right - Helium Street…

SHARON: Uhhhh…

BEN: "Light" and "Light"

> *Sharon gets it.*

SHARON: Oooooooh!

KENNY: Weird right?

SHARON: Totally weird.

BEN: They planned it that way back in the 60's. If you go to the corner of Sunshine and Route 20, there is this big brick sign that fell backwards a long time ago…20 years ago? It's all overgrown with weeds and Ivy. But if you peel some of it away you can see the original engraved sign "Bright Houses. Come to the Light"

KENNY: How'd you find that?

BEN: I had a friend who lived here in High School. We were just messing around.

KENNY: It's still there?

BEN: I think so.

*Weird beat. Will the conversation shift?*

SHARON: Oh shit! I forgot the appetizers.

BEN: That's OK.

SHARON: No they're just inside. I'll be right back.

*Sharon goes inside. Ben goes up to the deck, kind of "testing" it.*

KENNY: Hey, man thanks again for all the advice.

BEN: Oh, its not me, it's the book.

KENNY: Yeah but I never would have read that book.

BEN: I'm glad it helped. The deck's sure coming along.

KENNY: Yeah it's gonna be nice. We should sit down again sometime soon.

BEN: Sure thing.

*Ben looks at the grill*

What is it burgers?

KENNY: Yes with a ball of American cheese inside. It melts while it cooks.

BEN: *(As in, shit yeah)* Yeah.

KENNY : You have to be careful though you'll burn your mouth. Hold on I need some salt.

*Kenny moves towards the house.*

You need anything?

BEN: Maybe another beer.

KENNY: You got it.

*Kenny goes inside as Mary comes outside. She has a very big plastic cup of vodka tonic. Mary goes to Ben, speaking with her voice a little hushed.*

MARY: Ben, there's nothing in there.

BEN: What?

MARY: They've lived here 5 weeks. And there is no furniture in there. Nothing. Except the coffee table we gave them and this one arm chair with stuffing coming out of it. It looks like a dog ate it. And a tiny TV sitting on a cardboard box....

---

BEN: Well they said they had no furniture.

MARY: Yes, but NO FURNITURE.

BEN: They're starting from scratch.

MARY: And I think there is a smell. Like a bad carpet smell. Like a sick carpet smell.

BEN: Oh come on.

MARY: Even the bedroom—

> *Mary takes a big gulp of vodka tonic.*

BEN: You went in their bedroom?

MARY: There's not even a bed. I mean there is this mattress looking thing, and some sheets barely hanging off it, onto the floor, and that TJ Maxx suit hanging like a carcass in the closet.

BEN: You looked in the closet?

MARY: I don't know it just makes me feel strange, I mean who are we talking to?

BEN: They're getting it together. I'm sure they have no credit cards, no nothing. I don't even know how he bought this lumber.

MARY: They did buy curtains.

BEN: Only for the front, did you notice?

MARY: Well. They're trying to be good neighbors, I guess.

> *Mary and Ben look at each other and breathe one breath. What have they gotten themselves into? No, Ben thinks its awesome, dammit.*

BEN: I don't know, I think they're great.

MARY: No furniture, no clothes.

BEN: Mary will you just shut up about it? You're being judgmental. Kenny's got a good game plan.

MARY: Well, you're the expert.

BEN: How much vodka is in there?

MARY: It's not yours.

BEN: I can smell it over here.

MARY: It's just strange. I feel strange.

> *Kenny enters.*

KENNY: Ladies and gentlemen, drumroll please!

> *Kenny holds the door open. Sharon enters with a rusty cookie sheet with some snacks on it.*

SHARON: Alright so you all the theme is white trash because

I'm trying to own up to what I am these days ha ha and anyway the Cheetos are always the first things to go at a party right? Even when they're sitting right next to the Brie. SO, we've got cheetoes, saltines, a canned bean dip and cheese wiz, and then I made Delta Caviar, ha ha no really its like anti-caviar so we don't kill Kenny. Its got a can of corn, red peppers and yellow peppers, a can of black-eyed peas and some Italian dressing, and salt. At least we can afford salt! Wait till you taste it!

BEN: I have a weakness for the bean dip.

*Ben digs in.*

SHARON: Mary try some.

MARY: I'll have a Cheeto.

*Mary takes one cheeto. Kenny returns with Ben's beer and goes to the grill.*

BEN: God its so nice to just chill out like this. When I started working from home I imagined myself totally relaxed, working a couple hours, going for a jog, doing a little gardening—

MARY: You don't garden—

BEN: I know I just imagined it. But instead my days are so hectic. I'm always on the phone or learning more HTML for my website—

SHARON: Ha ask Kenny about trying to learn HTML—

KENNY: HTML can kiss my sweet ripe ass—

BEN: Running to STAPLES Jesus Christ how many times a day can a man go to Staples! Anyway I am totally fried by the time Mary comes home and kind of panicky because I feel like I didn't get enough done.

KENNY: When do you "launch"?

BEN: Well it was supposed to be this past Monday. But everything always takes longer than you think.

MARY: I still don't understand how JUST A WEBSITE is going to attract customers. I mean it is just hanging out there in the ether. Is someone just going to decide they need a consultant and then POOF find your website?

BEN: I've got it baby—

MARY: No I just mean there are like what, a gazillion bazillion websites out there—

BEN: I've got it.

SHARON: Anyway I heard the "next internet" is coming out soon. Something that we can't even imagine. This super fast thing that will change everything. Change everything so much that like we won't even have to own things anymore. Because the whole thing will become obsolete. Like landlines.

BEN: Do you mean—I don't understand. I mean what will happen to websites. I don't understand.

SHARON: That's just it, I can't explain it, and it's outside of our understanding at this time—

BEN: I mean I'm sure there'll be some sort of conversion, a way to convert the website into—

SHARON: Ben. No worries. Our tiny brains can't conceive of it, it's totally new, like finding out......this table is actually alive, and has been for a long time. We can't understand it yet, but the inventors of the "next internet" are doing that part for us. So you, Ben, should just unfurrow – is that a word? Unfurrow that forehead and enjoy some bean dip and Delta Caviar.

*The distant sound of Sharon and Kenny's doorbell. Sharon looks puzzled.*

Is that our doorbell?

*Everyone pauses, listens, ambient sounds of the neighborhood. Are they the same as usual or have they changed? A moment. Another moment. Another doorbell.*

MARY: I think it is.

SHARON: Who on earth can be ringing our doorbell?

KENNY: Do you want me to get it?

SHARON: No you finish the burgers.

*Sharon exits.*

KENNY: Okay, two minutes.

*He yells to Sharon.*

HEY SHARON WHEN YOU COME OUT BRING THE BUNS AND THE KETCHUP AND STUFF!
She also made potato salad. She makes awesome potato salad.

MARY: I wonder why it was a meat locker.

KENNY: What?

MARY: In the dream.

KENNY: Oh. Who knows.

MARY: Do you dream, Kenny?

> *Kenny laughs, maybe for a long time, then shuts down this conversation.*

KENNY: No.

> *Kenny turns back to the grill. Mary might say the next line in a British accent.*

MARY: Ben would you get me another drink?

BEN: No.

> *Mary kind of pouts.*

I'll get you 7UP. I'll get you 7UP if you want it. Mary, will you please let me get you a 7UP?

> *Mary kind of clicks her tongue and sighs.*

MARY: Sure, alright.

> *She hands Ben her cup. Ben gets up and starts to go to towards the house.*

KENNY: Hey Mary Sharon was asking about those plastic plates you have—

> *Suddenly Ben falls through one of the boards of the porch. Either it breaks or there was like a slot that his foot could slide through. He falls one or two feet into the porch and catches himself with his hand.*

BEN: SHIT!

KENNY: Oh god—

> *Kenny goes to help him.*

BEN: Ow ow ow SHIT!

MARY: Is it broken?

BEN: The porch?

MARY: No your leg, you *fucking* imbecile.

KENNY: Let me help you.

BEN: I think its bleeding, ow OW wait take it slow shit…. Ahhh….

> *Ben is now sitting on the porch, his leg has a deep scratch or gash from the wood.*

KENNY: I'm getting some ice, and water, don't move. Are you sure its not broken?

BEN: No, no I don't think so.

*Kenny runs inside.*

MARY: *Fuckwad.*

BEN: MARY! It's not me it's the PORCH!".

MARY: That new internet is going to come and then where will we be?

*Kenny comes running out with a cup of water and some ice and a paper towel.*

KENNY: Man, this was totally my fault man, SHIT hold on let's pour some water in it, to clean it out –

*Kenny pours water on the wound, It HURTS.*

BEN: Ow Ow! This is so dumb!

KENNY: I think there are splinters in there. I think we need to pull them out with a tweezer.

BEN: Give me a second, man. Just give me a second.

KENNY: Aw Man do you have insurance?

MARY: Maybe hydrogen peroxide.

BEN: Just give me a second.

*We hear Sharon yelling at someone from inside the house.*

SHARON: Yeah you too you fucking nutcase! You're a fucking stinky cunt, you hear me? You are insane!

*Sharon enters carrying buns, a bottle of ketchup, a jar of mustard and a jar of hamburger dill slices. It is a little awkward. Oh and also she is furious. At some point during this tirade Mary slips in the house for some more vodka. Also at some point Sharon puts down the buns and the condiments. By the end of the tirade Mary is back outside.*

Kenny you are not going to believe this I am fucking losing it do you see me I am losing it! It was the pink jogging suit lady. At our door! Only she wasn't wearing a pink jogging suit she was wearing shorts and a blue T shirt. And she came over to ask us politely—sort of—politely if we could keep our dog from shitting on her lawn.

KENNY: We don't have a dog.

SHARON: WE DON'T HAVE A DOG. Exactly. And so I said to her, politely, I said "we don't have a dog" and she said "yes you do have a dog and it is quite fond of taking craps on my lawn." "Quite fond." Like slicing a razor blade across my face "quite fond". And I said "Lady, do you want to come in my house? We've got NOTHING in our house, especially a DOG. Especially we do not have a DOG." And she said "Listen, Missy." FUCKING MISSY! "Listen, Missy. I've lived in this neighborhood for 6 years, and I jog every morning. This dog appeared out of nowhere and started crapping on my lawn. I'm not asking you to get rid of it I'm just asking you to clean up his crap." And I practically started crying—look at me I'm crying now—and I said "Ma'am, people have accused me of many things before but they have never accused me of having a dog, you need to investigate further you need to knock on other doors—"And she said—her voice changed and she said "Look if it craps on my lawn one more time I am calling the police" and I said "Are you kidding? The police are going to fucking LAUGH IN YOUR FACE if you call them about some dogshit." And she said "AHA! So you DO have a DOG!" And I said "No, no, no, no, no fucking NO there is no dog here lady!" And she just shook her head and kind of kicked our plant and said "Ha I thought it was fake." And turned around I mean FUCK. KENNY. FUCK. This is like FUCKED UP.

*Sharon sees Ben.*

What the fuck happened?

KENNY: He fell through the porch.

SHARON: Fuck.

MARY: It's his own fault.

BEN: Can someone get me a wet towel? These paper towels are going to stick.

SHARON: Oh um, yeah, um—

*Sharon starts turning in circles.*

Oh wait also the potato salad.

KENNY: We only have one towel and I really think it is too dirty to put on your cut.

SHARON: I mean what kind of neighborhood have we moved into!

BEN: I think we have, Mary, can you—

MARY: Maybe we should move to the woods.

KENNY: Oh shit the burgers just a second.

> *Kenny goes to the burgers. Ben tries to pull a splinter out. Sharon looks at Mary.*

BEN: Ow.

SHARON: Yes, that's it. I'm moving to the woods with my friend Mary. With chipmunks and baby deer for neighbors. Fuck this bullshit place. Where nobody likes you and you get fired from your job because you went back to your car to get your weight lifting belt.

BEN: You got fired from your job? Kenny?

KENNY: Baby can we not—MARY: Ha! Now there's a game plan!

SHARON: It's a fucking crack of shit, crock of shit. And I thank the pink jogging suit lady for helping me see the light of day.

MARY: In the woods we could eat rabbits, and if hunting was hard we could eat grasshoppers.

SHARON: And we can put a spout into the tree to get the maple syrup out. Do you know how to do that, Mary?

MARY: Sure. And just like you said no men, baby, no men, just you and me in our tent with our fucking mess kits in the mesh bag and the one pot and the one pan—

SHARON: And the sunsets shit there will be sunsets!

MARY: And no phones.

KENNY: The burgers are OK. They're well done but they're fine.

BEN: You know I think I need to go to the emergency room.

KENNY: Really?

BEN: Yeah, I mean it's not stopping.

MARY: Paul Bunyan! We can meet Paul Bunyan!

BEN: I think YOU need to take me to the emergency room.

KENNY: OK.

BEN: I'll send Mary inside.

KENNY: She can stay here.

BEN: No no no no no no. She's drunk.

MARY: I'm not drunk! I'm planning a trip.

BEN: She needs to go home.

SHARON: Kenny help, Kenny help its happening—

KENNY: It's not happening.

SHARON: Just like they said it would happen in our meetings—

KENNY: Sharon—

SHARON: They said our old life would feel like real life and our new life would feel like a dream. I'm dreaming right now.

BEN: No you're not.

SHARON: *(Starting to hyperventilate)* I am. I can feel it. I'm dreaming—

> *Mary grabs Sharon in some awkward and intimate way. Ben and Kenny are trying to deal with Ben's cut leg.*

MARY: No you're not. You're here, Sharon. I am here. And we are going camping. For real. This is not a dream.

> *BLACKOUT*

*Night sounds.*

*The lights rise on Mary and Ben's backyard. Sharon is tiptoeing on to Mary's back porch wearing a T shirt and underwear. Maybe a ratty robe? Suddenly, Mary opens the sliding door. She is dressed in pajamas. They look at each other for a moment.*

MARY: Too excited to sleep?

SHARON: Yes!

MARY: Oh my god me too! I can't believe we're actually going! Do you know the campground is only twelve miles away from here? I've googled it so many times. In case of emergency. I sit there and look at the website and imagine.

SHARON: I got hot dogs and buns and coffee.

MARY: I got bug spray and bacon and toast.

SHARON: We can make bacon?

MARY: I'm bringing a frying pan!

*They kind of giggle like little girls.*

SHARON: I think nature is really going to help. Mary, every day really is a new day. But Mary, I open my eyes every morning and all I want is a pipe to smoke. It's like there's a fire burning in the center of my head, Mary, and the pipe is the water that will put it out. And I say this at our meetings, and they are all very supportive but the fire only goes down a little bit. Every day, all day. And in the middle of this burning I am supposed to envision my life, Mary. I'm supposed to set goals and maybe take night classes that will expand my horizons. And I guess that works, Mary, I guess so. But to be honest I feel like the real opportunities are the ones that fall into your lap. Like winning the lottery or someone's rich Uncle needing a personal assistant. That almost happened to me once, Mary. And everything would have been different.

MARY: Well, now you're here. Things are changing for you right now.

SHARON: Mary, two days ago I fell off the wagon. I called in sick and walked down to the gas station and bought a stash from the kid with the skateboard. And I got high right there, Mary, in the parking lot by the dumpster.

MARY: Okay. What did you do?

SHARON: I started walking, Mary, I walked around our neighborhood, and nobody fucking walks here so I stuck out like a sore thumb. Have you walked around our neighborhood, Mary? It soooooooo beautiful, especially when you let the street signs really sink in. This guy in a pick up truck pulled over and asked me if I needed help – by that time I had accidentally walked out of one of my shoes, and hadn't realized it. So I said yes, please and he drove me home and we were hanging out in his truck outside my house and he finally said "are you high" and I said "yes, I am" and he told me about all the ways he parties—He does ecstasy he eats mushrooms and every now and then but not too often he shoots heroin. But he's careful because he doesn't want to get hooked on it—

MARY: Right—

SHARON: Oh and sometimes he takes Ludes and sometimes he does whipits just to remind himself of high school. All like 3 streets away from here, on Solar Power Lane. And I said "what do you do for a living?" And he said: "I'm an electrician. I do house calls". And I said "how do you afford all that stash" And he said "Would you like a house call?" And I said no, our electricity is fine."

MARY: Sharon, I don't think he was talking about electricity.

SHARON: I know. But sex on smack just isn't my thing. And I love Kenny, I really do, you know that Mary, right? You can tell.

MARY: Of course.

SHARON: And so I said "do you want to be an electrician forever?" And he said well, actually, what he really wanted to do was be a marine biologist and we were just getting into this amazing conversation about the many varieties of sharks—the guy was rubbing my feet—

*Sharon starts to tear up.*

MARY: When Kenny came home.

*Sharon nods.*

SHARON: He knew immediately what I had done.

He was really nice to the guy, considering.

I spent the rest of the day drinking diet coke and watching Jerry Springer and then like four hours screaming my face off and trying to escape. Somehow Kenny tied me to the wall, to the door handles?

MARY: What?

SHARON: No, no he had to. He had to.

MARY: This all happened—

SHARON: Two days ago. Between the last time I saw you and now.

MARY: Jesus.

SHARON: I know.

MARY: I think I was at work pretending to type a letter while surfing the internet looking for plastic outdoor table-cloths.

SHARON: This is a nice table. You don't need a tablecloth.

MARY: I know I just get bored with it every now and then.

*Sharon notices the light on. She looks at it.*

MARY: He's working on his website.

*They both look for a second more.*

And Kenny's still letting you go?

SHARON: Kenny thinks you're good for me.

*Aw. Mary is a little touched by that.*

SHARON: And what about your life? Do you feel like a con-struction worker building a house, or a twig floating in the stream?

*Mary laughs.*

MARY: You say some funny things sometimes.

SHARON: Washing our faces in the fresh water. Gathering a few nuts.

MARY: Sharon.

SHARON: Yup.

MARY: Why don't you have any furniture in your house?

SHARON: Because we're broke. Crazy broke. I mean I'm 31 years old and I still eat ramen noodles for dinner a lot. Because we have to.

MARY: What's going to happen to you?

SHARON: What do you mean?

MARY: I just…I don't understand…how you and Kenny… are ever…I mean something's going to happen again… and you're going to be…I mean how many times do you get to…

SHARON: You've got to live this moment, Mary. That's all you can do. I'm as beautiful on the inside as you are.

*Sharon touches Mary's face.*

*The sliding glass door opens. Ben comes out. He is wearing a cast on one leg. He's not alarmed, just curious.*

BEN: What's going on?

MARY: We're too excited to sleep!

BEN: You girls are going to get eaten by bears!

SHARON: Stop it! I hate bears.

MARY: There's no bears around here. Sheesh.

BEN: Come get some sleep.

MARY: Goodnight, Sharon.

*Sharon mumbles good night. Mary and Ben go inside. Sharon scratches each of her arms. She goes towards her backyard.*

*BLACKOUT*

*What are the sounds? Is it the neighborhood sounds only processed? Or is it construction sounds, because they are knocking down the house a few blocks over?*

*The lights rise on Mary and Ben's front yard. Kenny and Ben are sitting on the front steps of Ben's house. Ben has a light cast or brace on leg almost up to his knee. It is the afternoon. They are each drinking a beer, like a Budweiser. They are quiet for a couple seconds.*

KENNY: Well whatever new job I get they're gonna garnish the paychecks.

BEN: Have you ever thought of sitting down with a credit specialist?

KENNY: I thought I was sitting down with a credit specialist.

BEN: And how much do those specialists usually cost? When you pay full price?

*Silence for a moment.*

I'm not asking for a lot of money. I just need to place some value on my time. Services cost money. If you offer something for free, it is seen as having less value. My book told me this.

KENNY: How is $25 going to make a difference to you right now?

BEN: It's the principle. I've got to stick by my principles.

*They both take a sip of beer.*

It's not a lot of money.

KENNY: Let's see, we'll see. I've got a court case I'm waiting on in Arkansas. It's gonna save us, if it comes through.

BEN: In Arkansas?

KENNY: I slipped and fell in a supermarket a few years ago. That's how I hurt my back. That's why I have to wear the weightlifting belt. The belt that cost me my job.

BEN: Right.

KENNY: When I get that settlement, I'll give you your $25 and you can give me more "advice."

BEN: Alright.

*A few seconds.*

Are you supposed to be drinking that?

KENNY: One is OK.

*They sip.*

KENNY: So are you ready to start taking "real" clients?

BEN: I better. I have one more month of severance pay.

KENNY: One more month and you'll be just like me.

BEN: I guess so, yeah.

KENNY: Bruh-thaaaz.

*Ben and Kenny clink beer cans.*

KENNY: How much you want to bet they're gonna call us any minute. Ah! There's snakes! There's roaches!

BEN: I don't know that their cell phones work out there.

KENNY: "Come out here! It's dark!" And you know what, we're not gonna go.

BEN: Well—

KENNY: No really, they're out there in nature, sitting in the menstrual hut, eating crickets, whatever, that's what they want, and we have to honor that. We have to let the women be women.

BEN: They better not come back wanting to burn that… that…

KENNY: Sage stick.

BEN: Yeah! I went to a wedding once where they did that. So weird.

KENNY: That stuff stinks.

BEN: Wearing feathers and a deerskin skirt.

*They both laugh.*

KENNY: So whaddaya say, brothah? Boys night out. There's Dan's Place and Déjà vu and Temptations and Barely Legal.

BEN: I don't know—really?

KENNY: I've only been to Dan's Place and Déjà vu. Déjà vu is upscale but Dan's Place is traaa-shee!

BEN: I mean really I should work.

KENNY: Work? It's Saturday. Our wives are away—

BEN: I know but maybe—

KENNY: We're just embracing our human nature, man –

BEN: But Kenny those clubs are expensive.

KENNY: We're just relaxing after a hard week's work.

BEN: The drinks alone are like 9 bucks. And it's usually a 3 drink minimum. It adds up, and then what?

*Lisa D'Amour*

KENNY: Aw man.

Aw man is that what this is about? You think its irresponsible? For us to have a night out? For ME to have a night
out?

BEN: No, I didn't say that. Its just…its just one night…if we
take a step back for a second—

KENNY: Oh god that fucking book!

BEN: I have….I have a vision for my life, Kenny.

KENNY: So do I, douchebag.

BEN: Hey, hey, hey. This is coming out wrong. I mean I don't
even know how….can we…can we just drink, please?

KENNY: Hmph.

*Both men take a sip.*

You're a good man, Ben.

BEN: I don't know.

KENNY: No really, you are.

BEN: In a parallel universe I'm a good man.

KENNY: I'm an asshole.

BEN: No you're not.

KENNY: I'm like "You too good for yellow mustard!?" right
in the middle of the store.

BEN: You're under a lot of stress.

KENNY: I'm an asshole, and its too late for me.

*Ben doesn't know what to say. The two men sip their
beers.*

BEN: I think this might be against the law.

KENNY: What?

BEN: Drinking beers in the front yard.

KENNY: You own this house right?

BEN: Of course. Well I mean the bank owns it -

KENNY: Shit then, private property.

You gotta hang on to this house, Ben.

BEN: Of course.

KENNY: Don't let anyone take it from you.

BEN: No, no we're fine. I mean we haven't even dipped into
our savings and I don't think we'll have to. We're not…
we're not anywhere near that yet.

KENNY: Hang on to that house. That's what my grandfather
always used to say to my Dad.

BEN: And did he hang on to it?

> *Kenny doesn't say anything. It is obvious his dad did NOT hang on to the house.*

> *Silence. Sound of the suburbs. Kids in the distance on bikes. A plane over head. The compressors for several Central A/C units. Maybe hovering a little closer than usual, pressing in.*

> *Ben contemplates boys' night out.*

BEN: I mean I've got this leg.

KENNY: I bet it could get you a sympathy lap dance.

BEN: I don't know.

KENNY: I'll drive.

BEN: It's just such a hassle to GO anywhere.

KENNY: We deserve it, Ben.

> *A few moments of silence where they kind of sit and watch and sip. Then Ben finishes his beer and crushes his can.*

BEN: Alright let's do it.

KENNY: Serious!

BEN: Yeah, you decide where we're going and you have to drive. Except I've been to Dan's too and it really is too skankified so not there.

KENNY: You've been?

BEN: Sure for an um bachelor party.

KENNY: Yeah right.

BEN: So maybe one rung up the ladder.

> *Ben looks down the street.*

KENNY: Temptations then, let's try Temptations.

BEN: Should we get dinner first?

KENNY: Nah man let's just eat something here.

BEN: We've got nothing in the house.

KENNY: Fuck it let's scrounge. I've got a can of Manwich.

BEN: I think we have hot dogs.

KENNY: Yeah we'll chop em up, mix em around.

BEN: Spaghetti? Over Spaghetti?

KENNY: Oh man no I think maybe no—

BEN: Alright we might have some white bread.

KENNY: My brothah we're good to go! Chow down and get there in time for happy hour.

BEN: I think its 2 for 1 navel shots.

*Kenny kind of dances and sings that line from the song "Hey-Ya" by OutKast.*

KENNY: awright, awright, awright—

BEN: That's what they advertise, anyway.

This next speech cracks Ben up.

KENNY: See! For two Brothahs on a budget! For two MEN whose wives are out playing survivor. For two men in need of a little R and R after a tough couple of weeks. For two men in search of a little good clean fun. For two men in need of a boys' night out. For two men who appreciate God's gift to this green earth: that special titty talent of the special titty dancer. For two men who want to feel more connected to their bodies and to the world. Who want to get out of the house and see the world—

BEN: Yeah!

KENNY: For two men who aren't afraid to have a good time even though their financial lives are swirling around in some kind of homemade toilet bowl—

BEN: Come on—

KENNY: For two men who are men. For two men who are going to have a great fucking night. For two men who are going to have a fucking great fucking night on the town, not far from their house.

BEN: It's all 10 minutes away!

KENNY: For two men who can take one night to not worry so much—

BEN: Yes!

KENNY: Not to question so much—

BEN: Yes!

KENNY: not to obsess so much about their lives and how they wound up here on Shiney Sun Lane or whateverthe-fuckitscalled, for two men who will forget all of that and go out. GO OUT. Go out on the town and engage with the night life, with the life of the night, who want to see what kind of

*Ben and Kenny almost say this together.*

BEN AND KENNY: Good clean fun

KENNY: is out there!

BEN: Out there!

KENNY: And if in the process they get their hands a little dirty well hey, it was in the name of good clean fun. For two men who oh shit...oh shit...oh shit...oh shit...

*Kenny sees something down the street. Ben looks.*

BEN: Oh shit.

KENNY: Oh shit.

*Ben takes the beer cans and tosses them behind the bushes.*

KENNY: Oh shit.

Shit.

*Sharon and Mary walk up. They carry pretty big backpacks, like camping backpacks, on their backs.*

MARY: Hi!

SHARON: Hello! We didn't make it!

MARY: We didn't make it!

BEN: I guess not.

*Ben hops up, hopping on one foot, and helps Mary take her backpack off.*

MARY: First we drove out onto the loop and got totally lost.

SHARON: We thought we were going TOWARDS the campground but actually we were going away.

MARY: And then all of a sudden we were in this tiny town called "Sooter"

BEN: Oh that's where the minor league baseball field is.

SHARON: And there was this store with a little lunch counter.

MARY: Can you believe it? It was like straight out of an old history book.

SHARON: And so we had sandwiches and diet cokes.

MARY: And the guy gave us directions BACK to the campground. And I went to pee and we got back on the road.

SHARON: And we were on our way and then I had to pee.

MARY: So we got off the interstate and stopped at a gas station.

SHARON: And I peed in this nas-tee bathroom while Mary flirted with the counter guy—

MARY: I did not! I bought a pack of Big Red.

SHARON: "Big Red"

MARY: Shut up!

SHARON: And then we were pulling out of the gas station and the car started making this crazy ass noise.

MARY: Like the gears were crunching together.

SHARON: Like the car was eating celery mixed with ice cubes.

MARY: So we stopped the car and the guy from the gas station came to look at it and he fooled around for like 30 minutes and did something with the gears—

SHARON: He rigged it with a coat hanger!

MARY: And we asked if he thought it was OK for us to take the car to the campground. And he said sure it should the campground is close. So we got in the car and we set off but we were really quiet.

SHARON: For like 10 minutes we didn't talk. And finally Mary said: Sharon, are you afraid of breaking down in the woods?

MARY: *(Pointing to Sharon.)* And she said: YES! I'm terrified! I never thought about breaking down before we left!

SHARON: There are bears in the woods!

BEN: There aren't really bears.

MARY: And I started thinking about my foot. And how I didn't have a clean bandage. And the wet ground.

SHARON: Slugs. Dead Frogs.

MARY: And I said well its late so maybe we should just—

MARY AND SHARON: Go home—

MARY: And right that second I saw the exit for Richfield Road, the back way home and so I cut across 3 lanes of traffic.

SHARON: I spilled my diet coke all over the window!

MARY: And I started laughing so hard I almost peed myself, even though I had just peed!

SHARON: And we kind of swerved to the side of the road. And BAM!

MARY: A flat tire! So I pulled over—I mean I've changed a flat tire before—

BEN: And you didn't have a spare.

MARY: I didn't have a spare!

BEN: I haven't had a chance to get a new one since we popped the old one.

MARY: And we cancelled triple A to save money so we were like well do we call the guys or maybe a gas station and

WAIT for them to come here?  Or do we HIKE the 20
minutes home?

SHARON: A hike. That's like camping.

MARY: Sure it is!

SHARON: So that's what we did!

MARY: We fucking hiked!!

BEN: *(Quick, re: her cursing)* Mary—

SHARON: And here we are! I hate camping anyway. All those
BUGS!

MARY: And rapists!

SHARON: Baby did you miss me?

MARY: We got cat-called.

SHARON: We thought maybe we could party here.

MARY: We thought maybe we'd grill.

BEN: We've got to get the car I guess.

KENNY: I've got a spare you can use.

BEN: Thanks, Kenny.

KENNY: Just a $15 charge. For the rental.

> *Quick moment of quiet.*

Just kidding!

BEN: Alright let's go.

MARY: We'll get together some snacks.

SHARON: It's so weird how nothing ever happens.

KENNY: I'll get my keys.

> *Kenny leaves and goes into his house.*

BEN: We were going to watch soccer.

SHARON: You keep thinking things are going to happen but
nothing ever does.

MARY: You don't watch soccer.

BEN: Kenny likes soccer. He lived in Ireland for a year when
he was a kid.

SHARON: No he didn't.

BEN: What?

SHARON: Jesus that stupid story.

MARY: It's funny, just making the effort to go camping made
me feel a lot better.

> *Kenny comes back with his keys.*

BEN: Alright well should we grill?

SHARON: Almost only counts in horseshoes and hand grenades.

MARY: *(A little over the top, a little dorky.)* It's Saturday night! Let's have a goooooooooood time.

*Quick moment where Ben, Sharon and Kenny are like "Huh? That was sort of dorky." Mary doesn't notice.*

*BLACKOUT*

*Night sounds. Then, the sound of music, low. Some kind of party music. Maybe music from Sharon and Kenny's Hotlanta days? It gets louder and louder.*

*Lights up on Mary and Ben's backyard. Ben, Kenny and Mary are dancing their asses off on Ben and Mary's porch.*

*Ben is dancing on a chair with his broken leg.*

*Kenny is maybe fake humping the grill.*

*Mary is spinning in circles.*

*They are all beer-wasted. Which is different from bourbon wasted. Bourbon makes you mean and switches on your regret.*

BEN: Yay-eah, Yay-eah, Yay-eah Yay-eah Yay-eah.

MARY: I'm a sexy mothafuckah on yo roof.
I'm a sexy mothafuckah on yo back porch
I'm a sexy mothafuckah in yo kitchen
I'm a sexy mothafuckah on yo lawn.

KENNY: *(Wailing, high-pitched R & B style)* I'm your lover I'm your daddy I'm your car tire I'm your devil I'm your sexy I'm your burger I'm your boyfriend I'm your superstar!

BEN: Yay-eah, Yay-eah Yay-eah Yay-eah Yay-eah.

BEN: *(wailing too)* I'm your superstar!

I'm your superstar!

MARY: Hey Ben do this! Do this! Ben do this!

*Mary does some kind of dance move she wants Ben to do. Ben does it. Kenny comes up behind Mary and dirty dances with her a little.*

MARY: Wait everybody do this! Do it!

*She does a dance move. They don't do it.*

DO IT!

*The two guys do it, they are all in a line.*

MARY: We're on that show! You know that show with the dancers.

BEN: Yay-eah, Yay-eah, Yay-eahYay-eahYay-eah.

KENNY: I was on that show when I was 16!

MARY: Really!

KENNY: No. Sometimes I just say shit.

BEN: Look I'm doing the one legged twist.

> *Kenny cracks up. Mary twists with Ben. Kenny cracks up more.*

KENNY: That is some funny shit.

> *Kenny starts doing some weird vaguely John Travola-esque humping of the air, almost like he is swinging his dick around. Or maybe using barbecue tongs as his dick?*

MARY: Kenny!

BEN: *(Kind of cracking up but kind of like "what?")* Holy Shit!

> *Kenny wails and grinds.*

KENNY: I'm a superstar!

MARY AND BEN: I'm a super star.

> *Sharon enters with two bowls – one filled with water and one filled with some other kind of food. She puts them on the floor and looks at them.*

KENNY: What are you doing?

SHARON: I'm feeding my dog. I have a dog remember? I'm feeding it.

KENNY: Oh that is fucking funny.

> *Kenny gets two beers out of the cooler.*

MARY: Oh right, your dog! You love your dog!

BEN: Ha ha that is fucking funny.

SHARON: Now I'm walking my dog.

> *Sharon fake walks her dog, it is on a leash and she kind of dances while she does it. The others crack up.*

KENNY: Walk that dog.

> *Sharon walks the dog sexier. The other take up fake leashes and walk their dogs, dancing while they do so.*

MARY: Oh no my dog just pooped! Look at me!

> *She pretends to pick up the dog shit with a fake bag and*

*throws the bag away. They all hoot and holler and cheer while she does so. Sharon steps up on to the table and walks her dog up there. Kenny hands her a beer and she gulps it down.*

MARY: Are you allowed to have that?

*Sharon keeps dancing.*

SHARON: Yeah sure its just beer.

KENNY: Her problem was really freebasing heroin anyway.

SHARON: Kenny!

MARY: That was a joke right?

BEN: Yay-eah, Yay-eah, Yay-eahYay-eahYay-eah.

SHARON: Yay-eah, Yay-eah, Yay-eahYay-eahYay-eah.

*Kenny gets up on the table and starts dancing with Sharon. Ben and Mary walk their dogs.*

MARY: Oh my god I just got the greatest idea?

SHARON: What?

MARY: We should all fake walk our dogs over to the lady in the pink jogging suits house! We should fake walk our dogs over there and have them take a fake crap on their lawn! And we'll be like whoooooo hoooooo!

BEN: Let's do it!

SHARON: Oh my god that's hilarious.

*Mary, Ben and Sharon start to go. Kenny starts herding them back: he is a seasoned partier and he knows that crazy shit could bring cops and spoil everything.*

KENNY: No no no we're going to stay back here.

MARY: Come on!

KENNY: Come on let's keep the party here. No no, come on.

MARY: Party pooper!

*Sharon cracks up.*

SHARON: Get it? Party pooper!

*Mary cracks up. Mary and Sharon fake poop or fake fart on Kenny.*

KENNY: Alright bitches!

*Kenny picks both ladies up and spins them around. The ladies squeal. He puts them down and the three of them dirty dance for a few seconds. Ben sits on the patio table with his feet on a chair.*

SHARON: Come on Ben!

BEN: Just a second I'm resting.

MARY: No! No resting! No resting! No resting resting resting resting!

*It becomes a chant. Ben kind of dances in his seat. Mary couple dances with Sharon.*

MARY: Oh my god I really needed this! Some down time!

BEN: It feels good just to release!

*The patio table breaks and Ben falls to the ground. A moment, they look, just music, then Ben jumps up.*

I'm Okay!

*They all chant and dance. Maybe do a little "He's Okay!" chant. Ben dances with everyone.*

*Sharon acts like she is holding a giant cup.*

SHARON: Guess what this is?

*Everybody says "What!"*

SHARON: It's a giant cup of party juice and I'm drinking it down!

*Everyone hoots and hollers as Sharon drinks.*

*Mary pretends to be holding something over her head.*

MARY: Guess what this is?

*Everybody says "What!"*

MARY: It's a big bowl of get down and I'm pouring it all over you!

*They all hoot, holler and get down as Mary pours the fake juice.*

*Kenny pretends to be holding something over his arm, like a purse.*

KENNY: Guess what this is?

*Everybody says "What!"*

KENNY: It's my hand basket and we're all going to hell in it!

*Everybody hoots and hollers "Going to hell! Going to hell!"*

*Sharon starts dirty dancing with Ben.*

*Pretty quickly they start to make out. Pretty quickly it is pretty hot.*

*Mary and Kenny are still dancing and saying "Going to Hell!" Then, Mary sees Sharon and Ben and stops dead in her tracks.*

*She reaches out for Kenny's arm, who is still dancing.*

MARY: Kenny, what's happening. What is that?

KENNY: Oh its nothing, nothing hold on.

*Kenny dances over and dances Sharon away from Ben. He dances with Sharon and whispers in her ear. Sharon kind of giggles and says "you're right, you're right" only to Kenny.*

*Ben is shell shocked for a minute and then starts dancing again.*

*Mary is shell shocked for a minute longer and starts dancing again.*

*Kenny is dancing with Sharon, and when Mary isn't looking Sharon looks to Ben and mouths the words "Sorry, I'm sorry" to him. Ben smiles at her and kind of shrugs his shoulders and laughs back.*

*Kenny and Sharon start making out. Ben and Mary get a little uncomfortable and sort of half dance. Kenny grabs Sharon's ass in this major way, like his finger is sliding down the back of her ass crack on top of her pants over and down between her legs. Sharon kind of rides his leg. Mary freaks a little.*

MARY: Okay okay okay okay! I think we are stopping! I think it is time for us to be stopping!

*Sharon breaks away from Kenny.*

SHARON: No, no, no no stopping! No stopping!

MARY: Weird things are happening!

SHARON: No, no, THINGS are happening. Can't you see?

BEN: It's OK Mary, don't worry.

MARY: I'm going to call the police.

KENNY: No you're not.

MARY: I mean somebody – somebody is going to call the police.

BEN: It's our house. We're on our lawn.

SHARON: This is nothing compared to what's going down on Solar Power lane right now.

---

MARY: Yes but they do it quietly.

SHARON: *(Yelling)* AND WE DO IT LOUD! Whoooo!

> *Kenny turns the music up a bit.*

KENNY: Just keep dancing Mary, it gets the endorphins going. We learned this in rehab. It can take the place of drugs. But you have to keep moving.

> *Mary keeps moving: half-dancing, half-exercising.*

SHARON: It's beautiful! Your beautiful, Mary.

> *Sharon kisses Mary deeply. Mary lets her. The guys watch. Sharon lets go.*

MARY: Did that really happen?

SHARON: Of course it did! Things can happen. You can just DO them. You have to just DO them. If you don't, then the world just stays the same.

> *Music. Music. Mary busts a chair on the cement patio. Music. Music. Is Ben going to be mad?*

BEN: Whooooooo—hoooooo!

> *Another mad round of dancing. On chairs, with each other. Nothing real sexual just mad dancing. At some point Ben breaks another chair.*

BEN: I hate these fucking chairs! Who wants a chair that you can break with one hand?

MARY: They were on clearance from Patio Depot.

BEN: Fuck patio Depot!

> *They cheer and dance. Sharon starts piling the wood from the chairs into a pile. Kenny downs another beer. Mary starts a chant.*

MARY: I'm feeling, I'm feeling, I'm feeling, I'm feeling

> *Kenny joins her.*

KENNY AND MARY: I'm feeling I'm feeling I'm feeling I'm feeling.

KENNY: Take it Mary!

MARY: I'm feeling electricity, electricity running through my arms and legs –

KENNY: Yeah!

MARY: It's in my blood, the electricity is in my blood!

SHARON: That's good!

KENNY: I'm feeling, I'm feeling, I'm feeling –

MARY: Yes, Kenny?

KENNY: I'm feeling like my whole body is filled up with some kind of sweet air, strawberry air, and strawberry shortcake air—

MARY: Whooo!

KENNY: And its making me feel like I can do fucking anything!

MARY: WaaaaaahhhhH!

KENNY: Look at me!

BEN: I'm feeling, I'm feeling—

*Kenny joins him—*

KENNY AND BEN: I'm feeling, I'm feeling, I'm feeling

BEN: I'm feeling like telling the truth!

KENNY: Yeah!

BEN: I'm feeling it!

MARY: *(with Kenny and Sharon joining in)* Tell it, tell it, tell it, tell it.

BEN: Should I?

MARY: *(with Kenny and Sharon joining in)* Tell it, baby, tell it. Tell it, baby, tell it.

BEN: *(Still in party chant mode.)* Alright!
    I have no website! I said there ain't no website!
    I have no website, I have no business cards I have no plan,
    I got nothing! Nothing nothing nothing!

KENNY: Yea-ah, Yeah-ah, Yeah-ah Yeah-ah Yeah-ah!

MARY: What?

*Kenny is dancing around.*

BEN: After seven whole weeks.
    I've got nothing!
    Nothing to show!
    Nothing to show show show!

MARY: What did your computer crash or something?

BEN: No. I just. I think I don't want to, Mary.

MARY: You don't want to?

BEN: I mean I've got a domain name. A domain name that I own. On the internet. But I don't think I want to run a financial planning business.

MARY: You're telling me this now?

KENNY: *(With Sharon joining in)*
  Ben's got nothing
  Ben's got nothing
  Ben's got nothing
  Ben's got nothing
BEN: There's so much you don't know, Mary! Like Mary, did you know that I have always wanted to be British?
SHARON: I knew it!
BEN: Yes, Sharon, Yes! When I was 10 I would watch "Masterpiece Theater" and read Agatha Christie, and when I would go to McDonalds I would order iced tea, because I thought that is what a British person would do.

  *Kenny is kind of cracking up.*

KENNY: Yeah!
BEN: And there was a whole year, when I was 8, when I ate all my sandwiches with the crusts off. Until one time I got beat up for doing that and so I stopped.

  *Falling asleep wondering what a crumpet was.*

SHARON: That's so sweet, Mary are you hearing this?
MARY: I'm hearing it.
BEN: And There is a website out there, Mary, called "Brit-Land" and it is designed especially for non-Brits who want to be British. I have an identity on that website. A British identity. It all plays out in real time.
KENNY: Who are you baby, who are you?
SHARON: Tell us.
BEN: My name is Ian. I'm a prep school teacher. I teach Geology. I like to bike. I have a cat. I am engaged to be married. I drink a pint of Ale each afternoon.
  Right now I am asleep, because I like to get up early to go for my jog and a cuppa tea before heading to campus.
  Right now I am asleep in my flat.
MARY: Huh?
BEN: Right now I am asleep in my flat. With my girlfriend Julia. I spend way more time in Brit Land than I do on my website, Mary. Maybe more time than I spend with you.
MARY: NOOO!

  *Mary kind of runs at Ben, to hit him. Sharon and Kenny catch her.*

SHARON: No no no Mary. It's a beautiful thing, Mary!

*Mary, Ben just told you the truth. And now he as at zero. No website. No secrets. No nothing.*

And guess what, Mary?

MARY: What?

SHARON: When you are at zero, anything can happen.

*It's like total possibility.*

BEN: Yeah, Mary

SHARON: He's like a tennis player with his knees bent, poised to jump in any direction.

MARY: But what are we going to do?

*A moment. Then Sharon.*

SHARON: We're going to start a fire.

BEN: Huh?

KENNY: Really?

SHARON: Yeah, just like we used to do in Plano.

KENNY: Yeah but that was Texas.

SHARON: Yes but its such a beautiful thing.

KENNY: True dat.

SHARON: It's a ritual, a healing ritual for Mary and Ben.

*Their clearance patio furniture will go up into the air, like a flower petal on the wind.*

And then you will be at zero, together. Together, Mary!

MARY: Um.

*Sharon couple dances with Mary.*

SHARON: We're going to do this. It's going to happen right here before your eyes. And it is going to open up a space.

MARY: What kind of space?

SHARON: You are living inside a tiny spectrum, Mary.

*She shows Mary with her fingers—like pinching her forefinger to her thumb.*

Like this small. And do you know how big the spectrum really is Mary? Do you know?

MARY: I don't know.

SHARON: Light it Kenny.

*Kenny lights a match. Somehow, the pile of wood instantly catches fire. A roaring fire. They are all mesmerized.*

MARY: A campfire!

BEN: Woah. Isn't that kind of big?

MARY: You're taking me camping!

SHARON: Yes I am.

MARY: Ben, Sharon is taking me camping!

*Sharon hugs Mary.*

SHARON: This fire is for everyone, Mary. For Mary and Sharon and Kenny and Ben.

*Kenny makes a torch out of a piece of patio furniture and dances around.*

MARY: I can feel the heat. And the wind. Going into my eyes. I can feel my eyeballs and my inner ear, my inner ears. And I feel a splitting feeling, like maybe in my bones down here, the bones that make up my hips I feel a splitting feeling Ben? Ben? Where are you?

*Ben hugs Mary. Sharon moves away.*

BEN: I'm right here with you Mary.

MARY: I think I am feeling another skin just below my real skin. It's been there the whole time.

BEN: That's beautiful.

*The fire is getting pretty big.*

MARY: My forehead separating from my skull.

BEN: Look at that burn…

*Kenny stands in the doorway to Mary and Ben's house with the torch.*

*Sharon stands apart from him, watching him, transfixed.*

*Kenny lights the curtains of Mary and Ben's house on fire. Its exhilarating.*

*Sharon walks to Ben and Kenny walks to Mary to join them. It becomes a group hug in front of the bonfire.*

SHARON: This is really happening, kids. Right now, right here.

BEN: He who hesitates is lost.

KENNY: Every day is the first day of the rest of your life.

MARY: That's terrifying.

KENNY: But it's true.

MARY: Yes but are the curtains supposed to be on fire too? Is
that really happening?

*They look into the kitchen.*

BEN: Oh shit look at that!

MARY: Somebody call the…oh shit my phone is inside.

SHARON: No, this is good! This is amazing!

*Sharon and Kenny dance.*

MARY: Ben let's go next door. Quick, let's go next door!

*Mary helps Ben off the porch.*

*Sharon and Kenny keep dancing as the lights:*


*BLACKOUT*

*We hear the sound of fire burning, of the fire getting bigger.
We hear neighbors and sirens and the crackling of wood.
We hear the shouting of firemen. We hear the "whoosh"
of water coming out of the fire hoses.*

*We hear the fire die down. We hear the neighbors start to
disperse. We hear the police arrive and ask questions. We
hear the wet wood smoldering. We hear the last cinder
popping. We hear the fire trucks drive away. We hear
the morning breaking. We hear no more voices. We hear
morning sounds, pretty much like any other early morning
in the Bright Houses subdivision.*

*The lights come up on Mary and Ben standing in front
of their burned down house. Sharon and Kenny's house
stands next to theirs. Their front door is wide open.*

*There is a man standing with them. He's dressed casually,
like maybe a plaid shirt and blue pants. Perhaps the style
of his clothes is just a little out of date.*

*This is Kenny's great-Uncle. The keeper of the house
Sharon and Kenny were living in. His name is Frank.*

FRANK: I knew Roger best when he was 9 years old. He'd
come over to the house for Thanksgiving, and I took him
fishing for perch a couple times—there used to be a pond
you know, at the end of Feather Way, where they keep the
bulldozers now. Got his line all tangled up in a tree. Fish
hanging there like it was a Christmas ornament.
Roger was my niece Donna's son. Donna never quite settled
down—She had Roger with her first husband, and then she
has two girls with the man I think she's still with now.
At first his troubles were typical boy stuff—graffiti, cheap
wine. Even when his son was born, when Roger was 17, it
seemed like things might be OK. I remember he got a job working for a construction company. The young woman, the mother
of his child, started cleaning houses. Sometimes those things
work. Sometimes a child focuses you towards your life.
BEN: We didn't know he had a son.
FRANK: Well, he was my great nephew, and I wasn't that close
with my niece Donna, his mother. She moved to Nebraska

five, ten years ago. I hear now she's a high school guidance counselor.

But I know Roger's troubles got worse. Drugs. And I think a spell in jail. Spells in jail.

And so when Roger appeared on my doorstep—all dressed up with that new girl—and asked me if they could stay in the house...well,I told him I'd think about it, and give him a call.

And I never gave him a call. It was a can of worms I thought best to keep closed.

They got in through a back window I guess. I bet he fixed it right away. Roger always was a handy guy. Got in through the back window and then probably never locked the door.

MARY: He went by Kenny. He told us his name was Kenny.

FRANK: Kenny huh? No, its Roger. It's always been Roger.

*Frank, Ben and Mary look at the burnt down house. The sounds of Bright Houses: cars, the hum of air compressors, kids in the distance, etc.*

Do you two have some help?

BEN: What?

FRANK: Help. Family, friends? To help you through all this?

BEN: Oh yeah, we have insurance. For this sort of thing.

FRANK: Insurance isn't going to bring you a home cooked casserole.

MARY: We're in a motel.

BEN: Our parents might come. And I have a brother.

FRANK: Whoo. Talk about a clean slate.

I lived around the corner for 29 years. We bought one of the model homes, the houses people would come pick from. There were five of them, and every house in this neighborhood is one of the five. Hard to tell now, because people have redone things, repainted, knocked down, rebuilt. But yes there were five model homes and you just picked the one you liked and they built it for you. You could choose your colors, or maybe move a closet from here to there, but mostly they just built from the model. It was no big deal that your house looked like a lot of the other houses. It was a new house! You were living in Bright Houses. It was like stealing second base. You were safe.

They were magic times. Kids running ragged everywhere, skinning their knees, catching beetles. All the fathers pulling into the driveways at 5:30 sharp in their Belvederes, their Furies. Kids running up into their arms. Our arms.

But now look at this place. Half the houses falling apart, the others so fancified they seem untouchable.

*He indicates a large house across the street.*

I mean how are you going to ask for a cup of sugar from someone who lives in THAT place? You'd have to buy a new pair of shoes just to walk up their driveway. This is not what the developers intended. They wanted you to have neighbors. They wanted you to be in it together…

Well I'm going to go down to Home Depot and buy some padlocks for the front and back doors. I don't think they'll come back, but if they do, I can't let them in. They've done enough already.

MARY: They really didn't have much of anything in the house.

FRANK: It's spooky in there. There's just a mattress and a coffee table and some dirty laundry. A few dishes. Sheet rock's all banged up in the bedroom. I think there's blood too.

BEN: They weren't bad people. They were trying.

FRANK: Mm Hmm.

MARY: We enjoyed them.

FRANK: Ma'am, they burnt your house down.

*Mary and Ben look at the burnt down house. Does Frank pick up an object from the wreckage? And then look out to the neighborhood?*

FRANK: Someone should really start an archive about this place, and the things that happened here. I'm going to get my granddaughter take me on the internet, help me find people who lived here over the years. We'll track people down and ask them for old photos of the way things used to be. And they could mail them to me parcel post and I could glue them all into one big book. Maybe with memories written out next to each one. An archive. And we could put it in the neighborhood somewhere…maybe where the old pavillion was…..and people could gather round…

*He looks back to Mary and Ben.*

You know if you two need a place to stay for a little while, you're welcome to stay at the house.

*He points over to Sharon and Kenny's house.*

It's true it's a little rough around the edges, but I wouldn't charge you anything of course—

BEN: Thank you but—

FRANK: I'd like to help.

MARY: We're thinking of moving to Britain.

*Mary looks at Ben like, "right honey?"*

BEN: Right.

MARY: Ian's got some family over there. I'd like to have a farm.

FRANK: Oh well Britain's great. Beautiful place. Nice people.

MARY: Not really. I find them a bit snooty.

BEN: *(In a British accent)* A bit snooty, yes.

FRANK: Oh well I don't really know anything about that.

> *Mary and Ben look at each other. Frank looks at the neighborhood.*

You really should have been there. Two Saturdays a month in the summer time were the Noontime at Night Dances. They'd light up the pavilion with colored lights and you'd dance till you had blisters on your blisters. Everybody's shoes tossed off to the side. All outdoors! Nobody had any money. We all doubled up on babysitters—we'd pick up little Walter and Katie from the floor of Ed and Shirley's house at 2AM, 3AM sometimes... Such a perfect memory, sometimes I wonder if it was real at all.

*Frank seems to be leaving.*

MARY: So long.

*Frank stop and points.*

FRANK: I think I had a picture of my sister Lois standing right there planting that tree...

> *Mary watches Frank go. Ben looks at the list in his hand.*

MARY: What's that?

BEN: They want a list of things that didn't burn. Something about our net worth.

*Lisa D'Amour*

*Ben and Mary look at their burned down house.*

MARY: But it all burned.

BEN: Right.

    A moment.

    I'll do whatever you want. We can do whatever.

MARY: Well we have the car...

    *Ben and Mary look at the remains of their house.*

MARY: What do you think this was before all that?

BEN: Probably farmland.

MARY: And before that?

BEN: Who knows. The wild?

    *Mary contemplates the wild that once was.*

MARY: I dreamed last night that I was sleeping alone in the room at the Super 8, and someone started banging on the door. And when I opened it, and you were standing there, but it was like I had never seen you before in my whole life.

BEN: Really.

MARY: You smiled and said "Oh, I'm sorry, I thought you were my wife." And you walked down the little outside hallway.

BEN: I slept like a rock last night.

MARY: You were turning to go down the stairs when I woke up. And there you were.

    The real you. And you opened your eyes, and looked at me...

    *Blackout*

*End Of Play*

# HONKY

*Greg Kalleres*

Produced by Urban Stages,
March 8th – April 14th, 2013

Directed by Luke Harlan
Set Designer: Roman Tatarowicz
Sound Designer: Brandon Wolcott
Costume Designer: Sarah Thea Swafford
Projection Designer: Caite Hevner
Production Stage Manager: Brian D. Gold
Lighting Designer: Miriam Nilofa Crowe
Production Manager: Sean Hagerty

CAST:
THOMAS HODGE: Anthony Gaskins
DAVIS TALLISON: Philip Callen
PETER TRAMMEL: Dave Droxler
EMILIA HODGE: Arie Bianca Thompson
ANDIE CHASTAIN: Danielle Faitelson
DR. DRISCOLL, WILSON, REPORTER,
ABRAHAM LINCOLN: Scott Barrow
KID 1, FREDERICK DOUGLASS: Chris Myers
KID 2: Reynaldo Piniella

GREG KALLERES received his BFA from Tisch's Dramatic Writing Program at NYU. Since, his plays have been produced in numerous cities including, New York, Los Angeles, Chicago, Berkeley, Bloomington, IN and Beirut, Lebanon. He received the Certificate of Excellence from the Kennedy Center and The Emerging Playwright Award from Urban Stages. His one-act plays have won top honors at the Samuel French Festival, Turnip Festival and Fusion Theatre One Act Play Festival. Greg's work has been published in the New York Times, TDF Stages Magazine, as well as United Stages' "Best of EATFest" Volumes 3 and 4.

In addition to playwriting, Greg has written and produced commercials for ESPN, Nike, Brand Jordan, Budweiser, New York Magazine and Twitter. Greg was a lead writer on the award-winning "This is Sports-Center" campaign and created ESPN's Monday Night Football campaign: "Is it Monday Yet?"

Greg's screenplay, *Last Day Man*, was optioned by Evamere Entertainment.
See more at www.gregkalleres.com

CHARACTERS:
(8 Actors required for following cast)

THOMAS HODGE:  30's, black male
DAVIS TALLISON:  40s-50's, white male
PETER TRAMMEL:  30's, white male
EMILIA HODGE:  30's, black female; Thomas' sister
ANDIE CHASTAIN :  25-35, white female; Peter's fiancee
DR. DRISCOLL:  35-60, white male
KID 1:  18-25, black male
KID 2:  18-25, black male
WILSON ELLIOT:  (Played by Dr. Driscoll)
REPORTER:  (Played by Dr. Driscoll)
FREDERICK DOUGLASS:  (Played by Kid 1)
ABRAHAM LINCOLN:  (Played by Dr. Driscoll)

*This play should be performed without
an intermission.*

PLACE:  New York
TIME:  Now

**hon·ky** *(hông'ke) n. Offensive Slang.*
A disparaging term for a white person

# ACT I

## Scene 1

*A projection of a poor, black, American neighborhood. A SOULFUL WOMAN sings to a slowly building, inspirational hip hop beat*

SOULFUL WOMAN: *(O.S.)* Oh, yeaaaah . . . .ooh, yeaaah . . . uh-huh . . .

*A silhouette of two BLACK KIDS dressed stereotypically "ghetto" strut toward each other like they're going to fight. One presents a basketball and they begin playing an aggressive game of one-on-one.*

*It's choreographed beautifully, like a dance. It's about more than basketball.*

SOULFUL WOMAN: *(O.S.)* When life is hard out in the street
It matters what is on your feet
Reach for the sky
When the ghetto's on your sole
And it's kinda like "The Wire" on HBO
Reach for the sky
Reach for the skyyyyy

*Kid 1 shoots—Kid 2 blocks—Kid 1 goes down! Angry, Kid 1 takes off his sneaker and aims it at Kid 2 like it's a gun! Kid 2 pulls off his Sky Max 16 shoe—a light shines on it. He aims it back at Kid 1, who realizes he's over-matched, raises his hands, and lowers his head.*

SOULFUL WOMAN: *(O.S.)* Reach for the skyyyyyyy!!

*BANG!*

ANNOUNCER: *(O.S.)* The new SKY MAX 16s.

*As projection that says: "Introducing the SKY MAX 16."*

KID 2: 'Sup Now!"

*Kid 2 blows on his shoe, like a gun.*

*Lights out.*

## Scene 2

*A nice office. DAVIS TALLISON, white, sits confidently behind a desk, scrutinizing a wildly colored basketball sneaker. Across sits THOMAS HODGE, black, 30's, waiting. And waiting.*

DAVIS: So, are they going to stay these colors?

THOMAS: Well, yeah. That's kinda the design.

*He examines it more. Thomas waits.*

DAVIS: Would you wear these?

THOMAS: You mean . . . ? Sure. I mean. What do you mean?

DAVIS: I mean would you wear them?

THOMAS: Well, I wouldn't design anything I wouldn't wear—

DAVIS: No, I understand that, pride in your work and I get that. But . . . would you?

THOMAS: *(With conviction)* Yes.

DAVIS: See, I think I looks like a circus shoe.

THOMAS: You don't like it.

DAVIS: I can't think of a pair of pants that would go with them.

THOMAS: You said the same thing about the 16s.

DAVIS: Right, well, the first question, the important one, is would *you* wear them? You say you would. The next question is, would *I*? And the truth is, I wouldn't wear them on a bet.

THOMAS: Well. With all due respect Mr. Tallison, they're not for you.

*This sparks something in Davis.*

DAVIS: No? Who are they for, Thomas?

THOMAS: They're for . . . well. Black kids. They're for black kids. That's our target. Urban youth; 14-24.

DAVIS: Ahh. That does exclude me, doesn't it? Guess my opinion doesn't carry much weight around here.

THOMAS: No, that's not—what I meant was—

DAVIS: They're for *your* people. Right? It's okay. That what you're saying?

THOMAS: *(beat; cautious)* I was hired to design shoes for the urban youth market. Sky Shoes . . . I'm saying, Sky Shoes is an urban—*primarily* —black brand.

DAVIS: Fair enough. Now, let me tell you why I was hired.

THOMAS: Mr. Tallison . . .

DAVIS: No, please. You don't get to go to all these boring positioning meetings that I do, so let me fill you in on our *position*. I was brought in last year because this company has a property. An unusual property. And currently it's not living up to it's potential. You know why?

THOMAS: No.

DAVIS: Because for the last 15 years, Sky has been selling to your people and only your people. Is it cool if I talk like this? I'm not making you uncomfortable, "my people, your people"—I grew up in Chicago. Point is, these are facts, yes?

> *(before Thomas can answer)*

Now, I wont bore you with numbers here but we've found a large sub-segment of suburban white kids who literally wont *wear* anything, *listen* to anything, *say* anything unless it's been legitimized by blacks first.

THOMAS: Legitimized.

DAVIS: By the urban market.

THOMAS: We don't sell to suburban white kids.

DAVIS: This is what I'm telling you—we do now! But see, turns out they won't trust us to sell them anything. That is, *they*, being *my* people, wont trust *us*, being *white* people. But they'll trust *you*.

THOMAS: My people.

DAVIS: There's this incredible phenomenon called white guilt. Have you heard of this? These kids who live off of Mommy and Daddy with their trust funds and private schools; it's like Kryptonite! We did a whole focus group on it. I'll show you the video, it's fascinating. Anyway, we can use this guilt to outsell our competitors. How? Because we have what Nike does not.

THOMAS: What's that?

DAVIS: We're really *black*!

> *(Thomas just stares blankly)*

So, yes. We market to African Americans. Why? Because they're the best salesmen we have! So, again, the first question is, would *you* wear them? The second question is . . . would *I*?

> *(Beat)*

---

I'll get back to you with more detailed feedback on the design later in the week.

*Thomas turns to leave . . . and then stops.*

THOMAS: What about when it becomes shit?

DAVIS: What's that?

THOMAS: Illegitimate. Watered down popular culture. "Whoot There it is."

DAVIS: In ten years we sell the "Whoot There it is" retro shoe.

THOMAS: That explains the ad for the 16s.

DAVIS: You don't like it.

THOMAS: I designed a basketball shoe. That ad has nothing to do with basketball.

DAVIS: We're not selling basketball; we're selling culture!

THOMAS: You're selling the ghetto. And that tag line? "'Sup Now?'" What is that?!

DAVIS: 'Sup Now. It's like . . . "what's up now", except—

THOMAS: I know what it means!

DAVIS: Oh. I see. I'm the white guy right now. Is that it? Hm? I can see that look you're giving me. It's okay. You're right. I'm just a salesman. The 16s were your design. Your brilliance. Personally, I found them silly looking but we've got black kids killing each other in the streets for those things! Now, white kids see that and they respect it. It's stupid, I agree, but they do. They're taking notice and we did that. How? By selling the ghetto!

THOMAS: You're serious.

DAVIS: Black kid shoots someone for a pair of our shoes, white kid says "now that's something real! Something authentic!" They want it because they don't understand it! We need our brand to accepted by *real black America* so we can become real to the *posers* of *white America*! You wanna know how we beat Nike? Hm? When it's *white* kids killing for our shoes. Then we win.

THOMAS: You're talking about the kid who was shot. Because of our commercial.

DAVIS: Who knows why people do these things. It's ghetto shit. I'm from Chicago and I still don't understand it. The point is, perception. Kid gets shot, in the ghetto, his shoes are missing—happens to be our shoes.

*Pause.*

THOMAS: Mr. Tallison . . . I love this company. Like every kid in the neighborhood, I developed an early obsession with sneakers. Sky Max 3's were my first pair. After that, I was hooked. Fetishized them. Sometimes I'd hardly ever wear em. I'd just look at 'em. Feel 'em. Smell 'em. To this day, the smell of leather on a brand new shoe is the closest thing to true happiness I know. And every year, the new Sky shoe would come out in February, just before spring. It was the only thing kids from my street, "my people," could talk about. And the only time a kid got hurt was when he scuffed someone's shit up. We loved Sky because it made no apologies. It was a black shoe for black people. And if we saw a white kid wearing 'em, he better be able to back his shit up on the court or he was gonna get his ass beat. There was a purity to it.

    *(beat)*

The kid who was killed? That was my little cousin. So, I'm sorry, but I don't quite share your enthusiasm for edging out the competition. You'll have my resignation by the end of the week.

    *Thomas turns for the door.*

DAVIS: Tom! Thomas!

    *Thomas stops.*

DAVIS: Is that . . . ?

    Jesus, I'm, obviously, I wouldn't have . . .

    This country, Thomas . . . and I'll tell you, there are things, like this, you see it day in and day out; violence and the divisions and a system that just, frankly . . .

    *(then empathy)*

    My wife killed herself.

    *A moment of complete and utter confusion.*

THOMAS: Excuse me?

DAVIS: That's right. Bottle of sleeping pills. Not a lot of people know that. First she stopped talking. Then she wouldn't leave her room. Started calling me by my middle name, Allen, which she only used when she was mad at me. One morning I walked in and . . . well, the whole thing is god-damn senseless.

*Pause. Thomas is still at a loss.*

DAVIS: Hey, look, you know what . . . let me take another look at these.

THOMAS: I'm sorry, I don't understand . . . .

DAVIS: You were right with the 16s, I have no reason to doubt you now. I want you with me on this one, Thomas. What do you say?

THOMAS: *(beat)* Whoot there it is.

> *Lights out.*

# SCENE 3

*A therapist's office. PETER, white, sits across from EMILIA, black. This is their first meeting and he's nervous.*

*Peter fidgets, awkwardly.*

PETER: I'm sorry, I don't really know what I'm supposed to say.

EMILIA: That's alright. Why don't you tell me what's on your mind.

PETER: *(Beat)* Getting married soon.

EMILIA: Congratulations.

PETER: Thank you, she's very white.

*(Awkward beat)*

I don't know why I just said that. I don't mean "*white*", like the distinction between the colors white or black. I mean, she's just very, you know . . . *white.* This is sounding bad. I don't mean "white" like, "*lynch you*" white—and shit! I don't mean "lynch" as in . . . !—Or even "*you*" as in—! Jesus. How did I—? I didn't mean to make it a thing about, you know . . .

EMILIA: Okay . . .

PETER: Because the truth is, I'm totally color blind. And I don't mean that figuratively either. I mean, I don't see color. You should see my socks—totally integrated!

*(Beat, careful)*

The point I'm making is that I'm getting married . . . to a woman . . . who is not a racist.

EMILIA: That's the point you're making.

PETER: It wasn't originally.

EMILIA: So, she's not a racist.

PETER: Or maybe she is! Who knows, right? I mean, they say everyone is kind of, you know, even if they don't think they are.

EMILIA: Does that include you?

PETER: Me?! Are you kidding?! My mom marched with Dr. King! Well, not technically. She overslept and missed the actual march. But she was a huge fan!

EMILIA: So, we've established that you, your fiancée and your mother are not racists.

---

*Greg Kalleres*

PETER: *(choosing words carefully)* Right. Well. To say you're not racist is ignorant and ignorance is the very seed of racism. What I mean is I don't hate someone because of the color of their skin or the slant of their eye. I don't mean *"slant"* as in . . . my point is, I like African Americans! *(Realizing this is stupid)* But obviously not just because they are so. I mean, I like some and I don't like some. Like I like some white people and *hate* some white people—like any race!

EMILIA: The Chinese?

PETER: Sure! *Hate* them too. *And* like them! My point is, I don't hate *because* they're Chinese. And I think that's what we're talking about here.

EMILIA: Is it?

PETER: Right? Exactly! "Is it?" And I didn't mean to imply that all racists are white either. I think racism is an equal opportunity kind of thing. Hell, you could be a racist.

EMILIA: I could.

PETER: Of course! You can be anything you want! That's what's so great about this country! And I don't mean to say that all racists are bad people. Some are very good people! Good people who just don't know because they didn't have the money for the education. My Aunt Judy? Total racist. But you can't blame her because she grew up poor, so it doesn't really count. And she's white!

*(Chuckles)*

Well, of course she's white.

*(beat)*

Or she might not be! I didn't mean to imply that because I'm Caucasian she has to be Caucasian. It's very possible, not knowing me or my heritage, that she could be African American. Or Chinese. Or Asian! Not that all Chinese are Asian, obviously.

EMILIA: *(correcting him)* Not that all Asians are Chinese.

PETER: Right. Some are Japanese. Korean. Oriental.

EMILIA: "Oriental" is not politically correct.

PETER: Well, we can't blame them for that; it's probably just a culture thing. I've written papers about this exact thing.

EMILIA: You have?

PETER: Yeah. One. In college. Same thing we're talking about.

EMILIA: And what is that again?

PETER: *(false modesty, comfort)* Oh, you know. This whole thing we're discussing. This whole silly race thing. It was actually in the school chronicle. Not a big deal really but the piece was very popular among the African American students. And Caucasians. All of them.

EMILIA: Hispanics.

PETER: Yes. They loved it too.

EMILIA: And the Asians?

PETER: Not a lot of Chinese at my school. Point is, I've written about this and I have a lot of strong feelings and I think that's kind of what we're both saying here.

> *Long awkward pause. Peter forces a smile, trying to look comfortable.*

EMILIA: Peter . . . before you came here today, did you know that I was black?

PETER: *(innocent)* Uh . . . why do you ask?

EMILIA: Because you seem a tad uncomfortable with it.

PETER: *(pretending to be floored)*
. . . . . . . . . . . . . . what?????

EMILIA: And, as a therapist, I want you feeling comfortable. If my being black keeps you from being honest or comfortable, I could refer you to another therapist.

> *Peter fidgets, trying to decide if he should take the out she's offered.*

PETER: Well, I'm just . . .

The idea that you think—because I know the people you're talking about and . . .

Whew! Man. I . . .

This is . . .

Okay. Okay. I'm going to be honest here. When I walked in and saw that you were not some whitey white, stuck up, Dr. Phil yuppie, I was so relieved. I gotta tell you, I can't wait to tell you my problems and stuff.

EMILIA: Okay. Why don't you tell me why you came to see me today.

PETER: *(pause, coming clean)* A kid was murdered for a pair of shoes and I think it's because of a commercial I wrote.

---

*Greg Kalleres*

EMILIA: Sky Shoes. You wrote that ad? "Sup now?"

PETER: *(Sheepish, trying to joke)* Not too much. How are you?

*Lights out.*

# Scene 4

*A bedroom. ANDIE sits in bed reading Vogue as she speaks to someone off stage.*

ANDIE: Oh, my parents called! They want to know what we're doing for the holiday weekend. I said I'd ask you but I think they want us to go up to Connecticut. They're gonna have the Brennans up. Remember the Brennans? Mr. Brennan's the one who smells like Mayonnaise. Apparently, they're family now! For the past few months my parents keep referring to them as Aunt and Uncle for some reason. Oh, that reminds me, I haven't told you this yet because my therapist and I are still kind of working it out but I'm pretty sure I have a repressed memory of Mr. Brennan touching me as a kid.

*Peter emerges from the bathroom.*

ANDIE: I mean, it's repressed, so you never know for sure but I get a queasy, after school special type of feeling around him. And whenever he sees me in a bathing suit he gives me this very specific sort of: "Whoa, I think I may have molested you once" kind of look. Plus when I go to sleep in my old house, I have this immediate craving for a turkey sandwich. You know. Turkey? Mayo? Probably means nothing but my therapist is gonna think about it. So, anyway, Mom asked the other day if we wanted Mr. Brennan to do our wedding service because he's some sort of judge and I was like, "are you kidding?" Can you see us up there saying our vows and I suddenly smell Miracle Whip and have a panic attack?!

PETER: I saw that woman today.

ANDIE: Oh good! How was it?

PETER: She was nice.

ANDIE: Don't be discouraged if you don't like her right away. It's normal. It took me four years to like my therapist.

PETER: I like her.

ANDIE: What did she say about the shooting? Did she tell you it's not your fault, or did she do that thing where she makes you figure it out on your own?

PETER: There was a witness.

ANDIE: In her office?

PETER: No, to the shooting. Just came forward. Saw the whole thing. Know what the kid said before he shot him? "'Sup Now?"

ANDIE: *(proud)*Honey, that's your line!

*(Realizing)*

I didn't mean that. Obviously. Hey, honey? It is not your fault. People kill. They buy guns and they shoot and they kill. It has nothing to do with you or your commercial. It's a testament to your talent that you even got people to buy those things in the first place!

*(off his look)*

Well, Peter, they're ugly shoes. What pants would even go with those things?

*She exits to the bathroom. We hear her brushing her teeth in the bathroom.*

ANDIE: *(O.S.)* Killing people for shoes. What is this the 80's??

*She pops her head out.*

ANDIE: Can you imagine women killing each other over shoes?! Not to be, you know, but can you?! Of course, I say that but Peg was wearing the hottest pair of Manolos the other day at lunch and I considered shooting her in the face myself!

*(Pointing her finger)*

'Sup Now, BITCH! Pow!

*Lights out.*

# Scene 5

*Emilia sits at her desk when Thomas bursts though the door.*

THOMAS: Reach for the skyyyy!

EMILIA: *(startled)* Thomas—?!

THOMAS: Reach for the sky mothafuckaaaas!!!

EMILIA: What are you doing? I have patients outside —!

THOMAS: I need you to look at my ass!

EMILIA: What?

THOMAS: Quickly! Look at my ass!

EMILIA: Okay! Okay!

*She bends down and looks.*

THOMAS: Are you looking?

EMILIA: Yes!

THOMAS: You sure?

EMILIA: I'm looking!

THOMAS: Do you see a white man's dick in there any-where?!

EMILIA: Jesus, Thomas!

THOMAS: I'm a bitch, Em! I'm a a white man's bitch!

EMILIA: Okay, calm down . . .

THOMAS: I knew it'd take a toll! Growin' up around all those rich, white people takes a toll. It takes a fuckin' toll!

EMILIA: Okay . . .

THOMAS: I knew eventually I'd be getting fucked by Clay Aiken, Cold Play and *Downton Abbey*! I'd wake up in a cold sweat needing to buy some $600 Nottingham Wall Sconce from Pottery Barn!

EMILIA: You said that sconce gave your place a nice classic feel.

THOMAS: Damn right it's a nice classic feel! It's also an el-egant way to disguise the lack of furniture in that part of the room—but you're missing the point!!

EMILIA: And that is?

THOMAS: This is not what black people talk about!!

EMILIA: Not this again. What are we supposed to talk about, Thomas?

THOMAS: I don't know—black shit!

EMILIA: Black shit.

THOMAS: Black shit that black people talk about and you and I have been living around whitey so long we don't know how to do it anymore!

EMILIA: Don't say "whitey."

THOMAS: Why, am I insulting you?

EMILIA: It's base.

THOMAS: What about nigger? Is that "base"? Because that's what my boss called me today!

EMILIA: Your boss called you—??

THOMAS: Not as in the *word,* no. But with his eyes, you know? His tone, his whole: "It's cool, I'm from Chicago"—I mean, did I miss something? What the *fuck* happened in Chicago?! Shit, Emilia, I'm black—I can say "whitey" whenever I want!

EMILIA: You've earned it, huh?

THOMAS: Damn right; my heritage!

EMILIA: Your heritage is Rumson New Jersey, and I don't think Bob Gammons would like you calling him whitey.

THOMAS: Bob Gammons?! Fuck Bob Gammons!

EMILIA: Fuck Bob Gammons?

THOMAS: Fuck him!

EMILIA: That's nice Thomas! He was like an uncle!

THOMAS: Fuck him! And fuck whitey!!

EMILIA: *(gesturing to the door)* Shhh! Thomas!

THOMAS: *(to the door)* Whitey! Whitey! Cracker! Honky! White . . . trash . . . K.K . . .

*(struggles for breath)*

I can't breathe . . .

EMILIA: Sit down.

THOMAS: I'm having . . . a . . .

EMILIA: You're having a panic attack. Sit down.

THOMAS: Panic? I'm having a damn . . . heart attack!

EMILIA: Shhh. Sit down. You're hyperventilating. Listen to me. Okay? Breathe in. Breathe out. Slow. Breathe in. Good. Out.

*He rests his head on her shoulder.*

EMILIA: Used to do that as a kid. Remember? Scared the hell out of Mom and Dad. Never knew what you were so nervous about.

*She gets some pills from a drawer.*

EMILIA: Take this.

*She exits to the bathroom.*

THOMAS: Black people don't hyperventilate!

EMILIA: *(O.S.)* It's an anxiety attack!

THOMAS: They don't have anxiety attacks neither!

*She emerges with water.*

EMILIA: You'd be surprised.

THOMAS: Oh yeah? How many black patients do you have?

*He takes a drink, lays his head back.*

THOMAS: I made a work of art, and they turned it into a rap video.

EMILIA: I know.

THOMAS: I shoulda quit. I shoulda left the moment they hired that white motherfucker to sell our shoes!

EMILIA: Thomas . . .

THOMAS: I'm not gonna let that happen to the 17, Em. It's the best thing I've ever done and I wont let another Charley Cross get shot because I let them put my shoes on thugs instead of black people.

EMILIA: C'mon, Thomas. Make it sound like you knew the kid.

THOMAS: *(smiles devilishly)* Yeah, well . . . I told Tallison he was my cousin.

EMILIA: You what?

THOMAS: You should've see his face. And I thought he couldn't get any whiter.

EMILIA: You lied to your boss?

THOMAS: Yeah and he believed me! So fuck him for thinking all black people know each other! And then he comes back to me with this whole "it's okay, my wife killed herself" bullshit!

EMILIA: His wife?

THOMAS: I know, right? Why you gotta top my shit!? Why does your wife's suicide beat my cousin's murder!?

EMILIA: He wasn't your cousin!

THOMAS: Yeah, but he didn't know that!!

EMILIA: Well, he didn't die because of his shoes or some stupid commercial and you know it.

THOMAS: They quoted the ad, Emilia.

EMILIA: The kid was a gangbanger!

THOMAS: And so he deserved to die?!

EMILIA: Will you cut that shit out!! Damn! I'm on your side!

> *(She calms, collects)*
>
> Look, I know you feel this guilt. This . . . conflict. Somehow you got it in your head that because you grew up with money and education you're not black enough. But getting yourself shot doesn't make you black, it makes you stupid.

THOMAS: Oh, he was stupid too!

EMILIA: You see this? You talk about how offended you are at this commercial, its portrayal of black ghetto youth as aspirational, and yet you defend the lifestyle. It's just like when we were kids. And you were always playin' ball with those gangsters from the neighborhood over—

THOMAS: You mean my *friends*?!

EMILIA: Friends?! You'd come home crying every time! All the shit they'd give you! Call you rich boy, call you white! Honky! Make fun of how you dressed, how you talked. And next day, sure enough, you'd go back for more.

THOMAS: Don't do that, alright? Don't analyze me like you do your white people.

EMILIA: That's the difference between us, Thomas. They are not white people to me. They're people with problems.

THOMAS: And you think they just see you as their doctor.

EMILIA: How else would they see me, Thomas?

THOMAS: No, see, they go home and they say, *(imitating a white woman)* "Jill! I'm seeing a new therapist, and you know what, she's *(whispers)* black! Isn't that interesting? And she's really smart and articulate; you almost don't even think about it."

EMILIA: Does everything have to be so heavy?! Is that what talking about "black shit" is? Mining for the diabolical subtext? Stereotypical conversations about the white man keeping us down? You don't seem down Thomas!

THOMAS: I'm gonna find him, Em. I'm gonna find the black ass motherfucker who wrote that ad . . . .

EMILIA: Thomas, what makes you think he's bla—

THOMAS: I'm not kidding. At the 16 party tomorrow night, I'ma walk up to him, take him outside and I'ma show his ass wa'sup now!

*Lights out.*

## SCENE 6

*Davis' office. WILSON ELLIOT sits awkwardly across from Davis.*

WILSON: Davis.

DAVIS: Wilson.

WILSON: I don't want to take too much of your time with this, or make too much of it, so I'll try to keep this brief. It seems there have been comments around the office concerning your . . . *insensitivity.*

DAVIS: Insensitivity.

WILSON: Some people have made mention. Some of the minorities. Do you see what I'm saying?

DAVIS: No.

WILSON: They, that is the people who have made mention, the minorities, they have made claims that you might be a little, well...*insensitive.*

DAVIS: Insensitive.

WILSON: *Racially.*

DAVIS: You're kidding.

WILSON: Let me make this clear, this is not me talking to you right now. This is the board. Unfortunately, my hands are tied.

DAVIS: They had you come down for this?

WILSON: Complaints have been filed. Measures need to be taken. By me. On the record. I have to have this conversation with you.

DAVIS: You do?

WILSON: Well, the board does. Technically, I'm not even here.

DAVIS: I see.

WILSON: Look, obviously you've been through something. Your wife. And my God, I mean, my God. So, don't think anyone holds anything against you. But it has to be on the record that you have heard what I've said and that steps will be taken. So . . . ..have you heard what I've said?

DAVIS: . . . yes.

WILSON: And will steps be taken?

DAVIS: I'm sorry, to do what?

WILSON: To be less . . . be more . . . *sensitive.*

DAVIS:  What exactly is it that I did wrong?

WILSON: No one is saying you did anything wrong. There are things, in the workplace, with people, certain situations in which one must exercise *caution.* The things one says, *how* they're said and, in turn, how they are *received.* Do you understand?

DAVIS:  Did this come from Thomas Hodge?

WILSON: Who?

DAVIS:  Then who said it?

WILSON: Well, it was more than one person.

DAVIS:  How many?

WILSON: I can't tell you that.

DAVIS:  Look, I'll guess a number and if you say nothing, I'll know it's a yes, okay?

    *(Beat)*

Okay?

WILSON: I was saying yes.

DAVIS:  Oh. Good. Two?

WILSON: No.

DAVIS:  Three? *(Beat)* Three people?

WILSON: Sorry, I was thinking about something else. Look, this is a delicate time. And things are very, well, delicate. And the board just doesn't want you to lose site of that.

DAVIS:  Okay. So, what, you're telling me . . . ?

WILSON: The *board* is tell you.

DAVIS:  Telling me what?

WILSON: Our goals, expanding Sky Shoes, widening our demo, selling to Nike—these things are the important things.

DAVIS:  I know that.

WILSON: No one is saying you don't but—and obviously this goes without saying—we don't want anything, whether it's this thing or something else, to get in the way of that.

DAVIS:  Let me get this straight . . . the board is concerned Nike will balk if it gets out that employees said that I'm racist?

WILSON: Whoa! Hey! Okay. Let's keep the "R word" out of it.

DAVIS:  But isn't that what they're saying?

WILSON: Yes, but it's their word. We can't really use it.

DAVIS:  *(fed up)*Look, I truly appreciate the opportunity you've given me here at Sky. But I've been in this industry for 20 years. I don't give a shit if someone is black, Arab, Chinese or Martian. All I care about is who's buying what, where they live and what they can afford. That's not racism, it's marketing. You wanna talk about stereotypes? We pay a premium for them. They're called demographics. Out there it may be racist to say that poor black people like malt liquor, fried chicken and McDonalds but in here it's just a Power Point presentation. So, if the board wants to fire me for doing the job they hired me to do it would be good to know. Meanwhile, if you'll excuse me, I have a black shoe company to paint white.

*Davis exits.*

WILSON: *(discomfited)* Yikes.

*Wilson writes it all down.*

*Light out.*

## Scene 7

*Peter and Andie's apartment. Both on their laptops. Peter in a chair, Andie on the floor.*

ANDIE: Have you sent me your list yet?

PETER: Huh?

ANDIE: Your new invitation list. Did you email it to me? I haven't gotten it.

PETER: Yeah, I haven't sent it yet.

ANDIE: Okay; let me know when you send it.

PETER: *(beat, confused)* Well, I'll just, you know, send it, and then you'll know.

ANDIE: I just wanna try to email it to my parents before they go to bed. I got mine down to 150. Which is good, I think. Assuming 25 don't come, I think we're okay. If you can get yours down to like 120, assuming 15 don't come, we should be in pretty good shape. Unless they do come. Which I doubt, but I don't want to over-assume. Or under-assume. I guess I'm wondering how much assuming you think we can do, over all.

*(Beat)*

Peter? Are you listening to me?

PETER: More people were killed.

ANDIE: For the shoes?

PETER: In the Congo. Six hundred deaths this week!

ANDIE: God.

PETER: Six hundred!

ANDIE: Horrible. What are Betty and Dell's kids' names?

PETER: August and Minnesota. This is genocide! It's genocide and it's like the country, we, because, what, I mean, we'll go where there's oil, right? But, hey, a good old fashioned holocaust?

ANDIE: AIDS too.

PETER: You're damn right, AIDS! Wait, what about AIDS?

ANDIE: In the Congo.

PETER: Yes! Right! And rape! Women over there, I mean, and I've read about this—it's like a national pastime! And what do we do? It's like because it's not here. Because it doesn't effect us—why are we inviting Betty and Dell's kids?

ANDIE: I'm assuming they wont come. How did they die?

PETER: Who?

ANDIE: The six hundred?

PETER: I don't know. I just read the headline. AOL's got a poll about it. I'm doing it. I am *fucking* doing it!

ANDIE: You should!

PETER: "Do you think the US should help in the Congo?" Fuck. Yes.

*He hits a button on his computer.*

ANDIE: Vote for me too.

PETER: Huh?

ANDIE: Vote for me.

PETER: You can only vote once per screen name.

ANDIE: Oh.

PETER: And you know why it is, don't you? And this is what kills me: it's because they're black! You know that, right? I mean, if this was a white, European nation we'd be over there in a heartbeat! But because African Americans have no power in this country, we just mail them food and a few pairs of jeans and be done with it.

ANDIE: Isn't our country run by an African American?

PETER: Right, well, one!

*A moment.*

ANDIE: I was talking to Tshombe at work. He's the guy I was telling you about. The one from Zambia? He hates it when white people refer to normal black people as "African American."

PETER: *(Defensive, insecure)* What do you mean?

ANDIE: Well, he's *African*, like *from Africa*, so for him it's annoying. I suggested a book to him and said that the author was African American and he said, "is he *really*?" You know, with this tone.

PETER: Who?

ANDIE: Tshombe.

PETER: No, the author. Who was it?

ANDIE: Oh. The guy who wrote "Another Country."

PETER: Ralph Ellison.

ANDIE: No the other one.

PETER: Langston Hughes.

ANDIE: No, the other one. Anyway, Tshombe said, "Is he from Africa?" And I said, "I don't think so" And he said, "then he's not African American. *I'm* African American. I'm from Zimbabwe."

PETER: Zambia.

ANDIE: I think it's Zimbabwe. Anyway, he doesn't like when white people refer to black people as African American because he *is* African. They're just . . . Americans.

PETER: *(beat)* I think I say black mostly.

ANDIE: Me too.

   *(Beat)*

Unless I'm talking to a black person.

PETER: We don't know shit.

ANDIE: Totally.

PETER: No, I mean, we have our little, you know, but out *there*? There's shit happening! Important shit! And what do we know?

ANDIE: Are you talking about the Congo or black people?

PETER: Both! Syria!! I mean, look at us!

ANDIE: Syria?

PETER: Yes, fucking Syria, Haiti!! People are dying is my point! And we are so…sheltered! So—I mean—YOU!

ANDIE: Me?

PETER: Well, yes, honey, you! You grew up, you had everything. Money, care, opportunity. A 300 person wedding?! You're living proof that the American dream is a congenital affectation!

ANDIE: That's not my fault.

PETER: But doesn't it bother you?

ANDIE: What?

PETER: This! Our whole *thing!* Don't you feel a little . . . you know . . .

ANDIE: What??

PETER: For this! All of this that we have!

ANDIE: We work; we have jobs.

PETER: But you have a job because you're educated and you're educated because you grew up in a wealthy, white family!!

ANDIE: What does being white have to do with it?

PETER: There's a plight! A struggle and a plight that you know nothing about because you were born the way you are!

ANDIE: I know the plight.

PETER: You don't know the plight!

ANDIE: Oh, and you know the plight?

PETER: Yes! I know—not all of it—but a lot of the plight, yes! My mom marched with Dr. King for Christ sake!

ANDIE: No, she didn't—!

PETER: Not *next* to him! Not *literally*! But she marched! As in "the march!" As in the idea. A movement.

ANDIE: Peter, just because you went to public high school doesn't make you Nelson Mandela.

PETER: I'm just saying when I grew up I was taught to feel a certain, you know, level of a kind of . . .

ANDIE: Guilt?

PETER: Yes! Exactly! Guilt!

ANDIE: And that's good?

PETER: I think when you consider the plight, a smidgen of guilt is the least you can feel!

ANDIE: So because you're a neurotic mess, I should be too?

PETER: Neuro—?? Is that what you've gleaned from this whole thing?! I'm talking about suffrage here! Plight!

ANDIE: Stop saying plight!

PETER: Struggle!

ANDIE: I think this is *your* struggle, not theirs.

PETER: Don't say "theirs" like they're a "*they*!" They are not a "they!"

ANDIE: Who are you talking about?!

PETER: Who are *you* talking about?!

ANDIE: Are you still in therapy?!

PETER: God, you are so fucking white!!!

　　　*Lights out.*

## SCENE 8

*A newscast. A REPORTER in the field.*

REPORTER: Early this morning, in the quiet, suburban town of Greenwich Connecticut, Felix Sanders, a white teenage boy, was shot in the leg for what appears to be his basketball shoes. A possible reaction to what occurred two weeks ago when an African American teen was shot and killed for the same brand of shoes. Sky Max 16s. This time, however, witnesses claim the crime was committed by a group of young white males. All of whom were wearing crooked baseball caps, extra large shirts and baggy jeans. Some of the clothes were actually being worn …backwards.

*Lights out.*

# Scene 9

*A subway car. Davis sits staring out when two BLACK KIDS get on the train, laughing and being very loud.*

KID 1: Nah, nah, nah, nigga, that movie was the shit!

KID 2: Nigga, whatchu smokin'?! That ending can suck my dick!

KID 1: What, you telling me, you sittin' there, gang a hard mothahfuckahs come up to you—you ain't got no choice!

KID 2: Nah, I ain't takin' it like a bitch.

KID 1: Nigga! Five hard niggas! Whatchu gonna do?!

KID 2: Run.

KID 1: They catch up.

KID 2: I do what that guy did in the movie.

KID 1: Yo, daz cuz nigga had a knife son!

KID 2: I'd have a knife!

KID 1: You ain't gotta knife now. Nah. Dat shit happens now, you gotta take it. Question is, after you take they shit . . .

DAVIS: Excuse me . . .

KID 2: I'd get a damn gun, son, blow the nigga's joints off!

DAVIS: Excuse me . . .

KID 1: Nigga, you lie!

DAVIS: Excuse me!

KID 1: *What?!*

DAVIS: Wondering if you wouldn't mind keeping it down.

KID 1: Last I checked, it was a free country.

DAVIS: Freedom doesn't mean we can't express a little courtesy.

KID 2: My man, how we not being "courteous"?

DAVIS: Well, frankly, you're being very loud. And there are children and you're using words like, "shit" and "nigger" …

*Suddenly the tone changes.*

KID 1: What did you just say mothafuckah?!?

DAVIS: Nothing; I was repeating what you said.

KID 2: Nah, my man called us "nigger!"

DAVIS: What? No! I said—you said —

KID 1: What?!

DAVIS: You called him . . .

KID 2: What?!

DAVIS: Nigger.

KID 2: He said it again, nigga!

DAVIS: *You* just said it again!

KID 1: What?

DAVIS: Uh—he—nigger!

KID 2: Nigga-*what*-nigga!?!?

DAVIS: Listen, let's take the N word out of the conversation!

KID 1: I think that'd be wise for you.

*Kids approach, threateningly. Just then we hear:*

TRAIN CONDUCTOR: *(O.S.)* This train is being held in the station due to train traffic. We apologize for the inconvenience.

DAVIS: Obviously, I've said something to offend you and I apologize. It's been a very bad day. Plus, the truth is, my wife . . . *(stops himself)* Point is, I think I can clear this up. I see your wearing Sky shoes—

KID 2: What about my shoes, bitch?

DAVIS: I'm the president of the company.

KID 1: You're kidding.

DAVIS: Well, I'm on probation now but for all practical purposes . . .

*He pulls a card from his pocket.*

DAVIS: Here, now, you take that to any Footlocker retailer, they'll give you a free pair.

KID 2: Do I get one? I want one.

DAVIS: Well, I only have the one with me.

KID 1: Why you givin' me this?

KID 2: I think he was scared.

DAVIS: No. I just don't want any trouble.

KID 2: What did you think we was gonna do?

DAVIS: Nothing.

KID 2: Damn, man. Give the racist his damn card back.

KID 1: Easy for you to say! You didn't get one!

KID 2: Fine, nigga, keep it! Uncle Tom mothafuckah.

KID 1: *(looks at Kid 2, guilty)* Damn.

*He throws the card back at him.*

KID 1: Racist mothahfuckah!

*The kids exit the car, leaving Davis alone.*

*Lights out.*

# SCENE 10

*DR. DRISCOLL's office. Davis listens, reluctantly, as DR.*
*DRISCOLL points to a map of the human brain projected*
*on the wall.*

DR. DRISCOLL: Driscotol works to isolate a small portion of
the occipital lobe and numbs it, just slightly. This area here.
Not coincidentally, it's the occipital lobe that is responsible
for our memory and vision. Damage to this area can cause
amnesia, hallucinations and what is referred to Color Ag-
nosia. Loss of color. The drug itself was discovered after
examining the head wound of a KKK Grand Wizard, whom
while re-shingling his roof, fell and damaged his occipital
lobe. When he came to, he was perfectly fine with one
simple change:

DAVIS: He was scared of heights.

DR. DRISCOLL: All men were created equal, Mr. Tallison. He
no longer hated or discriminated on the basis of color. And
through years of tests we found that we can successfully end
racial bigotry if we can just replicate this brain damage.

DAVIS: Okay. Let's. First of all, I am not a racist. This is more
of a formality. For my job.

DR. DRISCOLL: Okay.

DAVIS: Sure. I mean, what, I'm intelligent, I understand that
everyone has an inkling of, I mean—you, right, a little?

DR. DRISCOLL: No.

DAVIS: Exactly, me either! Hell, I run an urban shoe company.

DR. DRISCOLL: Urban?

DAVIS: It's a euphemism for African American. The point is,
I spend a lot of time with African Americans. I know the
African American culture and sell to the African American
a product—

DR. DRISCOLL: You don't have to say "African American"
every time Mr. Tallison. You can simply use . . .

DAVIS: Urban?

DR. DRISCOLL: I was gonna say "a pronoun."

DAVIS: Oh. I sell basketball shoes to them.

DR. DRISCOLL: Well, now the pronoun's offensive.

DAVIS: My overall point is, I don't think I'm a racist.

DR. DRISCOLL: Of course you don't. That's precisely why you are one. Do you understand?

DAVIS: No.

DR. DRISCOLL: We have a saying at the office, Mr. Tallison, that I think will appeal to you: "One who thinks, *is*. One who does *not* think, *is*. But *one* who is not one, thinks he is. One."

DAVIS: I don't understand a word you just said.

DR. DRISCOLL: You've proven my point perfectly.

DAVIS: I know what you're doing. Okay? I'm in marketing too. You sell the disease to sell the cure.

DR. DRISCOLL: Do you feel you need to be cured of something?

DAVIS: *(annoyed)* Listen: My dad was a salesman. My grandfather was a salesman. I'm a salesman. That's all I know and, frankly, all I care about. For the first time, I have a chance to succeed at a level they never could. And I won't let that be taken away because of some silly rules about what you can and can't say. I take this pill, the board is happy and I can run the company again! That's why I am here. So, write me a script and I'll get out of your hair.

DR. DRISCOLL: That's not how it works. I need to know you need it.

DAVIS: You just told me I needed it!

DR. DRISCOLL: For legal reasons, I need to hear it from you.

DAVIS: *(beat, sighs)* Fine. I was on the subway today. I don't usually ride the subway but today I did. And these kids come in. They were . . . urban kids. And they were being very loud. Laughing and shouting as if they wanted the entire subway to know they were having a good time. And all I could think was, "Jesus, are all black people this loud?"

*(beat)*

So, what do you think?

DR. DRISCOLL: What else you got?

DAVIS: How racist do I have to be?

DR. DRISCOLL: We like to cover our bases.

*Davis takes a moment.*

DAVIS: Okay. It's possible I may have . . . exploited the murder of a young black teenager to sell more shoes.

*Driscoll just stares.*

DAVIS: What?

DR. DRISCOLL: No, nothing, that's just really racist.

DAVIS: Okay, you know what . . . !

DR. DRISCOLL: No, please, it's good!

DAVIS: You know, I don't know how appealing brain damage sounds . . .

DR. DRISCOLL: I assure you, it's perfectly safe.

DAVIS: Are there side effects I should know about?

DR. DRISCOLL: Different people react differently. Like any drug. Which is exactly why we conduct these little interviews. But I wouldn't worry. You seem like just the right kind of racist.

DAVIS: Thanks.

*He hands him a bottle of pills.*

*Lights out.*

# SCENE 11

*A quiet corner of a party. Signs up all over that say: "Sky Max 16" and "'Sup Now?"*

*Thomas drinks alone at the bar. Andie, a little tipsy, sits a few seats down.*

ANDIE: *(pause)* I love these things.

> *(nothing)*

I'm kidding. I don't really love these things. I was being ironical.

THOMAS: Yeah, I know. I love irony.

ANDIE: Oh. Aha. Now you're being ironical.

THOMAS: You like that word.

ANDIE: It was my dictionary.com word of the day. I try to use it at least once.

THOMAS: Good, so you're done then.

> *Slighted, she turns back to her drink. But only for a moment.*

ANDIE: Pretty ugly shoe, huh?

> *Now she has Thomas' attention.*

ANDIE: I mean, I wouldn't wear those things on a bet, much less shoot someone for them.

> *(Whispers conspiratorially)*

It's okay, I can say that. I know someone who kinda works for the company.

THOMAS: Must be nice.

ANDIE: Right? I guess it's like how if you're Jewish you can make fun of Jews and it's funny but if you're not, it's offensive.

THOMAS: Are you Jewish?

ANDIE: Me?? No! But I had this friend in college who was always using the word "retarded." "This is retarded, that's retarded, what a retard?" Even made jokes about retarded people; impressions, the whole thing. You know how retarded people have that voice? That like deaf person voice?

THOMAS: *(uncomfortable)* Uh-huh.

ANDIE: Well, he would do that.

THOMAS: What a talent.

ANDIE: Right? So, finally I said, "look, maybe you should cool it on the whole retarded thing. It's kind of offensive to retarded people."

THOMAS: Not to mention the deaf.

ANDIE: Yeah but they can't hear it. So then he says, "no, it's cool, my brother and my aunt are retarded. I can make fun of retards all I want!"

THOMAS: Sounds like he comes from a whole line of retarded people!

ANDIE: Right?! He's got like a free pass!

THOMAS: If he were Jewish, he'd have endless material!

ANDIE: He is Jewish!

THOMAS: Well, there you go!

ANDIE: Makes fun of Jewish people all the time!

THOMAS: What a comic genius!

ANDIE: He is funny.

*(Beat)*

Like you can pretty much make fun of anyone you want.

THOMAS: *(Interested in this)* Is that so?

ANDIE: Oh yeah! African Americans? God.

THOMAS: Didn't realize I had such a cultural advantage.

ANDIE: Are you kidding? You can make fun of anyone! Well, except for Native Americans but they're not that funny anyway.

THOMAS: No.

ANDIE: I mean, their names.

THOMAS: Their names are hilarious.

*Andie stops, realizing . . .*

ANDIE: I'm offending you.

THOMAS: Don't worry about it.

ANDIE: No, I'm sorry, I do that sometimes, I think. I say things and people suddenly tell me I've said something I shouldn't have—

THOMAS: No, stop apologizing. Really. You haven't offended me.

ANDIE: Oh. Good.

THOMAS: Can't speak for Jews or retarded Native Americans but . . . actually, I find your honesty refreshing. You know, for a cracker bitch.

*She laughs, shocked.*

THOMAS: It's okay, I can say that. Our cleaning lady was a cracker bitch.

ANDIE: Yeah, well, you can say whatever you want, you're African American!

THOMAS: *(mocking her whiteness)* I certainly am African American!

ANDIE: I don't sound like that!

THOMAS: That is exactly how you sound.

ANDIE: Shut up!

THOMAS: "Oh my god! Shut up!"

ANDIE: *(laughing)* Stop!

> *(Smiles, beat)*

So, why are you back here alone? All broody and disconsolate.

THOMAS: Dictionary.com?

ANDIE: That obvious?

THOMAS: Inimitably.

ANDIE: What's that mean?

THOMAS: Check your inbox.

> *Andie scoots closer.*

ANDIE: So, are you like one of those angry black men?

THOMAS: *(incredulous laughter)* What?! Girl, seriously, you better be careful! Some of the shit you say . . . ?

ANDIE: What?

THOMAS: I'm just saying, some of the things you say . . . you should consider your audience.

ANDIE: You're my audience.

THOMAS: Yeah, well, you don't know me. You can't just say the things you say to a complete stranger. Jewish people and blacks and shit like that—there are consequences. You have to be responsible for the things that come out of your—

> *(change of subject, tone)*

—and what if I am angry? Huh? Does my anger deserve your condescension?

ANDIE: I wasn't condescending you; I was just asking.

THOMAS: No. You said "angry black man". Like my anger only exists in a stereotype. That's condescending. I mean, does it occur to you that I might have something to be angry about?

A reason that has nothing to do with my being black?

ANDIE: You're right. I'm sorry.

*(Beat)*

Someone accused me of being too white today, so do with that what you will.

*Thomas starts laughing.*

ANDIE: Is that funny?

THOMAS: I've known you five minutes, you're whitest chick I ever met.

ANDIE: Thanks. Maybe you guys should hang out.

*(Beat)*

So, what are you angry about?

THOMAS: Maybe that's private.

ANDIE: Well, then what are you doing at a party?

THOMAS: I was expecting to see someone here tonight.

ANDIE: A girl??

THOMAS: No. A guy.

ANDIE: *(assuming he's gay)* Oh.

THOMAS: *(realizing)* No!

ANDIE: No?

THOMAS: No.

ANDIE: Oh.

THOMAS: I mean, a man—*a dude* I've never met. He's supposed to be here tonight. All I got is his name.

ANDIE: What is it? Maybe I know him.

*Before Thomas can say, Davis enters.*

DAVIS: Thomas! There you are! Where have you been?

THOMAS: Oh, I was just . . .

DAVIS: How was the funeral? Your family? Everyone okay?

THOMAS: Uh. Yes. Thanks for the flowers. It was very thoughtful.

ANDIE: I'm sorry, I didn't know—someone in your family die?

THOMAS: Oh, this is . . . I'm sorry, I don't . . .

ANDIE: Andie.

THOMAS: Andie. Andie this is Davis Tallison. The president of Sky. Andie was just telling me how much she loves the 16.

DAVIS: Well, I'm just the suit. It's all Thomas' design.

ANDIE: Your design???

*Thomas smiles.*

DAVIS: He didn't he tell you?

THOMAS: I was hoping to keep it a surprise. Hey, so, what are those Nike guys doing here?

*Davis looks. Then he bluffs.*

DAVIS: What do you think? Taking notes.

*(Changing the subject)*

So, do you work for the company?

*Andie is still flustered, and Thomas loves it.*

ANDIE: Me? No. My fiance writes your commercials.

*Thomas' smile drops.*

THOMAS: Peter Trammel?

ANDIE: You know him? He was supposed to be here tonight but I think he ditched me.

DAVIS: Probably for the best. Thomas wasn't the biggest fan of the 16 spot.

*The two stare at each other though Davis. Awkward beat.*

DAVIS: Okay. Well, I gotta run. Come over when you have a minute?

THOMAS: *(Still staring at Andie)* Sure.

DAVIS: Nice meeting you.

ANDIE: *(still staring at Thomas)* You too.

*Davis exits.*

ANDIE: I don't really think they're ugly, like in a bad way. They're probably very nice with the right pants—God, you just let me talk!

THOMAS: Peter Trammel. That's your fiance?

ANDIE: You know him?

THOMAS: He the one thinks you're too white?

ANDIE: Yeah.

THOMAS: Marrying a black dude?

ANDIE: Peter? Yeah, he wishes he was black!

THOMAS: He's white?! The guy who wrote the 16 ad?

ANDIE: Yeah. Why?

THOMAS: *(chuckles to himself)* How ironical.

ANDIE: Look, you have to let me make it up to you. Let me buy you a drink. Okay? Please.

THOMAS: *(considers)* Sure.

*She turns to the bar but he stops her.*

THOMAS: You kidding? Drinks here are free. Let's get outta here.

ANDIE: *(blushing)* Okay.

*Thomas takes her hand and they exit together.*

THOMAS: *(O.S.)* Oh, hold up a minute—!

*Thomas re-enters to grab his hat. He turns to exit and bumps right into—*

*—Peter who rushes in!*

THOMAS: Shit, sorry man— !

PETER: —oh, God, no! I'm sorry! I'm such an idiot—!

THOMAS: It's cool, man, it's cool.

*Thomas exits as Peter shakes off his guilt and looks around for Andie.*

*Lights out.*

# Scene 12

*Davis' apartment. Late night. There's someone in the shadows, looking around for something, singing to himself. Davis enters holding a baseball bat. He turns on a light to reveal FREDERICK DOUGLASS. White beard, white hair, etc.*

DAVIS: *(startled)* AHH!!

FREDERICK: SHHH! Damn! Wanna wake the whole neighborhood!?

DAVIS: Who are you?! How'd you get in here?!

FREDERICK: You know who I am, shit!

DAVIS: *(beat)* I do?

FREDERICK: You sure as shit better!

DAVIS: *(thinks)* My high school Principal, Lani Bishop??

FREDERICK: Man, I ain't no Lani Bishop! I'm Frederick Douglass!

DAVIS: *(beat) The* Frederick Douglass?

FREDERICK: Bingo mothahfuckah!

DAVIS: I don't understand.

FREDERICK: You're on drug's bitch! I'm just a side effect!

DAVIS: Driscotol.

FREDERICK: Ain't that some shit.

*Awkward pause.*

DAVIS: Right. So. Can I help you?

FREDERICK: You got somethin' to eat up in this mug?

DAVIS: Uh. I have some left over salmon. And risotto.

FREDERICK: I'll take it.

*Davis, bewildered, exits the room.*

DAVIS: *(O.S.)* Well, I'd just like to say, I really respect what you've done for your people. I mean that. Quite an accomplishment.

*He enters with the food and hands it to Frederick who begins eating.*

FREDERICK: Oh yeah? What did you think of my books?

DAVIS: Your books. Yes. Well, I didn't read them all, but . . .

FREDERICK: Which one did you read?

DAVIS: Which one? Uh, I think it was the . . . slavery one.

FREDERICK: Nigga, you didn't read a mothahfuckin' word!

DAVIS: You really developed a potty mouth, didn't you?

FREDERICK: Damn bitch! "Narrative of the Life of Frederick Douglass" is only 75 mothahfuckin' pages! No wonder you got me talking like this!

DAVIS: I'm sorry, how long does this side effect last?

FREDERICK: Shut yo ass up! Now! We got's to change some shit!

DAVIS: The honey glaze is too much, I know.

FREDERICK: Nah, nigga! I mean real shit! You have some power now! It's time to use it. Time to look at the world and say, "shit, you ain't even close!"

DAVIS: Close to what?

FREDERICK: Being a country where people don't use the black man!

DAVIS: I don't use the black man.

FREDERICK: You don't use the black man?!

DAVIS: I don't think I use the black man.

FREDERICK: Mother fucker you use everyone! Damn, there is way too much honey glaze on this motherfucker!

DAVIS: What do you mean I use everyone?

FREDERICK: What do you think I mean, "Allen!?"

DAVIS: *(catching the reference)* My wife? I don't use her.

FREDERICK: Bitch off"ed herself five years ago and you still use that shit like Charmin! Anytime yo ass get dirty, yo wife's suicide come clean you right up.

DAVIS: Jesus, that's really vivid.

FREDERICK: What, you think cuz you had some pain in yo life, gives you a right to be a racist?!

DAVIS: No, I just—

FREDERICK: I'm no math wiz but I don't think one sad little white bitch equals an entire century of oppression, Allen. Do you?

DAVIS: I tried to help her. I did. She just, she wouldn't get better. No matter what I did, she just wouldn't get well!

FREDERICK: *(snaps fingers)* Hey! Focus Allen! These is white people problems!

DAVIS: Black people don't get clinically depressed?

FREDERICK: Hell, no! Now! Tonight at the party! Those Nike guys wasn't there to just suck yo dick and leave now was they?

DAVIS:  No, they wasn't. Weren't. They wanna see the 17. If our numbers are good and they like the new design, they're going to buy us out.

FREDERICK: And after Nike buys this bitch, you'll be selling each shoe with a Josh Grobin Christmas album! But this shit was the plan all along, wasn't it? Water down the black culture 'til it melts into a creamy whiteness!

DAVIS:  I wouldn't say a creamy whiteness . . .

FREDERICK: And you don't use the black man! Shit, I don't even wanna talk about Thomas' cousin. That's some sorry ass shit right there!

DAVIS:  *(realizing)* I used his shit like Charmin, didn't I?

FREDERICK: Damn Skippy.

DAVIS:  My God . . . you're right.

FREDERICK: No shit I'm right! I'm Frederick mothahfuckin' Douglass!

DAVIS:  I'm using the black man!

FREDERICK: Good mo'ning, bitch!

DAVIS:  It's like a whole new brand a slavery!

FREDERICK: Uh-huh.

DAVIS:  Except this time it's American consumerism! MTV! Microwave popcorn. It's Orville fuckin' Redenbacher!!

FREDERICK: You know he lynched some mothahfuckahs in his time!

DAVIS:  Whoever owns the media, owns the country!

FREDERICK: And it ain't no black man writing for yo shoes.

DAVIS:  No! It's this one creamy white son of a bitch!

FREDERICK: Now you got white boys shooting each other for our kicks?!

DAVIS:  That's fucked up!!

FREDERICK: It's an insult! I heard some Jewish kid on the upper west side, nicknamed J-Fresh, shot hisself for his own damn pair!

DAVIS:  Well, to be fair, he was also retarded.

FREDERICK: Mentally handicapped.

DAVIS:  Good call.

FREDERICK: It's one thing to take the blues and turn it into rock and roll. That's respect. But this shit?!

DAVIS:  It's time for a change!!

FREDERICK: A-Men!!

DAVIS:  Damn!

FREDERICK: Shit!

DAVIS:  Bitch!

FREDERICK: Motherfucker!

DAVIS:  How's the risotto?!

FREDERICK: DRY AS SHIT!

DAVIS:  FUCK!!

*Beat.*

FREDERICK: Alright. I gotta run. Read the fuckin' crib notes next time so I don't sound like no white man tryin' to sound like some fuckin' gang-bangin' mothahfuckah. I'ma take this.

*(takes the salmon)*

Peace, my brother.

DAVIS:  Good night, biznitch.

*Lights out.*

# Scene 13

*Peter on his cell phone.*

PETER: *(nervous, leaving a message)* Hello! Dr. Hodge. Emilia. Dr. Emilia. Hodge. This is Peter. I just wanted to call and apologize if I said anything the other day that made you . . . anyway, just confirming I'll be there Thursday! And so. It's confirmed and all set. Officially. Okay. Alright. I'll see you then. Cool.

*He hangs up, embarrassed. Lights out.*

*A bedroom. Andie is bed, reading US Weekly and speaking to someone off stage, like her first scene.*

ANDIE: So, after all that, my therapist puts me under hypnosis and it turns out I was totally wrong about the being-molested-thing. Which, I have to admit, was a little disappointing. I mean, you put that much emotional energy into anything it's exhausting but to not have it pay off . . . ? He did get me to remember that I once walked in on my parents naked in bed discussing an episode of *MASH*.

*Thomas emerges from the bathroom, shirtless. He approaches the bed.*

ANDIE: I'm sorry, I'm talking a lot, I know. I've never done this before and I mean . . . God, you're very attractive, aren't you? Oh. Okay; were doing this again, I see. Well, oh. How nice.

THOMAS: God, you are so white.

*They lie back in bed, as the lights slowly fade out.*


*END OF ACT 1*

# ACT 2

## Scene 14

*Peter sits across from Emilia.*

PETER: "The most monstrous monster is the monster with noble feelings."

*(Beat)*

It's a quote that's been haunting me lately. Faulkner.

EMILIA: Dostoevsky.

PETER: I was close. I knew it was someone I'd never read.

EMILIA: And what does that mean to you?

PETER: You're the therapist.

EMILIA: I didn't read it either, I just know the quote.

*(beat)*

What's bothering you Peter?

PETER: Are you angry with me?

*She sighs, and collects herself.*

EMILIA: I think it's lazy. He wrote it to describe a character or a thing or an action, not for us a hundred years later to apply it to ourselves however we please. Words are not islands. They're connected to sentences, which are connected to stories and ideas. To take words out of the pyramid of meaning, out of context, is ignorant. Irresponsible.

PETER: Like my job! I take a reference from one thing, a movie, a book, a painting, and I steal it to sell a bar of soap. I once stole a line from Sylvia Plath to sell a new contraceptive device! Client said it sounded too optimistic.

EMILIA: And "'Sup Now"?

PETER: I heard it in a rap.

EMILIA: Do you like rap?

PETER: Sure, some. Actually, no. I find it violent and tasteless.

EMILIA: But you used it.

PETER: They say we're selling to kids who listen to it and so I listen. I hear the phrase, "'Sup Now?" Sounds urban. So I steal it and slap it on a sneaker ad.

EMILIA: Out of context.

PETER: Out of the pyramid of meaning, yes. No knowledge of the origin behind hit. In fact, contempt.

EMILIA: And then you take the attitude, the very attitude you find so offensive in rap music and attach it to this shoe.

PETER: Yes! Which is then taken out of context again just before shooting a kid for these very shoes. Is that not monstrous?

EMILIA: *(a calm breath, suppressing)* It's not your fault.

PETER: I can't work. I'm paralyzed by that stupid commercial I wrote. And they play it over and over!

EMILIA: You should be proud. I understand sales have doubled.

PETER: Yeah, and now you have rich, white kids shooting each other over them! I mean, doesn't that offend you?

EMILIA: *(sincerely confused)* Why would that offend me?

PETER: Because these are kids who can afford the shoes, ignorantly imitating the struggle African Americans actually experience!

EMILIA: Not all African American experience that, Peter.

PETER: No, but they're making a mockery of your plight.

EMILIA: My plight?

PETER: Yes! These are idiots! Oblivious to what they're imitating and why! Which is exactly what I was doing when I wrote that commercial!

EMILIA: Peter—

PETER: I don't know shit about the Congo!

EMILIA: I'm sorry?

PETER: I think you should know that.

EMILIA: Are you talking about Africa?

PETER: Africa, Syria, here; I don't know shit! This is my point—everything blends!

EMILIA: What do you mean? What blends?

PETER: The issues! The words! Everything I say is wrong. Everything that comes out of my mouth is offensive because what do I know of struggle? Nothing! I am untouched! Unscathed!

EMILIA: Peter, I think maybe we should—

PETER: I look at you, the last month I've been in here and I think, "what you must think of me?"

EMILIA: Why me?

PETER: I spend a maximum effort avoiding the banalities of my life! To not tell you what I do in a day, what my fiancée talks about, what we eat!

EMILIA: Why would I care what you—?

PETER: What we listen to! The time we spend discussing, God knows what! I even lied to you just now. 'Sup Now? I never heard it in a rap. It just sounds like something a black person would say! My ignorance, ultimately, do you see, is monstrous!

*(then quickly)*

Would you go to dinner with me?

*(Regretting)*

I'm sorry, that was—would you?

EMILIA: I think our time is up.

PETER: Right. Of course. I'm sorry. I'm. God. What you must think.

*He exits. She sighs, relieved. Suddenly, a voice in the darkness.*

VOICE IN THE DARKNESS: That was rude. Throwing out a paying Caucasian like that.

*A light reveals ABE LINCOLN sitting in the corner. Hat, beard and all.*

EMILIA: Oh, no, not you again…

ABE: You don't look too good, Doc. Something I can do?

EMILIA: Please leave me alone!

ABE: *(ignoring)*Hey! Did I mention that I freed the slaves? Yep, totally freed 'em! You know, lots a people did big things, invented coffee makers or signed some shitty bill. But I'll tell you what feels really good. Telling people you FREED THE SLAVES! Man. And they called Bill Clinton the first black president.

*She finds her bottle of Driscotol.*

ABE: Not sure how appropriate this is but you've got a whole Condoleezza thing going on and it is smokin'!

EMILIA: Please go away!

ABE: Michelle Obama?

EMILIA: Why do you do this to me!

ABE: You tell me, you're the one taking a race pill.

EMILIA: I take it so I don't have to think about race!

ABE: Oh, c'mon, Doc! It's okay to express a little pent up rage! You're an oppressed people! Peoples! Is it people or peoples? I never know. It's like monies. When is it appropriate to use the plural there?

*He sees that she's ignoring him and pretends to feel feint.*

ABE: Whoa . . .

EMILIA: What's wrong?

ABE: My head. I don't know. I'm burning up.

*She feels his head.*

EMILIA: You don't seem hot.

ABE: You sure? Because it feels a little like . . . jungle fever!

*He stuffs his face in her breasts and she pushes him off. He chuckles, devilishly, as she collects herself.*

EMILIA: I am a therapist!

ABE: You're a black therapist. Totally different.

EMILIA: What does it matter that I'm black! Things were fine before he showed up! I like my life! I like my job! Why doesn't this godforsaken pill work with him—!!

ABE: Okay, okay! Calm down. We're gonna get through this. Together. Breathe in. Breathe out. Breath out. Breath through, breathe in, breath in and out through and around and good. Now . . . what's that *adorable* little mantra you have?

EMILIA: "They're not white people. They're people with problems."

ABE: And problems have no color.

EMILIA: The strong help the weak!

ABE: And you are?!

EMILIA: The strong!

ABE: Good! Now . . . what's the deal with black people and wine bars?

EMILIA: Excuse me?

ABE: I never see them there! I mean, do they not drink wine? Or just object to the idea of a bar that doesn't serve liquor? Because I can actually can get on board with that.

EMILIA: I go to wine bars.

ABE: No, I mean like real black people.

*She collects herself. And then, strong:*

EMILIA: I want you out of my office. And if you want to see me again, I suggest you make an appointment.

ABE: Fine! Sue me for trying to free one more black person!

*Lights out.*

## Scene 15

*A subway car. Peter sits, staring out. The two Black Kids from before enter but this time speak much differently.*

KID 1: No, no, no, that movie was brilliant!

KID 2: You liked it? Really? That guy at the end? It made no sense!

KID 1: You're not taking into account the character's moral ambiguity.

KID 2: Oh, here we go again!

KID 1: Look, if he is an atheist, like he says, then what makes him feel like he's doing anything wrong? What is immoral to a man who has no moral system. No God?

KID 2: That is so trite. Please. Moral standards are not defined by God, they're defined by man.

KID 1: Who in the absence of a God has no reason to act moral.

KID 2: Kindness. For his fellow man. How about that?

PETER: Excuse me . . .

KID 1: You just contradicted yourself!

PETER: Excuse me?

KID 2: No, I didn't. I am saying if there is no God, then there are still rules, of the human condition.

PETER: Excuse me?! I was overhearing your conversation. And, well, I find it very interesting.

KID 2: *(confused beat)* Okay?

PETER: Look, this is kind of strange but I see you're wearing Sky shoes. I actually work for their advertising company. If you take this card here to any Footlocker retailer they'll redeem it for one free pair.

*He hands it to Kid 1.*

KID 2: You're giving us free shoes? Because you like what we said?

KID 1: Hey, don't question it. It's a very kind gesture.

KID 2: You're right. That's very kind of you. While you're at it, would you mind removing your watch and wallet, please?

PETER: Excuse me?

*Kid 2 pulls out a gun.*

KID 2: How about pretty please, sir.

KID 1: See?! This is what I'm talking about!

KID 2: No, no, you can't use this as an example!

KID 1: This is a perfect example! You steal and don't feel wrong about it.

PETER: I'm sorry, are you serious?

KID 1: I'm afraid he is.

PETER: You're robbing me?

KID 1: This is so embarrassing.

KID 2: Will you please hurry up! My stop is coming.

PETER: Of course! Uh. Here. Just don't shoot.

KID 2: Shoot?! Listen to this. Just because I'm black he thinks I would shoot him!

PETER: No! Of course not! I was just, you know, with the gun and everything . . .

KID 2: Oh, I see how it is! A black man can't brandish a gun at someone in this country without people thinking he's a cold blooded killer!

PETER: No! You're right!

KID 1: He is?

KID 2: I am??

PETER: Yes! An African American man should be able to, you know, bear arms at someone and not be stereotyped.

KID 2: Right. Exactly. See? Thank you.

KID 1: Well, that's a first.

KID 2: Alright. Well, thanks for the card and watch and everything.

PETER: You're welcome. Just let me know if you need anything else.

KID 2: We will.

*The Kids exit. Peter's smile drops as he crumbles onto the seat.*

*Lights out.*

## Scene 16

*Thomas' bedroom. Andie strokes his hair, as he lies in her lap. Thomas seems relaxed for the first time.*

ANDIE: Have you ever thought about wearing eyeliner?

THOMAS: What?!

ANDIE: It's not gay if that's what you're thinking.

THOMAS: It's not straight either!

ANDIE: A lot of celebrities are doing it now. I was reading this article the other day that said Jude Law and Leonardo Dicaprio wear eye liner and they're not gay.

THOMAS: They're gay enough.

ANDIE: C'mon, it'll be fun. Let's try it!

THOMAS: No way!

ANDIE: C'mon!! Don't be whiny.

> *She grabs her purse from the ground and straddles him. She starts to apply it.*

THOMAS: *(half laughing)* Girl, don't you put that shit on me . . .

ANDIE: Now DON'T move . . .

THOMAS: Whoa—careful!

ANDIE: *(laughing)* I haven't even touched you yet! Don't be a baby!

THOMAS: I'm worried about being a blind baby!

> *She starts applying again.*

THOMAS: A blind . . . gay baby.

> *They both giggle. They kiss. And she continues to apply the eyeliner.*

ANDIE: I was watching this shampoo commercial the other day. It had this woman taking a shower and having an orgasm while putting it in her hair. Have you seen this? It was so stupid. Of course, then I bought it. I mean, I know I'm not gonna have an orgasm, right? I don't care how deep cleansing it is, or where it cleanses deeply, but I bought it on the off chance because, I don't know, what's the difference, really, between any of them, and I might as well get the one that says it'll make me cum.

> *Thomas turns cold.*

THOMAS: Alright, stop.

ANDIE: I'm almost done with this first one—

THOMAS: C'mon—cut that shit out!!

*He pushes her off, and gets out of bed.*

ANDIE: Uh. What's going on?

THOMAS: Do you talk to him the same way you talk to me?

ANDIE: Who—?

THOMAS: Peter! You tell him the same things? Your therapist, your magazines, that one show with that one guy, and then come here and rehash the whole thing?

ANDIE: He doesn't really listen anymore. Everything has to be so "heavy". But when I talk to you it's . . . easy. You know?

THOMAS: *(bothered by this)*No! No, I don't. You know what . . . ?

*He begins putting his clothes on.*

ANDIE: Where are you going?

THOMAS: You know, you talk and you talk and you have no regard for what you're saying! None! No respect for your audience!

ANDIE: You're my audience.

THOMAS: Exactly! This is what I'm saying! You, you, you talk about celebrities and napkin rings like we're two regular people! We're not two regular people! I mean, shit, what makes you think I give a flying fuck about that shit! What makes you think I don't have more important things . . . things I think about. Heavy. Profound shit!

ANDIE: *(beat)*Is this a black thing?

THOMAS: Okay. See? This. No.

ANDIE: What?

THOMAS: You! Trying to suck all my power from me.

ANDIE: What power? How?!

THOMAS: By talking! By saying the things you say. Looking at me like that. Like I'm just a normal guy. By not acknowledging this!

ANDIE: What?!

THOMAS: *This!*

ANDIE: You're not making sense. What are you missing?

THOMAS: The guilt! Okay? The fucking white guilt!! Where is it??

ANDIE: Jesus, not you too!

THOMAS: You have no idea, do you? You think you can just walk around saying whatever you want, and there will be no repercussions.

ANDIE: What am I saying that is so illegal?!

THOMAS: Why are you here? Huh? With me. Why!?

ANDIE: I like you.

THOMAS: Bullshit! I'm black! Plain and simple!

ANDIE: Well, that too.

THOMAS: What?

ANDIE: What?

THOMAS: You're here because I'm black?

ANDIE: In the beginning, sure, that was part of it.

THOMAS: *What?!*

ANDIE: *What!?* You just said that's what it was!

THOMAS: But you're not supposed to admit it!! You're supposed to get all defensive and be like, "uh, no, no, I'm color blind, I had a black friend once!" Shit like that!

ANDIE: But it's true! In the beginning. Peter was being so self righteous, acting like the man of the people, calling me white and . . . then I saw you, and you were, of course, black . . .

THOMAS: And . . . ?

ANDIE: And then we started talking.

THOMAS: And that's it.

ANDIE: Pretty much. I actually don't have any black friends. Except Tshombe. But he's like *really* black, like from Zambia, so it doesn't really count.

THOMAS: There! Right there! You can't just say that!

ANDIE: Sorry! You're right! African American.

*He begins breathing heavily.*

ANDIE: Well, then explain it to me! I want to understand! I mean, if there's something I need to learn, something I'm missing, some secret code then . . . Thomas? Are you okay?

THOMAS: I can't. This thing. I've done what I came to do.

ANDIE: What is that supposed to mean . . .

THOMAS: I means it's over!

ANDIE: Thomas . . . Thomas? Tell me what you want?

THOMAS: Stop saying that! Stop acting so innocent!!

ANDIE: I don't get it. One second you like how honest I am, the next you want me to feel bad because you're an oppressed peoples!

THOMAS: Peoples?!

ANDIE: Look, I'm the one taking the risks here! Have you considered that? I'm engaged! For the last month I've been creating different reasons for working late, inventing errands on the weekends. You want me to feel guilty for something—try that! That's my guilt. That I fell for you. And until a minute ago, I thought you were falling for me! And you wanna hear something else I'm probably not supposed to say?! Ready for this!?—Your blackness?? Not that interesting!!

*Thomas looks totally confused.*

THOMAS: What?

ANDIE: That's right! I could take it or leave it! How you like that? In fact, if you were white, I'd still have sex with you!

THOMAS: You're crazy.

ANDIE: How is that for "stealing your power?" You could be Irish and I'd "tap that shit!" Polish! German! White Russian!

THOMAS: Alright . . .

ANDIE: Canadian!

THOMAS: You lie!

ANDIE: Yep! A white-ass, Canadian, Mounty mother fucker, and I'd ride that Canuck shit all night long, EHH?!!

THOMAS: *(Covering his ears)* Stop it!

ANDIE: Deal with it, Thomas! You're "blackness," while it might have turned my head, is now nothing more than a minor detail in all of "this!"

THOMAS: You're a crazy white lady.

ANDIE: I think I love you.

THOMAS: *(Beat)* You're engaged.

ANDIE: I don't have to be.

*He looks at her, breathing harder now.*

THOMAS: No, that's . . . not what this was.

ANDIE: What was it?

THOMAS: Revenge.

ANDIE: For what?!

THOMAS: Charley Cross!

ANDIE: Who the hell is Charley Cross?

THOMAS: I DON'T KNOW!

*(beat, chuckles sadly)*

I don't know.

*(Beat)*

But when he looked at me like that, in his office . . . "my people, your people," talking about his death like it was another commercial . . . winking at me like I was just black enough to lend him the credibility and just white enough to let it all slide. I had to let him know. I had to make him feel something. And guilt is the only power I have.

*He begins to hyperventilate. Andie goes to him.*

ANDIE: Shh. Come here . . .

THOMAS: . . . it's like a . . . weight . . . on my chest . . .

ANDIE: Shh. Take a deep breath. That's it. Let it out. You're breathing too fast. In . . . out. That's it. Just keep breathing. In. Good. Out.

*(beat)*

Tell me what I need to do, Thomas. You want me to watch what I say? I will. I'll filter everything. You want me to acknowledge this? Okay. Guilt? I can do that. Just don't leave yet. Don't go and tell me what you want.

*Thomas turns to her, perhaps considering the offer…but then exits.*

ANDIE: Thomas! Thomas, wait! Don't go!

*Lights out.*

# Scene 17

*Davis' office. It's late, dark. Thomas sneaks in wearing a black hoodie; a bag over his shoulder. He quietly looks around the room for something when . . .*

DAVIS: They fired me, Thomas.

THOMAS: *(startled)* Shit!

DAVIS: Course you already knew that, didn't you?

THOMAS: Tallison?

*Davis is sitting in the dark, drinking.*

DAVIS: Little advice: this day and age, a black man sneaking around at night like that could be misconstrued. I'm just saying.

THOMAS: What are you doing here—?

DAVIS: I did everything they asked. Tried to be more sensitive, say the right things—you can ask Frederick Douglas! He says I'm using the black man. Fine. So, I killed the 16 ad.

THOMAS: You killed it?

DAVIS: And they killed me. So, congratulations, Thomas. You win.

THOMAS:  didn't have anything to do with—

DAVIS: *(explodes)* BULLSHIT! This is all you. So...'Sup Now, Nigga?!

*(off his look.)*

Oh. What? You don't like me using that word? Did I steal from you? Rob you of the one thing you have that's yours? A word? Yeah, well, Sky Shoes used to be yours too, didn't it? "A black shoe for black people." Guess we stole that too. Welcome to America! Welcome to creamy whiteness!

*Thomas turns to leave.*

DAVIS: I'M NOT FINISHED!

*Thomas looks at him, almost pitiably.*

THOMAS: Yeah. I think you are.

*He turns to leave again but—*

DAVIS: Came for these, didn't you!?

*Davis holds up the Sky Max 17 prototype.*

THOMAS: Give 'em to me.

*Greg Kalleres*

DAVIS: Where do you think they'll put the Swoosh? Hm? Over here?

THOMAS: They're mine.

DAVIS: Yours? Didn't you hear what I just said?

THOMAS: Give 'em to—

DAVIS: No, this is good; let's think about this! What is yours? What does the black man, Thomas Hodge, have when all the dust has settled? Hm? Your history? Your so-called culture? Nope! Bought and sold years ago—just like ours. Watered down. Processed and paid for. Hell, your identity has been whittled down to nothing more than a, a, movie, a rap song—a fucking commercial about a basketball shoe! You want some truth? You are a cliché, Thomas! Borrowed from clichés that we created! So, reach for the sky, bitches!

*Thomas turns from him.*

But, hey, no; you have your pain, right? Your daily struggles? A black man in a hard white world? Bullshit! No one owns their pain! The second you use it for currency, it's lost forever. Trust me. So don't rely on your pain for your power. That guilt "your people" love to push on us is nothing more than an advertisement for a product you don't own anymore. Nothing is yours! Your cousin...? Far as I'm concerned, he's the only real thing in this world.

*Beat.*

THOMAS: He wasn't my cousin.

DAVIS: What's that?

THOMAS: Charley Cross. The kid who was shot? Never met him before in my life.

DAVIS: *(beat)* Are you fucking with me?

THOMAS: Nope.

*Davis slumps. Thomas takes the shoes from him and exits.*

DAVIS: *(existential)* Ain't that some shit.

*Davis stares out, lost.*

*Lights out.*

## SCENE 18

*Emilia's office, late. She sits with a bottle of Driscotol.*
*There is a frantic KNOCKING at the door, and she pockets*
*the pills.*

EMILIA: Who is it?

PETER: *(O.S.)* It's Peter! I need to talk to you!

EMILIA: It's late, Peter!

PETER: *(O.S.)* I was mugged!

*She opens the door. Peter enters disheveled, possibly*
*drunk.*

EMILIA: Are you okay?

PETER: Yeah, I'm fine. How are you?

EMILIA: Are you drunk?

PETER: Why won't you go out with me?

EMILIA: Excuse me?

PETER: I've been perfectly nice to you, haven't I? Shown you
every courtesy?

EMILIA: Peter . . .

PETER: And I'm trying to learn! Surely, you can see the effort
I've made to show you that I'm willing to be taught!

*He approaches. She retreats.*

EMILIA: Okay. I'd like you to leave now.

PETER: I don't deserve your condescension, do I?! I mean, it's
me! Peter! I'm one of the good ones, remember?! Look,
if it's about my fiancée you don't have to worry. It's over
between us. She totally doesn't get me.

EMILIA: Peter, you're not thinking straight. You don't mean
what you're saying.

PETER: Which part? That I'm in love with you or that you're
condescending?

EMILIA: You're not in love with me! You feel bad about what
happened to that boy; it made you examine some things
in your life: your fiancée, perhaps, your job; now you're
sublimating.

PETER: Do you prefer the term black or African American?

EMILIA: What?

PETER: I never know what's more PC. You say one, it could be
viewed as insensitive, the other, a little contrived, right?

EMILIA: Peter, please leave before I stop accepting your insurance!

PETER: C'mon! One date! I promise, I'm very charming when I'm not in therapy.

EMILIA: I don't want to call the cops!

PETER: The *cops?!* I'm asking you out, I'm not gonna hurt you! I just —

*He reaches and she slaps him away.*

PETER: Ah! What?! What is wrong with me!??!?

*Emilia is frightened.*

PETER: What more do I have to do?! Huh!? I feel for your people! Okay? The struggle? The, the plight?! I have professed my sins! Every week I come to you, contrite! And out there, all the time, in different ways! I am sorry! Okay?! I AM SORRY FOR MY PEOPLE! They suck! Whatever they did, whenever they did it, I renounce them! THEY ARE RENOUNCED! Jesus! I'm tired of paying for shit I didn't do! Slavery! Oppression! 40 acres and the Jim Croce Laws! I didn't bring you people over here!!

*(beat)*

So, I see these black kids on the subway. They look a little sketchy and I think, "hey, maybe I should go to the other side of the train"— but no! Because then I say to myself, "who are you to judge?! They're probably very smart educated kids! Who am I to assume that just because they're African American, they don't read Sartre?!" But guess what?! They pulled a fucking gun on me anyway! It didn't matter what I thought! So fuck them! And fuck *guilt*!! I'm tired of it!! Watching my tongue, policing every syllable that comes out of my mouth! So, do me a favor, will you? Tell every black person or African American that you know that it wasn't me! Can you do that? Vouch for me?! Huh? IT! WASN'T! ME!

*He has her backed against the wall, shaking. He then steps back, takes a deep breath.*

PETER: Whoa. That felt really good. Was that a breakthrough? Is that what they call it or whatever? I'm sorry if I scared you—did I? Jesus, that was amazing! Well, I guess I should probably go. Thank you.

*Peter turns to the door.*

EMILIA: And Charley Cross? Are you sorry for him too?

PETER: Who?

EMILIA: That's funny. I thought that was the entire reason you were in therapy. A 14 year old African American boy shot in the face because of a commercial.

> *(beat)*

> Imagine me listening to a man apologize over and over without the first clue as to what he's sorry for. He thinks it's because he's white. Well. Isn't that a shame. Even his contrition is out of context. His shame, ignorant and ir-responsible.

> *(beat)*

> This was never therapy. It was a confession. To the only black person you know. And you thought if we went out, if you charmed me and we connected as people it would somehow magically pardon you of all wrong doing. An instant hall pass that would walk you past every negro you meet with a fist bump.

*She approaches him. He retreats.*

EMILIA: I come in here every day and listen to the problems of white folks. Crackers with cracker problems and cracker guilt!

PETER: Did you just say cracker?

EMILIA: I tell myself to be objective. Listen to the issues. Be understanding. "They're not white people," I say, "they're people with problems." But after a while it doesn't take. No matter how many pills I swallow, it doesn't suppress. But this is my job. To tolerate it. To pretend, like you, that I un-derstand. That I don't seethe with my own disgust. My own shame. But the problem, Peter, is that I do understand. Your fortunate problems? I get it. I too am unscathed. Untouched. Like you. So, I donate to the NAACP and I volunteer to the United Negro College Fund. And I do it all to absolve myself. Ignorantly. Out of context. Just. Like. You. So, you see, you came to the wrong nigger for exoneration. You feel ashamed for your whiteness? So do I, Peter. So do I.

*Now she has him against the wall.*

*Greg Kalleres*

PETER: So, I should kind of go.

EMILIA: Not until you get what you came for.

PETER: What was that?

EMILIA: Absolution.

PETER: Really? I feel like we made a lot of progress today.

EMILIA: A few minutes ago, you were gonna leave your fiancee for me.

PETER: I was subjagating—

EMILIA: Sublimating.

PETER: Sublimating. And I think I thought about it, what you said, and it makes sense, so, thank you.

EMILIA: Am I not black enough for you anymore?

PETER: No! You're totally black enough!

*She forces Peter into the chair and straddles him.*

EMILIA: Put your hand on my breast.

PETER: Am I being charged for this?

EMILIA: What, you're no longer attracted to the chocolate?

PETER: Yes! Sure! I like the chocolate! I'm just—I'm engaged!

EMILIA: Peter! I am offering you forgiveness killing my cousin!

PETER: Your cousin!?

EMILIA: Now put your hand on my breast!

*He puts his hands on her breast.*

EMILIA: Call me a nigger.

PETER: I can't say the N-word!

EMILIA: Kiss me!

PETER: No!! And it's not the chocolate thing, I promise!

EMILIA: Barging in here, filled with all that righteous indignation! How I'd rejected you! And now you don't want me?

PETER: Look, if things were different—

EMILIA: I don't want you, Peter. Anymore than you want me. I do, however, want to help you.

*She pulls out her bottle of Driscotol.*

EMILIA: Now . . . open your mouth.

PETER: I just wrote a commercial.

EMILIA: And I'm offering you forgiveness.

PETER: It was just a commercial.

EMILIA: Open. Your fucking. Mouth.

*He opens his mouth and she puts a pill on his tongue, like communion.*

EMILIA: Good boy.

*She takes one herself.*

PETER: What will it do?

EMILIA: Cure us.

PETER: Of what?

EMILIA: Hatred. Anger. Righteous indignation.

*She pops another in his mouth.*

PETER: I'm not a racist.

EMILIA: Sure you are; we all are.

PETER: Who says?

EMILIA: Everyone. The TV, the radio, Abraham Lincoln. It's the rhetoric of our times.

PETER: And this will fix me?

EMILIA: You tell me. Do you want to be absolved?

PETER: *(pause)* Yes.

EMILIA: Then open. Really. Wide.

*He opens his mouth and she dumps the bottle down his throat.*

*Lights out.*

# SCENE 19

*A subway car. Thomas sits, holding the bag with the Sky Max 17s. The two Black Kids walk into the car.*

KID 1: You gotta be kidding me with that shit. That movie was incredible!

KID 2: Nah, man, that ending was bullshit.

KID 1: It was real!

KID 2: You telling me that kid couldn't get away if he wanted? He was running like that retarded nigga from across the street.

KID 1: He's not retarded, he's got Turret's Syndrome.

KID 2: I don't care what he's got, nigga runs like a retard.

KID 1: Whoa, whoa. We got company.

*They approach Thomas.*

KID 1: Hey brother, you looking for something?

THOMAS: Me? No. Thanks.

KID 1: You sure? We got some good shit.

THOMAS: I don't do crack.

KID 2: Crack?! Do we look like crack dealers to you?!

THOMAS: No! You're right. My bad.

KID 1: *(proud)* We sell top of the line pharmaceuticals!

KID 2: Under the counter, over the counter and through the woods.

KID 1: And from what I can tell, you could use a little something.

THOMAS: Why do you say that?

KID 1: Two in the morning, sneaking out of the Sky Shoes office . . .

KID 2: Is-sues.

THOMAS: How did you know I was—what issues?

KID 2: Panic attacks?

THOMAS: Huh?

KID 1: You get em? Accelerated heart rate, sweating, trembling . . .

KID 2: Shortness of breath, nausea . . .

KID 1: Abdominal stress? You know!

THOMAS: Uh, yeah, sometimes.

KID 2: Do you ever experience feelings of intense fear in response to ordinary situations?

KID 1: What about the sensation that you're trapped, the world is coming to an end, doom, gloom . . .

KID 2: Helplessness, hopelessness, loss . . .

THOMAS: Not really.

KID 1: Feelings of extreme nervousness in social settings . . .

KID 2: Loneliness, night sweats, nightmares . . .

KID 1: Restless leg syndrome?

KID 2: Restless arms?

KID 1: General restlessness?

THOMAS: Uh . . .

KID 2: What about periods of weightlessness?

KID 1: Heaviness?

KID 2: Bloating?

KID 1: Whatever the opposite of bloating is?

THOMAS: No.

KID 1: Have you ever felt as though a particular pain hurt more than it was supposed to?

KID 2: Or less?

KID 1: Or, strangely, exactly as it should?

THOMAS: I sometimes hyperventilate.

KID 1: Impossible.

THOMAS: Why?

KID 1 AND 2: Black people don't hyperventilate.

KID 1: Stick out your tongue.

*He does.*

KID 1: Uh-huh.

THOMAS: What is it?

KID 2: How's your erection?

THOMAS: Right now?

KID 1: Do you have one right now?

THOMAS: No!

KID 2: Then when you have one.

THOMAS: It's fine, I guess.

KID 1: Nigga, you wearin' eye liner?!?

*Thomas looks embarrassed.*

KID 2: What about feelings of conflict?

THOMAS: Sure.

KID 2: Am I black, am I white . . . ?

THOMAS: Yes!

---

KID 1: Hate?

THOMAS: Yes!

KID 1: Uh-huh. Who? Mother, father?

KID 2: Sister?

KID 1: Childhood friends . . . ?

KID 2: The ones you abandoned 15 years ago.

KID 1: Your white girlfriend . . . .?

KID 2: The one you abandoned 3 hours ago.

KID 1: Guy who wrote a commercial that killed your cousin.

KID 2: Who wasn't your cousin.

THOMAS: Yes.

KID 2: The kid who started all this shit.

KID 1: The one you never even knew.

KID 2: But you made a flag from his corpse and sold a shoe!

THOMAS: Okay—yes! All of it! I hate them all!

KID 2: But you're tired of the hate!

THOMAS: Yes.

KID 1: Tired of being tired of the hate!!

THOMAS: My God, yes!

KID 2: Well, you happen to be in luck, brother. Cuz we got some premium shit, fix you right up.

KID 1: Make you forget you was ever black.

KID 2: Make you forget you was ever white.

THOMAS: What is it?!

KID 2: Brand new. Just hit the market.

*He pulls out the bottle of Driscotol.*

KID 1: Driscotol!

KID 2: Or as we call it on the street, "Bleach."

THOMAS: Is it safe?

KID 2: Perfectly safe.

THOMAS: Is it addictive?

KID 1: How addictive is bliss, motherfucker?

KID 2: Just one pill a day and you'll be able to work without that sting in your side!

KID 1: Am I white, am I black, shit—am I a man?!

KID 2: And best of all, you can tap that white bitch up in yo crib, conflict free!

KID 1: Guilt free.

KID 2: Revenge free.

KID 1: But you should definitely take it with food.

KID 2: What we're offering you is life without weight.

KID 1: Words without meaning.

KID 2: Text without subtext!

KID 1: Faith without the burden of God!! And all we ask in return . . . is that bag you holding.

THOMAS: This? You don't even know what's in here.

KID 2: Prototype for the Sky Max 17s.

KID 1: I'm thinkin' that's definitely somethin' I could put on Ebay.

KID 2: C'mon man, what do you need it for? Prove your black? Sky ain't even a black brand no more.

THOMAS: This shoe is.

KID 1: Oh yeah? And you don't want them to have it.

KID 2: Like Noah takin' his shit on the Arc before the big wave!

KID 1: That it? You think you're saving us?

THOMAS: No . . .

KID 1: I mean, shit, you ain't Dr. King cuz you made a basketball shoe for black folks.

THOMAS: It's something. It's pure.

KID 2: Like the Sky Max 16 was pure?

KID 1: Sky Max 15?

KID 2: 14? 13? 12?

KID 1: Nigga, ain't nothing pure in this world got a logo on it!

KID 2: You don't own the 17 any more than I do.

KID 1: You think working at a black shoe company made you one of us?

KID 2: You were never one of us and you never will be.

KID 1: But once you take this, you wont give a fuck who you are!

KID 2: And if you buy now…we'll even throw in some crack.

*Thomas looks at the bottle . . . and slowly reaches for it.*

THOMAS: *(quiet)* I think . . .

KID 2: What's that?

THOMAS: I think . . .

KID 1: You think what motherfucker?

THOMAS: I think, maybe, I think . . . . . . .thank you but I think I'm okay.

*Pause.*

KID 2: C'mon man, this was a waste a damn time!
KID 1: Yeah. Shit. See you 'round. Racist motherfucker!
*The Kids exit.*

> *A lightness comes over Thomas for the first time. He takes off his shoes . . . and replaces them with the Sky Max 17s.*

> *Lights out.*

## Scene 20

*Thomas' apartment. Andie sits on the bed staring at Thomas who stands in the doorway wearing his new shoes.*

THOMAS: Hey.

ANDIE: You came back.

THOMAS: You're still here.

ANDIE: I got worried.

THOMAS: It's funny. Ever since I left all I could think of . . . was that commercial. You know, the one where the woman's shampoo gave her an orgasm? And I thought, my God. An actress actually had to act that out. In front of people. And not smart people, but advertising people. Marketing people. Executives discussing her performance behind the camera. Offering suggestions to the director for a more realistic performance. "More moaning, I think we need more moaning here, I don't believe our product is making her cum enough!" And it was nice. To think about something you had said. This stupid commercial, which has nothing to do with anything. So . . . weightless. Subtextless. And I thought, this is Andie. This is what I feel when I'm with Andie.

ANDIE: That's good, right?

THOMAS: I want you only to talk to me.

ANDIE: You mean . . . ?

THOMAS: Dinner parties, US Weekly, who's dating who on what series, which Starbucks is better, and what your therapist thinks of your latest dream. All of it. Spare me nothing about your day. The whiteness of your week. Your irresponsible honesty. I want you to talk, I was wrong before, say the things you say; filter nothing. I just want you to say them only to me.

ANDIE: Okay.

THOMAS: *(smiling)* Okay?

ANDIE: Only you.

*She buries her head in his chest. He strokes her hair. The only two people left in the world.*

*Lights out.*

# Scene 21

*Straight from previous scene, new age music plays. A spot on Dr. Driscoll, as he addresses the audience, like a commercial.*

DR. DRISCOLL: Hi. I'm Dr. Leonard Driscoll. Do you suffer from racism and bigotry and just hate it? Do you ever have thoughts that make you say to yourself, "Whoa. That was really racist. Glad I didn't say it out loud." Of course you do. And we have the answer: Dristcol. Just one tiny caplet a day and all your hatred, deep seeded or on the surface, will fade away. Driscotol has become the top selling pharmaceutical in the country. After Viagra. And is helping people all over the world. But hey, don't take it from me.

*Spot on Davis talking to the audience.*

DAVIS: My name is Davis Tallison, recovering racist and former exploiter of the black race. Since taking Driscotol I'm not only more sensitive, I'm more employable. And now I'm not just a satisfied client . . . I'm Driscotol's new Marketing Director.

*Spot on Emilia.*

EMILIA: I'm Dr. Emilia Hodge. I am a psychiatrist. With Driscotol, I am now able to be objective in my sessions and treat people, not white or black, Latino, Asian, South Asian, Middle Eastern, Native American, East Indian, European, or "other" . . . .but simply people with problems. Which is why I prescribe Driscotol to all my patients.

DR. DRISCOLL: So, remember, if you're feeling like you *might* be, and chances are you're right, and even if you think you're *not,* because that kind of means you *are*—consider Driscotol. Isn't that right, Peter?

*Spot on Peter. He tries to talk but the words barely come out. Like he's about to say something but then changes his mind. Comes up with the right way to say it and retreats.*

PETER: I . . . . We. I mean! What I mean is . . . actually . . . let me rephrase that.
The thing I wanna . . . without meaning to offend or upset . . .

What I mean to say . . . and I don't want to speak for every-
one here . . . .or anyone or upset . . . .someone!
My thought is . . .
And really, what is that? My thoughts?
The words . . . my uh . . . my words?? . . . My . . . . . .

*(smiling, happy)*

Driscotol.
DR. DRISCOLL: Driscotol. For the racist inside of you.
ALL ACTORS: Inside of all of us!

*Lights out.*

*End of play.*

# THE NORWEGIANS

*A play about gangsters.*
*Really, really nice ones.*

*C. Denby Swanson*

THE NORWEGIANS was originally produced by
The Drilling Company in New York, NY
from March 7 to April 14, 2013.

Creative Director: Elowyn Castle
Choreographer: Megan Sipe
Scenic Design: Jennifer Verbalow
Costume Design: Mimi Maxmen
Lighting Design: Tyler Learned
Sound Design: Nicholas Simone

Cast
Olive: Veronica Cruz
Gus: Dan Teachout
Betty: Karla Hendrick
Tor: Hamilton Clancy

**C. Denby Swanson** graduated from Smith College, the National Theatre Institute, and the University of Texas Michener Center for Writers, where she was a fellow in playwriting and screenwriting. She has been a Jerome Fellow, a William Inge Playwright in Residence, and a McKnight Advancement Grant recipient. Her work has been commissioned by the Guthrie Theater, 15 Head a Theatre Lab, Macalester College, and The Drilling Company, and featured in the Southern Playwrights Festival, the Women Playwrights Project, the Lark Theater's Playwrights Week, PlayLabs, the WPA Festival at Salvage Vanguard, JAW: A Playwrights Festival at Portland Center Stage, and multiple residencies at New York Stage & Film. Her full length adaptation, *Atomic Farmgirl*, was developed by the Drilling Company, at the Culture Project's Impact Festival and at the Icicle Creek Theatre Festival, and won a prize in the 2009 Earth Matters on Stage Festival at the University of Oregon. She won a 2008 Susan Smith Blackburn Special Prize for her short play *The Potato Feast*, which was also nominated for a 2008 New York Innovative Theater Award. Her blues play *Blue Monday* was developed at ZACH Theatre Center as part of the NEA/TCG National Theater Residency Program for Playwrights. She is a former Artistic Director of Austin Script Works and on the faculty at Southwestern University. Her work is published by Smith & Kraus, Heinemann, and Playscripts, Inc.

CHARACTERS
GUS and TOR, the Norwegians
OLIVE and BETTY, good friends. Sort of.

# Act I

1.

*(A room. A table. It is today. There is a red checkered table cloth. Single dingy light bulb dangles overhead. TOR pulls the string and turns it on, revealing: OLIVE. Nervous. Sitting in the chair. TOR and GUS stand behind her. This does not make her less nervous.)*

TOR: So.
OLIVE: I was—I was—I was referred by uh a friend.
GUS: A friend.
OLIVE: Yes.
GUS: A friend.
OLIVE: Is that wrong? Is that the wrong thing to—
GUS: What's this friend's name?
OLIVE: Uh name?
GUS: Tell me the name of your friend.
OLIVE: I don't really – Why do you need –
GUS: Marketing purposes.
OLIVE: Marketing? Marketing purposes?
GUS: Yes.
OLIVE: Is that a um a euphemism? Or …
TOR: Uff da.
OLIVE: No?
GUS: We don't use euphemisms, Olive.
TOR: We're Norwegians.
GUS: Minnesotan Norwegians.
　　　*(Pause. Possibly threatening.)*
And a little bit of other stuff.
TOR: Stay focused, Gus.

GUS: It's actually for marketing.

OLIVE: Oh.

> *(It may seem to OLIVE that GUS advances on her. She backs away. GUS extends his hand. OLIVE cringes. GUS stops.)*

GUS: Tor.

TOR: What.

GUS: I need a—bulb.

TOR: A bulb?

GUS: A light bulb. This one is too dim. I can't even see her face, Tor.

TOR: Uff da.

GUS: How can I do my job if I can't even see her face?

TOR: Wait just a second.

> *(GUS pulls the string and turns off the light. He unscrews the light bulb. TOR: comes back on with another light bulb.)*

Low watt bulbs are great for mood, aren't they, Gus.

GUS: And the environment.

TOR: But mood isn't everything, is it now?

GUS: The environment isn't everything.

TOR: What is everything, Gus?

GUS: Trust.

TOR: Trust. Trust is everything.

GUS: Light.

TOR: Light helps trust grow.

GUS: That's profound, Tor.

TOR: Oh, sure.

> *(GUS turns on the light again. It is much brighter now. Disconcertingly brighter. At least to OLIVE.)*

OLIVE: You are gangsters. Right? you're—

TOR: Norwegian.

GUS: Gangsters.

OLIVE: Um. Okay.

TOR: The nice kind.

OLIVE: Nice?

TOR: So, Olive—before we agree to kill your ex-boyfriend—

OLIVE: I didn't say it was my my my my—

GUS: 83% of our clients want to take out their ex.

OLIVE: 83%?

TOR: Breakups are very hard.

GUS: Especially on Norwegians.

TOR: Marketing.

OLIVE: I'm not a Norwegian.

TOR: We know.

OLIVE: I'm from—

TOR: Texas.

GUS: Texas.

OLIVE: Is it that obvious?

TOR: Uff da.

GUS: Still. She has a pretty face.

OLIVE: I do?

TOR: Gus.

GUS: I'm a little bit of a mutt myself.

TOR: Gus, remember what happened the last time.

OLIVE: The last time?

TOR: The last time he thought a woman was pretty.

OLIVE: Is she … Is she not pretty anymore?

GUS: She's fine.

OLIVE: I would really like to keep my face the way it is.

TOR: You look like your mother.

OLIVE: How did you know that?

TOR: We're the Norwegians.

GUS: From Minnesota.

TOR: We are magical.

GUS: Minnesota Norwegians.

> *(Pause.)*

So you were referred.

OLIVE: Referred. By a friend. Isn't that the way it works for hit—hit—hit people?

GUS: Gender neutral. That's very progressive.

TOR: When our client is un-Norwegian the risks inherent in our business are significantly greater.

GUS: Double, actually.

TOR: Did you fill out our optional demographic form?

OLIVE: No.

TOR: Your people, your Texas people, were what, French and Scottish? A little… oh, I don't know, what do you think, Gus, do you think she looks German?

GUS: Tell us the name of your friend.

OLIVE: Is this like a job interview where you check my my references?

GUS: We'd like to send our thanks.

OLIVE: Your thanks?

TOR: No, really. We want to send our thanks.

*(GUS stares at her. OLIVE clears her throat. Again, a little threatening.)*

Maybe she's thirsty. Are you thirsty? Would you like something to drink?

*(GUS sets down a bottle. Bang. TOR opens it. GUS sets down glasses. Bang. Bang.)*

GUS: Give us a name.

*(Bang.)*

TOR: I would do what Gus asks.

GUS: Have a drink.

*(There is a sudden shift.)*

## 2.

*(An uptown wine bar. Not today, maybe like yesterday, or the day before. OLIVE and BETTY have dealt death blows to a couple of half-price bottles at this point in the happy hour, and are maybe also into a cheese plate.)*

BETTY: It's a bad idea.

OLIVE: No.

BETTY: It's a really bad idea.

OLIVE: It's my only option.

BETTY: It can't be your only—

OLIVE: It's my only option.

BETTY: Killing your ex-boyfriend can't be your only option.

OLIVE: Betty. Do you have to—

BETTY: What.

OLIVE: I'm not—

BETTY: You're not going to kill your ex?

OLIVE: Oh my god.

BETTY: You just said you were planning to kill your ex.

OLIVE: I didn't actually say — I whispered it. I didn't say anything. Ha ha ha ha. Betty, this is a bar. With people in it.

*(She looks around the bar.)*

BETTY: Come on, Olive. Is killing the man who jilted you what you are planning to do? Because I, you know, I'm in the same spot. As it happens. I got jilted also. As it happens. I think this is a great opportunity to really talk things through.

OLIVE: It's happy hour. Can we not be happy? For just like a minute?

BETTY: Do you think we can be happy? The way we are? Now? Alone?

*(OLIVE comes very close to a ginormous wracking sob. And then she catches herself.)*

OLIVE: Yes. YES. I can be happy because because he'll be dead. I can be happy, see? I have a plan.

BETTY: A plan.

OLIVE: Well, maybe not a plan but whatever. A plan.

BETTY: Why not do it yourself? If you want him dead, I mean. Do it yourself.

OLIVE: Because because he might be expecting that.

*(Pause)*

From something I said.

BETTY: I like you, Olive.

OLIVE: Oh, Betty, me too. You're so nice.

BETTY: Fuck you, Olive.

OLIVE: Minnesota nice, isn't that what they say?

BETTY: No, but you are actually nice.

OLIVE: What do you mean?

BETTY: I think it's because you're from someplace warm. The cold just begins to affect the soul. You know? If you're not from here, raised here, indoctrinated in it. Your first Minnesota winter changes you. Makes you a little mean.

OLIVE: Mean? People here are mean? No.

*(BETTY takes a drink.)*

I mean, a cold winter makes you Makes you help people, right? All the ice and snow.

My ex helped me with that. Once. You have to help people or they die. I mean, I don't know if it does that I've just I've heard that winter here is as bad as a Texas summer. Only, you know, The opposite. We don't really help anybody though if it gets hot. Old people just die. Old people and children. They get heat stroke and we let them just die.

BETTY: Here in Minnesota, you gotta find a lover before the first freeze or else it's just too late, you're iced in for a very long time, all alone. They don't tell you that when you move here but it's true. You are iced in for all the short days, there are so many short days before the sun comes back and it begins to thaw. Short days and long nights. Long cold nights all alone, just the sound of the radiator in your apartment turning on, the knocking and the whispering of steam. Just leftover soup heated up mid-afternoon before the light fades. In fact, you make so much borscht that your poop turns red and you think it's blood and you have to have a tube with a camera on it shoved up your ass. On camera. In February. And the doctor aims the tube at you and says, "Here we go!" and then you watch your looming butt cheeks docked like the international space station by a tiny camera on a tube, like the space shuttle, right there on TV. It's that kind of cold, Olive. It's the cold of those bulky purple and yellow sweaters that you have to put on to take out the garbage, so that you're shapeless, like a big purple and yellow potato. That's you: a big plate of starch. You're just purple and yellow and shapeless and starchy, and you've just had a camera up your ass. On TV. Unless of course you find a lover, and hold on to him, and you make your own steam, and knocking, and whispering, and you feed each other food from your hands, not soup but solid food, and you draw lines with ice cubes down each other's body, no one's cold then. No one's cold. No one's alone. So did you do that, Olive? Did you find someone before it froze? No. Oh, you tried, now, didn't you. But you failed. You didn't get a lover. No. No, you didn't. Because he left you. He froze you out. He left you to die.

*(OLIVE sobs.)*

That is Minnesota nice, my new little friend. What I just did to you. That's what Minnesota nice feels like in your heart after five years. Five winters. That's all it takes. Unless of course you were raised here. Which I wasn't. I am from Kentucky.


## 3.

*Back at the red checkered tablecloth. Today.*

OLIVE: Okay. So I uh a friend told me sort of told me it was a she she indicated, she thought maybe I should call you.

GUS: For a job?

OLIVE: Yes. A job. *(Pause)* A job? Am I saying it right? The right emphasis?

GUS: Killing your ex. That kind of job.

*(Pause)*

OLIVE: I—I think—So. Yes.

TOR: Look at that face.

GUS: It's sweet.

OLIVE: I've never uh I'm a little—Um.

TOR: Nervous.

OLIVE: Yes.

GUS: She's nervous.

TOR: Don't be nervous, Olive. My goodness.

OLIVE: You guys are so nice.

GUS: Yes.

TOR: You can trust us.

OLIVE: That's what that's what I want.

TOR: We're just not sure yet that we can trust you.

OLIVE: What? But I mean. What? You're the criminals. Right? I'm just I'm a paying customer.

GUS: From Texas.

OLIVE: No, but. We're the friendly state. "Tejas" means "friendly."

TOR: Friendly enough to want someone dead.

OLIVE: You don't trust me because because I'm a paying customer?

TOR: We've learned from experience.

GUS: And we've had some customers who are—

TOR: A little unsettled.

GUS: I don't know if I'd say unsettled.

TOR: Therapeutically challenged.

GUS: Moody.

TOR: Fair enough. Olive, is this friend, is she a good friend?

OLIVE: Good?

TOR: Yes. Good. Would you call her a good friend?

OLIVE: Um we recently both uh had Bad Romantic Experiences. Breakups. So we're good. I'd say we're good. Good enough.

TOR: Good friends are important when bad things happen. Aren't they, Gus.

GUS: Tor and I are good friends.

TOR: Friends.

GUS: We have lots of good friends.

TOR: Oh, now don't brag, Gus. Sorry, Olive. Bragging is not part of a Norwegian's cultural landscape.

GUS: Some. Good friends.

TOR: We have friends.

GUS: A few.

TOR: Each other.

GUS: We're on Twitter.

   *(Pause)*

OLIVE: Oh my God. Are you cops? Did she set me up? Are you cops?

GUS: No.

OLIVE: You whack—

GUS: Yes.

OLIVE: You take out—

GUS: Yes.

OLIVE: You you you you

GUS: We're gangsters, Olive.

OLIVE: See? That's what I want.

TOR: We are the nice kind of gangster.

   *(Pause)*

OLIVE: I guess I don't understand how that works.

TOR: We are the Norwegians.

GUS: From Minnesota.

OLIVE: I'm hiring you to kill my ex-boyfriend.

TOR: Yes.

OLIVE: And you'll be able to kill him?

GUS: Have some wine.

TOR: I'd do what he asks.

> *(OLIVE takes a shaky sip of her beverage.)*

**4.**

> *(The wine bar.)*

BETTY: Texas.

OLIVE: Yes.

BETTY: You grew up in—

OLIVE: Texas.

BETTY: Huh.

OLIVE: What.

BETTY: Nothing, it's just—

OLIVE: What.

BETTY: You don't come across, you know, like that.

OLIVE: Like what?

BETTY: Like Texas.

OLIVE: What, like an accent?

BETTY: No.

OLIVE: I don't have much of an accent. Until I drink.

BETTY: I'm not sure if you know this, but in the rest of the country, Texas has kind of a bad reputation.

OLIVE: Nationalistic. All the talk about seceding. We're an easy target.

BETTY: If you left the union, no one would really try to stop you. You understand that, right?

> *(Pause)*

OLIVE: We're just sort of bullshitters. Texans are bullshitters. I mean, I'm not. I mean, Texans in general.

BETTY: So did you have a horse as a kid?

OLIVE: A horse?

BETTY: Did you have a horse?

OLIVE: Not all Texans have horses.

BETTY: You did, though, didn't you. Come on.

OLIVE: I grew up in suburbia. Houston. It wasn't. It was the

Johnson Space Center. Astronauts.

BETTY: Did the astronauts wear spurs? Giddy up, Space Shuttle!

OLIVE: Houston was mission control it wasn't God it wasn't the actual Launch pad. Jesus. Don't salt the wound. Fucking Florida.

BETTY: I bet you like cowboys. You keep thinking, where's my cowboy? Don'tcha?

OLIVE: Texas isn't just hicks and ranchers and cow shit Betty. Betty.

BETTY: The movie that you're in, in your head, it's a Western. Like a gambler gone bad, or some kind of—no no no—

OLIVE: I'm not in a you think I'm in a movie?

BETTY: At first it was a Wild West romantic comedy, right? Then he broke your heart and the genre changed, so now it's, like, High Noon in the middle of the Butch Cassidy Bolivian desert.

OLIVE: Those were very good movies.

BETTY: And now you're evading the mercenaries, the sheriff, the police force, you're building up to some kind of shootout with the—

OLIVE: Well of course.

BETTY: Of course.

OLIVE: I want a shootout, don't you? I want to find the guys who will like, the good guys.

BETTY: There aren't any good guys. Haven't you realized that yet?

OLIVE: I mean, in the movie. In my head. In the metaphor of the movie.

BETTY: Look at me. Okay? You and I, we're in the same movie. This is my situation, too, okay? Your situation is my situation. You got ditched. I got ditched. My heart, yours. We're both sitting here in the saloon, empty whiskey glasses overturned on the bar.

OLIVE: You know I always wanted to be a princess. I really like the dresses. I wanted to be the Lunar Princess. Lunar Princess, we had the –the beauty pageant.

BETTY: You're drunk.

OLIVE: I'm not drunk. Bullshit. I'm an earth sign. I can't be drunk.

BETTY: An earth sign? Seriously?

OLIVE: You're drunk. You're the Pisces.

BETTY: There's a reason the astrology column was always in the section of the newspaper with the comic strips and the weird little narratives about bridge games. Or the back of the magazine. Or the add-on to Facebook, like Farmville, or what, like what, like some stupid little app. But you take it seriously? Seriously? You take it seriously? You're one of those people? You, like, have an actual, like you have a person that you call? Jesus. Did your astrologer tell you that an awful man you loved was going to break your heart? Did she tell you, don't go to the fancy Italian restaurant that he Yelped and got all excited about, because it's a set up? Because you will be ambushed? Did she happen to mention that your boyfriend is a fucking power hungry fucking asshole, by the way, clue number one is that he picked someplace special and expensive so that you won't scream and cry – he thinks you might, by the way, and he thinks he's being nice when he – when he pulls the plug and leaves you there to gasp for air and die. Weren't you wondering, sitting like a dumb ass, not breathing, not moving, as he says what he says, watching the truck come at you, bam! There's a $45 entrée and another glass of wine on its way, he says, graciously, Get whatever you want, it's on me, and you don't wonder why you hadn't been warned by your FUCKING ASTROLOGER? Instead you quietly sob with your head in your hands and people stare but you don't make a sound. Do you think your ex just had a better planet in his house that day than you? (Pause) I had a horse. Is why I asked. I had a horse. Growing up. But she was – it was not like horseracing Kentucky, it was like white trash Kentucky and I had old coffee cans stuck into the dirt for markers, and she was not a very good horse. She probably was at one time, but by the time I got her, she was a broken down, very mean little bitch.

OLIVE: In Texas, sometimes we say rode hard and put away wet.

BETTY: Similar. Right. (Pause) One very mean little bitch.

*(Both women take a slug of their drinks.)*

**5.**

*(The red checkered tablecloth.)*

TOR: Now what was it that brought you to Minnesota?

OLIVE: I-35.

*(Pause)*

TOR: Oh, sure.

OLIVE: I mean that, I mean—

TOR: What? What?

GUS: It's irony, Tor.

OLIVE: I mean, I mean—

TOR: Irony? I don't get it.

GUS: A linguistic mechanism that indicates a mockery of something or someone.

TOR: Oh. *(Pause)* Maybe I've never experienced it directly before.

GUS: We're not big on irony up here in Minnesota, Olive. It's not, shall we say, appreciated. I mean, for me, sure, but the pure bloods, well, it's just not in their nature.

OLIVE: That wasn't irony because because it was sarcasm.

GUS: Nice.

OLIVE: Yes. Yes. Like that. And also it's just factually correct. I drove up here on I-35. I got in my car and I went pretty much straight north and then I turned slightly to the left. Can I have another some more?

TOR: A little bit of a drinker, hmm?

*(GUS pours another glass. OLIVE sips.)*

OLIVE: What is—What am I drinking?

GUS: Elderberry wine.

TOR: Homemade.

OLIVE: Elder what?

TOR: You've never had Elderberry wine before, Olive?

OLIVE: Me? Uh no. We don't have it where I'm from. We like our wine new and bitter. Or we like it to be beer. This is good. It's sweet. It tastes like—

TOR: Manischewitz.

OLIVE: Like the dessert—

TOR: Manischewitz.

OLIVE: Yes.

TOR: Norwegians invented Manischewitz..

OLIVE: They did?

GUS: Tor.

OLIVE: Norwegians made—

TOR: From an ancient, even mythological recipe.

GUS: No, Tor.

TOR: Okay.

GUS: No. For the last time.

TOR: Okay. *(Pause)* Elderberry wine is a traditional Scandinavian beverage.

GUS: Thank you.

OLIVE: It's very good.

GUS: Thank you.

TOR: Gus made it.

GUS: Well.

TOR: He grows and ferments the berries himself. Just like his father did. And his father's father. And his father's father's mother, because Norwegians are also very progressive.

OLIVE: Gus. You're a Renaissance Man. Gangster. Renaissance gangster.

GUS: Have to separate the berries from the stems. That's the most important step.

TOR: There's this waxy business that comes from the stems, and if you don't get all the stems out before you start fermenting, there is wax everywhere, and it's just—

GUS: Terrible.

TOR: Terrible.

GUS: And deadly.

TOR: Uff da.

OLIVE: Excuse me? Deadly?

TOR: The leaves, twigs, roots, seeds, and branches of an elderberry plant contain cyanide.

   *(OLIVE puts down her glass.)*

GUS: I only use berries to make the wine. I don't—

   *(OLIVE pushes the glass away from her.)*

Oh, Olive.

TOR: We aren't going to poison you, Olive. Gus won't poison you.

GUS: No.

TOR: You're a client. We like our clients.

GUS: Sometimes we like them very much.

OLIVE: So you won't kill your clients but you'll kill your clients' exes?

GUS: Olive, most of our clients are very nice people.

TOR: Most of our clients, yes, except the ones who are a bottomless hole of need.

GUS: You just didn't like her.

TOR: I'm not saying that specifically about one person.

GUS: You didn't like her.

TOR: I didn't even use her name.

OLIVE: I'm not a nice person.

TOR: Everybody wants someone dead at least once in their life. This is just your time.

OLIVE: I'm hiring you to kill my ex.

GUS: Because you wouldn't do it yourself, now, would you? Pull the trigger yourself?

OLIVE: I might. I mean, I told him that I would might kill him.

TOR: But instead you called us.

OLIVE: I did.

TOR: You have boundaries.

OLIVE: I do.

TOR: Boundaries are nice things to have.

OLIVE: I don't want to be mean.

GUS: You're not.

TOR: And neither are we.

GUS: "The very, very nice gangsters."

TOR: Gus is our Vice President for Marketing. He keeps metrics.

GUS: I came up with that slogan.

OLIVE: You should put it on your business cards.

*(Pause)*

TOR: We did.

OLIVE: You did? Because the one that I—That my friend gave me was just Gus' name on it.

TOR: Well, Gus has several different business card designs.

GUS: I am the Vice President for Marketing. I have to have my own nice cards.

TOR: Olive, can I just explain something to you a little bit? Just a little bit. Norwegians aren't showy, okay. No. We're very—Restrained.

*(Restraint.) (Restraint.)*

See? We're restrained. As a people. Norwegians evolved—
this is your basic sociological evolution, not your biology—
to conserve the energy we might spend on emotions and
use it for heat instead. Norway is very cold. It's cold. Have
you been? No? Minnesota has nothing on the homeland. I
mean, I love Minnesota. It's a very nice place. But my little
reptile brain goes right back to Norway. Every single time.
It is an almost primal instinct. If Norwegians were primal.
And reptiles. Which of course we're not.

OLIVE: You're restrained.

GUS: We're not restrained. Not all of us, not entirely.

TOR: And, Olive, what you need to remember is that Gus is
not 100% Norwegian. He has a little bit of something else
in him, don't you, Gus? A little bit of something else. It
explains a lot. The needy clients, the slightly questionable
ethics, all the different business cards, all that drama, all that
variety. True Norwegians don't need either of those things.
Certainly not variety. We are a true people, a committed
people. A loyal people. Frankly, we are just more content.
But Gus. Well. It explains a lot.

GUS: Just tell us about your friend.


**6.**

*(The wine bar.)*

OLIVE: So we're the same.

BETTY: Uh, no.

OLIVE: You just said we're the same.

BETTY: No, I said—

OLIVE: Will you help me?

BETTY: No.

OLIVE: Help me.

BETTY: No.

OLIVE: He broke my heart.

BETTY: The little shits do that sometimes, Olive.

OLIVE: But why why are we letting them get away with it?

BETTY: We?

OLIVE: We're in the same movie. That's what you said.

BETTY: I didn't say I was letting anybody get away with anything.

OLIVE: So what? What?

BETTY: Having your ex killed is always a terrible idea.

OLIVE: No.

BETTY: It's a terrible, just from a practical perspective, it's a—

OLIVE: It's a good idea. It's a very good idea.

BETTY: Olive.

OLIVE: You can't stop me.

BETTY: I'm saying it's a terrible idea. I'm not saying you shouldn't do it.

*(Pause)*

OLIVE: See? This is why we're friends.

BETTY: We're friends because we were both in the can at the same time and you needed a tampon.

OLIVE: Fate.

BETTY: And that was ten minutes ago.

OLIVE: The stars aligned.

BETTY: The stars are bullshit. Didn't we just have this conversation?

OLIVE: You'd make a good Texan, Betty.

BETTY: Flattery does not work in Minnesota. It makes the locals very uncomfortable.

OLIVE: You're not a local.

BETTY: True.

OLIVE: You've been here five years?

BETTY: Five winters. Yes. Five long winters.

OLIVE: Does it ever stop snowing?

BETTY: No.

OLIVE: When does spring come?

BETTY: Never.

OLIVE: At home it doesn't snow. Snow 11 inches! A foot! In April! I had to call him to dig out my car! Him meaning my ex.

BETTY: And he came over and dug out your car, didn't he.

OLIVE: Minnesota nice.

BETTY: Little shit.

OLIVE: This is hell. I'm in hell.

BETTY: Then go home.

OLIVE: I have to kill him first. I made a sacred vow. *(Pause)* Or whatever. It was a vow.

BETTY: You need to get a haircut and go to the gym.

OLIVE: I need to follow through. It doesn't matter if it's sacred or not.

BETTY: A haircut is better. He doesn't make the new you, you do.

OLIVE: That's a nice slogan.

BETTY: I have experience in Marketing. Why don't you just wait?

OLIVE: Wait?

BETTY: We're all going to die. He will, too.

OLIVE: That could take forever. Also, I have a desire to punish.

BETTY: Look. Olive. Once you've done it, you can't go back.

OLIVE: Why would I want to go back? I don't want to go back.

BETTY: What if he called?

OLIVE: He is poison. He poisoned me. He's like a snake. I want to cut him in half. Do you think a hit man would cut him in half for me? I really want I'm feeling very dramatic about my about my vow. Do you think he might actually call?

BETTY: With a new haircut, you force yourself to be a different person.

OLIVE: Is that what you're trying to do with yours?

*(Pause)*

BETTY: Yes. It is what I'm trying to do with mine.

OLIVE: What I meant was—

BETTY: And do you know why?

OLIVE: I really like your hair. Don't be mad.

BETTY: Olive, killing someone is extreme.

OLIVE: Okay. Okay. But he said—listen—He said, "I want to dance at your wedding, whether it's to me or to somebody else."

BETTY: He—

OLIVE: He said that to me In the restaurant. The fancy Italian place. He said that to my face. *(Pause)* I don't really know what it means.

BETTY: Me, neither.

OLIVE: He said it, like like—

BETTY: It's a little… staged.

OLIVE: I know. It's appalling. Like he practiced.

BETTY: But I mean, it's also kind of poetic.

OLIVE: Poetic? Poetic?

BETTY: At first glance.

OLIVE: Like, what, like like he'd been thinking about it or or something? Like he planned how to break my heart?

BETTY: Like he had been figuring out what to say to cause you the least harm.

OLIVE: You mean maybe maybe he was trying to be an ok guy? *(Pause)* No. He's a dick

BETTY: Yeah.

OLIVE: He should be killed.

BETTY: Yeah.

OLIVE: You think so too?

BETTY: I'm killing my ex and his breakup shit was a lot less weird.

OLIVE: Oh, you're just saying that to make me feel better.

BETTY: No.

*(Pause)*

OLIVE: What?

BETTY: What. I'm having my ex killed.

OLIVE: What?

*(Pause)*

BETTY: I actually like my haircut. But it's not enough.

OLIVE: You're actually going to—

BETTY: He needs to be dead. So I made a call.

OLIVE: You actually—You called a, like a—

*(BETTY takes a drink.)*

Like a hit man?

*(BETTY drinks.)*

And has he—Hit Anything? Yet?

*(BETTY drinks.)*

Betty?

*(Bang. BETTY's glass is empty.)*

BETTY: It's in progress.

OLIVE: In progress. You mean, like—

BETTY: When he's dead I'll get a text

OLIVE: So you have a um a phone number?

BETTY: I've got a fucking business card.

OLIVE: There are business cards for for—that kind of—I didn't know, I wasn't sure how to reach the Italians. Are there Italians in Minnesota? I don't know where they'd be here.

BETTY: Wisconsin.

OLIVE: What?

BETTY: They're in Wisconsin. I have to pee. Watch my shit.


## 7.

*(Red checkered table cloth.)*

GUS: What's her name?

OLIVE: It was a referral.

GUS: Come on, Olive. What's her name?

TOR: Gus. You're not acting very nice.

GUS: I got a bad feeling, Tor.

TOR: Bad feelings aren't Norwegian.

GUS: I know. That's why I have them and you don't.

OLIVE: Referrals are nice, right? Referrals are like a business theme. Right, ya'll? Can't you just be nice? And happy that can't you just be happy?

GUS: Why the resistance, Olive?

OLIVE: I just want to be happy. Why is that so hard? I don't know maybe I shouldn't actually kill anybody.

GUS: You're not going to kill anybody. You're going to get us to kill somebody for you. And I really want to kill somebody.

TOR: Tell us who your friend is and we'll give her a gift certificate.

GUS: Gift certificate!

TOR: Don't you think that's a good idea, Gus? A gift certificate.

OLIVE: Why would she need a gift certificate? Like for her next assassination? Is there like a Groupon or something?

GUS: That's actually a good idea.

TOR: A Groupon.

GUS: On it.

TOR: Vice President for Marketing!

GUS: What's her name.

OLIVE: I mean, she didn't really—

GUS: What.

OLIVE: Give me—

GUS: She didn't give you? What?

OLIVE: Like like the referral wasn't direct. I'm thinking now that I have second thoughts, maybe.

GUS: I want her name, Olive.

TOR: Oh, Gus.

GUS: No, Tor, I really really need to take someone out right now. I'm feeling very wound up.

TOR: Gus.

OLIVE: Look, she didn't actually—

GUS: She didn't actually what?

OLIVE: I just don't want to sabotage the because now you're all distracted the work you're doing for her.

GUS: Work?

OLIVE: The project. The job. Did we say job is the right terminology?

TOR: She said we were doing a job?

OLIVE: It's in progress. It's an in-progress job.

    *(Pause)*

TOR: Uff da.

OLIVE: What.

GUS: We don't have any jobs in progress.

OLIVE: You don't?

TOR: How exactly did you get our number?

**8.**

    *(The wine bar. OLIVE eyes BETTY's unattended purse.)*

**9.**

*(Red checkered tablecloth.)*

TOR: So you're a spy.

OLIVE: A spy?

TOR: Who are you spying for? For the Swedes? The Danes?

GUS: The Finns?

TOR: The Finns are weasels.

OLIVE: I'm not spying for any other ethnic Committee or business or co-op of Scandinavian murderers.

TOR: Uff da. Gus.

GUS: She knows about the co-op.

OLIVE: There's actually a co-op?

GUS: It's Minnesota, Olive. Of course there's a co-op.

TOR: Is this a sting, Olive? Are you trying to sting us?

OLIVE: No. No.

GUS: Find the wire.

TOR: Where's the wire, Olive?

OLIVE: I'm not—

GUS: You're wearing one, aren't you.

OLIVE: No—No—

TOR: Pat her down, Gus.

OLIVE: There's no wire. There's no wire. Gus, there's no—Tor. Listen. The only wire I have on is in my bra, okay? The only wire anywhere on my body is holding up my ta-tas. I could show you my ta-tas but that's not very that's like a South Padre Island kind of it's not Tejas friendly or Minnesota friendly, it's not the nice theme that we've been that you've been selling me on.

*(GUS stops.)*

TOR: Uff da.

GUS: She's right.

TOR: Okay.

OLIVE: Okay.

GUS: Is there actually a friend?

OLIVE: Yes.

*(Beat)*

Well, friend.

TOR: She's not your friend?

GUS: Don't confuse him, Olive. The sarcasm thing.

OLIVE: I met her at a bar. We were both at this bar.

GUS: Just tell us her name.

OLIVE: Betty. Betty. My friend's name is Betty.

GUS: You're friends with Betty?

## 10.

*(The wine bar. BETTY is in the bathroom, staring at her new haircut. Which she hates.)*

BETTY: Fucking stylist was Norwegian, too. Wasn't she. Wasn't she! Fucking Annika. I should have known.

## 11.

*(The red checkered tablecloth. GUS reels from the information.)*

TOR: Are you okay?

GUS: Betty.

TOR: Gus.

GUS: Betty.

OLIVE: I'm not a cop. Or a Swede. Except on my dad's side I'm a little Swedish. And Scottish, which I think is sort of like being Taurus and Libra, You know, contradictory. Which I am also, sometimes.

TOR: Uff da.

OLIVE: What.

TOR: Astrology.

OLIVE: Betty doesn't believe in it either.

GUS: Betty.

TOR: It's so not Norwegian.

GUS: Betty.

OLIVE: Gus. Breathe through your nose.

TOR: Why are you so upset?

GUS: Nothing. Nothing.

OLIVE: I thought she said she was going to call you. She didn't call you?

TOR: For what?

OLIVE: For a job.

TOR: Another one?

OLIVE: What do you mean another one? Another job? Another job?

TOR: She's one of the 83%.

OLIVE: You mean she's had an ex killed before?

GUS: Betty Betty Betty is a client.

TOR: She was the client we were discussing earlier. The one that Gus nicely described as "moody." Well, sure she's moody. Oh, sure. Isn't she, Gus? A little moody. But we forgive her. Don't we. Not because we're Norwegian, but because of marketing. She gave you our business card. Oh, they turned out so nice, don't you think?

OLIVE: Yeah, I mean simple, just the phone number and a name.

TOR: And great slogans: "We're the kind of guys you want to bring home to your mom. Depending on how you feel about your mom."

*(Pause)*

GUS: I wrote that, too.

TOR: Gus wrote that one, too.

OLIVE: Well, like I said, mine was really just the and I don't know if I would have you know positively. I like my mom. But I'm sure the right the right demographic ou know loves it.

TOR: There are three variations. Well, four. Your basic design, which is me, and three variations, which is Gus. He needs to be show-offy. But online printing is cost efficient, oh sure. A package of a thousand. Just upload that little logo and—

OLIVE: Logo? What logo?

TOR: The Tor logo.

GUS: God, I hate that logo.

TOR: You hate the logo?

GUS: I just—

TOR: Tor is the God of Thunder in Norwegian mythology. I found it in Clip Art. I love clip art. Don't you love clip art?

But I'm not judging you at all, Olive. Very few shiksas can identify the God of Thunder anymore. It's not taught in schools the way it used to.

OLIVE: Shiksa?

GUS: Tor, Olive is not a shiksa.

TOR: Technically, she is.

GUS: Shiksa is a Yiddish word, Tor.

TOR: It can be—

GUS: It means she's not Jewish.

TOR: And she's not. She's from Texas.

OLIVE: There are actually Jews in Texas.

GUS: "Shiksa" doesn't mean "not Norwegian."

TOR: There's no way that Olive, who is from a very hot place, and who is named after an ingredient in pesto, which we don't eat ethnic food anyway, there's no way Olive would know the cultural reference of Tor the God of Thunder.

OLIVE: Tor is like Zeus.

TOR: Oh, sure. Easy comparison.

OLIVE: Like a god of Olympus. Right? That's what I'm saying.

GUS: She knows the Greeks, Tor.

TOR: Of course she knows the Greeks. Everyone knows the Greeks. Even Texans, who removed Thomas Jefferson out of American history, on purpose, even they know the Greeks.

GUS: Wait, Texans did what?

OLIVE: It's we are an easily misunderstood people.

GUS: He's a Founding Father.

OLIVE: And a liberal.

TOR: Norwegians! Norwegians were the Founding Fathers! Norwegians are the liberals!

GUS: Thomas Jefferson wasn't a liberal. He owned people.

OLIVE: It's just very hot in Texas, Gus. Okay? Things get all melty and it's just very hot.

TOR: And the Greeks stole Olympus, they stole Zeus, from Norwegians. The rest of the world are thieves. Everybody is a thief!

OLIVE: The business card that I stole from that I got from—

GUS: Betty—

OLIVE: There's no God of Thunder on it.

TOR: Our cards prominently feature Tor the God of Thunder.

---

*C. Denby Swanson*

OLIVE: Well, not the one I saw.

TOR: But you just said that's how you called us, Olive.

OLIVE: No. I called Gus.

TOR: You called Gus?

OLIVE: That's why I said the card was so simple. It was just, like, "Gus" and then a number.

   *(Beat.)*

GUS: My card was in her purse?

OLIVE: And handwritten.

TOR: Handwritten?

GUS: What was my card doing in her purse?

TOR: Why do you have your own card with your name and title—I printed three different variations!—and then another entirely other card with just your name on it? And handwritten? No one handwrites things anymore, Gus, not unless you are going to make the pigment yourself, which the bachelor farmers already do—that's why the sexually active Norwegians invented computers and email. I mean, don't you think four cards is excessive, even for you? How many different business cards does one non-Norwegian actually need?

GUS: It's not a business card. I don't use it for business. It's a personal card. I use it for personal. Things.

TOR: So why did Betty have it?

   *(Pause)*

GUS: We were uh—

OLIVE: You were sleeping with Betty?

TOR: Uff da.

GUS: Yeah.

TOR: She's a client.

GUS: I know.

TOR: You can't keep sleeping with our clients.

GUS: I know.

TOR: You remember what happened with the pretty-faced one.

GUS: Yes.

OLIVE: Oh Oh you're the Asshole.

GUS: She called me that?

OLIVE: She said she wants to kill you.

GUS: I can believe it.

TOR: This is why we're falling in market share.

GUS: But I was the God of Thunder, Tor. For, just, a brief moment.

TOR: No, you weren't.

OLIVE: The God of Thunder?

TOR: Olive, for just a little background on this, okay, so Tor, The God of Thunder, is not only the head of the Norwegian pantheon, it is also a sacred position of love, written down in the Old Time and illustrated in a sacred book. Did you know that? No, I bet you did not. I am, of course, because of my heritage and because of my name, an expert on that book, and on all its contents. It's still in print. You can get it at Barnes & Noble. Or Amazon.

GUS: That's the Kama Sutra.

TOR: Which the Hindus stole from—

GUS: Tor.

OLIVE: No, Gus. Listen. Betty literally wants to kill you. She hired a hit man. She's going to have you killed.

*(Pause)*

GUS: Yeah.

## 12.

*(Light comes up on BETTY . She's holding, maybe putting on, a large, shapeless, gender-neutral coat, scarf, hat, gloves.)*

BETTY: The Norwegians. They are insidious. Dangerous. Clever. Strong. They are weather proofed, as children, to not mind extreme cold or large flying bugs. Or Canada. They don't mind being close to Canada. They are insulated, somehow. Well trained for outdoor survival. Even babies. They kayak. Babies! Yes. They ski. It is like they are all little baby Navy SEALS. They learn to drive on frozen rivers, they learn how to slam on the brakes and spin wildly into the snow. Not babies. But teenagers. And on purpose, not like the rest of us, as an act of rebellion, or inadvertently because we don't know how to brake, but sanctioned, organized, they are trained to do it the right way. All their driver education classes take place outside in the winter on frozen rivers. All of them. On purpose. Training little Norwegian Jason Bournes. They are well fed, despite the limited window for agriculture, but they rarely get fat. In fact, they appear wholesome. And charming. And handsome. And perfect. And pure. But they're not. Don't be fooled. They prioritize social services, like elder care—they even call it elder care—and drug rehab for teenagers and independent living programs for the mentally ill—and they give to the arts with an unshakeable ferocity, even in difficult economic times, even in deficit years, as if they actually believe in those things, in the worth of those things, in the benefits of community. I asked one, I asked why, why these donations, why all this money going to artists and addicts and museums and public gardens? And he said, Because otherwise it would be like living in Omaha, only further north. I swear, it's what he said directly to me. Asshole. Think they're loyal, upstanding citizens? Think again. Norwegians started colonizing this country five centuries before Columbus. Greedy bastards. Never in large numbers. Secretly. Under the radar. Until they dominated the lumber trade and farming and fishing and crafts trades and back home there was a crisis and they decided to take over the flat, fertile land of our precious Midwest. Like they take over our flat, fertile women. There are five million of them now, in this country, committed to their homes and parks and neighborhood watch groups and to their extended families, too. "Family," right? You've seen The Godfather. But note this: In the last hundred years, almost no Norwegians have become Mormon. Okay? Right? You don't find that suspicious? Who can resist the Mormons these days? They knock on the doors of Jehovah's Witnesses and walk away with new converts. I mean, Mormons are freaking everywhere, and they have that pitch about saving the souls of your dead relatives, despite the fact that they're dead, if their souls are anywhere they're in Hell, you can imagine your great aunt suddenly yanked out of the fire, Oh, she says as the flames recede, I knew I could count on that one, my niece, she is such a nice person. But Norwegians, no. They're like, Well, now there's a hot dish, oh sure. I'm telling you, a practical people. Warm. Thoughtful. Destructive. Evil.

THE NORWEGIANS

**13.**

*(The checkered tablecloth.)*

OLIVE: This is beginning to wig me out.

TOR: What is?

OLIVE: What? What? What do you mean what?

TOR: Oh.

OLIVE: "Oh" is right. Damn right.

TOR: Gus and Betty dating was unprofessional.

OLIVE: No no no—You're wigged out about—

TOR: You have my word, it will not happen again.

OLIVE: I'm not wigged out about love about people loving each other—

TOR: Gus and Betty were not—in love.

OLIVE: I don't care. What I'm really I'm wigged out about assassination, Tor. Tor. Hit hit hit hit people. Jobs.Everybody whacking each other.

TOR: But Olive, you have to understand, that's what we do.

OLIVE: I just want to be happy. Don't you want to be happy? What would it take for you to be happy?

*(It's possible that TOR considers this question.)*

GUS: She kept my card in her purse.

TOR: Uff da, Gus.

GUS: It was in her purse, where she could reach in—

OLIVE: I think instead of of killing him my ex I'm just going to give him a call.

TOR: You can't do that, Olive.

OLIVE: No. Of course I can't. Not if he's dead.

TOR: You've already engaged our services. You signed a contract.

OLIVE: Well well

GUS: My card was right next to her hand. Tor, it was right next to her hand.

TOR: Gus.

GUS: She has a great hand. Great fingers.

TOR: Gus.

OLIVE: But what if I just don't want him Dead Anymore? My astrologer my therapist told me I wouldn't.

TOR: Your therapist was obviously not Norwegian. Tor the God of Thunder has a very vindictive thunderbolt that he uses to strike down—well, anybody he feels like betrays him.

*C. Denby Swanson*

OLIVE: It didn't matter to me what she was. She answered whenever whenever I called.

GUS: I was the God of Thunder with Betty. For a brief moment. The Kama Sutra version. I was the God of Thunder.

TOR: GUS! *(Pause)* Was your ex-boyfriend mean to you, Olive?

OLIVE: Mean? He was um—

TOR: Was he mean? Like Gus was mean to Betty?

GUS: What? I wasn't mean to—

OLIVE: He was a nice man. He was a very nice man. Just just sometimes we were badly matched. I thought we were well matched. Earth sign like me and Cancer like him, his birthday was in July, so he was a and it turns out we were badly I don't think he was He wasn't purposefully mean Or an asshole chickenshit motherfucker pencil dick. *(Excuse me.)* On purpose. Not on purpose. He was he was very kind a lot of the time.

TOR: Until he broke your heart.

*(OLIVE withholds a tremendous, wracking sob.)*

Everybody is kind until they break your heart. Right, Gus?

OLIVE: God, I hate men sometimes.

TOR: Me, too.

OLIVE: I just, I just killing him I mean, if he stays alive someday we could talk again.

TOR: You want him dead, Olive.

OLIVE: I do?

TOR: You do. You may think, One day he will want me back, but he won't.

OLIVE: He won't?

TOR: He won't.

GUS: He will. He might.

TOR: He may call you someday. Like on your anniversary.

OLIVE: Really?

TOR: And you will answer.

OLIVE: I told him not to call me again unless he means it.

TOR: And he nodded solemnly, didn't he.

OLIVE: Yes.

GUS: Men do that.

TOR: They're shits.

GUS: Not on purpose. Sometimes on purpose. Not all the time on purpose.

TOR: Your ex will call, on your anniversary, a year after breaking up with you at that Italian place.

OLIVE: How did you know it was—

GUS: It's always an Italian place.

TOR: Too much garlic and pepper for anything but sadness.

GUS: Your ex will say some nice things. Because sometimes they do.

TOR: What he will say is that he's been thinking about you this whole time, and he's come to the realization that you are still the one he loves. Your breath catches in your throat. And he will tell you that breaking up was the biggest mistake of his entire life. You think, I told him not to call unless he means it, and then he called, he must mean it! Like Gus meant it when he said he would stop sleeping with our clients.

GUS: I did mean it. In that moment I meant it.

TOR: Once you are reassured, once you are softened, once you think you can be happy again, together again, he will mention that he has this recurring fantasy about running into you somewhere downtown, in public, and you and his new fiancée get into a catfight in the middle of the street.

OLIVE: That's not that's not really bearable. Is it.

GUS: He wanted commitment, he wanted family—

TOR: He just didn't want them with you. *(Pause)* Gus is like that sometimes.

GUS: I was like that once.

OLIVE: With the fiancée and everything?

TOR: You can't let him live. Your ex.

OLIVE: You're right.

TOR: See? Regular people don't trust women. But Norwegians do. Norwegians trust your instincts. We trust every single one of your—

> *(It's GUS standing there but in him OLIVE sees her ex-boyfriend. With that vision, TOR continues to talk, but the world slides sideways for a second, all the sound goes sideways with it and warps, strangely. GUS moves. It all returns to normal.)*

OLIVE: You what?

TOR: What?

---

OLIVE: You trust my what? I'm sorry, I didn't hear you, it got blurry for a second.

TOR: Your instincts.

OLIVE: You trust my instincts?

GUS: Is that unusual?

OLIVE: I don't think—I don't think I have any. Instincts, I mean. Do I have instincts?

*(Pause)*

GUS: Oh, wow. He got you bad.

TOR: You deserve so much, Olive. Sure you do.

GUS: You must really hate your ex.

TOR: You must.

GUS: You must.

OLIVE: I must?

TOR: You understand?

*(Pause. OLIVE nods.)*

OLIVE: Of course I have instincts. And they're telling me to kill my ex until he's dead. Or whatever. To have you guys do it.

TOR: We will kill Olive's ex.

GUS: I'll get the equipment.

*End Of Act I*

THE NORWEGIANS

# Act II

## 14.

*(BETTY stands in a pool of light, like a streetlight. She's waiting, on edge, ready for something.)*

BETTY: The Norwegians. And their Lutheran Church. Home of orphan and refugee relocation services all over the world. Their revered social services. Fuck me. Fuck them. The Norwegians and their gravlax. Does anyone even know what that is? An alien word for, I don't know, something fishlike. And fermented trout. Fermented. Trout. And lutefisk—fish steeped in lye and then covered in ashes. I mean, my god, fish, lye and ashes. Fish, Lye & Ashes. It sounds like a band name from the 1970's. Like, a white r&b band. And their perpetually cheerful snow suits and their stupid local customs. They will stop in any weather and help a stranger change their tire. I just want to scream at them, I know you don't really mean that. You cannot love people who make gravlaks. You can not love people who make lutefisk. You cannot FUCK people who make elderberry wine, not an actual fuck, not a true heartfelt beautiful intimate fuck, as I discovered. Late. Or lingonberries. Lingonberries. If that doesn't bring up dirty images in your head, I don't know what would. What lover would let you serve them lingonberries? And my god, hotdish: meat and Stovetop drenched in mushroom soup and covered in tater tots. That's not even—that's like casserole death. But Norwegians hand this "food" out in the neighborhood when new people move in. When there are pot lucks. They think hotdish is welcoming. They think lingonberries are—Well. These are fearful, terrifying, terrible, very frightening things to serve people.

*(She checks her phone. Nothing. )*

If I could have hired him to kill himself, it would be over by now.

*(She pulls a baseball hat down low over her face, she is hidden, almost anonymous.)*

**15.**

*(A dimly-lit street. TOR, GUS and OLIVE are lying in wait.)*

OLIVE: Look at the stars. So bright. So beautiful.

TOR: So Norwegian.

OLIVE: The stars are Norwegian?

TOR: The quality of the night sky, Olive. The clarity of the air.

OLIVE: Leo, right?

TOR: What?

OLIVE: You're a Leo.

TOR: That is so sweet. You are very observant.

OLIVE: Gus, what are you?

GUS: What am I?

OLIVE: What sign?

GUS: Come on.

*(He turns away. Then he realizes that TOR & OLIVE are staring at him.)*

We're lying in wait. Aren't we lying in wait?

TOR: What's your sign, Gus?

GUS: You don't believe in astrology, do you?

TOR: I don't?

GUS: You do?

TOR: I believe in the stars.

GUS: But they don't orbit around us or send us secret messages. Come on. They just don't. It wouldn't be very Norwegian if they did.

TOR: Who are you decide what meets the guidelines for Norwegian-ness?

OLIVE: They have power, Gus. They have those cute little rays of energy—

GUS: They're too far away to send little rays of energy on purpose. They're millions of light years out in the universe.

OLIVE: Yeah but maybe—

GUS: It can't be intentional, I mean, Olive, my god, think about it. When the light first left them, there were dinosaurs roaming the earth.

TOR: Maybe they were Norwegian dinosaurs.

OLIVE: My astrologer said She said It was all for a purpose.

GUS: "It" being your heartbreak? Us taking somebody out for being mean to you, this is not predicted by a fortune cookie. It's not dependent on your ridiculous chart that you spend hard-earned dollars on each month. It's a choice you make, to engage our services. He hurt you, that was his choice. You have hired us to hurt him back. That is yours. And we're sitting here waiting on him to show up, because we are professionals, because you have hired us to kill him. You have decided on at least that. You can also choose to be happy. You can choose not to kill someone. We're particularly good at it, especially me, and I actually really like the work, but it's a choice you're making to engage our services, you're paying us to take someone out. And you may not feel any big difference afterwards, unless you just want to. Unless you want to be happy, whether or not your heart has been broken. A ball of gas two hundred million miles away from us has nothing really to do with what happens next.

TOR: That's not very good marketing, Gus.

GUS: I got most of that speech from Betty, actually. *(Pause)* Scorpio.

OLIVE: What?

OLIVE: You're a Scorpio.

GUS: Scorpio.

TOR: She's right, Gus. You were born in November.

GUS: I am whatever sign it is that carries this:

> *(He presents a large, threatening baseball bat.)*

These notches carved into the wood? Our stats.

OLIVE: You mean—

GUS: Completed contracts.

TOR: We're going to put your ex-boyfriend right here.

> *(He points to an empty spot on the baseball bat.)*

OLIVE: This is what you use?

GUS: Every time.

TOR: Gus uses it. I'm more on the management side.

OLIVE: I thought you were the nice the nice the nice gangsters.

TOR: Oh, we are.

OLIVE: A baseball bat seems awfully awfully awfully awful.

TOR: Gus isn't Norwegian on his mother's side.

GUS: Gives me an edge.

TOR: And you know what's funny? The bat is also our company accounting system. Tax season we just hand it to the CPA.

GUS: Refund every year.

TOR: She's so good to us.

*(The NORWEGIANS spot a shadowy figure nearby.)*

Is that him?

GUS: Let's take him out, Tor. I want to take him out. I want to take someone out.

OLIVE: Oh. Oh. Oh. Oh.

*(GUS and TOR head toward the figure, stealthily; they look, strangely and for a brief moment, a lot like professionals.)*

TOR: Now, Gus.

*(GUS raises the baseball bat above his head and is about to bring it down.)*

I am the God of Thunder!

*(The figure spins around.)*

OLIVE: Wait! Wait!


## 16.

*(TOR stands by himself.)*

TOR: Here's what I'm thinking in that moment. The moment of ending a life. It is the single most important moment they will ever have. The end. It's an event they will get to experience only once. Only once. They don't expect it to be happening now. But it is. It is. It is happening now. I want it to go well. Is it possible that a baseball bat isn't the best choice? Might seem that way. Sure. To an outsider. In 1991, the Minnesota Twins won the World Series. It was a magical season. Just magical. We haven't had one like it since. And I was there for the whole thing. The Twins and the Braves were the first two teams in Major League history to start out last and end up first. It's so biblical. Almost prophetic. So restrained. And so—so—so Norwegian. And the last shall be first. So deeply Norwegian. It took the whole seven games. Four at home. We could have been nice and come in second. We could have been true to our nature. But we got up our nerve and we actually won. That's the way that I think about growing the business as well. The Norwegians could be second in market share. Second in revenues. Third, even. And that would be fine. Because inside, we would know ourselves champions, gracious to the competition, we would know it in our hearts. We would even be nice about it. Or we could beat the living crap out of the other team, and win. I love the Minnesota Twins. I love them with all my heart. And this is their winning bat.

## 17.

OLIVE: Wait! Wait!

*(On the dimly lit street, everything stops.)*

Gus. That's not him. That's not my ex-boyfriend.

GUS: It's not?

TOR: Who is it?

BETTY: Olive. Tell the Vikings who it is.

*(OLIVE aims her flashlight at the figure.)*

OLIVE: Oh my lord.

*(It's BETTY, of course.)*

TOR: It's—

GUS: Betty. Betty. Betty. Betty.

*(BETTY takes off her baseball hat and shakes out her hair. The big jacket slides off her shoulders as if it were suddenly liquid.)*

## 18.

*(In some little dive bar somewhere, maybe a year ago, maybe 18 months, we see the first moment when GUS met BETTY. It's winter, of course, and she is taking off her heavy coat and shaking the snow out of her hair. GUS is mesmerized.)*

GUS: Your name is—

BETTY: Betty.

GUS: Betty. Betty. Betty. It's Betty.

**19.**

*(Back on the dimly lit street.)*

BETTY: It's Betty. Fabulous. Now I'm an It.

TOR: We didn't think you were an It.

BETTY: No?

TOR: We thought you were a man.

GUS: Tor.

BETTY: You know, the last time I wandered around Minneapolis under this kind of shit ton of insulation, I was near the river, in February, it was ten degrees outside, and I was wearing 4 layers of silk underwear and polar fleece, three pairs of socks, a big scarf, two sets of mittens, a hat, and a fluffy ski jacket. I looked like a giant purple doughnut. Some Norwegian perv drove past, rolled down his window, and let out a wolf whistle. And the coat I'm wearing now is like lingerie compared to that outfit. So you, plural, you, Tor, thought I was a man?

TOR: We're not trying to be mean.

BETTY: Yes, you are. You are naturally mean. You say you're not, but you are.

TOR: Gus is the mean one.

GUS: I'm sorry, Betty. I'm sorry. I'm sorry.

BETTY: Save it.

TOR: What about me, Gus? Are you going to say sorry to me?

GUS: For what? She brought us business.

OLIVE: Betty, they could have killed you.

BETTY: Yes. I know.

TOR: We could have—What?

BETTY: You—Or rather—Gus could have killed me.

*(A moment happens. The beginning of the revelation. Sound begins to slide uncertainly across the world.)*

TOR: If we had actually—

GUS: If I.

TOR: Killed Betty. Whom you love.

*(It might be the same kind of wah wah wah thing that OLIVE experienced with the word "intuition." Or it might be different. But it keeps going. It extends.)*

GUS: Don't think about it.

TOR: What if you had killed—

GUS: Don't think about it.

TOR: What killed—

GUS: Don't think about it!

TOR: What is this feeling?

OLIVE: I think it's called irony.

*(Bing.)*

TOR: I have never experienced irony directly until now.

BETTY: I popped his irony cherry.

OLIVE: Are you okay, Tor?

TOR: That's sweet of you to ask, Olive. Oh my god, Olives aren't sweet!

BETTY: He might be sore for a couple of days, baby.

TOR: Everything is different now. The world is different now. Colors. Everything. This—this—is irony?

BETTY: I'd be gentle with him, she said cynically.

GUS: Betty, I still love you.

BETTY: Gus, I'm going to have you killed.

GUS: I know.

OLIVE: Betty? Um hey, Friend. Can we talk for a minute?

BETTY: What do you want to talk about?


## 20.

*(At the bar. BETTY returns to the barstool, a little wobbly.)*

OLIVE: Are you okay?

BETTY: That bartender is an asshole. Every time I come here he roofies my wine.

OLIVE: He does?

BETTY: It's Minnesota, Olive. People play hard ball.

OLIVE: Maybe you just drink a lot.

BETTY: Where's my purse?

*(OLIVE hands it to her.)*

Let's go.

## 21.

*(The dimly lit street. The women stand apart.)*

OLIVE: You left it when you went to pee.

BETTY: I did.

OLIVE: Did you want me to look through it?

BETTY: I had to pee.

OLIVE: And you didn't take your purse?

BETTY: For what, for ID?

OLIVE: For your purse.

BETTY: I didn't need my purse.

OLIVE: You gave me a tampon, when when we were in the bathroom together, when we first started talking. You gave me a tampon. You had tampons in your purse. Did you not need a tampon when you went to pee?

BETTY: I just. I keep spares.

OLIVE: They help you make friends? Or do you always enlist a Texan to help you have your ex killed By Norwegian assassins?

*(Pause)*

BETTY: You got the business card on your own.

OLIVE: You wanted me to.

BETTY: A Wild West Romance. A gambler gone bad. A police thriller. What movie are you in now?

OLIVE: I'm not really that big a movie buff.

BETTY: I'm in Thelma and Louise.

OLIVE: Oh.

BETTY: I liked that one.

OLIVE: Me, too. Me, too.

BETTY: I like convertibles.

OLIVE: Me, too.

BETTY: We need to live someplace not so fucking cold so that we can drive around in a convertible, like all the time. Wouldn't that be nice? No idiot boys. Just two friends.

OLIVE: But Betty, you tricked me. But we don't do that in Texas. Texas is the friendly state.

BETTY: You're having your ex-boyfriend killed.

OLIVE: So are you. Again. Again!

BETTY: I needed you to get Gus out into the open. He was kind of hiding from me.

OLIVE: You could have just asked.

BETTY: I will next time.

OLIVE: Are we ever going to be happy? Do you think we will ever love someone again and not be broken up with and be happy?

BETTY: All I know is that there's a target on Gus' back. Which is where it should be.

OLIVE: He seems like such a nice guy.

BETTY: He's a hit man.

OLIVE: Still.

BETTY: Olive, he hurt me. He hurt my heart.

OLIVE: I know, Betty.

BETTY: He assassinated my heart.

OLIVE: There, there.

BETTY: I really, really want him dead.

OLIVE: Let him kill my ex first.

BETTY: Okay.


## 22.

*(The dimly lit street, over where GUS and TOR stand, watching the women.)*

GUS: What do you think they're talking about, Tor?

TOR: I don't know, Gus. What do non-Norwegian women talk about?

GUS: I don't know.

*(They watch.)*


## 23.

*(OLIVE has a fantasy moment. It's a dance sequence; specifically, it's a two-step sequence. She may or may not be dressed as a Lunar Princess. She's two-stepping with a shadowy man. This might be on film. The movie that she's in. Music twangs underneath their movements. He spins her. Steps away. The dancing frame between them is*

*broken. The man is distracted by BETTY, who also wears a*
*Princess outfit. One of the two women pulls out a baseball*
*bat from some hiding place in her voluminous skirts. I'm*
*not sure which it is. You pick. She beats the man with the*
*baseball bat until he is flat on the floor, motionless.)*


## 24.

*(Back in the dimly lit street.)*

GUS: I love her.

TOR: Uff da.

GUS: I know. I know.

TOR: Oh, Gus.

GUS: I just—I can't help it.

TOR: You love her so much you want to marry her? *(Pause)* Oh, that's not nice.

GUS: I don't want to—

TOR: Gus.

GUS: You mean, right now? Marry her right now? Today? No.

TOR: The Norwegian High Council will be very displeased.

GUS: The who?

TOR: The Norwegian High Council.

GUS: What are you, on Star Trek?

TOR: What?

GUS: Which are the ones that have a High Council? The Vulcans? The Cardassians? You're something on Star Trek.

TOR: I don't know what you're talking about.

GUS: You've never watched Star Trek?

TOR: I am Norwegian, half-breed.

GUS: Don't be a dick.

TOR: You're the dick, dick.

GUS: I thought the Norwegian High Council didn't like foul language.

TOR: It's your own anatomy.

GUS: True.

TOR: You were a dick to Betty.

GUS: Yes.

TOR: Well, it's good of you to admit it.

GUS: Oh, I mean, I love Betty, I really do, but I was being honest with her about our long-term, about this particular moment and the long term—well, I was just being honest. I'm just not ready for a thing, a permanent thing, you know?

TOR: A permanent thing.

GUS: I mean, I got fucked over in my first marriage. She had an affair. For a long time. I found out and I let her stay. And then she was out mowing the lawn and I took her a lemonade, and she broke down and said I was too nice, she couldn't take it any more. Packed her bags and left.

TOR: Oh, geez, Gus. That's rough. *(Pause)* Why was your wife the one mowing the lawn?

GUS: She was very strong, okay? Big boned. Kind of an Austrian thing. Look, I just I want to sleep with a lot of women now. Plow through their fields. Dominate. You know? It's a fantasy I have, before I risk settling down again.

TOR: Did you find many takers?

GUS: I just got started with the handwritten cards.

TOR: Maybe you just aren't very attractive.

GUS: Uff da, Tor.

TOR: I'm not trying to hurt your feelings.

GUS: No. Of course not.

TOR: It doesn't seem like you're really ready for a thing with me, either. A permanent thing as my business partner.

GUS: You're a nice man, Tor.

TOR: Yes.

GUS: I wish I was as nice as you.

TOR: You're not Norwegian, Gus. Deep down inside, you're something else.

   *(Pause)*

GUS: Yeah. I tried to get my uncle Vigo interested in helping us out, taking on some jobs, but he's got a lot of business as it is building his brand in Madison. Actually, he offered me a gig, there, with him, not just because my mom called in a favor, I had to apply and everything, fill out some forms. Write an essay. Kill a guy. But he said you could keep the red checkered tablecloth as long as you like. Which he didn't think would be very long. He said that he thought "the Norwegians" was a sinking ship. Like, you know, who'd arrange a hit with a strange-looking blue-eyed albino pussy? Those are his words. Not mine. Also, he thinks you have a funny accent. *(Pause)* I am the God of Thunder.

> *(He laughs.)*

GUS: You kill me.

TOR: Yeah.

## 26.

> *(GUS holds the bat. He walks up to the plate. Takes his stance. He concentrates. He stares hard. He waits. He swings.)*

## 27.

> *(The red checkered tablecloths. TOR pours a round of elderberry wine.)*

BETTY: He's just not ready for a thing?

TOR: That's what he said.

BETTY: He's just not ready?

OLIVE: Betty.

> *(Pause.)*

BETTY: Well, damn.

OLIVE: I'm so sorry.

BETTY: No. It's okay. It's okay.

OLIVE: It's what? It's not it's not okay, Betty—

BETTY: He's not ready.

OLIVE: I heard what Tor said.

BETTY: Which means he could be. He could be someday. Ready. For a thing.

OLIVE: Um. No. That's not—I don't think that's what that means.

BETTY: I'm going to text him and call it off.

> *(She digs in her purse.)*

OLIVE: You're going to text Gus? But he's out killing my ex. I need him to do that. Kill my ex.

BETTY: I mean the guy. The guy I got.

TOR: To do your hit?

BETTY: The hit guy. The hit man.

TOR: Olive, I really liked it when you used the phrase, Hit Person. That really resonated with me. So welcoming.

OLIVE: Thank you, Tor.

TOR: So you are still feeling okay about your decision?

OLIVE: Betty promised to let Gus go through with my job first.

BETTY: I know. I know.

OLIVE: How long will it be?

TOR: Any minute.

OLIVE: And then—What.

TOR: I hope you'll be happy with the results.

OLIVE: I hope so, too. Do you think it's possible?

TOR: Customer satisfaction is very important.

BETTY: I can't find the—the—Where is the damn card?

TOR: Who'd you go with?

BETTY: I can't remember his name. Swiss. He's Swiss.

TOR: Very prompt, the Swiss.

BETTY: If I could find his damn card—

TOR: Then you could rescue Gus and avert tragedy and then what?

BETTY: Then what?

TOR: Wait around for him to be ready?

OLIVE: Tor, telling Betty about Gus just not being ready yet—It gave her hope.

TOR: That was mean, wasn't it.

OLIVE: Yes. Yes, it was. It was very mean.

TOR: I'm sorry, Betty. I apologize.

OLIVE: You are so nice.

TOR: You think so?

BETTY: The business card. The business card. Where did I? God damn it, Olive, did you put it somewhere?

OLIVE: Me?

BETTY: When you were digging around in there at the bar.

*(TOR's cell phone buzzes.)*

TOR: A text from Gus.

OLIVE: It's done?

BETTY: Fuck!

---

*C. Denby Swanson*

TOR: Olive. Congratulations.

OLIVE: Oh. Oh. Oh, god.

TOR: How do you feel?

OLIVE: Great. I feel I feel kind of shitty actually. Wait, what am I supposed to feel? Great. Great. It's what I wanted, right? I feel awesome. Liberated. I feel terrible. Like a really bad person. Why didn't I do this before? God, it's like a vortex. It's like a great big vortex of I don't know. I don't know how I feel. I don't know how to describe myself now. Am I happy? Is this happy? I'm a scorned heartbroken conspiratorial murderer. It's so big so dangerous so mythological. Pleased, maybe, kind of pleased. Electric. If I had to pick one word? I guess I'd say Texan.

TOR: Texan?

BETTY: I thought Texans were bullshitters. This was not a bullshitter move. Assassination. Not bullshit.

OLIVE: No. Oh, no. Because I'm like the cheerleader's mom. Remember her? They made a TV show, it was like I'm like the astronaut who who drove across the country to kill her lover's girlfriend wearing adult diapers so that she wouldn't have to stop to pee. I'm a cowboy, a cheerleader, and an astronaut. And a TV show! I'm finally a real Texan. Betty, how did you describe yourself after killing an ex for the first time?

BETTY: I don't know. That's when I met Gus. Everything sort of slid sideways for a minute, and I don't really remember anything else until the Italian restaurant.

OLIVE: I made a vow. A sacred vow.

TOR: You must feel so empowered.

OLIVE: Yes! And sad, too. Of course. A little.

TOR: So you are free now, Olive, you are free to find your someone else.

OLIVE: My what?

TOR: Your someone else.

*(Beat)*

OLIVE: I still don't get it.

TOR: There's someone else for everybody.

OLIVE: You mean there's someone for everybody.

TOR: No.

OLIVE: He was he was my someone.

TOR: And now he's dead. Gus just killed him.

OLIVE: I know. I paid him to. I paid the Norwegians to kill my kill my

TOR: Here, have some wine.

*(She does.)*

Olive, it might be a good moment to think about the next person in your life.

OLIVE: Next?

TOR: Your next great love. Your next partner.

OLIVE: Oh my god, he's dead. He's actually—

TOR: Drink.

*(She does.)*

BETTY: I had his card. I had his business card. I had it. I just had it.

TOR: The Swiss was going to do your job after Gus did Olive's, right Betty?

BETTY: Yes. Yes.

TOR: They are very prompt.

BETTY: I know. They were my second choice the first time. I should have fucking gone with them, lesson learned. I mean, the Swiss, he was, like, no questions, you know, he didn't ask why. He didn't need to have any other data. He didn't flirt. He didn't cause trouble. No weird romantic subtext, it didn't even matter to him if my tits were nice. He was just, you know, Swiss. Those people are like their own trains.

TOR: We can all learn from the Swiss.

BETTY: I told you, Olive, that this was a bad idea. Didn't I? I did. In the bar. I said it, I said, Killing your ex is a bad idea. And it is. It is. It is a terrible, terrible, terrible idea.

OLIVE: What would you do instead, forgive him? Would you forgive him?

*(BETTY holds back a big wracking sob.)*

BETTY: Yes.

*(OLIVE erupts.)*

OLIVE: I WILL NEVER FORGIVE MY EX BOYFRIEND. NEVER NEVER NEVER NEVER NEVER NEVER NOT EVEN NOW THAT HE'S DEAD. He was a cusp. You know what that is? He was on the cusp of Cancer and and whatever that next one is. You know sort of one foot in each sign. Like me. I was a cusp, too. Taurus/Aries. But no longer. He's dead and I'm a—

*(She sips her wine.)*

OLIVE: Wait. Is this elderberry, Tor? It tastes different.

TOR: It's a Pinot.

OLIVE: Oh. Weird. Norwegians drink Pinot?

TOR: There's someone else for you, Olive, just like there is some other wine for me.

BETTY: I loved a Norwegian. I just have to say it. I loved him. I did. Gus. A Norwegian. Part Norwegian. Whatever. I loved him with all my heart. My Kentucky heart. And it's not okay. It's not okay. My relationship track record. Hiring the first hit man. Falling in love with him. Hiring the second hit man. Scandinavia just in general. Seducing Olive to help me—

OLIVE: Seducing what?

BETTY: Seduction, like friend flirting. Haven't you ever done that? I mean, you walked in to that bar and it was, target acquired. You were made.

OLIVE: Me? Honey, I made you.

TOR: Thinking like an assassin, Olive.

OLIVE: Assassin. Assassinator. Assassinette. Assassin person.

BETTY: Assassin has two asses in it. Both of us. Ass Ass In. Even though, when it comes down to it, Olive, I actually do think we're good friends. Like a southern thing: Kentucky, Texas. You know, southern girls, we could run off together and have misadventures. Use my horse. After I save Gus from the Swiss guy.

OLIVE: That would be nice.

BETTY: Whatever the hell his name was. Sven? Lars?

*(She dumps the whole purse.)*

TOR: It may seem impossible right now that there's someone else, Olive. But you'll find him. I have faith. You'll find someone else. Someone kind. Someone loyal. Someone true.

OLIVE: There's no someone else for me. I mean, that's a nice thought. But my ex, I think he was the one person. He was it.

TOR: He was the wrong person.

OLIVE: I know.

TOR: You Texans are tragic. Almost as tragic as Norwegians. Are all your movies black and white and sad and cold?

OLIVE: A lot of our movies are about the wide open the nothing and the heat. It's really hot. And trying to get away and not being able to even in a place that's just wide open and nothing. Still can't escape. Die trying. Like Butch Cassidy and the Sundance Kid.

BETTY: They died in Bolivia. Not Texas, Bolivia.

OLIVE: Still. That's why we're so religious. We're being punished by God Like, all the time. Also, we like to shoot things.

TOR: The western was actually invented by Norwegians.

BETTY: Olive, help me find this fucking business card.

OLIVE: Okay.

*(She joins BETTY in the archeology dig of the purse contents.)*

I just don't believe there could be someone else?

TOR: Everybody might have someone, but it goes terribly wrong and then that someone is no longer around. So then you get someone else.

OLIVE: That's kind of profound. Isn't that profound, Betty?

TOR: I overheard it at a party. A couple was comparing divorces.

OLIVE: Oh.

TOR: But they were couples. Different couples than they had been. Coupled differently. But they had coupled back up again. After. After the devastation. I mean, other people. Well, honestly, I have to tell you it was a little confusing. But the point is, Olive, you'll find someone else. You will. Someone who has an innate kindness, a strong set of values, compassion for others. Someone who is worthy of you.

OLIVE: You think that's possible?

TOR: Only in the Midwest.

BETTY: You're getting the hang of that irony thing, Tor.

TOR: All of us, even you will find someone else.

OLIVE: Gus will live. She's going to call off the hit.

TOR: Not without the phone number.

*(He holds up a business card. The missing one. BETTY's cell phone buzzes. It's a text.)*

BETTY: Oh, shit.

*(TOR brings out a wine bottle.)*

TOR: Betty, this is the a bottle of elderberry wine. I made it myself. Please take it as a thank you for your referral.

OLIVE: Tor, you are so sweet.

*End Of Play*

# PALOMA

*Anne García-Romero*

*Paloma* received readings at the
WordBridge Playwrights Laboratory,
the Open Fist Theater,
New Dramatists, the LoNyLa Lab
and the Los Angeles Theatre Center.

*Paloma* won runner up for the
2011 National Latino Playwriting Award
at the
Arizona Theatre Company.

*Paloma* received its world premiere on
20 July, 2012
at the
National Hispanic Cultural Center,
Albuquerque, New Mexico,

produced by Camino Real productions,
Linda López McAlister, producer,

with the following cast:
Ibrahim Ahmed: Abraham Jallad
Paloma Flores: Lena Armstrong
Jared Rabinowitz: Ron Weisberg

Director: Gil Lazier
Scenic and Lighting design: Richard Hogle
Costume design: Jaime Pardo

Special thanks to Juliette Carrillo, Mark Charney, Andres
Del Pozo, Rachel Ely, Nelson Eusebio, Laura Flanagan,
Alan Freeman, Leah C. Gardiner, Irene Meisel, Mahan
Mizra, J Dakota Powell, James Thompson, Chantal
Rodriguez, Elaine Romero, José Luis Valenzuela, Dave
White, Samir Younis, The Institute for Scholarship in
the Liberal Arts, College of Arts and Letters and The
Nanovic Institute at the University of Notre Dame.

**ANNE GARCÍA-ROMERO'S** plays include *Provenance, Earthquake Chica, Mary Peabody in Cuba, Land of Benjamin Franklin, Horsey Girl, Don Quixote de la Minny, Marta's Magnificent Mundo, Desert Longing, Juanita's Statue* and *Santa Concepción.* Her plays have been developed and produced at the New York Shakespeare Festival/Public Theater, The Eugene O'Neill National Playwrights Conference, Arielle Tepper Productions' Summer Play Festival (Off-Broadway), The Mark Taper Forum, Hartford Stage, South Coast Repertory, INTAR, HERE, New Georges, National Hispanic Cultural Center, Borderlands Theater, Nevada Repertory Company, Jungle Theater, East L.A. Repertory, Open Fist Theater Company, Wordbridge Playwrights Laboratory and LoNyLa Writers Lab. She's received commissions from the NYSF/Public Theater, The Mark Taper Forum and South Coast Repertory. She's the U.S. translator for *The Grönholm Method* by Spanish playwright, Jordi Galcerán. She's been a Jerome Fellow at the Playwrights Center of Minneapolis as well as a MacDowell Colony fellow. She holds an MFA in Playwriting from the Yale School of Drama and a Ph.D. in Theater Studies from the University of California, Santa Barbara. She's an Assistant Professor in the Department of Film, Television and Theatre at the University of Notre Dame. She's an alumna of New Dramatists and a Resident Playwright at Chicago Dramatists. www.annegarciaromero.com

*For my parents, José Antonio and Barbara*


CHARACTERS
Ibrahim Ahmed, late twenties
Paloma Flores, late twenties, his girlfriend
Jared Rabinowitz, early thirties, his friend and
            also his attorney

SETTING: 2003-2005. New York City as well as
various cities in Spain.

Note: This play contains excerpts from *Ring of the Dove* by Ibn Hazm, a meditation on love written in 11th century Muslim Spain. The texts are my own English translations of the Spanish.

The scenes in this play must move swiftly between various months from 2003 to 2005. Time shifts can be achieved through minimal lighting, costume and sound design choices. The scene titles could be incorporated as projections or spoken aloud by one of the actors.

Italicized words ought to be pronounced as authentically as possible.

An asterisk (*) indicates an overlap or interruption in the dialogue. The next line should begin when the asterisk appears.

# 1. THE SIGNS OF THE EYES.

*NEW YORK CITY. SEPTEMBER 6, 2004. EVENING. IBRA-*
*HIM AND JARED IN IBRAHIM'S STUDIO APARTMENT.*

IBRAHIM: I want to feast my eyes on the curve of her hip.

JARED: I need you to focus.

IBRAHIM: I want to wink at the grin on her face.

JARED: I really need you to try.

IBRAHIM: I want to caress the nape of her neck.

JARED: The trial will go a lot easier if*

IBRAHIM: But all I can see is . . . twisted metal . . . smoke . . . flesh . . . blood.

JARED: We need to prep this.

IBRAHIM: I'm not talking to anyone.

JARED: Not an option.

IBRAHIM: My eyes. I can't bear to see it behind my fuckin' eyes, man. Not again. You down with that?

JARED: Ah . . . no I'm not . . . ah . . . down . . . with that.

IBRAHIM: Fuck. Off.

JARED: Tell me in pieces. Fragments. Bits. I'm not asking for like hours of testimony here.

IBRAHIM: Fragments? Bits? Really?

JARED: Come on. You know what I mean. You see . . .

IBRAHIM: Glaucoma. I've developed glaucoma along with amnesia. Tell the court that.

JARED: Ah . . . no. *(beat)* Come on, Abe . . .

IBRAHIM: Ibrahim.

JARED: You'll need to drop that.

IBRAHIM: So you want my name to be like John or some shit?

JARED: Go back to your nickname. Your childhood name. Abe.

IBRAHIM: Not happening.

JARED: The nick name you used your entire life until you arrived at NYU and took like some fuckin' cultural studies class and got in touch with your roots or whatever.

IBRAHIM: I'm not changing my birth name.

JARED: Do you want my professional help?

IBRAHIM: I don't know. Do I? *(beat)* So the other night I'm on the six train and I get off at Lexington and there's this guy pissing on the tracks and like no one reacts.

JARED: Just focus for a few minutes.

IBRAHIM: Or I'm on the one train and I get off at Christopher Street . . .

JARED: Abe. Dude.

IBRAHIM: And like this dude is shouting at someone, "Don't you touch my fuckin' hand" and the people just keep on going and ignore his sorry ass.

JARED: You can't ignore this law suit.

IBRAHIM: Got any smokes?

JARED: You smoke now?

IBRAHIM: And?

JARED: Isn't that like against your religion or something?

IBRAHIM: Not anymore.

JARED: So what . . . now you're like an atheist?

IBRAHIM: Whatever. Seriously, do you have any?

JARED: I quit. Trying to get back into shape, you know?

IBRAHIM: Smokes. Need them. Now.

JARED: Later. If we don't prep for this, they get the upper hand.

IBRAHIM: Jared, look, I can't*

JARED: Look, I understand this is*

IBRAHIM: You don't understand shit.

JARED: Let's just start with . . . like how you met.

IBRAHIM: Smokes. Need 'em. Now.

*LIGHTS SHIFT.*

## 2. On the essence of love.

*ONE YEAR EARLIER. SEPTEMBER 22, 2003. EARLY EVENING. IBRAHIM AND PALOMA STUDY IN THE NEW YORK UNIVERSITY LIBRARY. THEY READ TO EACH OTHER.*

PALOMA: *(reading)* Love, may God honor you, begins with riddles and ends in truth

IBRAHIM: *(reading)* and because it is sublime, its subtle definition cannot be deciphered

PALOMA: *(reading)* nor its essence understood without generous determination.

IBRAHIM: *(reading)* We know that the essence of attraction or the separation between created things arises from the affinity or repulsion between them.

PALOMA: *(reading)* In sum, love is a rebellious illness.

IBRAHIM: *(reading)* Whose medicine exists within itself, if we know how to treat it.

PALOMA: *(reading)* But it's a delicious illness and an appetizing sickness. Those who don't have it curse their health.

IBRAHIM: *(reading)* Those who have it don't want to find a cure.

*A FEW AWKWARD BEATS.*

PALOMA: And so apparently *Ibn Hazm* had it goin' on in eleventh century Spain.

IBRAHIM: And so he wrote *Tawq al-Hamamah. El Collar de la . . . Paloma.*

PALOMA: My name.

IBRAHIM: Paloma.

PALOMA: Uh-huh. Means dove. Then there's *Flores*.

IBRAHIM: *Paloma Flores.*

PALOMA: Flowers.

IBRAHIM: *Flores de Paloma.*

PALOMA: Flowers of the Dove. Right here. That's what I'm talkin' about. *(beat)* You have good pronunciation. You speak? *Hablas español?*

IBRAHIM: *Un poco. No mucho. (beat) (re: the book) El Collar de la Paloma.*

PALOMA: Ring of the Dove.

IBRAHIM: *Sí.*

PALOMA: *Ibn Hazm* described rules.

IBRAHIM: On how to love.

PALOMA: Kickass rules.

IBRAHIM: Do they still apply?

PALOMA: I think they just might.

IBRAHIM: So are you suggesting we try to . . . apply them.

PALOMA: Is that a come on?

IBRAHIM: Too obvious?

PALOMA: Kinda.

IBRAHIM: Oh.

*AWKWARD BEAT.*

PALOMA: I mean it's not like I'm not into obvious come ons. It's just in this context.

IBRAHIM: Yeah.

PALOMA: In the NYU library.

IBRAHIM: In a study room.

PALOMA: In the afternoon.

IBRAHIM: Early evening, actually.

PALOMA: Study session.

IBRAHIM: Random context, you're right.

PALOMA: Not a bad context, just kinda . . .

IBRAHIM: Random.

PALOMA: Unexpected.

IBRAHIM: Not always a bad thing.

PALOMA: Not always.

IBRAHIM: Could kinda fit with the study partner thing.

PALOMA: Huh?

IBRAHIM: Partner. Couple. Study. Learn. Just you know, different context.

PALOMA: Why're you even taking this class?

IBRAHIM: Attraction to . . .

PALOMA: Okay . . .

IBRAHIM: To this subject matter for my Masters . . . .

PALOMA: Because . . .

IBRAHIM: I so dig that period and location in history . . . in light of you know . . . now.

PALOMA: You mean like all the residual anxiety and antagonism in the atmosphere hovering over our entire society?

IBRAHIM: Ah . . . there is that. *(beat)* And you?

PALOMA: I wanted this course for my Masters . . . in World History . . . and this one covers transnational themes so . . . yeah . . . ancient Muslim Spain.

IBRAHIM: *Al-Andalus.*

PALOMA: Eight hundred years.

IBRAHIM: Three religions.

PALOMA: Islam . . .

IBRAHIM: Christianity . . .

PALOMA: Judaism . . . *La convivencia.*

IBRAHIM: Co-existing peacefully. Right. Exactly. I mean . . . yeah. And plus there are definite benefits.

PALOMA: To . . .

IBRAHIM: Taking this class . . .

PALOMA: And they are . . .

*IBRAHIM POINTS TO PALOMA*

PALOMA: Ah . . .

IBRAHIM: Yeah.

PALOMA: There is that.

*LIGHTS SHIFT.*

## 3. Guarding of the secret.

*SEPTEMBER 6, 2004. SAME EVENING. A FEW MOMENTS LATER. IBRAHIM AND JARED IN IBRAHIM'S STUDIO APARTMENT.*

JARED: So you never planned to tell your parents about Paloma?

IBRAHIM: My parents? *(beat)* At first, I was like, "No way. Never."

JARED: Never.

IBRAHIM: I knew how they were going to react. If I brought her there, they would seriously flip and she'd be like, "See ya'".

JARED: So you kept your relationship with her a secret.

IBRAHIM: I mean look, I knew my pop would completely freak and get all up in my face and be all, *(with slight Moroccan accent) "Ibrahim.* This is forbidden. Stop. Now."

JARED: Because she was not Muslim.

IBRAHIM: I mean, when my sister, Hailey . . . Halimah . . . snuck off to a Christian bible camp with her high school friends, she got home and my father hit her on the head with a *Qur'an*, repeatedly.

JARED: And you were concerned he'd be violent with you?

IBRAHIM: You've never experienced the wrath of my father.

JARED: No, but my dad's a pretty intense dude.

IBRAHIM: Your dad's chill compared to my pop.

JARED: Uh . . . chill? Not so much.

IBRAHIM: When we were at that posh restaurant . . . after your law school graduation . . . he's all relaxed and chill.

JARED: That day was the exception. Get him fired up about just about anything and chill is not the word. You do not want to cross him.

IBRAHIM: But your parents aren't as religious as mine are.

JARED: My dad only goes to synagogue on the high holidays but my grandfather . . .

IBRAHIM: So you're thinking if I told my parents before, we wouldn't have taken the trip but I couldn't . . . so we did.

JARED: That she still might be here if you'd told them right away about her but that wasn't an option.

IBRAHIM: That secret keeping. I had to.

JARED: But did you absolutely have to*

IBRAHIM: I just said, there was no other way*

JARED: Fly with her to Spain? Bullshit.

    *Beat*

IBRAHIM: Are you gonna be that mean to me in court?

JARED: Get used to it. Their attorney's a fuckin' ball buster.

IBRAHIM: So it is all my fault.

JARED: You will not be saying those words at any time on the stand, got that? *(beat)* So then if you couldn't tell your parents, you couldn't be with her here, why not break things off?

IBRAHIM: Being with her made my mind spin, my knees shake, my heart race and my dick hard . . . pretty much full body impact.

JARED: So you get this idea to fly her to Spain.

IBRAHIM: Yes, counselor, I get this idea to fly her to Spain. I get the idea. Like I said, all my fault. You're doing wonders for my defense, by the way.

JARED: It was not all your fault. She fully agreed to go with you on the trip, right?

IBRAHIM: She said, "Dude. We're so jetting there. Climbing those stone streets. Baking in the Andalusian sun."

JARED: Bingo.

    *LIGHTS SHIFT.*

# 4. On the lovers' union.

*TEN MONTHS EARLIER. NOVEMBER 10, 2003. EVE-NING. IBRAHIM'S STUDIO APARTMENT. IBRAHIM AND PALOMA READ TO EACH OTHER.*

PALOMA: *(reading)* One of the aspects of love is the lovers' union which is sublime fortune,

IBRAHIM: *(reading)* Renewed life

PALOMA: *(reading)* Perfect existence

IBRAHIM: *(reading)* Perpetual joy

PALOMA: *(reading)* Great mercy from God. *(beat) (looks up from book)* That's what I'm talkin' about. *(beat)* You religious?

IBRAHIM: Uh. Yeah.

PALOMA: Huh. You pray a lot?

IBRAHIM: Daily.

PALOMA: Really . . .

IBRAHIM: Five times.

PALOMA: Five? Wow. Huh. You don't strike me as . . .

IBRAHIM: A fanatic? I'm not.

PALOMA: I wasn't saying.

IBRAHIM: But you were thinking.

PALOMA: Do religious dudes bring their study partners back to their apartment after dinner to pray?

IBRAHIM: Maybe.

PALOMA: Seriously? We're gonna pray now?

IBRAHIM: That interest you?

PALOMA: Would we be clothed during this praying thing?

IBRAHIM: Ah. That. Well.

*THEY KISS. HE NERVOUSLY PULLS AWAY.*

PALOMA: You've lived in this place how long?

IBRAHIM: Since school started.

PALOMA: Decorate much?

IBRAHIM: Simplicity. Much preferable.

PALOMA: So you're like a monk?

IBRAHIM: You could say.

PALOMA: Seriously?

IBRAHIM: Wanna drink?

PALOMA: Oh. So we're gonna get hammered and then pray . . . in bed?

IBRAHIM: Not that kind of drink and we're not praying . . . in bed.

PALOMA: You don't drink or fuck?

IBRAHIM: If you wanna put it that way . . . no.

PALOMA: Not even a little?

IBRAHIM: Actually . . . no.

PALOMA: Purist.

IBRAHIM: You could say.

PALOMA: Religious reasons?

IBRAHIM: You down with that?

PALOMA: I mean, I was raised Catholic but I'm not that religious. And I dig the occasional cocktail and the frequent fuck, not necessarily in that order. So . . .

IBRAHIM: So you pray?

PALOMA: On Christmas. Easter. And when I'm really stressed.

IBRAHIM: Ah.

PALOMA: I dig that you do though.

IBRAHIM: Okay.

PALOMA: Really.

*THEY ALMOST KISS AGAIN BUT HE PULLS AWAY.*

PALOMA: What does your name mean?

IBRAHIM: *Ibrahim.* Father of a multitude. *Ahmed.* Highly praised.

PALOMA: As in you'll have thirteen kids or you'll be a highly praised leader of the people?

IBRAHIM: What do you think?

PALOMA: I'm intrigued is what I think.

IBRAHIM: We should go there.

PALOMA: Where?

IBRAHIM: *Ibn Hazm*-land.

PALOMA: Eleventh century Spain?

IBRAHIM: Cheap internet flight. Cheap internet hotel.

PALOMA: What. Now we're eloping or something?

IBRAHIM: Ah. Well . . .

PALOMA: And then we eventually get married and have thirteen kids?

IBRAHIM: Fourteen, perhaps?

PALOMA: Um. Okay. That wasn't a proposal by the way.

IBRAHIM: Okay . . .

*Anne García-Romero*

PALOMA: Dude. We're so jetting there. Climbing those stone
    streets. Baking in the Andalusian sun.

IBRAHIM: From your mouth to god's ears.

PALOMA: So . . . now . . . are we prayin'?

*THEY KISS AGAIN.*

*LIGHTS SHIFT.*

## 5. DIVULGING THE SECRET.

*SEPTEMBER 6, 2004. SAME EVENING. AN HOUR LATER. IBRAHIM AND JARED IN IBRAHIM'S STUDIO APARTMENT.*

IBRAHIM: So, I eventually called my father.

JARED: When?

IBRAHIM: That morning.

JARED: The morning you planned to travel from Madrid to Granada?

*IBRAHIM NODS.*

JARED: What time did you call?

IBRAHIM: One thirty a.m. Madrid time. Seven thirty p.m. New York time.

JARED: Why that day?

IBRAHIM: Paloma inspired me.

JARED: She did? Or threatened you?

IBRAHIM: At that point, Granada was in our sights. I could picture us walking beneath the intricately carved sandstone walls by the Patio of the Lions, strolling down the fountain walkways in gardens of the *Generalife*. Total inspiration.

JARED: You called him from the hotel?

IBRAHIM: I needed some space so I left the hotel, walked around for a while and then decided to take the Metro to *Sol*. I walked out of the station and up the stairs of this internet and phone place. I paid five euros for booth six and dialed, knowing my pop would be home, watching some shit on the History channel.

JARED: You left Paloma in the hotel room. Alone . . .

IBRAHIM: Yeah. We'd had this intense talk.

JARED: A fight?

IBRAHIM: More like a heated discussion. About belief and . . . stuff. And I needed some space so I went out for a walk and decided to call my father.

JARED: This wasn't like a fight where you were telling her she had to go to Granada?

IBRAHIM: No. So. I sat in that booth sweating, my stomach turning, my intestines cramping, my bladder aching, fight or flight, you know? . . . and that fucking phone kept ringing and ringing.

JARED: But he picked up.

IBRAHIM: Eventually. And I'm like, "Yo, pop." And he's like, *(with slight Moroccan accent)* "What the hell are you doing calling me at one thirty in the morning in Madrid?" And I'm like, "I wanted to chat with you." And then I'm starting to sound like I'm real nervous, you know?

JARED: And then you told him?

IBRAHIM: Not yet. At first I was like talking small talk and shit and I knew my pop was getting pissed. *(with slight Moroccan accent)* "What, you run out of money?" And I'm like, "No, pop. I . . . I met someone." And he's like, *(with slight Moroccan accent)* "You get a girl pregnant and I'll kick your ass." And I'm like, "Pop. Her name is Paloma." And he's like, *(with slight Moroccan accent)* "You meet a nice Muslim girl with a Spanish name?" And I'm like, "She's nice. She has a Spanish name. But . . . "

JARED: She's not Muslim.

IBRAHIM: And he's like, *(with slight Moroccan accent)* "What about *Sharzad*?"

JARED: Who?

IBRAHIM: This woman at the mosque my father wanted me to marry.

JARED: Okay . . .

IBRAHIM: And I'm like, "Pop. I'm not seeing her anymore." And he's like, *(with slight Moroccan accent)* "Your mother and I know." And then my stomach starts to fuckin' ache and I have to shit real bad and I'm like fuck, I know that tone in his voice. He's like, *(with slight Moroccan accent)* "She called us three days ago. She told us you went to Madrid with your new girlfriend. She told us her name is Paloma. She told us she is Christian." And he proceeded to cuss me out real rapid fire in Arabic, you know. I didn't know shit what he was saying but the energy was serious and I was like fuck.

JARED: And that's why you didn't tell him before you left?

IBRAHIM: And then in like his intense English he says things like, *(with slight Moroccan accent)* "You know, God will punish you for your sins and our family's reputation is ruined."

JARED: Has he ever come around?

IBRAHIM: Absolutely not.

JARED: Damn.

IBRAHIM: That was the last time I spoke to him. The last time I'll probably ever speak to him.

JARED: Shit.

IBRAHIM: So he hung up on me and I sat there in that booth and I cried. I fuckin' cried. Then I ducked into their bathroom and they have those kind that are like little rooms, you get your own little room, and I sat there and like heaved.

JARED: So your father doesn't know about everything that's happened?

IBRAHIM: He knows. My mother's seen me since I've been back. I talk to her on the phone.

JARED: So I can't even call him?

IBRAHIM: He won't answer your questions.

JARED: And this is like a forever deal? Having him testify could seriously bolster our case at this point . . .

IBRAHIM: Fuckin' forget it. This shit runs so deep, it's like this unconscious parasite that burrows in his brain and no matter how much you try to perform psychic surgery on his head this shit is lethal.

JARED: Do you think he talked to family members about it? Could I contact any uncles?

IBRAHIM: Forget it.

JARED: Aunts?

IBRAHIM: Nope.

JARED: Your mother?

IBRAHIM: Doubt it.

JARED: Your imam?

IBRAHIM: Not at this point. Fuckin' Sharzad's probably told everyone who goes to the mosque by now. I don't know how she found out.

JARED: You didn't want her to find out?

IBRAHIM: I didn't care but I didn't think she'd fuckin' try to ruin my life.

JARED: I guess that means Sharzad's out?

IBRAHIM: Ah . . . yeah. *(beat)* And you know the next morning, Paloma told me she wrote me some letter like while I was out that night at the phone place . . . but she wanted to wait to give it to me in Granada.

JARED: But she never told you what was in the letter?

IBRAHIM: And I didn't ask. I should've asked her to give it to me then but I couldn't. At that point, all I wanted to do was to get us to Granada. *(beat)* Do you know every night before I go to sleep I try to remember the feeling of having Paloma beside me in that hotel bed in Madrid? For like ten seconds I squish my eyeballs so hard in their sockets they burn until I can get like a millisecond of a taste of that feeling. I try every fuckin' night and each second the taste gets fainter and fainter until the feeling disappears altogether.

JARED: Right. *(beat)* So. In the absence of that letter and in light of the fact that the attorney for the other side is gonna to try to decimate your credibility, I'm still gonna need to build a list of character witnesses.

*LIGHTS SHIFT.*

# 6. On those who fall in love in dreams.

*NINE MONTHS EARLIER. DECEMBER 3, 2003. EVE-NING. IBRAHIM AND PALOMA IN IBRAHIM'S STUDIO APARTMENT.*

IBRAHIM: So I'm in this large desert-like space and it's sunset and there are these weird creeping critters on the ground like a cross between a scorpion and a snake and they start to try to wrap around my ankle and then you run up to me but your eyes are like zombie-eyes and your face is pale and your dress is torn and your hair is wild and I say your name but you look at me like you don't know who I am and one of those motherfuckers bites my pinky toe and you rush away and I turn to follow you but I fall down because my toe is like swelling and when I hit the sand it gives way and I descend into the earth and as I'm like falling through the earth I see you falling next to me and we're like encased in separate glass bubbles and falling like a speeding elevator race and you look ravishing yet sad and you mouth "I love you" and I bang on the glass but no sound comes out and then your glass bubble elevator thing zooms away into the earth and mine stops and slowly the oxygen runs out and I gasp for air and I wake up.

PALOMA: Dream much?

IBRAHIM: They're usually not that . . . vivid

PALOMA: Or spooky.

IBRAHIM: Any grand interpretations?

PALOMA: What would *Ibn Hazm* say?

*THEY FLIP THROUGH THEIR BOOKS SEARCHING FOR A PAGE.*

IBRAHIM: Ah . . . here. This one. *(beat)* Page one hundred and twenty three. *(reading)* One day I went to see my friend and I found him pensive and distressed. I asked him what was wrong and he said,

PALOMA: *(reading)* The strangest thing you've ever heard.

IBRAHIM: *(reading)* Which is . . .

PALOMA: *(reading)* "Last night I dreamt of a woman and upon waking, I noticed that my heart had fallen for her and I was helplessly in love with her. I'm in the saddest state because of this love."

*Anne García-Romero*

IBRAHIM: *(reading)* This went on for a month until I said, "Not even God can forgive you for what you're thinking about, obsessing about something that doesn't exist, that isn't real. Do you even know who she is?"

PALOMA: *(reading)* "By God, I do not."

IBRAHIM: *(reading)* "With your weak judgment and blind understanding, you love someone you've never seen, who's never been created nor walked this earth. You'd be more forgivable, in my eyes, if you'd fallen in love with one of the women in the murals on the bathhouse wall."

PALOMA: Well that doesn't apply so much here. Unless the woman in your dream wasn't me.

IBRAHIM: It was you but it wasn't you.

PALOMA: I'm not crazy about the fact that we never really connect and go zooming through the earth in glass bubble thingies. Then you suffocate? Do I suffocate you?

IBRAHIM: No.

PALOMA: Not even a little?

IBRAHIM: Paloma . . . .

PALOMA: And it's intense that he writes, "Not even God can forgive you for what you're thinking about . . . " That's kind of harsh.

IBRAHIM: Some people view God that way.

PALOMA: Do you?

IBRAHIM: On the whole, no. But sometimes . . .

PALOMA: Maybe he's being hyperbolic? *(beat)* Do your friends at the mosque view God that way?

IBRAHIM: Hard to know.

    *AWKWARD BEAT.*

PALOMA: Can I come with you?

IBRAHIM: Where?

PALOMA: The mosque.

IBRAHIM: If . . . you want.

PALOMA: You say that like I'm not gonna wanna set foot anywhere near a mosque.

IBRAHIM: You'll have to observe from the back or sit in the women's area.

PALOMA: They have a women's area?

IBRAHIM: Men and women pray separately.

PALOMA: Right.

IBRAHIM: And it's best if you wear long sleeves and a head-scarf, if you have one.

PALOMA: Done.

IBRAHIM: You really want to visit my mosque?

PALOMA: I need to know more.

IBRAHIM: About . . .

PALOMA: The faith that keeps us apart.

IBRAHIM: Does my faith keep us apart?

PALOMA: Not in all ways, but in some . . . well . . . .tangible ways.

IBRAHIM: Yeah. Right. That.

PALOMA: I mean, listen, I think it's not a bad idea to go slow, you know. I rarely do. It's like one-two-three leap into bed, go nuts for each other, and then all bets are off.

IBRAHIM: I didn't realize it'd be . . . I mean I thought maybe it wouldn't be so bad to go slow . . . you know?

PALOMA: Like I said, it's not a bad idea . . . just different than my usual. *(beat) (rapid-fire)* Okay-I-totally-wanna-have-sex-with-you. *(beat)* There. It's out there. Moving on, now.

IBRAHIM: And you think I don't?

PALOMA: Hard to tell.

IBRAHIM: Well. I. do. Just. Not. Yet.

PALOMA: Yet. That. Right.

IBRAHIM: Come to the prayer service on Friday. I just won't be able to talk to you.

PALOMA: You'll be with the men.

IBRAHIM: And I just can't risk anyone seeing us talking or anything.

PALOMA: Seriously? I mean I can't just walk up to you and be all, "Yo Ibrahim, whassup sucka?"

IBRAHIM: Seriously. *(beat)* I'd rather keep it that way for now. For our sake.

*LIGHTS SHIFT.*

*Anne Garcia-Romero*

## 7. On betrayal.

*SEPTEMBER 8, 2004. EARLY AFTERNOON. IBRA-HIM AND JARED OUTSIDE A MOSQUE IN LOWER MANHATTAN.*

JARED: What time does the service let out?

IBRAHIM: I don't know. Soon.

JARED: So we'll just go into the mosque, you'll introduce me to some of your bros, we'll see if any of them will want to testify on your behalf.

IBRAHIM: This is so wrong.

JARED: Why is it wrong? Your family's out of town. And we can't even ask your family anyway. You had like no other real friends at NYU except for Paloma. The other friends you had were from here.

IBRAHIM: No one'll betray the elders by talking to you.

JARED: What do you mean betray?

IBRAHIM: I'm a bad role model for these guys. The elder brothers have probably warned the younger brothers about hanging out with me. I mean I haven't heard from any of them since I got back.

JARED: How badly do you want to win this case?

IBRAHIM: Right at this moment? I don't know. Badly. Yeah.

JARED: Bad enough to feel awkward and embarrassed for a few minutes? I mean, come on, no one here is gonna go all extremist on us or anything.

IBRAHIM: When exactly did the perception of my faith get so inextricably linked with extremism?

JARED: Every faith has had their extremist elements in history. The crusades for one. Not the most Christian activity . . . that pillaging and murdering thing.

IBRAHIM: It's just we're total pacifists in this community. But the ignorance around us is staggering. People go into this blind hysteria.

JARED: That's why I need to get at least a couple of your friends here to testify . . . to break out of the stereotypical bullshit that the prosecution will probably pull.

IBRAHIM: I mean sometimes I used to wander around down here after evening prayers . . . lower Manhattan can be eerily quiet at night . . . and I would just silently meditate while I walked, you know? And then sometimes I'd go down there . . . and look at the emptiness of that hallowed, tower-less ground . . . and pray harder for those thousands of souls. Pay my respects, you know?

JARED: We could use that. That's good. They won't expect that coming from you.

IBRAHIM: What's that supposed to mean?

JARED: Listen, their attorney might try to play up some preconceived notions. Anything we can do to illuminate otherwise.

IBRAHIM: Surreal. The layers of betrayal.

JARED: I gotta be realistic here, dude.

IBRAHIM: I mean when people respond that way with those preconceived notions or some shit and like it feels like all fucking humanity is betraying me . . . .that social contract that says we are all created equal in these here fifty states . . . yeah . . . uh . . . .right.

JARED: Maybe you should drop the Masters in Islamic Studies and consider a JD. Wanna study Con law, perhaps?

IBRAHIM: Then family and friends betray me because they think I betrayed them and they have these preconceived notions of what happened and who Paloma was.

JARED: So can we go in and meet some of these betrayers? Please?

IBRAHIM: Expect nothing. The service ends in five minutes.

JARED: So then we'll go in that door?

IBRAHIM: You'll have to take off your shoes when you get inside. You can store them in the little shelves against the wall. But I gotta head out.

JARED: Ah . . . no you don't. You need to introduce me to*

IBRAHIM: You can ask around yourself. Alright?

JARED: Did you always plan not to go in there?

IBRAHIM: I gotta . . . doctor's appointment.

JARED: You so don't have a fucking doctor's appointment. Why won't you walk in there with me?

IBRAHIM: Because on some level I betrayed my community too, alright? Not by being with a non-Muslim woman but acting in a way that was not worthy of my faith . . . lacking in courage, honor, respect, et cetera. And I don't really feel like facing that right now, okay? Is that fucking okay with you?

*LIGHTS SHIFT.*

# 8. On verbal allusions.

*SEVEN MONTHS EARLIER. FEBRUARY 25, 2004.*
*NIGHT. IBRAHIM AND PALOMA IN WASHINGTON*
*SQUARE PARK.*

PALOMA: So we can't hold hands?

IBRAHIM: I'd rather not.

PALOMA: Really.

IBRAHIM: Yeah.

PALOMA: What, the PDA police are gonna show up and like arrest us?

IBRAHIM: NYPD? What?

PALOMA: PDA. Public display of affection?

IBRAHIM: There's like an ocean of love in my heart for you and I just can't risk that being taken away from me by any judgment.

PALOMA: Who's judging you?

IBRAHIM: You never know who you might see.

PALOMA: We're in fuckin' Washington Square Park at like fuckin' ten o'clock at night. Really?

IBRAHIM: Really.

PALOMA: Wow.

*AWKWARD BEAT.*

IBRAHIM: Watch out for that . . .

*IBRAHIM STEERS PALOMA CLEAR OF WALKING ON*
*DOG SHIT.*

PALOMA: Thanks. See right there. Even in my pissed off state, you're looking out for me so I don't step in a pile of dogshit. Wow. I'm so not used to kindness.

IBRAHIM: What kinds of dudes have you been in a relationship with?

PALOMA: We're in a relationship now?

IBRAHIM: Answer my question.

PALOMA: Don't poke me with your elbow.

IBRAHIM: You don't want my elbow?

PALOMA: Your elbow is pointy and cold. Your hand is soft and warm.

IBRAHIM: Answer my question.

PALOMA: Domineering men. Dramatic men. Artistic men. Comedic men. But in the end, they are mostly just sad and mean men. I tend to be attracted to heartless men.

IBRAHIM: And I'm not heartless.

PALOMA: I know. *(facetious)* So you're saying then that I'm
attracted to you?

IBRAHIM: Seems so.

PALOMA: Seems?

IBRAHIM: Is. Are.

PALOMA: Okay.

IBRAHIM: Here.

    *HE GIVES HER HIS HAND.*

PALOMA: Just your pinky.

IBRAHIM: Really.

PALOMA: Pinky link on the down-low.

IBRAHIM: Word.

    *A BEAT.*

PALOMA: So how's it lookin' for the . . . ?

IBRAHIM: The . . .

PALOMA: You know, the . . .

IBRAHIM: Right.

PALOMA: We can say it out loud, you know.

IBRAHIM: I know.

PALOMA: But we can't talk about "it" on the street?

IBRAHIM: Right.

PALOMA: Really?

IBRAHIM: Really.

PALOMA: *(loudly)* Yo, people of New York City, listen up,
Ibrahim and Paloma are gonna . . .

| PALOMA: *(simultaneous)* | IBRAHIM: *(simultaneous)* |
|---|---|
| *(loud)* have sex! | *(louder)* go on a trip! |

PALOMA: We're calling it a trip, now? Really?

IBRAHIM: No, really. We're taking a trip. To . . . *Ibn Hazm*-land.

PALOMA: Serious?

IBRAHIM: Spring break. We're so jetting there.

PALOMA: Andalusian sun here we come?

IBRAHIM: Uh-huh.

PALOMA: For real? And I mean you want to cross the proverbial
threshold over there . . . .

IBRAHIM: In Madrid. Toledo. Granada. Yeah.

PALOMA: Oh yeah.

    *LIGHTS SHIFT.*

*Anne García-Romero*

## 9. ON THOSE, WHO HAVING LOVED,
### CAN NEVER LOVE ANY OTHER.

*SEPTEMBER 20, 2004. MORNING. IBRAHIM AND JARED IN WASHINGTON SQUARE PARK. IBRAHIM SMOKES. JARED STANDS BY HIM.*

IBRAHIM: I wanna yell at priests.

JARED: Your anger is understandable but find another way to . . .

IBRAHIM: I wanna scream at rabbis.

JARED: Please don't.

IBRAHIM: I wanna shout at imams.

JARED: Bad idea.

IBRAHIM: This is fucked.

JARED: And just promise me you won't say those things on the stand.

IBRAHIM: Pigeons suck. Why are there so many goddamned pigeons in this city? Did you know the Spanish word for pigeon is the same word for dove. Paloma? Her name? She was not a fucking pigeon alright. She was a dove. A gleaming dove. Do you hear that you fucking flying rats?

JARED: Dude. Dial it down.

IBRAHIM: I don't wanna dial it down. I can scream at the top of my lungs if I want to in this crazy ass park.

JARED: Yeah, well, if you keep screaming at the top of your lungs in crazy ass Washington Square park that you want to verbally assault religious leaders, you might have to spend the night in a holding cell and I don't want to represent you for a misdemeanor as well.

IBRAHIM: I'm not like those militant dudes on the corner of Broadway who are like yelling at people.

JARED: I realize that.

*A BEAT.*

IBRAHIM: Her hair man, I will never touch her hair again, that long, soft, silky, mixture between ebony and chestnut and like like auburn in a certain light.

JARED: Look, Sharon said you can stay with us tonight, if you want.

IBRAHIM: Sharon? Who the fuck is Sharon?

JARED: We moved in . . .

IBRAHIM: You quit smoking. You work out. You meet some girl at a bar on Lafayette street and you're shackin' up now? Damn.

JARED: I get that this is an extremely hard day for you.

IBRAHIM: You don't get shit.

JARED: Look, I'm taking your case for free, dude.

IBRAHIM: Oh, so it's about money now? You resent that I can't pay you?

JARED: No. Look. Let's just catch a cab.

IBRAHIM: I'm not staying with you and bar girl number five tonight. I'm not. Alright?

JARED: Fine. Just chill.

IBRAHIM: I don't want to chill.

JARED: Well then find yourself another attorney.

*A BEAT.*

IBRAHIM: Look, man I'm sorry I . . .

JARED: It's okay, I . . .

*AWKWARD BEAT.*

IBRAHIM: Would you like keep me in your prayers? I mean I don't know if you even go to like synagogue any more or temple or whatever but like if you do, or if you know someone who does, can you like have them pray something for me?

JARED: Sure.

IBRAHIM: I can't walk in there today and face her parents. If I see Paloma's mother and she has that same gorgeous long hair and I . . . I may go off and then that would suck and then . . . Promise me I won't see her mother.

JARED: I can't promise you anything. But I will keep you informed. Breathe.

IBRAHIM: She was a dove, man. A sign of fuckin' peace, alright? *(beat)* Like Noah and the ark and that dove, man.

JARED: Come on . . .

IBRAHIM: Not like these damn pigeons, signs of fuckin' shit. *(beat)* More like that dove that flies over the water back to the ark, you know? *(beat)* Right, you probably don't even remember that part of the story.

JARED: I learned a thing or two in Hebrew school back in the day.

IBRAHIM: But so if she's the dove, am I Noah or the ark or one of those sorry ass animals all cramped up in that wooden piece of shit boat? Huh?

JARED: I don't know. Come on. Let's go.

IBRAHIM: Yeah. Okay.

*LIGHTS SHIFT.*

## 10. ON THE CONTINUATION OF THE LOVERS' UNION.

*TOLEDO, SPAIN. SIX MONTHS EARLIER. MARCH 9, 2004. AFTERNOON. IBRAHIM AND PALOMA IN A CHURCH.*

PALOMA: Used to be a mosque.

IBRAHIM: Then a synagogue.

PALOMA: Then a church.

IBRAHIM: They're removing parts of the altar to restore the synagogue to invite the community back here to worship.

PALOMA: As if taking down an altar could do that.

IBRAHIM: Why didn't you respond when I texted you from the hotel this morning?

PALOMA: I saw your text but my phone was just about out of juice so . . .

IBRAHIM: You could've called me from a payphone.

PALOMA: And then I was by the fountain of Neptune and hurrying to meet you at the train ticket booth-thing at *Atocha* and I thought I should call . . . but I didn't have any change for the payphone.

IBRAHIM: When you lie, your face does this smiling thing and your voice does this raised thing at the end of each sentence.

PALOMA: You don't believe me.

IBRAHIM: Not really.

PALOMA: Like I wouldn't want to call you . . . be here. With you.

IBRAHIM: My girlfriend is all, "I'm goin' out for a walk. Meet you at *Atocha*." and what am I supposed to think?

PALOMA: I'm here, aren't I?

IBRAHIM: Yeah.

PALOMA: I just needed some time.

IBRAHIM: For . . .

PALOMA: Thinking . . .

IBRAHIM: About . . .

PALOMA: Can we not talk about this right now?

IBRAHIM: You're probably weirded out about the no-sex-yet-thing.

PALOMA: Pretty much.

*Anne García-Romero*

IBRAHIM: Yeah. I knew it.

PALOMA: Look, I get that it's part of your religion. My heart is not made of stone, you know.

IBRAHIM: Nor is mine.

PALOMA: So . . .

IBRAHIM: Here we are. Two stoneless hearts.

PALOMA: The only stones . . . the ones beneath our feet as we climb the streets of this ancient city.

IBRAHIM: Did you know the river *Duero* begins in this city? A little trickle and then soon a gushing river.

PALOMA: You don't think I really want to be here in *Toledo* with you? Maybe it's actually you who feels unsure about this.

IBRAHIM: Nine hundred years ago, our worlds co-existed here. Living side by side. Each free to practice. Each free to live with respect.

PALOMA: And we can't have that today?

IBRAHIM: Nine hundred years later. Numerous wars. An Inquisition. Years of genocide. It gets complicated.

PALOMA: If I close my eyes, maybe I can feel *la convivencia.*

IBRAHIM: And if I kiss your eyelids when they're closed will I also see the co-existence in this space?

PALOMA: Your lips will see with my eyes.

> *PALOMA CLOSES HER EYES. IBRAHIM KISSES HER EYELIDS.*

PALOMA:  Only I don't just see peaceful co-existence. I also see what followed. Shrapnel. And smoke. And blood. And piercing wails.

> *PALOMA OPENS HER EYES.*

IBRAHIM: So maybe I can kiss your eyelids again?

PALOMA: I'll meet you outside.

IBRAHIM: Paloma . . .

PALOMA: This place spooks me.

IBRAHIM: Let me get one picture of us.

PALOMA: It says no photos.

IBRAHIM: Just one.

PALOMA: Okay. Quick.

> *IBRAHIM TAKES A QUICK PHOTO OF THEM.*

IBRAHIM: Why does it spook you?

PALOMA: Doesn't feel like co-existence anymore. Maybe at one point during the mosque days. But then co-existence ended and someone conquered someone and it's a synagogue. Then someone expelled someone and it's a church.

IBRAHIM: I don't see it that way.

PALOMA: It's not like, "Hey, do you mind if we steal this building, strip the interior and redecorate?" It's like, "Excuse me while I kill you and steal your house of worship."

IBRAHIM: Are you low-blood sugar right now because you seem kind of low-blood sugary?

PALOMA: You read the placard outside and you believe it or want to believe it or hope to believe it but co-existence doesn't last.

IBRAHIM: Let's go. Come on.

PALOMA: If you scratch beneath the surface of this paint, you'll hear howls not chanting, you'll see blood stains not like fuckin' mosaics.

IBRAHIM: You know, I think it's mealtime.

PALOMA: Feed me buckets of *gazpacho* but it won't change that fact.

IBRAHIM: In Granada, you'll feel differently. *(beat)* But for now, let's go drink buckets of *gazpacho*.

*LIGHTS SHIFT.*

# 11. On Forgetting.

*NEW YORK CITY. SEPTEMBER 20, 2004. MORNING. COURTROOM. IBRAHIM ON THE STAND. JARED CROSS EXAMINING.*

JARED: *(with improper pronunciation)* Mr. Ahmed (AH-MED). Abraham?

IBRAHIM: *(with proper pronunciation)* Ibrahim. With an "I". *Ibrahim Ahmed.*

JARED: Fine then. Ibrahim, can you tell us what you did on the morning of March eleventh?

IBRAHIM: My girlfriend and I . . .

JARED: Ms. Flores?

IBRAHIM: *Paloma.*

JARED: Paloma Flores.

IBRAHIM: Paloma and I woke up, left our Madrid hotel room, took the metro and entered the *Atocha* train station.

JARED: Are you a resident of New York City?

IBRAHIM: Yes.

JARED: Was Ms. Flores . . . uh . . . Paloma. Was she a resident of New York City?

IBRAHIM: Yes.

JARED: Both U.S. citizens?

IBRAHIM: Born and raised in New York.

JARED: Why then were you in Madrid on March eleventh in the Atocha train station?

IBRAHIM: On vacation.

JARED: Were you taking Ms. Flores . . . uh . . . Paloma there against her will?

IBRAHIM: The trip was my idea but she was excited to go too.

JARED: So, you didn't brainwash Ms. Flores into taking this trip?

IBRAHIM: No, I did not.

JARED: And where were you planning on traveling to that morning?

IBRAHIM: The city of *Granada.*

JARED: And why is that?

IBRAHIM: I guess you could call it a pilgrimage of sorts.

JARED: A religious pilgrimage?

IBRAHIM: More personal than religious.

JARED: Are you religious, Abraham?

IBRAHIM: *Ibrahim.*

JARED: Are you religious, Ibrahim?

IBRAHIM: Yes.

JARED: Could you elaborate please?

IBRAHIM: I am a practicing Muslim.

JARED: And did your girlfriend share your faith?

IBRAHIM: No.

JARED: Was this a problem?

IBRAHIM: To me? No. To our families? Yes.

JARED: And to Ms. Flores? Paloma?

IBRAHIM: I don't think so. No.

JARED: Were you planning on marrying Ms. Flores?

IBRAHIM: One day.

> JARED HOLDS UP A PLASTIC BAG CONTAINING A
> GOLD NECKLACE.

JARED: Do you recognize this item?

IBRAHIM: I do.

JARED: Can you tell us what this is?

IBRAHIM: A neck ring. A kind of necklace really. I bought one just like that for Paloma in Toledo. I gave it to her that morning.

JARED: As some sort of pre-engagement gift?

IBRAHIM: I don't know. More of a symbol of our relationship. We'd been reading this book, Ring of the Dove, a meditation on love and so it was because of that mostly.

JARED: So you weren't trying to bribe her with this gift to coerce her to take this trip?

IBRAHIM: No.

JARED: You weren't kidnapping her against her will to take this trip?

IBRAHIM: No.

JARED: Can you tell us what happened at seven fifteen that morning?

IBRAHIM: We boarded the train in the *Atocha* station. We were sitting there in car seven. Seats Nine A and B. Looking forward to our trip. I got up to use the restroom. The one in our car was occupied so I kept on going down the aisle to the next car, then the next one. Before I got to a vacant restroom. That's when it happened.

JARED: You're referring to the bombing of the Atocha train station?

IBRAHIM: Yes.

JARED: What is your cultural heritage, Mr. Ahmed?

IBRAHIM: I'm Moroccan-American.

JARED: Were you in any way involved in the planning of this attack?

IBRAHIM: No.

JARED: You were in no way involved in planning this attack on the trains pulling into the Atocha train station, an attack which injured six hundred passengers, killed one hundred and ninety-two people, including your girlfriend and soon-to-be fiancée?

IBRAHIM: Absolutely not. I'm a U.S. citizen. I'm non-violent. I'm a practicing, moderately devout Muslim. I was traveling with my girlfriend, a nominally devout Catholic . . . to a land where once many hundreds of years ago, a question like that would not only be offensive but completely preposterous . . . to *Al-Andalus*, a land where we could exist together without repercussion, further . . . to that land where our worlds could thrive and flourish together and neither of us would be injured, killed or sued for false imprisonment and wrongful death.

JARED: No further questions, Your Honor.

*LIGHTS SHIFT.*

## 12. On the signs of love.

*MADRID. SIX MONTHS EARLIER. MARCH 11, 2004. EARLY MORNING. IBRAHIM AND PALOMA ON A TRAIN IN THE ATOCHA TRAIN STATION.*

IBRAHIM: *(reading)* A sign. Persistence of the look, never blinking nor letting the beloved out of his sight.

PALOMA: *(reading)* A sign. Searching for an excuse to sit next to her beloved and be close to him.

IBRAHIM: *(reading)* A sign. The lover gives liberally as much as he can and rejoices as if he were himself receiving the gift.

*PALOMA TOUCHES HER NECKLACE.*

PALOMA: Feeling this next to my neck gives me this sensation of stillness inside.

IBRAHIM: And this?

*IBRAHIM KISSES HER NECK.*

PALOMA: Heart rate up. Heat through my chest, traveling down my stomach across my sweet spot down my legs and into my toes. Yeah.

IBRAHIM: And this?

*IBRAHIM KISSES HER LIPS.*

PALOMA: Ditto. Times ten.

IBRAHIM: Ten only?

PALOMA: To the tenth power.

IBRAHIM: Power. That.

PALOMA: That.

IBRAHIM: Yeah.

PALOMA: I can't wait to walk, hand in hand, through the *Generalife* gardens, in and out of the carefully manicured hedges and flowers around the eighteen tiny fountains of water simultaneously careening into the long rectangular pool.

IBRAHIM: And so it shall be.

PALOMA: *L'Alhambra.*

IBRAHIM: *El Generalife.*

PALOMA: *Granada.*

IBRAHIM: Moorish power.

PALOMA: A walled city.

IBRAHIM: Seat of power.

PALOMA: Centuries of power. *(beat)* Will we fuck in *Granada*?

IBRAHIM: Depends.

PALOMA: On . . .

IBRAHIM: The rules.

PALOMA: What *Ibn Hazm* wrote.

IBRAHIM: Exactly.

PALOMA: His rules are universal.

IBRAHIM: Applicable to all.

PALOMA: Yup. So . . .

IBRAHIM: We can apply them . . . in bed.

PALOMA: Really.

IBRAHIM: If you're down with that.

PALOMA: Uh . . . yeah.

IBRAHIM: And our little room will overlook the hills of *Granada*.

PALOMA: Serious?

    *IBRAHIM NODS.*

PALOMA: Because I get your whole religion thing but I also kinda thought you didn't want to . . . do it . . . with me.

IBRAHIM: It's never ever been about not wanting to do it with you. Are you kidding me?

PALOMA: I don't know. I mean . . .

IBRAHIM: P, come on.

PALOMA: Well . . . how am I supposed to really know?

IBRAHIM: Well, I do. And we will.

PALOMA: Fuck.

IBRAHIM: Ravish.

PALOMA: Screw.

IBRAHIM: Consume.

PALOMA: And it won't be like a Muslim Catholic guilt festival?

IBRAHIM: I'm not asking you to change anything.

PALOMA: Sure about that?

    *IBRAHIM KISSES PALOMA.*

    *A FEW BEATS.*

PALOMA: Ib? *(pronounced EEB)*

IBRAHIM: P?

PALOMA: What will it be like when we get back to Manhattan?

IBRAHIM: Crazy. Mad crazy.

PALOMA: Will we like meet each other's families and my mom will make *arroz con pollo* and your mom will make *couscous* and *tajine* and we'll have this feast with everyone shouting in Spanish and Arabic and English? It'll be mad crazy.

IBRAHIM: And so it shall be.

PALOMA: Say a quick prayer with me.

IBRAHIM: You're praying now?

PALOMA: And . . . you have a problem with that?

IBRAHIM: What are we praying for?

PALOMA: Safe travels. You know.

IBRAHIM: In a minute. I gotta . . .

PALOMA: Piss? Piss or pray. Pray or piss.

IBRAHIM: Be right back. Then we'll pray together for hours. Promise.

PALOMA: Ib?

IBRAHIM: Yeah, P?

*PALOMA LOOKS AT HIM.*

PALOMA: Just wanted to stare at you for another sec. Okay. You can go now.

*IBRAHIM STARTS TO LEAVE.*

PALOMA: Wait. One more thing.

*PALOMA GIVES HIM A KISS.*

PALOMA: Do you have to go?

IBRAHIM: I'll only be minute.

PALOMA: One?

IBRAHIM: Thirty seconds.

PALOMA: Twenty-eight.

IBRAHIM: Okay. Twenty-six.

PALOMA: Twenty-six.

*IBRAHIM EXITS. PALOMA SITS IN SILENCE FOR A FEW BEATS. SHE CLASPS HER HANDS TOGETHER, CLOSES HER EYES AND SAYS A QUICK PRAYER. SHE OPENS HER EYES AND MAKES THE SIGN OF THE CROSS. SHE LOOKS OUT THE TRAIN WINDOW AS THE LIGHTS FADE. BLACKOUT. A FEW BEATS. SUDDENLY A BLARE OF SIRENS.*

*END OF ACT ONE.*

## 13. On separation.

*MADRID. MARCH 12, 2004. AFTERNOON. HOSPITAL
ROOM. IBRAHIM IN A BED SLEEPING. A DOCTOR
AND NURSE ENTER (PLAYED BY THE ACTORS PLAY-
ING JARED AND PALOMA). THE DOCTOR READS
ALOUD WHILE LOOKING AT A MEDICAL CHART AS
THE NURSE CHECKS IBRAHIM'S VITALS.*

DOCTOR: *(reading) Una fractura del seno paranasal.* (Paranasal sinus fracture.)

NURSE: *La frecuencia cardíaca permanence estable.* (Heart
rate stable.)

DOCTOR: *(reading) Una lesión pulmonar.* (Blast lung injury.)

NURSE: *La fiebre ha pasado.* (Fever's gone.)

DOCTOR: *(reading) Un derrame pleural bilateral.* (Pleural
effusion.)

*IBRAHIM STIRS, DELIRIOUS FROM BEING HEAV-
ILY SEDATED. HE LOOKS AT THE NURSE AND THE
DOCTOR.*

IBRAHIM: *(to Nurse)* Paloma.

DOCTOR: *Ibrahim Ahmed.*

IBRAHIM: *(to Doctor)* Jared?

DOCTOR: : *(with Spanish accent)* You are a fortunate man.

IBRAHIM: *(to Doctor*) Jared, dude, what the hell? Why're you
in Madrid?

DOCTOR: You will stay here until you are stable enough to travel .
. . then we will help you arrange a flight back to Manhattan.

IBRAHIM: *(to Nurse)* Paloma?

NURSE: My name is *Nuria.*

IBRAHIM: *(to Nurse)* No it's not. It's Paloma. Come on. Don't
mess with me.

DOCTOR: Your physical injuries will heal. We have counselors
who speak English who can come speak to you. *(beat)* Unfortunately, we don't have any imams here at the moment
but we could—

IBRAHIM: Now you both wanna go to the mosque? What the
hell, dudes?

DOCTOR: We can discuss these options more later. First, you
must continue to rest.

IBRAHIM: *(to Nurse)* Paloma . . .

NURSE: Shhhh. You must rest.

IBRAHIM: Jared. Paloma. Paloma. Jared. *(beat) (to Doctor)* You came to Madrid . . . to meet Paloma? Dude, Jared . . . you're awesome. *(beat) (to Nurse)* Paloma, you finally met Jared . . . so awesome.

DOCTOR: We have contacted your family and also her family.

IBRAHIM: Jared, what's up with the accent? Come, on, dude. Drop it. *(to Nurse)* Paloma, he sometimes likes to joke around.

DOCTOR: But we can speak about the details more later . . . to make the arrangements . . .

IBRAHIM: What. Arrangements. Jared, what the fuck're you talking about? And cut it with the accent.

DOCTOR: Please. I prefer if you remain lying down. If you would prefer to raise your body, you can press the button here and the bed will move you.

*IBRAHIM TRIES TO SIT UP.*

IBRAHIM: Fuck.

DOCTOR: Please do not move, Mr. *Ahmed.*

*IBRAHIM CONTINUES TO TRY TO SIT UP.*

IBRAHIM: Paloma? What the fuck . . .

DOCTOR: Sir, Mr. *Ahmed.* Please lie back down.

IBRAHIM: I do not want to lie down. *(to Nurse)* Hold my hand.

*NURSE HOLDS HIS HAND.*

DOCTOR: Mr. *Ahmed.*

IBRAHIM: No mister. It's Ibrahim. *(beat)* Jared. Dude. What're you doin'?

DOCTOR: *(to Nurse) Aumenta la dosis a diez miligramos. (Increase the dose to ten milligrams)*

*THE NURSE ADJUSTS THE MORPHINE DRIP BY IBRAHIM'S BED.*

IBRAHIM: Paloma, please . . .

DOCTOR: It is necessary that you lie back down.

*THE DOCTOR FIRMLY PUSHES IBRAHIM BACK INTO HIS BED.*

DOCTOR: I am very sorry for your loss.

*Anne García-Romero*

NURSE: Now you will relax.

DOCTOR: Do your best to rest.

NURSE: Push the call button if you need anything.

DOCTOR: You will recover.

NURSE: You are very brave.

DOCTOR: You survived, Ibrahim.

NURSE: Very strong.

DOCTOR: Your girlfriend did not.

IBRAHIM: Paloma?

DOCTOR: : I offer you my condolences.

IBRAHIM: Jared. Dude. She's right here.

DOCTOR: Grief takes on many forms, Ibrahim.

IBRAHIM: She's right fuckin' here, alright?

DOCTOR: If you feel the need to talk to her, then . . .

IBRAHIM: Paloma. Please tell me . . . this is one of my nightmares . . . like that other one with the bubble thingy . . .
where I wake up and . . . and . . . my heart is pounding and
my mind . . . .it's racing and that feeling stays with my for
. . . .for fuckin' hours. Are we in a bubble thingy?

NURSE: Rest.

IBRAHIM: Don't go anywhere, okay?

NURSE: I will stay right here.

IBRAHIM: I don't know what Jared's talkin' about. But he's
fuckin' rude, alright?

DOCTOR: I will leave you with . . .

IBRAHIM:  Paloma.

   *LIGHTS SHIFT.*

# 14. On loyalty.

*NEW YORK CITY. SEPTEMBER 20, 2004. AFTERNOON.*
*IBRAHIM AND JARED IN JARED'S OFFICE.*

JARED: Why the fuck did you do that?

IBRAHIM: Because I put my hand on the bible swearing to tell the truth.

JARED: Jesus.

IBRAHIM: Exactly. He told the truth.

JARED: And look where that got him. Do you want to live out the rest of your days as a convicted man and die a grisly death?

IBRAHIM: Fuckin' chill, man.

JARED: This is bullshit. We prepare and you pull that shit?

IBRAHIM: I spoke my truth.

JARED: You gave the other side exactly what they wanted. A man with an Arabic name, a Muslim, who speaks emphatically*

IBRAHIM: Passionately*

JARED: From the stand, proclaiming allegiance to Al-Andalus.

IBRAHIM: So the fuck what?

*A BEAT.*

JARED: I don't think we're gonna get off, Abe. I know this judge and he's a hardass.

IBRAHIM: So you wanted me to lie about who I am?

JARED: Cut it with this holier than thou, bullshit. Alright?

IBRAHIM: I'm not gonna lie about who I am at this point, Jared.

JARED: I asked you to stay on script. You made me look like a fool and you sabotaged your own case.

IBRAHIM: By saying my name is Ibrahim and passionately speaking my truth?

JARED: By reneging on our rehearsed remarks.

IBRAHIM: I felt inspired.

JARED: That's fucked.

IBRAHIM: Fucked? What's fucked is being sued for wrongful death and false imprisonment. Like I caused her death by kidnapping her and fucking pushing her onto the train tracks?

JARED: Your inspired performance fucked up our case.

IBRAHIM: False imprisonment is like those sick bastards who lock little girls up and do evil shit to them and then kill them. That is not me.

JARED: I just kinda don't recognize you anymore.

IBRAHIM: Isn't that convenient.

JARED: What?

IBRAHIM: No, really, because I think you actually want me to lose this case. You were jealous of me and Paloma and on some level you want to punish me.

JARED: Dude. Give me a fuckin' break.

IBRAHIM: You jump from girl to any girl who's DTF and you've never had what I had.

JARED: DTF?

IBRAHIM: Down to fuck.

JARED: Fuck off.

IBRAHIM: I thought you were on my side. I thought, "Hey, cool, my bro Jared, college bud, hookin' me up with legal help." But really, you're not helping me at all.

JARED: Oh, I'm not helping you at all, busting my ass for hours for fucking free? Really?

IBRAHIM: Because basically you were jealous of me.

JARED: You are out of your mind.

IBRAHIM: I mean why didn't you ever meet up with me and Paloma? Why didn't you ever make the goddamn effort?

JARED: Because you were so secretive and then finally when you tell me about her, you ask me out like once and dude, I'm not in grad school anymore. I'm working my ass off at the firm. I have a life. It had nothing to do with you, dude.

IBRAHIM: Fuckin' sharky liar. As long as I've known you, you have never been with a girl for more than like three months.

JARED: Don't go there.

IBRAHIM: And so here I have this amazing new fucking phenomenal girlfriend and you can't deal so you avoid me and her.

JARED: Holy shit. Now you're gonna fuckin' psycho-babblize me on top of everything else? My relationship history has nothing to do with this.

IBRAHIM: Like hell it doesn't.

JARED: Would you stop?

IBRAHIM: Because I know you, dude.

JARED: What difference does it make if I was a little jealous maybe on some subconscious level or some shit. What does it fucking matter? I am not bringing that into the case.

IBRAHIM: I fuckin' knew you were.

JARED: Whether or not I felt one iota of jealousy for you and Paloma doesn't change the fact that you royally screwed us today.

*A FEW BEATS.*

JARED: Look, man, I know it fuckin' sucks shit that Paloma's gone. I get that you're angry and beyond pissed and stressed and flipped out by this case. But you have to try to chill.

IBRAHIM: She had this thing she used to do. She would put her hand on my chest sometimes and then she would say my name, "Hey Ib," or she'd be like "Yo, yo, Ib," and then like squeeze my hand real tight. And her palms were always like so soft. *(beat)* You never got to meet her, man.

JARED: I know. I know.

*LIGHTS SHIFT.*

## 15. ON SUBMISSION.

*MADRID. SIX MONTHS EARLIER. MARCH 8, 2004. EVENING. IBRAHIM AND PALOMA IN THEIR HOTEL ROOM.*

PALOMA: *(reading)* One of the most marvelous moves in love is the submission of the lover to his beloved and the forceful change he suffers when he adapts to his beloved.

IBRAHIM: *(reading)* Therefore, one sees a man who is asocial, obstinate, stubborn, contrary, fierce, severe, incapable of yielding yet when the slightest little love breeze blows or he descends into the gulf of passion . . .

PALOMA: *(reading)* he drowns in his own ocean, tricks his severity into sweetness, his pigheadedness into passivity, his frenzy into faith and his anger into austerity.

IBRAHIM: Maybe let's read a different chapter.

PALOMA: Are you afraid of submitting to me?

IBRAHIM: I'm not big on tricking and drowning.

PALOMA: But in exchange you get sweetness and faith.

IBRAHIM: And passivity and austerity.

PALOMA: I'll throw you a flotation device. Promise.

IBRAHIM: I bet you will.

PALOMA: You'll be doing more than floating, my friend.

IBRAHIM: Dare I say surfing?

PALOMA: Boogie boarding?

IBRAHIM: Jet skiing?

PALOMA: Now that's what I like. Power. Vroom. Vroom.

IBRAHIM: So tomorrow Madrid, Wednesday, Toledo, Thursday, Granada.

PALOMA: Why not *Madrid* then *Granada*?

IBRAHIM: I want to see Toledo which is sort of a precursor to Granada. A place where co-existence truly flourished. And once the capital of the country. And so close to Madrid.

PALOMA: You have this all planned out, don't you?

IBRAHIM: Uh-huh.

PALOMA: So how 'bout we also have some PDA in *España*.

IBRAHIM: Okay . . .

PALOMA: Let's hold hands on the Metro.

IBRAHIM: Sure.

PALOMA: And cuddle on a bench in the *Reina Sofia* museum.

IBRAHIM: Done.

PALOMA: Then smooch in *El Retiro* park.

IBRAHIM: Smooch?

PALOMA: Neck.

IBRAHIM: A peck or two and then we neck.

PALOMA: And then when we return to the hotel room after a full day of sights and *Madrileño* PDA and . . .

IBRAHIM: Ah. That.

PALOMA: Yeah. That.

IBRAHIM: Well.

*AWKWARD BEAT.*

PALOMA: Fine. Let's not talk about that now. Let's plan for tomorrow. So . . .

IBRAHIM: So breakfast then *Picasso* at the *Reina Sofia*?

PALOMA: Like, *Picasso* had this fucked up relationship with women. Have you seen how fractured those women look? A few months with *Pablo* and their eyes are on their nose and their mouth is on their arm. Is that how you want me to look?

IBRAHIM: Fine. So then maybe you'd rather see the *Velazquez* at the *Prado* or the Crystal Palace in *El Retiro* park or climb the Pyrenees mountains or take a dip in the Mediterranean or fly to *Barcelona* and gawk at the *Gaudí* towers.

*ANOTHER AWKWARD BEAT.*

PALOMA: Whoah. Wait. I'm suddenly ravenously hungry.

IBRAHIM: Clearly.

PALOMA: Let's go for pastries then *Picasso*.

IBRAHIM: Deal.

PALOMA: Just don't fracture me, okay?

IBRAHIM: Never.

*LIGHTS SHIFT.*

## 16. On the ugliness of sin.

*NEW YORK CITY. OCTOBER 5, 2004. EARLY EVENING.*
*IBRAHIM AND JARED IN A MIDTOWN BAR.*

JARED: I know it's ugly but . . .

IBRAHIM: I've like sinned against God, alright?

JARED: That's not why this happened.

IBRAHIM: A steel-toed boot is fuckin' lodged underneath my solar plexus and the pressure is getting fuckin' unbearable.

JARED: We're going to appeal the decision.

IBRAHIM: The sin is committed. The punishment will continue.

JARED: Bullshit. I'm gonna keep working my ass off. We'll work to get the verdict overturned.

IBRAHIM: Now I get why people jumped out of office buildings when the stock market crashed in 1929.

JARED: Don't jump out of a window.

IBRAHIM: The weight pushes you out of the structure. The insurmountable weight of crushing, soul deadening debt.

JARED: We will get this reversed.

IBRAHIM: You know that in some versions of the Christian prayer they say, "Forgive us our debts as we forgive our debtors." Her parents would never pray that about me.

JARED: I'm buying. What do you want. Coke? Club soda with lime?

IBRAHIM: Vodka tonic.

JARED: No seriously.

IBRAHIM: Bartender, vodka tonic, please.

JARED: Fuck off.

IBRAHIM: No you fuck off. Alright. You fuck off. I'm ordering two vodka tonics, three dry martinis, five Heinekens and ten shots of Jagermeister because at this point what does it matter? My sins are so massive I'm gonna get plastered, eat pounds of pork and spend the next twenty-four hours with a hooker.

JARED: Come on, let's get outta here.

IBRAHIM: I'm not movin' my ass from this seat until I'm fuckin' blitzed.

JARED: Come on, man. Chill.

IBRAHIM: Chill? Fuckin' chill? I can barely afford to eat right now. I'm unemployed. On leave of absence from school. No savings. And I owe my dead girlfriend's family four point seven million dollars. I don't even have four point seven thousand dollars.

JARED: It wasn't your fault.

IBRAHIM: Then why couldn't you convince the jury of that? Why?

JARED: Dude. I did my best but we couldn't compete with her father's testimony.

IBRAHIM: I didn't force her to do anything.

JARED: And that's why we're appealing because this is bullshit.

IBRAHIM: If my name were John Jones and I looked like ivory with a blonde buzz cut, this would not be happening.

JARED: Dude. We'll file the motion to appeal as soon as humanly possible.

IBRAHIM: Why did I have to take a leak that morning? Why does my bladder have to be so goddamn small?

JARED: You have the body God gave you.

IBRAHIM: Why didn't I just stay and pray and get to leave the planet with her?

JARED: Because God wanted you to stay for a while longer.

IBRAHIM: I want that drink, bartender.

JARED: You are not drinking any fuckin' booze, okay, so just chill.

IBRAHIM: Why do you even care? I'm sure this is doing wonders for your career, at this point.

JARED: My grandfather. That's why.

IBRAHIM: What . . . is he a shitty lawyer too?

JARED: No. I never met him. He was a rabbi from Poland. Didn't survive the war. Okay? And that is why. That is why I bother with your fuckin' case alright? God is not punishing you. Some evil motherfuckers killed your girlfriend and my grandfather and fuckin' hundreds of thousands of people who, like you, were just trying to search for some sliver of hope. So I'm not getting you a fuckin' drink not because I don't think you need it and not because I'm concerned you'll be breaking some laws but because it'll make you even more miserable than you are right now and I'd rather avoid that for all parties involved. You're here, Ibrahim. You're breathing, walking and for fuck sake talking. So enough with your punishment shit alright?

*LIGHTS SHIFT.*

## 17. On the excellence of chastity.

*MADRID. SEVEN MONTHS EARLIER. MARCH 10, 2004. EVENING. IBRAHIM AND PALOMA ON THE BED IN THEIR HOTEL ROOM.*

PALOMA: *(reading)* One of the best things a man can do in love is protect his chastity.

IBRAHIM: *(reading)* There is the one who sees his heart enamored and his thoughts invaded . . .

PALOMA: *(reading)* Blooming desire and multiplied passion . . .

IBRAHIM: *(reading)* Who, as soon as he is possessed by his beloved, feels his eagerness begin to dominate his understanding . . .

PALOMA: *(reading)* And his concupiscence subjugates his faith.

IBRAHIM: Concupiscence.

PALOMA: Sexual hunger.

IBRAHIM: Hunger.

PALOMA: Thirst.

IBRAHIM: That.

PALOMA: Hungry?

IBRAHIM: God.

*IBRAHIM GETS UP OFF THE BED.*

PALOMA: I mean as in food hungry.

IBRAHIM: Right. I knew that.

PALOMA: Liar.

IBRAHIM: Yeah. I'm hungry.

*PALOMA TAKES FOOD OUT OF A PAPER BAG.*

PALOMA: *Tortilla de patata.* My grandma used to make this all the time when we were little. Her mother was from *Barcelona.*

IBRAHIM: So you're actually part Spanish? Seriously? Why didn't you mention that before?

PALOMA: Great grandparents left here during the Civil War. Moved to *Puerto Rico.* My mom was born there. Met my dad. Married. Moved to New York. So *Barcelona. San Juan.* Manhattan. Yeah.

*IBRAHIM TRIES THE SPANISH TORTILLA.*

PALOMA: Egg. Potato. Onion. Garlic. Olive oil

IBRAHIM: You know how to make this?

PALOMA: Kinda.

IBRAHIM: You'll make me this?

PALOMA: And lots of other things.

IBRAHIM: Okay. So what time is our train tomorrow?

PALOMA: Seven fifteen. A.M.

IBRAHIM: Maybe we should wait then.

PALOMA: Wait.

IBRAHIM: Until Granada. Just one more night to wait.

PALOMA: What're you afraid of?

IBRAHIM: Completely losing my faith.

PALOMA: How will you lose it?

IBRAHIM: Hard to describe.

PALOMA: Try.

IBRAHIM: Like falling away from something inside. Like being tossed into the ocean and no preserver and swimming is treacherous.

PALOMA: What would happen then?

IBRAHIM: It'd be like someone carved a hole in the center of my torso and my flesh slowly rots until gangrene sets in and I die.

PALOMA: Seriously?

IBRAHIM: Ever since I was little, faith has been a huge part of my life . . . going with my family to the mosque . . . the deep stillness I experience during prayer with my forehead touching the ground . . . the inner assurance I sense as I read the *Qur'an* . . . the connection I feel in my bones to the centuries of reverence . . . the inner guidance . . . all that could potentially be lost. And then . . .

PALOMA: But no one will know. You. Me.

IBRAHIM: And *Allah*. God.

PALOMA: If you honestly think God really really doesn't want you to do this, why are we here?

IBRAHIM: What if we got married?

PALOMA: Wait. What?

IBRAHIM: Would you want to?

PALOMA: Ib . . . that's huge and . . .

IBRAHIM: Okay. We don't have to talk about it . . .

PALOMA: I mean I think I might but I don't know and*

IBRAHIM: Fine. Whatever. Don't worry about it.

PALOMA: I mean, wouldn't you want to at least meet my parents?

IBRAHIM: Well . . .

PALOMA: Shouldn't we like be going out for a while before this even comes up? And like . . . hello . . . religious differences . . .

IBRAHIM: There are a few ways that it would be okay.

PALOMA: Really.

IBRAHIM: A Muslim man can marry a woman of the book . . . who actively practices another faith which shares the same roots as those in the *Qu'ran* . . . so a Christian or Jew.

PALOMA: I'm Catholic.

IBRAHIM: But you don't really practice.

PALOMA: You want me to be all religious now and go to mass every day or something? That's not happening. What're the other ways?

IBRAHIM: It'd be okay if we were in a Muslim city . . .

PALOMA: *Granada's* not a Muslim city.

IBRAHIM: Granada could technically be considered a Muslim city.

PALOMA: No it can't. The Muslims were expelled over five hundred years ago.

IBRAHIM: But the history lives in the stones.

PALOMA: So what's the third way?

IBRAHIM: Or you could convert.

PALOMA: I'm not converting.

IBRAHIM: But you barely practice your own faith.

PALOMA: Maybe not as much as you but . . .

IBRAHIM: So . . . I thought . . .

PALOMA: I still wanna be able to hold the wooden rosary my mother gave me when I was ten and say the occasional Hail Mary and Our Father or go to midnight mass on Christmas eve and hear the choir sing, "Silent Night" while the candles burn in our hands and we walk out into the winter coldness.

IBRAHIM: O . . . kay.

PALOMA: I mean I visited your mosque. I sat with the women. I watched how they prayed with their hijab's touching the rug. I listened as the imam shared his wisdom. I witnessed the peaceful reverence. But apparently my respectful observation isn't enough.

IBRAHIM: I'm honored that you visited. Truly. But . . . if you were more observant of your own faith then . . .

PALOMA: What if I'm observant on the inside? Does it matter so much to you how many times I go to Mass or not?

IBRAHIM: Kind of. Yeah.

PALOMA: That is so legalistic.

IBRAHIM: There is power in the ritual.

PALOMA: How do you know? Have you ever attended a Mass before?

IBRAHIM: Once. At a wedding. With my family. A co-worker of my father's invited us. But I'd visit with you.

PALOMA: That is not the point.

IBRAHIM: Fine. Whatever. Forget it.

*AWKWARD BEAT.*

PALOMA: Ib, I'm mad crazy about you . . . why do you think I came on this trip? But you can't pressure me like this.

IBRAHIM: Who's the saint of impossible causes?

PALOMA: Jude.

IBRAHIM: Maybe you could pray to him for me. Then ask him for some guidance for you.

PALOMA: Like now?

IBRAHIM: Or later.

*IBRAHIM KISSES PALOMA THEN SUDDENLY PULLS AWAY.*

IBRAHIM: P. Can we just lie here?

PALOMA: Ib. I dunno. *(beat)* Can we?

IBRAHIM: I need to wait until Granada.

*IBRAHIM AND PALOMA LIE ON THE BED HOLDING HANDS.*

*LIGHTS SHIFT.*

## 18. ON THE ONE WHO SLANDERS.

*NEW YORK CITY. OCTOBER 8, 2004. MORNING.
IBRAHIM IN WASHINGTON SQUARE PARK. MRS.
FLORES ENTERS (PLAYED BY THE ACTOR PLAYING
PALOMA ).*

MRS. FLORES: *(with a slight Puerto Rican accent)* I did not lie. My husband did.

IBRAHIM: I know.

MRS. FLORES: I did not want this. I told my husband, "*Enrique*, this boy has suffered enough. We have all suffered enough."

IBRAHIM: You have suffered more.

MRS. FLORES: Suffering cannot be measured, *m'ijo*. It simply is.

IBRAHIM: I can never pay you.

MRS. FLORES: I know.

IBRAHIM: He said I threatened her. I never threatened her.

MRS. FLORES: My *Paloma* would have never gone with you if she did not want to. My *Palomita* was a wise young woman.

IBRAHIM: Did she ever talk about me?

MRS. FLORES: To me? Yes. She told me about your eyes, your smile, your intelligence and your nice *culito*.

IBRAHIM: My what?

*MRS. FLORES TAPS HER OWN BUTT.*

IBRAHIM: *Culito*.

MRS. FLORES: She called me from *Madrid*. She told me you saw the most beautiful *iglesia*, the church that used to be the mosque, the place where your ancestors worshipped.

IBRAHIM: *Toledo*.

MRS. FLORES: My husband is a strict Catholic. Me. Not so strict.

IBRAHIM: So you didn't mind your daughter . . .

MRS. FLORES: *Con un hombre musulmán*? With a Muslim man? No.

IBRAHIM: Your husband said I forced her onto that train. I did not.

MRS. FLORES: When she was little, *Paloma* said one day she would grow up to be a belly dancer or a nurse. Or maybe a belly dancing nurse. I do not know why because she was always afraid of . . .

IBRAHIM: You don't have to . . .

MRS. FLORES: Of a bloody finger or a broken bone. And I said, "How can you be a belly dancing nurse if you feel sick when you see illness?" And she said, "*Mami*. I will be a nurse who takes care of bellies only."

*IBRAHIM HANDS HER A BOOK.*

IBRAHIM: For you. She bought this in a bookstore in Madrid.

*MRS. FLORES TAKES THE BOOK.*

MRS. FLORES: *El collar de la paloma.* The ring of the . . .

IBRAHIM: Dove. This is a book we both studied in our class, where we met. We read an English translation from the Arabic but when she found this Spanish version she told me, "*Mami* must have this."

MRS. FLORES: *El libro mas ilustre sobre el tema del amor en la civilización musulmana.*

IBRAHIM: *Por favor?*

MRS. FLORES: The book most illustrious on the theme of love in the Muslim civilization.

IBRAHIM: We read from this book constantly, almost daily.

MRS. FLORES: Like about *el sexo*?

IBRAHIM: No. We never did that.

MRS. FLORES: Now that must be a lie.

IBRAHIM: We were going to . . .

MRS. FLORES: My daughter was not beautiful enough for you?

IBRAHIM: More than beautiful enough.

MRS. FLORES: And so . . . you have a little trouble with the . . .

*MRS. FLORES MAKES A GESTURE WITH HER FIN-GER REFERRING TO AN ERECTION.*

IBRAHIM: No. Not that.

MRS. FLORES: You prefer *los hombres* . . . men?

*IBRAHIM SHAKES HIS HEAD.*

IBRAHIM: We wanted to wait until we got to *Granada*.

MRS. FLORES: *Ay, m'ijo.* You should not have waited.

*MRS. FLORES HANDS HIM BACK THE BOOK.*

IBRAHIM: Keep it. Please.

MRS. FLORES: My husband might find it.

IBRAHIM: Hide it.

MRS. FLORES: I cannot.

IBRAHIM: She wanted you to have it.

MRS. FLORES: I cannot take it.

IBRAHIM: Please.

MRS. FLORES: I do not want it. Why did you ask me here?

IBRAHIM: I wanted to ask . . .

MRS. FLORES: What. More about my daughter? I came here because I had pity on you. I came here because I knew what my husband did was wrong. But I cannot stay. Any longer.

IBRAHIM: Your forgiveness.

MRS. FLORES: I can never forgive you. Walk away from you? Yes. Forget about you? Maybe. Forgive you? No.

IBRAHIM: Mrs. Flores, I adored your daughter. I would never, ever in a million years do anything to harm her.

MRS. FLORES: What kind of world is this where I outlive my child? Eh? Do I blame you like my husband does? No. Do I have pity on you? Yes. Can I be reminded of *Paloma's* last days by seeing you ever again? Absolutely no.

IBRAHIM: Please, Mrs. Flores . . .

MRS. FLORES: My husband and I came here from *Puerto Rico* for a better life. Your parents came here from *Morocco* for a better life. This is not a better life.

*LIGHTS SHIFT.*

# 19. On the messenger.

*OCTOBER 15, 2004. AFTERNOON. JARED AND MR.
AHMED (PLAYED BY THE ACTOR PLAYING IBRAHIM)
SITTING IN JARED'S OFFICE.*

JARED: So, if the appeal is accepted, it would really help the case if you could . . .

MR. AHMED: *(with a slight Moroccan accent)* My wife made me come here today. I do not want to be here.

JARED: And I appreciate very much your making the effort.

MR. AHMED: Does Ibrahim know that we are meeting?

JARED: Actually, no, he does not.

MR. AHMED: What would your father think?

JARED: Excuse me . . . my father?

MR. AHMED: Would he accept if you married a Muslim girl?

JARED: I rather we stay focused on this case, if you wouldn't mind.

MR. AHMED: He would not. I can tell.

JARED: It wouldn't be his first choice, no. But I think after he saw how much I cherished her, he'd come around. He might be opinionated but he wants me to be happy.

MR. AHMED: He wants you to marry a nice Jewish girl, yes?

JARED: That's actually more my mother, really. My father isn't so religious.

MR. AHMED: Did you meet her?

JARED: Who now?

MR. AHMED: This Paloma.

JARED: Actually I did not.

MR. AHMED: Do you think she seduced my son?

JARED: I don't think so, no.

MR. AHMED: I always wanted my son to marry a virtuous woman who is a believer.

JARED: Can I ask you about that night when Ibrahim called you . . . the last time you spoke with him . . .

MR. AHMED: He made me very angry. In our family, we do not keep these kind of secrets. We do not have relations of this kind. It is against our beliefs.

JARED: Did Ibrahim say or sound like he was trying to force Paloma to stay in Spain?

MR. AHMED: Force? My son is disobedient but forceful in that way? We are a peaceful family.

JARED: So he didn't mention he wanted to keep her there against her will?

MR. AHMED: He started to cry. I am yelling at him and he says he wants to come back home. He doesn't want to lose his faith. He is sorry he is disappointing me. But would I please meet this Paloma. And I tell him, he cannot come home. He can go wherever he wants but he cannot come home. And he continues to cry and then he hangs up.

JARED: So it's possible that Ibrahim might have flown with Paloma back to New York instead of taking the train to Granada?

MR. AHMED: Maybe if I had said, "Yes, come home. All is forgiven." But the anger was too big. What he did was too much disrespect. My wife yells at me after I hang up the phone with him. She says I do not have to say these things to our son . . . that he must stay away from us.

JARED: Would you be willing to say these things in court, if our appeal is accepted? During our previous trial, Mr. Flores, Paloma's father, gave compelling yet false testimony, depicting your son as a manipulative, fanatical man. Having you testify on behalf of your son would be a significant contribution to our appeal.

MR. AHMED: I came here to this country from *Morocco* with my wife thirty five years ago. We live an honorable and respectful life. We work so hard and then our son does this to us? Is this honor?

JARED: If you testify on behalf of your son, you can restore his honor.

MR. AHMED: That is not possible.

JARED: To speak in court?

MR. AHMED: To restore his honor.

JARED: Mr. Ahmed, I know this is very hard for your family.

MR. AHMED: You have no idea. Do you think your father would really be happy if you married a nice Muslim girl? What about your grandfather?

JARED: My grandfather died many years ago. I never met him. But they tell me he preached tolerance.

MR. AHMED: I'm not intolerant, Mr. Rabinowitz. I am practical, faithful and protective of my children. I like people of all religions. But I know how hard a married life can be. I want my son to have many years of happiness where he and his wife can go to the mosque together as a family, *Insha'allah* . . . God willing.

JARED: I suppose that is still possible.

MR. AHMED: We are a humble family. We cannot pay this money. Four million? Not possible.

JARED: It's your son who owes the money, not you.

MR. AHMED: I take care of my children, even in their disobedience.

JARED: So you'll testify then?

MR. AHMED: Many years ago, my wife, Miriam, and I traveled from *Marrakesh* to *Granada*. We walked up the stone streets, saw the ancient architecture, and felt the majestic history beneath our shoes and such pride mixed with sadness. The beauty of the land, the holiness, and yet filled with centuries of loss. I told my son about this place many times.

JARED: So for him it truly was a kind of pilgrimage.

MR. AHMED: The *Alhambra* tried to become one of the seven wonders of the world but someone decided it was not wondrous enough. They were wrong. It is quite wondrous.

JARED: Indeed.

MR. AHMED: Architects, artists, poets, mathematicians, scientists . . . all lived there, worked there . . . while the rest of Europe barely knew how to read and write. Do people know this? In these times? *(beat)* If you want, I will testify.

JARED: Thank you, Mr. Ahmed.

MR. AHMED: But will you please give my son a message? *(beat)* I may do this for him, but I still want to kick his ass.

JARED: Ass-kicking. Duly noted.

   *LIGHTS SHIFT.*

# 20. On Correspondence.

*MADRID. SEVEN MONTHS EARLIER. MARCH 10, 2004. NIGHT. PALOMA IN A HOTEL ROOM ALONE. PALOMA WRITES A LETTER WITH PEN AND PAPER.*

PALOMA: Madrid. March 10, 2004. Midnight.

Dear Ib,

I will never alter my tenuous belief system for you . . . scratch that . . . for anyone. So . . . if you think you're going to take me to *Granada* and I'm going to magically convert, you're awaiting . . . failure. *(beat)* Isn't the truth of that ancient city that we don't change each other but we co-exist peacefully . . . knowledgeably . . . respectfully . . . intelligently . . . maturely and tolerantly? *(beat)* Am I crazy . . . no . . . Am I foolish to think we can live like that together? If I am, I'll mourn the loss of this man who I love but cannot be with . . . because if you insist on my conversion, then our relationship can no longer be.

*Te quiero para siempre.*

Love always,

Paloma

p.s. Did you know that my cousin Roberto used to call me *palomitas* which means popcorn? *(beat)* Don't you wish you could slather me with butter right now? Okay. Must rest. I hope you come back to bed soon.

*LIGHTS SHIFT.*

## 21. On the Perpetuation of the Favorable Friend.

*NEW YORK CITY. MARCH 9, 2005. EVENING. IBRA-HIM AND JARED AT JFK AIRPORT.*

IBRAHIM: Routine security check, my ass.

JARED: Relax.

IBRAHIM: *(imitating security woman)* "Mista' Ahmed, would ya' mind steppin' aside for one moment?"

JARED: Drop it.

IBRAHIM: So you're gonna order me around now . . . what . . . to make sure I don't flee or some shit?

JARED: Hell yeah.

IBRAHIM: Well, I don't need this shit anymore. Traveling in or out of this country is a bitch.

JARED: Okay.

IBRAHIM: Like I'm some fucking ferocious lethal human being.

JARED: Say that a bit louder and we're not flying anywhere.

IBRAHIM: And the security woman is African-American. We look at each other eye to eye and she doesn't flinch when she says that. Deep, man. Deep. I gotta take a leak.

*IBRAHIM EXITS. JARED SITS READING HIS BLACK-BERRY PHONE. IT RINGS. HE PICKS UP.*

JARED: Hey babe. I know. I know. Me too . . . Look, I've told you a ton of times it wouldn't be my first choice either if I were him but he's all, "Granada, dude. Granada." . . . Yeah, whatever, it might be bizarre but it's what he wants . . . I wouldn't say that I'm a *mensch* or Anything . . . What . . . I seriously do need to do more discovery . . . there . . . Uh huh honestly the team doing prep for the appeal cannot go . . . right, uh-huh . . . I'm gonna be fine . . . would you relax? . . . for now, I told you . . . he can travel wherever he wants but . . . believe me, he's not gonna leave my sight . . . Okay. Right. Six hours ahead. I'll call you once we land in Madrid. I will. *(laughs)* Yeah. Me too. Really.

*IBRAHIM ENTERS.*

JARED: Just can't do that here. Now . . . Soon. Yeah. Gotta go, babe. Love you too.

*JARED HANGS UP.*

IBRAHIM: Cheryl? Shari? Whatever her name is?

JARED: Sharon.

IBRAHIM: Can't have phone sex for another eight hours. Damn.

JARED: Fuck you.

IBRAHIM: Just warn me so I'm out of the hotel room.

JARED: I got an international calling plan.

IBRAHIM: So you can roam the streets of Madrid until you rub one off in the stall of some public restroom.

JARED: Fuck. Off.

IBRAHIM: I'm just sayin'.

*THEY SHARE A LAUGH.*

JARED: When we get back, maybe you should . . .

IBRAHIM: Go to bars and hook up with random girls who are DTF and then move in together and have phone sex in airports? Not my style.

JARED: Sharon has this friend at work.

IBRAHIM: At Burger King?

JARED: Fuck off. At the salon where she works.

IBRAHIM: You're dating a girl who paints toenails and shit?

JARED: She's a licensed reflexologist. And its really more of an upscale spa. She does body work.

IBRAHIM: You date a girl who massages people's feet for a living? And you want me to date her friend who massages people's god knows what?

JARED: I'm just sayin'.

IBRAHIM: Not interested.

*A FEW BEATS. IBRAHIM TAKES OUT A NEWSPAPER AND STARTS TO READ.*

JARED: Wouldn't Paloma want you to be happy?

*A FEW BEATS. IBRAHIM IGNORES HIS COMMENT AND KEEPS READING.*

JARED: Sorry dude. It's just with Sharon. Things are kind of working out and it's bizarre. In like a good way. And I guess I just wanted . . .

*IBRAHIM PUTS DOWN THE NEWSPAPER.*

IBRAHIM: I get it.

JARED: And you know, I think you're probably right about the jealous thing on some level. Sharon's into therapy and so like we went as a couple and I actually learned some shit.

IBRAHIM: You went to a shrink? Yeah. I saw one for a while. Until my insurance ran out. Sort of helped. I guess.

JARED: And it's like because you know with my grandfather and everything . . . my father was pretty distant . . . didn't want to lose anyone close to him again so didn't want to invest much of himself.

IBRAHIM: Your grandmother?

JARED: I could see the pain in like the corners of her eyes. And so on some level I didn't want to lose anyone either. So why get close, right? . . . If you might just fuckin' get your heart ripped out of your chest, dude.

IBRAHIM: Exactly.

JARED: But what a shitty way to exist your whole fuckin' life. Three months. Two months. Two weeks. And the door keeps revolving without any girl actually staying. But like Sharon. She wants to stay. And so, yeah, it's like hard sometimes but way better. And so I thought, I don't want you to get like that. Like I've been. Without anyone. Forever. You know, dude?

IBRAHIM: Yeah, thanks man. Just not ready.

*A FEW BEATS. IBRAHIM PICKS UP HIS NEWSPAPER AND GOES BACK TO READING.*

JARED: So you're gonna be miserable during this entire trip?

IBRAHIM: You're paying for most of it so now I have to put out or something?

JARED: Fuck off.

IBRAHIM: I'll pay you back. God knows how but I will.

JARED: You don't have to pay me back.

*A FEW BEATS.*

JARED: When we get back, you should register for Fall semester, man.

IBRAHIM: Can't afford it.

JARED: The court accepted the motion to appeal. We will reverse this.

IBRAHIM: *(re: newspaper)* Yo . . . there's this rockin' music festival in this town in Morocco by the ocean. Muslim Woodstock. We should go, man.

JARED: We are not going to Morocco.

IBRAHIM: And there are these dudes with like long flowing white robes who wail and play these steel castanets. Fierce, man. It's not that far from Granada.

JARED: That's as far south as we're going.

IBRAHIM: Granada . . . .The *Alhambra*, wonder of the ancient world . . . so I can catapult through some portal and back into the eleventh century.

JARED: You better not pull any crazy shit.

IBRAHIM: Where I'd be a poet writing verse, you'd be an astronomer perfecting your astrolabe and she'd be a philosopher translating Plato into Arabic.

JARED: What the hell is an astrolabe? Sounds kinda kinky.

IBRAHIM: And we'd all be living harmoniously together and when the *muezzin* calls me to prayer, and the *shofar* draws you to synagogue and the cathedral bells beckon her to mass we'd all meet up later in the evening and discuss the wonders of the spirit over a cup of cinnamon tea.

JARED: Time travel back to the present, dude.

IBRAHIM: I'd rather search for a portal.

JARED: Where none exists.

IBRAHIM: Another time. Another moment. Another instance where . . .

JARED: Where you and she could be together? Well you're not and won't be. For the time being.

IBRAHIM: Is this the part where you say, "Get over her, dude?"

JARED: No, this is the part where I kick you in the ass, slap you on the face and say, "Wake the fuck up."

IBRAHIM: Since when are you allowed to be so hostile?

JARED: I'm allowed.

*LIGHTS SHIFT.*

## 22. On Death.

*GRANADA, SPAIN. MARCH 11, 2005. AFTERNOON.*
*IBRAHIM AND JARED ATOP A CASTLE TOWER AT*
*THE ALHAMBRA.*

IBRAHIM: *Granada. Alhambra. Alcazaba. Torre de la Vela*, Tower of the Candle. This is the portal I've been waiting for.

JARED: What the fuck is this portal shit?

IBRAHIM: Like a break in time and space . . . a tunnel to a former world.

JARED: *(sarcastic)* Oh . . . so like that movie where the kid drives that souped up Delorean and jumps back in time?

IBRAHIM: Jumping. Yeah.

JARED: Do not get near the edge if that's what you're fuckin' thinking about.

IBRAHIM: What if you're completely wrong?

JARED: You're so full of shit. You think you can drag me here, someone who's helped you to no end to then dream up some scheme to join her? You don't fling yourself off a tower because of love.

IBRAHIM: I wouldn't fling myself.

JARED: What . . . you'd toss yourself?

IBRAHIM: Better option.

JARED: You're here. For a reason. And you want to deny that? Whenever I say my name, Jared Rabinowitz, meaning descendant, son of a rabbi, I think of my grandfather's legacy, that I wish I'd met him, that I bust my balls to live a life worthy of his service and his sacrifice.

IBRAHIM: And you do.

JARED: I try.

IBRAHIM: But as for me . . .

*IBRAHIM SWIFTLY JUMPS UP ON ONE OF THE*
*STONE WALLS.*

JARED: Ibrahim, get the fuck down.

IBRAHIM: I can see the entire city of *Granada* in all its ancient wonder . . .

JARED: Ibrahim . . .

*JARED GOES TO GRAB IBRAHIM. IBRAHIM MOVES*
*FARTHER AWAY.*

JARED: And this is the best way to honor her memory?

IBRAHIM: Red tiled roofs, distant grey mountains, angular sandstone monuments, towering green forests . . .

JARED: Think of her legacy, then bust your balls to live a life worthy of her sacrifice.

*IBRAHIM STARES OUT OVER THE HORIZON AND APPROACHES THE LEDGE OF THE WALL, PREPARING TO JUMP.*

*LIGHTS SHIFT.*

## 23. On the One Who Falls in Love With One Sole Look.

*IBRAHIM AND PALOMA IN A LIMINAL, SPIRIT-WORLD SPACE.*

PALOMA: Live a life worthy of our time together. That's what you need to do, Ib.

IBRAHIM: P . . .

PALOMA: I don't want you here, with me . . . yet.

IBRAHIM: Why even show up then, appear or whatever it is you're doing right now in wherever it is we are . . . the do-I-stay or do-I-go portal?

PALOMA: You need to move onward. In your life.

IBRAHIM: Why move onward when the intolerance is so thick and the outlook so bleak? Why not dive into a past life where*

PALOMA: *(sarcastic)* We all lived harmoniously . . . with joyously tolerant neighbors and life would be*

IBRAHIM: Life would be tolerable.

PALOMA: You think this potential leap is a noble choice?

IBRAHIM: *Ibn Hazm* would understand.

PALOMA: *Ibn Hazm* isn't the ultimate authority.

IBRAHIM: But *Ibn Hazm* was our authority.

PALOMA: He wouldn't want this.

IBRAHIM: He wrote our guidebook so we could try to navigate through this minefield. *(reciting)* On he who falls in love with one sole look. Often love takes root in the heart with one sole look. There are two modes. First a man falls in love with the external figure of a woman without knowing who she is, without knowing her name or where she lives.

PALOMA: So you think you'll get some prize of like sleeping with many dark eyed virgins?

IBRAHIM: Day one. NYU. Literature and Society of Muslim Spain. Classroom door opens. In walks this woman. Eyes. Face. Body. Mind. Voice. Muslim? No. Christian? Probably.

PALOMA: Is that what you're really angling for?

IBRAHIM: *(reciting)* Second, a man falls in love with one sole look with a woman whose name, home and background he knows.

PALOMA: Heavenly fornication?

IBRAHIM: Day fifteen. NYU. Library. Study partners. Paloma. New York City. Puerto Rican. *Boricua*. Catholic. Body. Mind. Voice.

PALOMA: Ibrahim. New York City. Moroccan-American. Muslim. Body. Mind. Voice.

IBRAHIM: *(reciting)* In both cases the same thing happens. That which grows quickly, is consumed quickly . . .

IBRAHIM AND PALOMA: *(reciting)* that which takes time to be born, also takes time to end.

IBRAHIM: *(reciting)* On Death. Augmented in certain circumstances by the grief of love, the vitality of the lover is so weakened and the anguish grows to such a degree to cause death and departure from this world.

PALOMA: *(reciting)* In the devout traditions the following is found:

IBRAHIM: *(reciting)* He who falls in love and is chaste and dies . . .

IBRAHIM AND PALOMA: *(reciting)* Dies a martyr.

IBRAHIM: We should have . . .

PALOMA: Made . . . love. *(beat)* I know. We could have . . . early that morning in the hotel room in Madrid . . .

IBRAHIM: Yeah. So. Chaste still applies.

PALOMA: So you come here, to the *Alcazaba*, to Granada, climb this *Torre de la Vela*, Tower of the Candle, climbing a candle to become a martyr or . . .

IBRAHIM: And get to be with you . . . now.

PALOMA: I. Do. Not. Want. This. *Ibn Hazm* would not want this.

IBRAHIM: Paloma. Pigeon? Dove. *Palomita*. Popcorn? Nourishment. Pa. *Papá*. Father. Lo. Like "Lo and behold a babe is born in swaddling clothes." Or "Lo, looks who comes here." Ma. *Mamá*. Mother. Paloma. Family. *Familia*? All contained in your name. The universe in your name. *El Collar de la Paloma*. Ring of the Dove. Dove equals love. Ring equals bling. Bling of love. *(beat)* But we are . . . East and West. North and South. Male and Female. Muslim and Christian. *(beat)* I need . . . a portal. To another dimension. A window. To another reality. Because I had this opportunity to transcend these stone walls, these sandstone barriers and live with you and I fucked up. Instead of being bold and being with you in the land of my birth, on that island, I had to whisk you away to this foreign mythical place where I had some idea that we could live together and then return home transformed. Sin. Cowardice. Lust. Faithlessness. And the list goes on, tied around my neck like a lead plumb line leading me down to the center of the earth, underground, burrowed next to some pillar of a tree, where I can nourish the soil with my bones.

PALOMA: Ibrahim. Onward!

IBRAHIM: Now?

*LIGHT SHIFT.*

## 24. Paloma.

*MADRID. THE NEXT DAY. MARCH 12, 2005. LATE AF-
TERNOON. IBRAHIM AND JARED IN EL RETIRO PARK,
STANDING BESIDE A SMALL FOREST OF TREES.*

JARED: One hundred and ninety two trees.

IBRAHIM: Olive.

JARED: Cypress.

IBRAHIM: A river surrounding. *(beat)* Which one is hers?

JARED: You pick.

IBRAHIM: That one.

JARED: And so it is.

IBRAHIM: With the tall branches swaying to the right. A new way to see her.

JARED: Weeks later, my grandmother found a letter my grandfather had written to her only days before he was taken away. In the letter, he told her how much he loved her and their children and that if anything ever happened to him, he would be looking out for her and their family from the other side. She kept that letter tucked into her pillow for years after that. She used to tell me, "I see your grandfather in my dreams. We sit. We talk. We argue. We eat." *(beat)* There'll be other ways to see Paloma too.

IBRAHIM: Forest of the departed. *Bosque de los ausentes.* Why do they translate absent as departed? Absent means you're not around at the moment. Departed means you're not ever returning.

JARED: You can come back here any time. JFK. Madrid. Nonstop. Cheap internet flight.

IBRAHIM: This is enough. For a while.

JARED: This memorial will always be here. The trees will grow higher. The roots deeper. The water will continue to flow.

IBRAHIM: How does your version of the story about Noah and the flood and the dove go?

JARED: My version?

IBRAHIM: The version you learned as a kid in Hebrew school?

JARED: You mean when they've been in the ark and then the bird appears?

IBRAHIM: That part.

JARED: After forty days, Noah sends out a dove. The dove comes back with nothing.

IBRAHIM: 'Cause there was no land in sight.

JARED: Exactly. So after seven days, he sends the dove out again. And this time the dove returns with an olive branch.

IBRAHIM: A sign.

JARED: Right and then Noah sends out the dove a third time and the dove never returns.

IBRAHIM: The *Qur'an* version doesn't mention the dove. Both versions acknowledge the aquatic destruction and Noah's obedience. But the dove . . .

JARED: Paloma saved you from destruction. She could have insisted you stay with her to pray in that train compartment. But she did not.

IBRAHIM: So I'm left here, looking up at her tree in this park in Madrid.

JARED: One time when I was like five, I didn't get it and I asked my grandmother why my grandfather didn't take her away with him. And she said, "Because I wasn't supposed to go yet, *bubelah*." And I asked her why and she just shrugged her shoulders and said, "So many questions."

IBRAHIM: If her tree is olive, I'd buy a dove and build a bird house in its branches if I could.

JARED: Dove. Olive branch. A sign. So people could know.

IBRAHIM: Paloma.

*IBRAHIM AND JARED CONTINUE TO STARE AT THE FOREST OF TREES AS THE LIGHTS FADE.*


*END OF PLAY.*

# THE VANDAL

*Hamish Linklater*

First Produced in New York City
by The Flea Theater

Jim Simpson, Artistic Director
Carol Ostrow, Producing Director

Opened on January 31, 2013
Directed by Jim Simpson

WOMAN- Deirdre O'Connell
BOY - Noah Robbins
MAN- Zach Grenier

The design team featured:
David M. Barber (Set Designer)
Brian Aldous (Lighting Designer)
Claudia Brown (Costume Designer)
Brandon Wolcott (Sound Designer)
James McSweeney (Props Master).

**HAMISH LINKLATER** has acted in TV, film, and theater. He lives in Los Angeles with his daughter, Lucinda. This is his first play.

*For Jack*

WOMAN, forty
BOY, seventeen
MAN, fifty

Kingston, New York
Present time

Property List:
$20 Bill
Six-pack Budweiser
Bottle of Jim Beam
Pack of Camel Lights
Sun Chips and Cool Ranch Doritos
Credit cand and I.D.
Telephone and phone book
Tube of lipstick

Sound Effects
Bus arriving/departing

## Scene 1.

*Night, cold, a bus stop in Kingston. A woman waits. A boy comes up.*

BOY: Has it come yet?

WOMAN: No.

BOY: Late. *(Woman nods.)* Always late. *(Woman nods.)* Unless you miss it. Then you're late, you're the one who's late. Not the bus.

WOMAN: Yeah. I guess.

BOY: I guess. I guess if it came, if it weren't late, you wouldn't be here, right? I mean, like, why would you be here if it had come on time? You would be on the bus, and not here, keeping me company. *(Pause.)*

WOMAN: It may have, I was, I was a little late, so it may have already come . . .

BOY: Then we're in trouble, we are in trouble! It's like 20 minutes till the next one, right?

WOMAN: I think—

BOY: Oh my God, we're gonna freeze! We're gonna have to totally like, huddle together for warmth, just to survive *(Woman looks at boy.)* Kidding, I'm kidding. *(Pause.)* Where you headed?

WOMAN: Home.

BOY: Where's that? *(Beat.)* Sure gets dark early, huh . . . You come from the cemetery?

WOMAN: What?

BOY: The cemetery? *(He points off.)* That's where I was. I had a friend who died, about a year ago. I like to visit sometimes after school, say a prayer, check in, y'know, if it's a mess I clean up a little, get rid of the leaves.

WOMAN: Oh.

BOY: Is that where you were?

WOMAN: No. The Hospital. *(She points off in another direction)*

BOY: Oh right! I think that's hilarious, I always do, that, like, the hospital and the grave yard are right next door, it's like, what genius city planner . . . ?

WOMAN: I know.

---

*Hamish Linklater*

BOY: I mean, I guess it's practical, it's like economical, if things don't go well in one place it's a short drive to the next, but still, if you're going to the hospital and you're really sick, which you probably are because you're going to the hospital, it's not very—

WOMAN: Encouraging.

BOY: Ha! Exactly. Or even if you're not sick, if you're like having a baby, you can't get too psyched cuz there's the cemetery as you drive up, you're like, "Yay, New Life! Oooooooo right, we're all gonna die, shoot almost forgot. Thanks city planner."

WOMAN: *(Pointing off.)* And then there's the liquor store around the corner.

BOY: I know! That's like the one thing the city planner got right, like if you have to go to one or other of the other two places, and you're able to stumble out alive, at least there's the liquor store waiting for you. We're at the center of the triangle, *(Points at the hospital.)* Dying, *(Points at cemetery.)* Dead, *(Points at liquor store.)* Drunk. Are you sick?

WOMAN: What? No, why?

BOY: Is that why you were at the hospital?

WOMAN: No, my friend. I went to see a friend.

BOY: A friend, a-ha. Are you the friend, or do you really have a friend? Like when people say, "I have this friend who likes you", or "I have this friend who had a gay experience, but he's totally straight", or "I have this friend who pretends he's clumsy, but his dad beats the shit out of him", or "I have this friend who's freezing his ass off right now" but it's really you who's the friend—

WOMAN: I have a friend. An actual friend.

BOY: Oh no, I bet you do. Me too. I just told you about like 5 friends of mine, except the last one, the freezing one, that was me. No, I bet you have lots of friends.

WOMAN: What's that mean?

BOY: You're pretty. You're a little cold, but that might just be the weather. But I think you're probably nice too, when you warm up. So I bet people want to be friends with you.

WOMAN: Ok. Well. Thank you.

BOY: Hey, would you buy me a beer?

WOMAN: What?

BOY: I was, while we wait, could you buy me a beer, from the liquor store?

WOMAN: Why can't you buy your own? *(boy looks at her)* I don't think you can just drink beer outside, on the street.

BOY: Why not?

WOMAN: It's the law.

BOY: I'm the law.

WOMAN: Well then why can't you buy a beer for yourself, Law Man?

BOY: Because the Liquor Man has a bat and he doesn't believe me.

WOMAN: That you're 21?

BOY: That I'm The Law.

WOMAN: *(Laughs.)* How old are you?

BOY: How old are you?

WOMAN: Rude.

BOY: Why? Why is it polite to ask young people their age? Why is that gracious and charming?

WOMAN: You look 17.

BOY: You look old enough to be my sexy aunt.

WOMAN: How old's your sexy aunt?

BOY: I don't have one—yet.

WOMAN: If you are 17, I'm old enough to be your mother.

BOY: My mother's dead. She's up there too. That's not who I was visiting, just now, that was my friend.

WOMAN: I'm sorry.

BOY: It's ok, it's not bad, she died before I was born. Or like, she had died, and they had to do an emergency c-section to save me, but so, I never knew her. It's not so bad missing someone you never knew, though, y'know what I mean? It's not so bad.

WOMAN: Still, I'm very sorry.

BOY: So, will you buy me a beer? I'll pay.

WOMAN: I don't think so.

BOY: You're not conservative, are you?

WOMAN: What do you mean, politically?

BOY: Temperamentally. Not "a conservative," my dad's "a conservative," I just meant "conservative."

WOMAN: Because I wouldn't buy a kid alcohol? If that's . . . then, yeah, I guess I'm like your dad on that one.

BOY: You don't wanna be like my dad.

WOMAN: Oh no?

BOY: What about when you were younger? I bet you were more liberal.

WOMAN: When I was younger? I don't remember.

BOY: Because you were drunk all the time?

WOMAN: Sure. People were much nicer than me in my day. They'd buy beer for you at the bus stop no problem.

BOY: I miss the old days.

WOMAN: You're funny.

BOY: We both are.

WOMAN: I'm not. I'm not.

BOY: I bet you're hilarious when you get your drink on.

WOMAN: Well that's not happening tonight, so I guess we'll just have to live in the . . . I can't remember—

BOY: Why not tonight? Because of your friend? *(Pause.)* I had a teacher just like you.

WOMAN: Oh, now I'm your teacher, I thought I was your sexy aunt.

BOY: I told you, I don't have an aunt. But I had a teacher, Mrs. Blau— Wait, you might know her. Do you live in the area?

WOMAN: I do. I live here.

BOY: Why don't you have a car?

WOMAN: It's at the mechanic.

BOY: You can't afford it?

WOMAN: It's at the mechanic.

BOY: You had to sell it?

WOMAN: It's at the mechanic.

BOY: When'll it be ready?

WOMAN: Soon.

BOY: Is that why you can't afford to buy me beer? I told you, I'll pay—

WOMAN: You had a sexy teacher?

BOY: I didn't say that she was sexy, I said you reminded me of her.

WOMAN: Oh.

BOY: She had sex with a senior at my school, Matt Hoop—wait you might know him too.

WOMAN: I don't, I mean why would I—

BOY: He killed himself. It was in the paper.

WOMAN: If it was in the paper, why can't you say their names?

BOY: You might not have bought the paper that day; they've gotten expensive, newspapers. She got pregnant, Mrs. Bl— and she wanted to keep it because she was—how old are you again? Doesn't matter. She was much older than you and she didn't think there was any way, I mean there probably wasn't, this was her shot, it wasn't that she was ugly, she had dated this French guy, I don't know his real name, we called him Pierre, and they had been together for like 10 years, he didn't believe in marriage, maybe his father had fucked around, like Mitterrand, so he didn't believe in it—

WOMAN: How do you know?

BOY: My friend Tim Ross' mom was talking, or drinking wine and guessing, and Pierre was either against having kids because of coming from a broken home, or just sterile, and then Mrs. Bl—, the teacher, when she turned 40, he left her, just went back to France, or met someone else, Tim Ross' mom didn't know for sure, anyway Pierre was suddenly gone and the teacher was suddenly 40 and crying all the time in class which was just embarrassing for the kids, it was so pathetic, and as a result we had like, as a class, the lowest A.P. French scores in the county—

WOMAN: She taught—

BOY: French, so it was like torture, every word she said was part of a conversation with Pierre she would never have again, just *(French accent.) bleh, bleh, bleh,* blub, blub, blub all the time, I even went to the principal to get her fired, or sent on sabbatical till she got her shit together, not because I loved French so much, though I'm pretty good at it, *"On n'apprend pas aux vieux singes a' faire des grimaces"* (that's a french proverb), but no, I wanted her fired because it was just so disgusting the sob fest, and then, so, when she got pregnant and it was Matt Hoop—who was only in AP French because his dad was an undertaker and had like a chain of funeral homes, started with nothing but a shovel and a pair of black pants, put himself through Wesleyan, he was determined Matt would go to Wesleyan too, (but then Matt was a legacy so it shouldn't have been that hard, maybe he just needed an AP attended on his admissions,) anyway Matt got like straight F's, he was always zonked out in the back of class, Zoloft probably, all in black like his dad, but ironically, I think, to piss his dad off, but so that's why—I mean I thought it even before I heard Tim Ross' mom say it—why Mrs. Bl—chose Matt to get pregnant by, because Matt would never learn to say shit in French, not *merde*. But then, when she told him she was keeping it? Matt killed himself in that crazy way.

WOMAN: What way?

BOY: It was on TV. You don't even own a TV?

WOMAN: I own a TV, I just don't remember—

BOY: Or did you have to sell it with the car?

WOMAN: I just don't remember this story—

BOY: Self-entombment.

WOMAN: What?

BOY: That's what he died by: self-entombment.

WOMAN: What do you mean?

BOY: He buried himself alive. *(Silence)*

WOMAN: How?

BOY: It was kinda genius. There was a funeral that his dad was handling and he just swapped himself for the guy who was being buried. It was a closed casket deal, the dead guy, the already dead guy, Mr. Quinn I think, had died of some horrible like wasting disease, like Ebola of the head, and Matt's dad was like, "I can spruce him up and you can have the open casket but it'll cost you an arm and a leg to fix his face", and the Quinn family, they were Catholic and poor, not unrelatedly, and Mrs. Quinn, formerly Fleischer, was still kinda young so maybe she wanted to save a little heading into the second chapter of her life, not Tim Ross' mom's favorite, Mrs. Quinn nee Fleischer, so they went closed casket, but then when Mr. Quinn, or maybe it was O'Keefe, anyway when he was found in the woods by the road looking even more wasted, half eaten by woodlen creatures and all, everyone wondered who they had just buried, cause the coffin definitely had a body in it, it was heavy. Imagine it, Matt had to lay so still . . . . So when they dug up the casket, it was too late of course, he'd suffocated, or just, I don't know what kills you in self-entombment, dehydration maybe, but at some point he had changed his mind because it was a mess in there, he'd torn at the insides of the lid, all the lining, the stuffing was torn out, and it stank of course because you lose control of your functions when you die, you literally lose your shit, but it was also supposed to be beautiful with him all covered in ripped out white stuffing—like he was laying in a cloud, or a bath of angel feathers.

WOMAN: Was that who you were visiting?

BOY: What? No, I didn't really like Matt, I know tons of people who have died. This is Kingston. Just from my high school Becky Morse took heroine before going to the dentist and ODed on the Novocain, Marshall Swee's older brother died in Afghaniston, Kellen Hertz died of MS or ALS, I always get them Confused; my friend who I was visiting? A year ago he and 3 other kids were in a car that just wrecked on the way to school cuz it was icy and the tires were a little bald and they all died, just from a slippery road.

WOMAN: Jesus.

BOY: What? It happens all the time, everywhere. What would be really crazy is if people stopped dying, everywhere. That would be a story for the paper. So anyway, Mrs. Bl– had to quit, but she had her daughter 7 months later, it had a cleft pallet or something, it wasn't perfect, but it was something you could fix, and she never cried again.

WOMAN: That's who I remind you of?

BOY: Yeah.

WOMAN: Maybe you should have stuck with the sexy aunt line if you wanted a beer.

BOY: I just meant you both seem like women who see life, that it's short, and like, much easier to waste than use. And when you see a chance, y'know, to have sex with some AP French burn-out so you can have a life with a baby instead of one without, or when you see a chance to buy a funny kid a beer so that your freezing wait for a bus is noisy and entertaining instead of quiet and boring, you both choose life! Life! Life! Rah, rah, rah! *(Woman looks for the bus. It isn't coming. She laughs, opens her purse.)*

BOY: Oh no. I got it. I insist. Here, pay with this. *(He gives her a $20.)*

WOMAN: What do you want?

BOY: Just Bud.

WOMAN: Bud. Just, what? One or—

BOY: They come in 6; we can share.

WOMAN: Ok. We'll see. *(Woman takes the $20, goes off toward liquor store. Boy does something magical, like a front flip off the bench. The sound of the bus, he looks for her, it goes black as the bus pulls in front of him.)*


## Scene 2.

*Liquor store. Man behind counter. Woman puts 6-pack of bud down.*


MAN That it?

WOMAN: Yep.

MAN: Just the Budweiser?

WOMAN: Uhuh.

MAN: No chips or cigarettes or—

WOMAN: I don't smoke.

MAN: So, just the Budweiser?

WOMAN: Yes.

MAN: Ok.

WOMAN: Is that a problem?

MAN: You just don't strike me as a Budweiser drinker.

WOMAN: Oh no?

MAN: Not really.

WOMAN: What do I strike you as?

MAN: More of a wine drinker maybe.

WOMAN: That's—

MAN: I'm not being sexist. If I thought you were French I'd think you drink wine too. That doesn't mean I think all French people are women. Just playing the percentages. Because I sell a fair amount of Budweiser, but very rarely to middle aged, non-smoking women . . . But you're right, it's wrong, profiling people. *(Woman laughs)* What?

WOMAN: Nothing. French. Private joke. Nothing.

MAN: You sure you don't want some chips. Lotta beer on an empty stomach.

WOMAN: I don't want chips.

MAN: You have food already? Maybe a pizza in the car?

WOMAN: That's right. *(Man looks out the window.)* I parked round the corner.

MAN: That's weird. We got parking out front.

WOMAN: My spot's fine.

MAN: It's a cold night.

WOMAN: My coat's very warm.

MAN: Doesn't look it.

WOMAN: It is.

MAN: Not a great neighborhood. You got pepper spray?

WOMAN: I do.

MAN: I got a bat.

WOMAN: *(Beat.)* That's good.

MAN: You have to defend yourself. Against lawlessness. Maybe I should walk you to your car.

WOMAN: I'm fine. I'll be fine.

MAN: So just the six Budweisers, huh?

WOMAN: You know what, I will get some chips. I'm low on chips. Thank you, thank you for the suggestion. *(Woman grabs some chips.)*

MAN: He doesn't like Sun Chips. He likes Cool Ranch Doritos.

WOMAN: Who?

MAN: My son. Robert. He likes Cool Ranch Doritos. If you're gonna get chips too.

WOMAN: I don't know who you're talking about.

MAN: You shouldn't buy beer for minors. It's illegal.

WOMAN: Why would you think—

MAN: You're buying Budweiser.

WOMAN: It's a popular beer.

MAN: It's his favorite.

WOMAN: It's many people's favorite. Hence its popularity.

MAN: "Hence". Oooooo. *(Silence)* First Friday of the month. Little shit always sends someone in to buy him Budweiser first Friday of the month. Mostly they're homeless though. Not that I'm profiling you as not homeless. Just, they're usually the type of person that buys a kid a beer because they need one for themselves. And they're usually not women, or I should say attractive women. So, how's he doing? Did he tell you my wife is dead? To get you to come in here? Little shit.

WOMAN: I never met your son.

MAN: He says stuff like that to manipulate a situation to his advantage. Which is fine, no one wants to manipulate a situation to their disadvantage.

WOMAN: You don't get a lot of people buying Budweiser on a Friday night?

MAN: Oh, I'm not the most popular small business in Kingston.

WOMAN: Can't imagine why; are you gonna let me pay for this?

MAN: $12.49. *(Woman lays down the $20.)* Out of twenty. Without going over. Y'know that's his allowance money? Y'know that twenty came out of this till? I know it's not much of an allowance. I know, I'm not much for inflation. But once a month some derelict comes in here, buys Budweiser and whatever else without going over twenty, and I know who it is they're buying for. Where is he? By the bus stop?

WOMAN: I wouldn't know.

MAN: You can tell me. It's not like I'm gonna run out there and try to catch him. Give him a beating for making a pretty lady buy him beer.

WOMAN: You're not gonna do that?

MAN: He's too fast for me. Time I reach the corner Robert's gone, every time. It's like I set off his spidey sense. How did he seem to you?

WOMAN: I don't know your son.

MAN: I could call the police if you're contributing to the corruption of a minor.

WOMAN: I'll take a half-pint of Jim Beam, and a pack of Camels. Ultra light. Am I over twenty dollars now? Do I fit the profile of a lady Budweiser drinker now?

MAN: I thought you didn't smoke.

WOMAN: I used to, but I quit, and now I'd like to start again.

MAN: They'll kill you.

WOMAN: What won't?

MAN: Oooo lala.

WOMAN: Oui, Oui.

MAN: $26.63. *(woman pulls a few singles out of her purse,*

*fishes around, then puts the $20 back and hands him a credit card, he glances at it.)* Can I see some ID?

WOMAN: ID?

MAN: You're purchasing alcohol.

WOMAN: I'm over 21.

MAN: I'm sure you are. But we card anyone under 35.

WOMAN: I'm over 35.

MAN: You don't look it to me.

WOMAN: Are you flirting?

MAN: Would you like me to?

WOMAN: Now you are.

MAN: Now I am.

WOMAN: What would your wife think?

MAN: We're divorced, Libby lives in Long Island with her new family, they play tennis. She'll never know I was flirting.

WOMAN: Ok.

MAN: So can I see some ID?

WOMAN: Is this still flirting, or just annoying?

MAN: Probably annoying. But still store policy.

WOMAN: Who makes the policy?

MAN: Me. It's my store. I'm the Liquor Man.

WOMAN: Fine.

    *(she fishes through her bag again, hands over ID)*

MAN: Nice to meet you Margaret Cotter. I'm Dan.

WOMAN: Ok.

MAN: Do you go by Peggy or Maggie?

WOMAN: I don't.

MAN: You are over 21 and 35. I wouldn't believe it if I didn't have certified proof from the State of New York.

WOMAN: Thank God we're back to flirting.

MAN: But then who's Mary Willits? *(He holds up the credit card.)* I mean, I know who she is, she works at the hospital. Beautiful. Like a stunner, and so nice. And I guess there may be two Mary Willits', but according to your driver's license it looks like you're not one of them.

WOMAN: *(Beat.)* Mary's a friend.

MAN: Oh?

WOMAN: She loaned me her card.

MAN: She loaned you her credit card?

WOMAN: Yes.

MAN: You don't have your own credit card?

WOMAN: It's just, it's for emergencies.

MAN: Why would Mary loan you her credit card for emergencies?

WOMAN: She's my friend, and I've had a hard time, financially, and she was worried for me, if I ever got in a tight spot, she wanted me to have a fall back.

MAN: That's a good friend.

WOMAN: She is.

MAN: Did you go to school together?

WOMAN: No.

MAN: Because you're a little older than she is—

WOMAN: I know her from the hospital—

MAN: Do you work together?

WOMAN: Forget it, I'm leaving.

MAN: I'll call the police.

WOMAN: For a borrowed credit card?

MAN: Then I'll call Mary.

WOMAN: Do you have her number?

MAN: I have a phone book. *(Man pulls out a phone book starts flipping through.)*

WOMAN: My husband died.

MAN: My wife died too, according to my son.

WOMAN: You're saying my husband didn't die?

MAN: I'm saying it looks like bullshit is catching.

WOMAN: You're saying I'd make something like that up?

MAN: I'm saying I think my son's out there at that bus stop.

WOMAN: *(furious, pulls a picture from wallet)* This is my husband Paul Cotter, he fucking died 6 months ago of fucking cancer at Benedictine fucking Hospital, right up on that fucking hill there, and his nurse was Mary Willits! *(Man stops flipping through phone book, looks at picture.)*

MAN: I'm sorry.

WOMAN: Did you kill him?

MAN: No.

WOMAN: Then save your sorries, and let me have my ID and fucking credit card back.

MAN: You're young.

WOMAN: Oh now I'm young again, that's great.

MAN: For a widow.

THE VANDAL

WOMAN: That has to be the worst complement ever given.

MAN: I wasn't trying—

WOMAN: Then give me my cards back.

MAN: You don't want the Budweiser?

WOMAN No.

MAN: My son will be disappointed.

WOMAN: Your son, who I never met, can go fuck himself for all I care. *(Beat. woman holds her hands out for cards, man doesn't give them.)*

MAN: Ok, Miss. I'll give you back your ID, and I'll even give you back Mary's card, but I'm gonna call her first. I have to, that's only fair—

WOMAN: I can't believe—

MAN: And I'm having trouble believing, "hence" our little impasse here.

WOMAN: You need a better explanation than—

MAN: Yeah.

WOMAN: Than a friend helping a friend in need?

MAN: No sure, that's a friend indeed. I just think it's a little far fetched, nurses handing out their credit cards—

WOMAN: *(More furious.)* Ok, you look. Look me in the eyes, you asshole. My husband got diagnosed with stage 4 testicular cancer. He was 45 years old. They gave him 6 months to live. It took him 3 years to die. And Mary was his nurse, at his bedside, that whole time.

MAN: And that's how you became friends?

WOMAN: That's right. She's my friend, our friend, became our friend—because we lost everything—

MAN: You lost everything—

WOMAN: Everything, my husband quit his job when they told him and I did too, so we could spend those last months—

MAN: Ok.

WOMAN: But then he didn't die, and she was there for all of it, the chemo, the radiation, for the loans, the second mortgages, she was there for us losing everything, and she was great!

MAN: She is great.

WOMAN: I know.

MAN: A real angel.

WOMAN: I know. I know. So sympathetic, so beautiful. Everybody loves Mary.

MAN: Well it's good you had that time.

WOMAN: You think?

MAN: To say goodbye, say what you needed to—

WOMAN: *(Enraged.)* Oh my God, people say that!—y'know what time's good for? Nothing. A heart attack's better, a car crash, a bolt from the blue—you wanna tell me it's better to watch my husband die for three years—

MAN: No—

WOMAN: Getting a little hope up maybe, and then getting punched in the gut, over and over, that's better? If he's gonna die, fucking kill him already! Here's how you say good-bye for three years, "goooooooooooooooooooooooooo ooooodbyyyyyyyyyyyyyyyyyyyyye,IIIIIIIIIloooooooooooo oooooooveyooooooooooooooooooou".

MAN: Ok.

WOMAN: *(More enraged.)* And you wanna know why? Why he didn't die? I'll tell you why. Mary fucking Willits, that Angel. We'd joke the only reason he wouldn't kick off was her, that he'd fallen for her,—cuz like you said, she was such a ray of sunshine, you know washing him, all angelic, I mean we'd laugh about it, Paul and I, it was ridiculous, him staying alive so he could just keep going in to see her, gorgeous Mary Willits, keep getting cared for by this heavenly. And then, as if to prove the joke, and it's hilarious, after 3 years Mary got married to this doctor, Dr. Stevenson, and he, my husband Paul, he took a turn that was bad, and he finally did die, and I don't even think she really loved the doctor, Dr. Stevenson, I mean he was successful, but nothing to look at, or talk to. I think she just knew, I think she knew, after they took the car away, she knew; so she married this guy she didn't love so my husband could die, and I could, you know, move on.

MAN: And that's why she loaned you her credit card?

WOMAN: It's only for emergencies.

MAN: Like buying Budweiser for my son?

WOMAN: I don't know anything about your son. *(Man flips through phone book.)*

MAN: Willow, Wilmot, Winston, oops, wrong way—Williams, Williams, Williams, there must be like 30 Williams, here we go—*(Man dials phone.)*

WOMAN: *(Grasping)* Fine. I took it. Everything else is true. *(It rings.)* We lost everything, I don't know if he loved her or not, but he died, she hugged me, said how sorry she was, and I took her credit card. *(It rings)*

MAN: For emergencies?

WOMAN: For revenge. *(It rings)*

MAN: How does my son look? Is he ok? *(From the phone: "hello?".)*

WOMAN: Yes. *(Man hangs up. He looks at the credit card.)*

MAN: Does it still work?

WOMAN: Yes.

MAN: Do you use it much?

WOMAN: Groceries, twice a month.

MAN: Nobody cards anymore. Why hasn't she cancelled it?

WOMAN: Because she knows what it's being used for. Because she knows what she did.

MAN: Because she's an angel. *(Man runs the card. They wait. It goes through.)* It worked. Oh, I should have asked: Any cash back?

WOMAN: No, no thank you.

MAN: Wait. *(Man replaces the Sun Chips with Cool Ranch Doritos.)* Just take these, for Robert, as a trade. Ok? Take these, as your gift to me. *(She does and goes)*


## SCENE 3

*Bus stop, still cold. Boy there, woman returns with bag.*


BOY: How'd it go in there?

WOMAN: Easy Peasy. *(Woman hands him bag.)*

BOY: Cool Ranch! My favorite, how'd you know?

WOMAN: Lucky guess.

BOY: You want a Bud?

WOMAN: I want the bottle. *(Woman drinks Jim Beam, boy Bud.)*

BOY: You were gone a long time.

WOMAN: I had a problem with my card.

BOY: You paid?

WOMAN: My treat. *(She returns $20.)*

BOY: Why'd you pay?

WOMAN: Because I did.

BOY: Did something happen?

WOMAN: Just drop it, ok? Or change it, it's just, enough. Enough. Ok?

BOY: Ok. *(He bites a chip.)* You know what I like with Cool Ranch, any Dorito really, as opposed to like a Sun Chip? Or a, I don't know, regular tortilla chip? The flavor dust that gets stuck to your fingers when you bite your chip. See? With Cool Ranch it's like, a blue and gold flavor dust. It's not really the color of ranch dressing. Maybe it's a metaphor: "Cool Ranch" . . . But then look at this: so like, you lick it off, the flavor dust, *(He licks his fingers.)* Voila. But then when you go for the next chip, your fingers are like wet and sticky, *(He eats another chip.)* so more flavor dust sticks to your fingers, so you lick em again, and your fingers get wetter and stickier, so there's gonna be more flavor dust, there's gonna be more licking, and eventually it'll just like coat your fingers, your tongue and lips get all coated too, and who knows eventually if the licking is actually cleaning your fingers, or just shellacking on more layers of pasty flavor dust. It's just like this passing back and forth of smoosh that's losing flavor. It's just this cleaning which isn't even tasting anymore, this cleaning that's only making a bigger mess. It's a negative feed back cycle. And the chip, the start of the whole thing, is like beside the point.

WOMAN: Huh.

BOY: Do you think that's a metaphor?

WOMAN: I'm not sure I'm following

BOY: Is, like, the chip our Life, the flavor dust our dreams, the fingers reality, they moosh together, and then your mouth is like death? *(He licks his fingers.)*

WOMAN: I'm definitely not—

BOY: Or maybe the chip is your heart, the flavor dust is love, the fingers are heartbreak, and then time just gobbles them up? *(He bites a chip.)*

WOMAN: What if you just let me drink?

BOY: Wait, no, what if the chip is the soul, the flavor dust is magic, the fingers what you do with your soul, and the mouth Deep Space . . . or Oblivion, or whatever that massive thing is which doesn't even know the world exists or we exist or that existence exists, that Vastness which is deafeningly neutral, neither good nor bad, just there, just true, just bigger than thoughts can think, and eyes can see, and mouths can say, and when you think about God, Who no one should really think about, look what happened to Job who was a good guy, and always tried to be good, and God said, "You think you know me? You think you know what I want?" And then he bent Job over and fucked him so hard Job was like, "Ok! I get it, I get it," and God was like, "What? What do you get?" and Job was like, "I get that I don't get it, I won't get it, I can't get it, I get that there is nothing to get, there is only God, and He can fuck you up the ass whenever he wants to!" and God came in Job and blew out Job's brains and humankind has never thought of God, or conceived of the enormity of God since, because the part of our brains that could was blown away that day; that God, the real God, who we don't dare know the omniscience of, the omnipotence of, the plan, the rules of, that God, if He does exist, is only a blue flavor dust speck in the mouth of the True Vastness. We do not matter. More likely we are anti-matter. More likely it's not a metaphor. Most likely it's just a Cool Ranch Dorito.

WOMAN: You really do like those chips.

BOY: Don't get me started on Bud.

WOMAN: I won't.

BOY: I'll give you a hint. Bud's the counter argument to Doritos.

WOMAN: The counter argument.

BOY: The yang to the ying.

WOMAN: The vice to the versa?

BOY: Bud says there is only you. And everything else – time, space, God, blah, blah—everyone else—the drunk, dying, dead, blah, blah – exist inside you, if they exist at all, which is up to you, because only you know, and only you matter. You are the Vastness.

WOMAN: How does it say that?

BOY: Taste it. *(Woman puts down her bottle, opens a bud, sips it, slugs it.)*

WOMAN: Gotcha.

*Hamish Linklater*

BOY: Good, right?

WOMAN: Now gimme a Dorito so I can regain some perspective. No, you're right. I like mattering. Mattering, nattering about mattering. Wait. Who am I thinking of? Who's the girl? The one from the book, or the movie, with the blonde hair?

BOY: Does she have a blue dress?

WOMAN: Yes.

BOY: Is there a cat?

WOMAN: Yes.

BOY: And a tea party?

WOMAN: Yes!

BOY: I don't know.

WOMAN: Fuck you, tell me you brat, what's her name?

BOY: I'll give you a hint: she has a Restaurant.

WOMAN: What?

BOY: And Gertrude Stein loved her.

WOMAN: Shut the fuck up and tell me who I'm thinking of!

BOY: She doesn't live here any more—

WOMAN: Jesus are you a smartass! What school do you go to?

BOY: Kingston High.

WOMAN Bullshit.

BOY: Bull true.

WOMAN: I went to Kingston High! We didn't have AP French and AP Metaphor and AP Smartass at Kingston fucking High.

BOY: Maybe they introduced them in the 2000s. Or the '80s?

WOMAN: Smartass!

BOY: Intelligence is 20% education, 20% environment, and 60% hereditary.

WOMAN: So now you're taking shots at my parents?

BOY: I made that up.

WOMAN: So it's a shot at me?

BOY: It's a shot in the dark you dove in front of.

WOMAN: No wonder your father beats you. *(Silence.)*

BOY: He said he was my father?

WOMAN: Oh come on.

BOY: He knew I sent you?

WOMAN: Based on my purchases, he interpolated.

BOY: Why would you think he beat me?

WOMAN: He said he had a bat, and you said you had a clumsy friend, and I extrapolated.

BOY: My friend is Kevin Dumphy, I am not the friend.

WOMAN: And he's not your father.

BOY: He's my Dad, and he never touched me, and you should believe me.

WOMAN: He also said you have problems with the truth.

BOY: He has problems with the truth.

WOMAN: He also said your mother was alive. I don't care, he said it. It's just that's pretty messed up. I mean of all the things you've made up tonight, that's the messed uppedest. I don't care. I like it, the talk. But if I was your mother I'd be pretty hurt knowing that my son was walking around saying I'm dead when I'm actually just playing tennis in Long Island with my new family because my old one consisted of an abusive husband and a pathologically lying son. I'd be pretty hurt.

BOY: My father never touched me.

WOMAN: Ok.

BOY: He shouts sometimes. His wife died. The mother of his child died, so he shouts. That's allowed.

WOMAN: Ok.

BOY: Because that's not fair, losing your partner.

WOMAN: I know.

BOY: You don't know anything, you think you do, but unless you're me, or my Dad, instead of you, you don't actually know anything about what we've been through.

WOMAN: If you say so.

BOY: You don't because you're you, and I'm me, and Dad's Dad, and what happened to us only happened to us the way it happened to us.

WOMAN: No two snowflakes are the same.

BOY: You don't know.

WOMAN: Eskimos have a thousand words for snow.

BOY: What are you talking about?

WOMAN: If all the snowflakes in the world got together and made the world's biggest snowball and the Eskimos called it Germuchnik, and Tinkatink, and Spooldybooldy and a thousand other names and the snowball went to hell it would still melt, so . . .

BOY: I don't know—

WOMAN: I'm saying I don't care, I'm saying looks like snow, I'm saying where's the bus.

---

*Hamish Linklater*

BOY: She died giving birth to me.

WOMAN: Your Dad says different.

BOY: Why won't you believe me?

WOMAN: I don't not believe you.

BOY: But you believe my Dad?

WOMAN: I don't not believe—

BOY: He needs help. *(Boy cries.)*

WOMAN: Oh no. Oh no, sssssshhhhhh. You're gonna get, all your tears and snot are gonna freeze to your face, sssssssh-hhh. This is a mess, what a mess.

BOY: He's lying.

WOMAN: Oh gosh, what do you want me to say?

BOY: Say he's lying.

WOMAN: Oh sweetheart, everyone lies.

BOY: No they don't.

WOMAN: Of course they do, come on, you've got to, it's expected, it's common courtesy. Hey, I lied to you earlier.

BOY When?

WOMAN: When I said I had a friend, at the hospital. You guessed it.

BOY: What's wrong with you?

WOMAN: Nothing it was just a check-up.

BOY: Then why'd you lie?

WOMAN: Because it wasn't your business and it was nicer than saying "fuck off".

BOY: When was the last time you went to the doctor?

WOMAN: Fuck off.

BOY: You have to be vigilant, at your age.

WOMAN: Other things came up.

BOY: Why haven't you gone, do you have a death wish? *(Beat.)* It's ok, if you do, I used to want to die.

WOMAN: No, sweetheart.

BOY: *(Still sniffly.)* Oh my demographic's suicide rate is surreal. What with the hormones, you get zits and erections and suicidally depressed all the time, and you feel like nobody loves you, which with my mom is true since she never met me, I said that already—but there you are just going around like this, I don't know, this pimply, boner-fest, suicide bomb

WOMAN: But you don't want to die now.

BOY: Well, let's just say mostly I think I'd be happier to be alive than dead.

WOMAN: You know your mother loved you.

BOY: Oh yeah?

WOMAN: Of course she did.

BOY: When? When I was in utero?

WOMAN Sure

BOY: How do you know?

WOMAN Because she did.

BOY: Did you know her? Did you talk to her when she was pregnant with me? Were you her friend?

WOMAN No.

BOY: I'm gonna go. *(He starts to leave.)*

WOMAN: What about the bus?

BOY: I'm gonna walk.

WOMAN It's freezing.

BOY: I don't care.

WOMAN: How far's your house?

BOY: I'm not going home.

WOMAN: Wait, come on, what if I said I was your mother's friend? Would you believe me then?

BOY: I wouldn't believe you.

WOMAN: No, come on, what if I said, when your mom was pregnant, I was her friend, and she said she loved you, and she said she was so excited to meet you, and she couldn't wait?

BOY: *(Beat.)* What else?

WOMAN: What else? She said, she said she couldn't wait, and she, she was so excited to have a son, and she wanted you to be a baseball player so your Dad's bat would go to good use.

BOY: Uh huh.

WOMAN: It's true, she said you were her little blessing and and you were gonna to bring purpose to her life—

BOY: She wasn't happy?

WOMAN: No, she was. But your Dad, he could be a little stoic, a little strong silenty. But you, you were gonna be a talker. She was gonna see to that, read to you, get cd's of musicals, she was always listening to- what's the name of a musical?

BOY: *My Fair Lady?*

WOMAN: I don't know that one: *Mary Poppins*. She'd put the speaker right up against her belly, so when you came out you'd be all, "superfragalistic" and no one would be able to get a word in edge wise.

BOY: How did you guys meet?

WOMAN: We went to school together.

BOY: She didn't go to Kingston High. She was from Schenectady.

WOMAN: Which is where we went to middle school together. Before my parents moved here. Did she ever tell you the name of her middle school?

BOY: No.

WOMAN: St. Mary's Middle School, Schenectady, New York. We were thick as thieves. I was a bridesmaid at your parents wedding, she made me wear the ugliest dress, etcetera. So yeah, I was with her when she was pregnant, which is how I know she loved you, her little baby, her Robert. *(Pause.)*

BOY: Did my Dad tell you my name? In the store?

WOMAN: He didn't have to, I'm one of Libby's oldest friends *(Pause.)*

BOY: Can I ask you another question? You don't have to tell me the truth.

WOMAN Sure.

BOY: Are you my mother?

WOMAN What?

BOY: Are you the friend? Again?

WOMAN: Ummm.

BOY: Did you somehow survive giving birth to me, have you come back from the dead? Are you her? *(Pause.)*

WOMAN: What if I was?

BOY: How did you do it?

WOMAN: *(Gradually.)* Well, ok ... what if that night, after you were delivered and sent home with your Dad, ok what if I suddenly came to? What if they had given me this powerful sedative while I was giving birth, lexi-something, and I flat lined. But Dr. Stevenson, my ob/gyn, he used those paddle things and he brought me back to life. And what if when I came to I had amnesia—from the drugs and the paddles and shock. And what if Dr. Stevenson had always been a little in love with me, since Schenectady even, and when

THE VANDAL

he discovered I had amnesia and couldn't remember you or your Dad, he told me that he was my husband. That a new job had opened up in Long Island and we would have to be moving as soon as I was feeling better from my appendectomy. So we moved, and had a family, a family of tennis players. But it wasn't my fault, or anyone's really.

BOY: And what are you doing here now?

WOMAN: *(Beat.)* Well the other day, in Long Island, we were playing doubles, and your half sister, Helen, she hit a lob, and I went back and your half brother, Troy, he came forward, and Troy's so uber competitive, he jump slammed his return, and whacked me in the head with his racket. I got concussed, but it shook free this memory, this memory of a little boy, with a little blue hat, who smelt like me and paradise combined, a baby named Robert who I loved more than my new children and who I had to find at all costs, who I had to put my arm around *(she does this)* who I had to tell: Your mother is here. She loves you. She never meant to leave you. And now she's here.

BOY: I love you too.

WOMAN: I know. *(Pause.)*

BOY: Are you really her? *(The bus comes, the stage goes black. The bus drives off, the stage is illuminated, woman and boy are still there.)*

WOMAN: I'm not your mother.

BOY: Who are you?

WOMAN Margaret Cotter.

BOY: We're not related?

WOMAN: We're strangers.

BOY: I don't believe you.

WOMAN It's true.

BOY: You've never had children?

WOMAN: Never.

BOY: You weren't my mother's friend?

WOMAN: I never met your mother.

BOY: How'd you know how to make all that up?

WOMAN: Maybe I do know something about something.

BOY: Let me see your stomach.

WOMAN What?

BOY: I wanna see if you have a c-section scar.

WOMAN: I don't have, I'm not showing you my stomach.

---

BOY: Please.

WOMAN: What are you talking about?

BOY: Please!

WOMAN: It's freezing!

BOY: I knew it, I knew you were her!

WOMAN: Fine. There! *(She opens her coat and pulls up her shirt and down the front of her pants.)* There, see my stupid, horrible, scarless, stomach. *(He looks.)*

BOY: What's that?

WOMAN: What?

BOY: That line?

WOMAN: What line?

BOY: That horizontal line? *(He pokes at her belly.)*

WOMAN: Don't! That was a crease, just a crease, from my pants or panties, I've been sitting! It's not a scar you freak!

BOY: It's all made up?

WOMAN: There is a Dr. Stevenson, but I don't really know him, otherwise, yes, it was all a story.

BOY: Why'd you tell it?

WOMAN: To stop your crying, to lighten the mood, we were just talking, Jesus, I was trying to make you feel better.

BOY: I feel worse.

WOMAN: The point I was trying to, the point, the moral of my story was, whether you're mother, if she's dead or not, I don't care, it's just, come on, it's okay, you're not the first person that's gone through whatever it is you're going through.

BOY: Or the opposite.

WOMAN: Or the opposite, yeah . . . .—Alice!

BOY: What?

WOMAN: Alice! Through the Looking Glass, Alice!

BOY: Alice.

WOMAN: Alice! Why was I thinking of Alice?

BOY: Because you drank the Bud which made you feel big, like Alice after she drank the "Drink me" drink. And then you wanted to bite the Dorito, like Alice bit the "Eat me" cake, so you could feel small again.

WOMAN: That's stupid, why would Alice want to be small?

BOY: Because, she was too big to get through that teeny tiny door.

WOMAN What door?

BOY: You wanna get out of here?

WOMAN: And go where?

BOY: I'll show you the answer to all your questions.

WOMAN: I don't have any questions.

BOY: Then I'll show you the question to all your answers. *(Boy leans in and kisses woman.)*

BOY: Let's just walk. To stay warm. *(He goes. She sits.)*

## Scene 4

*Cemetery, several graves, the half finished bag of Doritos on one.*

WOMAN: *(Off.)* Robert! Hey! Hallooo! Robert! *(She enters carrying her remaining beer and bottle in a bag.)* Where are you, you little shit. I nearly just ripped my shitty coat on that shitty fence you just made me shitting hop. I don't hop fences Robert, I'm a lady! Worse yet I nearly broke my bottle! Not that there woulda been much to lose in a breaking, as much or most of the contents are gone. But I coulda been cut! Plus the remainder beers are all shook up now. Gotta quarter tap em to keep from getting sprayed all over. And I don't have a quarter. Or a nickel or dime. And worse yet I'm freezing! and drunk! thank god, or else I'd be worse freezing. "Worse freezing". Who says that? Drunk ladies in cemeteries chasing 17 year old boys putting on lipstick in case they catch em, that's who. What're we doing, a little graveyard hide 'n seek? *(She starts sneaking up and peeking behind headstones.)* Peek . . . a . . . boo! Peek . . . a . . . boo! Peek . . . a . . .

MAN: *(off)* Boo! *(Man emerges, ghostlike, from behind a grave.)*

WOMAN: Holy Jesus! Fuck You, Fuck you, Fuck you in the face, forever. That is bullshit!

MAN: What're you doing up here?

WOMAN: Jesus Christ, that was horrible. I nearly just threw up out of fright!

MAN: Why are you up here?

WOMAN Jesus—

MAN: Are you chasing after my son?

WOMAN What? No!

MAN: Because I could hear you screaming his name through the cemetery all the way down at my store. *(Beat.)* It's ok. I just figured, I sold you a lot of booze, and it's cold, and if he ran off, which it looks like he did, you might get lost and hurt yourself.

WOMAN: I'm not drunk.

MAN: That bag looks lighter.

WOMAN: I'm not saying I haven't drunk ... some beers ... and whiskies. I'm saying the drinking of the drinks didn't make me drunk. Should I be worried about where your son's gotten to?

MAN: Most likely he saw me coming and hurried on home. Did you guys come up here to make out?

WOMAN: No! I'm old enough to be his—

MAN: You're older. I've seen your ID.

WOMAN: Har har har.

MAN: Got a flashlight. Need help getting outta here?

WOMAN: Why don't you have a beer and calm down?

MAN: You're asking me to have a drink with you?

WOMAN: Beggars can't be picky. *(Woman hands a beer to him. He opens it. It sprays him.)*

MAN: Motherfucker.

WOMAN: Oh my god! That's terrible! What kind of novelty joke shop are you running down there, selling exploding beer cans to the public?!

MAN: So if you didn't come up here to score with my son—

WOMAN: Vandalism.

MAN: Better.

WOMAN: Yeah, we came up to do some tagging. Tag a couple graves.

MAN: Where's your spray paint?

WOMAN: Hardware store was closed. You got a Sharpie? *(She fishes in her purse.)*

MAN: I don't think kids tag any more.

WOMAN: What do they do then?

MAN: They post. And tweet.

WOMAN: They call it what?

MAN: Actually, you can be tagged in a photo.

WOMAN What?

MAN: On the internet?

WOMAN: My computer's at the mechanic. I'm talking about tagging. Outside.

MAN: My son's generation does its vandalism inside.

WOMAN: Your son's generation is sad.

MAN: They know. I read all about it on my son's Facebook page.

WOMAN: Oooo, look at you, modern man.

MAN: Why not charge a new laptop on that credit card?

WOMAN: That's right, mock the poor lady. No computer, no car, no dignity, no pen—

MAN: Probably no bra neither.

WOMAN: Ha! You're right! *(She flashes her breasts at him.)*

MAN: Whoa.

WOMAN: What? I already flashed my stomach tonight, compared to that the rest of my body's a ten.

MAN: You flashed my son your stomach?

WOMAN: He wanted to see my appendix scar.

MAN: Wait, so, you were gonna write your name—

WOMAN: Tag my tag name—

MAN: On a gravestone?

WOMAN: On as many as I can. Yeah.

MAN: Isn't that a little preemptive?

WOMAN: It's more a little fuck you.

MAN: To the deceased?

WOMAN: To the capital A Authorities. I just gotta think of a good tag name. I had this boyfriend in high school, your son and my's alma mater, straight edge kid. Benjamin Schuler, his tag name was TERD, T. E. R. D. It was so disgusting, and like the misspelling made no sense, it was an acronym, I can't remember the beginning, but the R and D were Random Destruction, maybe Rampant Destruction, Total Everywhere Random Destruction, so stupid. Because he could have spelled it T.U.R.D. right? With a U like for Utter, or Ultimate; but he was like, "I'm not writing T.U.R.D. all over the neighborhood, that would be gross." So it was Terrifying Extra Random Destruction everywhere, on benches and doghouses and mailboxes; it was totally redundant in bathroom stalls. And then one night he just died in his sleep.

MAN: How old was he?

WOMAN: 28. He passed out drunk in his truck, drove into a lake.

MAN: So he drowned.

WOMAN: I like to think he fell asleep and never woke up. He's around here somewhere. My husband's just down the hill there. And then there's gotta be Mr. Quinn, or O'Keefe, and Matt Hoop, and all those other kids. Your son was telling me about all these kids. Wow, I can't remember ever talking so much about death in a night. I mean it makes sense. We all have it in common, like sports, or the weather. But, wow, there is so much, and we don't, y'know, talk about it. I mean do you mind? Talking about it? In a cemetery?

MAN: I don't mind. If there's beer. *(He takes another beer, quarter taps it, opens it, drinks.)*

WOMAN: It's, I find it relaxing.

MAN: TITS. That could be your tag name, T. I. T. S.

WOMAN: What does it stand for?

MAN: You have nice ones.

WOMAN: I like it. Ooooh, lipstick. *(She finds lipstick in her purse, she starts writing TITS tagger style, in lipstick on all the graves.)*

MAN: So, what were you doing in this neighborhood?

WOMAN: I had a check up at the hospital.

MAN: Everything all right?

WOMAN: I'm clean.

MAN: That's good.

WOMAN: Friend where I used to work got me my old job back. Thanks, great, like I even asked. They needed the check up to get me on their insurance before I start.

MAN: What's the job?

WOMAN: Real estate. Bullshit.

MAN: Gotta work.

WOMAN Who says?

MAN: They do.

WOMAN: Fuck them.

MAN: At least the check up was good.

WOMAN: It was nothing, you fill out a form, they weigh you, take your blood pressure, temperature.

MAN: Quick though.

WOMAN: But, c'mon, run some tests, take some blood, something. Juice up the mammogram. Dig around a little.

MAN: Sometimes it's better not knowing.

WOMAN: No, but I mean, I'd been kind of getting my hopes up, y'know? When I got the appointment? There's no way I'm going back to that job, but that appointment. I mean I've got some symptoms, I've got no appetite, can't get out of bed.

MAN: Symptoms.

WOMAN: Symptoms, sure. So I got kind of hopeful. Crazier things have happened. It really got me out of bed, got me down to the doctor's. But then like, she's all done, and she's just a nurse practitioner, and I go, "so how's it look doc, how long do you figure I got?" She looks at my chart, "Oh I'd say 30, 40, maybe 50 years".

MAN: What does she know.

WOMAN: The fuck does she know, exactly, I could still be sick, she doesn't know. You didn't see a lump or anything? When I flashed you?

MAN: They looked healthy to me.

WOMAN: Perv.

MAN: Run into Mary?

WOMAN Day off.

MAN: Lucky.

WOMAN: Sure, lucky for me, I didn't have to give her her card back and now I can keep charging groceries for the rest of my endless healthy life.

MAN: So, this is why you're out all night, trying to intoxicate my son and have your way with him in a graveyard?

WOMAN: Fuckin A! I'd fuck you too, if I could just get drunk enough!

MAN: You're still gonna die eventually.

WOMAN: Yeah, that's not a huge fucking comfort.

MAN: Still pretty angry, huh?

WOMAN You betcha.

MAN: That's cool. I'm good with anger.

WOMAN: Oh, you're good with it?

MAN: Yeah. Anger's a standalone for me. I don't think it's gotta be part of a process, a larger process. I think it can be it's own thing . . . Like negative feelings, anger, depression, what have you, they say they're always part of a process. Something that you go through to get to, I don't know, acceptance, right? So you can be happy again, right? But then positive feelings, like happiness or confidence, they don't have that stink on them, of just being part of a process. Of being something you should get over. People don't preach, "you should work through your happiness to get to acceptance that there's nothing to be happy about." Not that I'm against happiness. I just think it's hypocritical thinking. Let happiness be happiness, and let anger be anger, and don't tell my rage to run on your schedule. Man.

WOMAN: That must have been some divorce.

MAN: Yeah, right? I was speaking more generally, in a general way. Sorry, I got a little tipsy.

WOMAN: Tipsy?

MAN: Buzzed, whatever, a little buzzed.

WOMAN: On two beers? The Liquor Man's a light weight?

MAN: I didn't say drunk. But give me another; I'll get there. *(She flips him another beer, he quarter taps it, drinks.)* This the last one?

WOMAN: Your son drank the rest.

MAN: Me and my boy splitting a sixer. Warms you up, a cold beer. That's weird. Shit, it's cold.

WOMAN: Someone oughta make a run to the liquor store.

MAN: Ha. Yeah.

WOMAN: Really?

MAN: What? No. Come on, we can't stay out here all night, right? Eventually everyone's gonna have to pile in their cars and head home. Right?

WOMAN: Ugh. My car is like, the running joke of the night.

MAN: Then the bus, whatever.

WOMAN: I missed the bus. Literally. I keep missing the bus.

MAN: Well then you want a ride? I could drive you.

WOMAN: I don't know.

MAN: Why not?

WOMAN: You're kinda creepy.

MAN: A second ago you were ready to take advantage of me.

WOMAN: I was being charming. Now I'm feeling vulnerable, and I don't really feel comfortable riding in cars with strangers.

MAN: I'm not a stranger.

WOMAN: Do we know each other?

MAN: In a way.

WOMAN: See that's what I'm talking about, that's creepy.

MAN: I mean that we're not strangers in that that's my wife's grave you just vandalized.

WOMAN: Oh my god, I'm so sorry.

MAN: It's ok, you didn't know.

WOMAN: How could I? Stupid, stupid—

MAN: It's just a stone, I didn't mean to get sentimental, it's just—

WOMAN: I'm so, so sorry—

MAN: It's ok. It's good. I'd almost forgotten where this place was actually. It's been a while since I've been here.

WOMAN: I didn't know.

MAN: No, I'm sure. Just, just my kid being a wise ass. Leading you up here. *(Beat.)* I know my wife is, this isn't a surprise, y'know?

WOMAN: Ok.

MAN: I just didn't want to talk about it anymore at some point. Not that I have a lot of people to talk to.

WOMAN: Ok.

MAN: But you get sick of the pity party.

WOMAN: Yeah?

MAN: With divorce, it's disgusting, people don't ask follow-ups generally; try to make you feel better for fucking up a marriage.

WOMAN: Yeah.

MAN: They leave you alone.

WOMAN: Which is what you want.

MAN: Right.

WOMAN: Should I go?

MAN: Not yet. Unless you need to.

WOMAN: I don't need to.

MAN: Then do you mind staying just a little more? I haven't been up here for a while. It's a little scary.

WOMAN: Sure.

MAN: And this is nice. Opening up. With you.

WOMAN: I'm glad.

MAN: It's just when you have a kid you want to shield them from that, too. Having everyone feeling sorry for their dad, and for them.

WOMAN I'm sure.

MAN: But then—You know, I had almost the exact same conversation with him about Santa Claus. One day, he's around 5, he goes, "Was mommy real?" And I go, "yes" and he goes, "Where is she?" and I—, "she died" and he's, "well then, where is she?" And there's no answer to that, unless your religious, which I've always thought was the quitters way out of using your head. But I try and I say she left, she went "home", and he asks, "to the north pole?" and he cries cuz it's so far, and you try to soothe, and you sort of bumble out, "No, closer—Long Island." And he's all, "What's it like, what's it like in Long Island?" And finally I say, "It's like heaven". And he's finally satisfied, so, so, so are you, finally.

WOMAN: Yeah, well, kids.

MAN: Of course, he figured it out, eventually, 3rd grade, first time a kid from his school went to East Hampton for the summer, Robert couldn't believe he came back alive in the fall. So we talk it out again, but I still didn't have a better explanation than Long Island, so I stuck to it, like a mule, shrugging, going "Long Island Long Island Long Island". And then when he was in that crash with the kids, my son, and when he, when Robert didn't survive, that sealed it for me. I couldn't come up here anymore, with the two of them side by side, and me, no idea where they'd gone—*(He breaks down. she looks at the two graves of his wife and son.)*. He didn't tell you? *(Silence.)* Makes sense. Who buys beer for a dead kid? *(She goes.)* Please don't go.

WOMAN: I have to . . .

MAN: Please, I'm scared.

WOMAN: I can't stay. *(She walks off.)*

MAN: Don't go. You don't know what's out there. *(Pause, she returns.)* I've never seen him. Since. I've tried running after him, out to the bus stop. I don't know. He probably knows I couldn't really take that. Seeing him. *(Silence)* And what difference would it make anyway, right? *(Silence)* But it's nice huh? How he takes care of me? Sending me visitors, And then sending a nice woman like you. Who gets it. To make me come up here? Get me to open up. It's nice. *(Pause.)* Are you alright?

WOMAN: No.

MAN: I'm sorry.

WOMAN Alright. *(Pause.)*

MAN: How, what was he like, Robert?

WOMAN: What?

MAN: How was he? What did he look like?

WOMAN: What did he look like?

MAN: Yeah.

WOMAN: He had on a hoodie and black jacket.

MAN: What else?

WOMAN: Jeans. Sneakers?

MAN: How did he seem?

WOMAN: I don't know.

MAN: Ok.

WOMAN: He talked a lot.

MAN: Oh yeah?

WOMAN: He wouldn't shut up.

MAN: What did he say?

WOMAN: I have no idea. He just talked, and talked, and talked.
*(Pause.)*

MAN: What was your husband like?

WOMAN: I don't—

MAN: Alright.

WOMAN: It's all a little much, I'm still a little in shock I think . . .

MAN: Me too, always. It's like a state of perpetual fucking shock. *(She begins to weep.)*

MAN: Oh come on.

WOMAN: I'm sorry.

MAN: No, I'm sorry, I'm sorry if this all was upsetting.

WOMAN: It was upsetting.

MAN: He looked like a nice man, your husband.

WOMAN What?

MAN: From the store. The picture, you showed me his picture.

WOMAN: Oh my god. I thought—

MAN: *(Realizing.)* Oh, you thought, no, no, the picture, his picture, I know what he looks like from that, not from—

WOMAN: From him haunting your store—

MAN: Yeah, no, not that!

WOMAN: He's not walking around out there somewhere, drinking beers, asking after me—

MAN: No, no, not as far as I know. But who knows, y'know?

WOMAN: Right. *(Pause.)*

MAN: What happens now?

WOMAN: Now? *(Beat.)* Now, you should give me a ride, because I'm too sloppy and it's too freezing to wait on the bus.

MAN: Can I, could I give you my phone number?

WOMAN: Why would you do that?

MAN: I'm just asking if I could.

WOMAN: *(Beat.)* Sure, you could give me your number.

MAN: And maybe you'd call me sometime?

WOMAN: Sure, if my phone hasn't been disconnected.

MAN: What would we talk about, if you called?

WOMAN: I don't know, sports, the weather, movies. Anything.

MAN: Really?

WOMAN: Why not? We'd talk. We'd talk and talk and talk.

MAN: And that'd make things better? *(Beat.)*

MAN: It's so cold.

WOMAN: So we should go. *(They don't move.)*

*End Of Play*

# WILD WITH HAPPY

*Colman Domingo*

WILD WITH HAPPY was originally produced by The Public Theater and ran from October 9th through November 18th, 2012.

Directed by Robert O'Hara
Sets and costumes by Clint Ramos
Lighting by Japhy Weideman
Music and sound by Lindsay Jones
Projections by Aaron Rhyne

CAST:
GIL: Colman Domingo
TERRY: Korey Jackson
MO: Maurice McRae
ADELAIDE/AUNT GLO: Sharon Washington

"Wild with Happy" was developed, in part, with the assistance of the Sundance Institute Theater Program, New York Theater Workshop, The New Works Festival with Theatreworks Silicon Valley and The Public Theater New Work Now Festival.

AUTHORS NOTE

With this work, I am exploring many composites of African American men and their relationships to their mothers. I wanted to examine religion, sexuality and the surreal that surrounds extraordinary circumstances such as death and eventual healing. This is not my story. These are many stories and they started to speak to me and tell me more about themselves as I wrote at my desk at home, while running on the treadmill, and being pushed to be as creative as possible by my visionary director Robert O'Hara in the snowcapped Canadian Rockies until I became "Wild with Happy." This play thrived with the support and nuturing of fellow artists such as Raul, Robert, Sharon, Maurice, Ariel, Phillip, Mandy, Oskar, Maria, Liz, Doug, Jen, Sarah, Philip, Christopher, Kelley, Meredith, Leslie, Jim and Linda.

**MR. DOMINGO'S** *Wild with Happy* received its world premiere Off Broadway at The Public Theater under the direction of Robert O'Hara. *Wild with Happy* received developmental support from The Sundance Institute Theater Lab, Theatreworks, New York Theater Workshop, The Public Theater and The New Black Fest. *Wild with Happy* has been produced by Theaterworks and Baltimore Centerstage. He won the 2010 Lucille Lortel (Best Solo Show), GLAAD Media Award (Best Theater Broadway or Off Broadway), and the Internet Theater Bloggers Award for his play *A Boy and His Soul*, which had sold out runs for The Vineyard Theater, Joe's Pub, The OMAI Festival for University of Wisconsin/Madison, Theater Development Fund and Thick Description in San Francisco. *A Boy and His Soul* was nominated for the Drama Desk, Drama League and Audelco Awards. *A Boy and His Soul* has also received productions at the Philadelphia Theater Company and the Tricycle Theater in London.

He has penned the plays *Up Jumped Springtime* (Theater Rhinoceros Studio and Mainstage, "Best Solo Show" mention by The San Francisco Chronicle and Oakland Tribune), *The Big Idea* (San Francisco Foundation commission) and *Mission of a Saint* (Movement Theater Company). He has been an artist in residence/artistic fellow for The Sundance Institute Theater Lab, New York Theater Workshop, Thick Description Theater Collective and Hartford Stage Company. He is an OBIE, Connecticut Critics Circle, Bay Area Theater Critics Circle, and Dramalogue Award winning and Tony Award nominated actor that has starred on Broadway in The Scottsboro Boys, Passing Strange and Chicago. He has directed for Berkeley Rep, New Professional Theater, The Working Theater, Geva Theater, Campo Santo, Inquiline Theater, San Francisco Mime Troupe, All for One Festival, The Beat Festival and The Lincoln Center Director's Lab/American Living Room Festival and workshops for the Roundabout Theater Company.

Mr. Domingo is on faculty at The National Theater Institute at the Eugene O'Neill Theater Center and a recurring "Visiting Artist" with The University of Wisconsin, Madison Office of Muticultural Arts Initiative First Wave. Mr. Domingo is under commission from The American Conservatory Theater in San Francisco and People's Light and Theater Company in Pennsylvania. Mr. Domingo is a Burian Lecture Fellow with The New York Writer's Institute.

# CHARACTERS

GIL: Forty-year-old African American male. Ivy league educated. Bitter. Sardonic. Deep down inside a romantic and believer. He is our deconstructed cinderella.

ADELAIDE/AUNT GLO: African American woman that is versatile to play twenty-five to sixties. Wide range of kind and good natured to hell on wheels. From the fairy godmother to the evil step mother.

TERRY AND OTHERS: thirty-year-old very good looking man, very bright spirit. A healer. Prince charming.

MO AND OTHERS: forty-year-old African American male, vain, and sassy. Masculine looking, well built, with a dash of 'lady'. The fairy.

NOTE: (* overlap) and Silences are to be played. They are key to the rhythm. This moves at a brisk pace. Acting ON the line is imperative for this surreal dark comedy of manners.

*Preshow Music: Every possible version of the classic song "Get Happy." Ending with the end all to be all version . . . Judy Garland and Barbara Streisand. Lights Up!*

# GET UP AND GET US SOME JESUS!

*Lights up on GIL, a forty-year-old African American man, dressed impeccably, standing in front of a theatrical curtain.*

GIL: As a matter of fact, the last time I was in a church it was very upsetting! We hadn't been to church in a really long time and Adelaide, my "mother," said to me one Sunday morning that we had to "get up and get us some Jesus!" "Get us some Jesus?" I thought, as a precocious ten-year-old, I thought that Jesus had moved or something by the way that she had been throwing parties and cussin'! You see, the Saturday night before we went to this church service, we had a rent party. Why? Cause we needed the rent. Everyone was smoking and drinking and carrying on. Well, Adelaide was nowhere to be found until her latest boyfriend, Ray Ray was caught showing some woman the backyard and stayed out there a little too long. My mother leapt out into that backyard as if she was that Bruce Lee doll with the Kung Fu Kick! You remember those? How old are you? Never mind! My mother cussed and turned that party OUT! I handed out coats from the bedroom with exceptional velocity! Adelaide went to bed drunk and shattered as I cleaned the entire house and sampled all of the left over cocktails. So when Adelaide yelled into my room first thing Sunday morning, that we were going to "Get up and get us some Jesus," I thought, was this heifa crazy??? I was trying to get up and get us some sleep!

*The curtain opens and reveals a gigantic Black Jesus nailed to the cross. It is lit up with bright white lights. GIL shifts into his ten-year-old self. He holds ADELAIDE'S hand. Suddenly ELDER BOVANE played by the actor that plays MO and the CHURCH NURSE played by the actor that plays TERRY appear. This is the church service to end all church services. It is from 10 year old Gil's perspective. In technicolor.*

ELDER BOVANE: So glad to see you sister!

CHURCH NURSE: Lawd, look what the cat done dragged in!

ELDER BOVANE: Mmm, mmmph, mm mph!

CHURCH NURSE: I hope the choich don't fall down! She got a ton of Fashion Fair on!!!

*Colman Domingo*

ELDER BOVANE: Welcome Sister, we ain't seen you in a month of Sundays! Hey Heeyy!!! The Lord will root you out of the devils house and bring you—BRING YOU BACK HOME! Hi Dee Hi Dee Ho!

CHURCH NURSE: *(to an unseen parishioner)* Sinning Adelaide and her little limp-wristed Gil! Thank you, Jesus! Praise him!

ELDER BOVANE: SINNERS! YOU'VE COME ON HOME! COME ON HOME TO JESUS! You have been running and you cain't run no more. Drinking! Living with Lucifer. Carrying on! Smelling like Saturday night while staring Sunday dead in the eye! Have you ever noticed that when nothing is going right in your life you can't run from your problems? It is because you have what?

CHURCH NURSE: Left yourself!

ELDER BOVANE: Can I get a Cheech and Chong??? It's because you what???

NURSE: Left yourself!!!

ELDER BOVANE: Just like your man left you! Hakalakalaka! Somebody told me about a party. Mmm hhhmmm. Do you hear me? A partay! Where a woman! I said a WOE-man! Who was a member of this very church many moons ago! This WOE-man!

CHURCH NURSE: Who has a limp-wristed spawn of Satan!

ELDER BOVANE: Praise God! This woman got tired of the devil's work! And like the great M.C. Hammper said, "Turned that motha' out!" She turned that mother out and has crawled like a child wrapped in a Donna Karan dress, back into the loving embrace of this here house of the Lord! Can I get an Amen?

CHURCH NURSE: AMEN!!!

ELDER BOVANE: ADELAIDE!!! *(pause)* YOU HAVE FALLEN AND YOU CAIN'T GET UP!

ADELAIDE: Boom chic a poom poom!

ELDER BOVANE: WE ARE SO GLAD THAT YOU'VE COME BACK HOME! SHAKE A HAND SHAKE A HAND! Shamalakadingdong! PEAS AND CARROTS, PEAS AND CARROTS, PEAS AND CARROTS! *(sings)* And it feels like fire!

CHURCH NURSE: FIRE!!!

ELDER BOVANE: Allll shut up in my bones. Like Jeremiah, won't leave me alone!

*The NURSE and ELDER BOVANE continue to stomp and clap. The NURSE riffs and sings hard over the song with Hallelujahs etc!*

ADELAIDE: PRAISE GOD! THANK YOU, FATHER! HALLELUJAH!

*ADELAIDE has caught the Holy Ghost. She is doing what appears to be an Irish Jig. She does the "Jitterbug" and the "Watusi." She does the "4 corners" and "The Cabbage Patch" dance. Her hair is wild, she is crying and speaking in tongues! ELDER BOVANE joins in and their dance becomes exaggeratedly African.*

GIL: WHAT ARE YOU DOING TO MY MOTHER! STOP!

*Silence*

ELDER BOVANE AND ADELAIDE: *(whispered)* We're gonna do this right? Right now? You ready?

*ELDER BOVANE raises his mighty hand and smacks ADELAIDE on the forehead! The slap is heard across the world. Birds chirp around Adelaide's head.*

ELDER BOVANE: HAKALAKALAKALA!!!! HEY HEY!!!

*ADELAIDE passes out. The CHURCH NURSE throws a red cloth over ADELAIDE'S face. She praises and applauds.*

NURSE: That's GAWDT! That's GAWDT!!

*The red curtain closes. GIL shifts back into his 40 year old self.*

GIL AND I HAVE NEVER, EVER, BEEN TO CHURCH SINCE! So . . . no church!

*He looks back at the shadow of a man. It is Terry.*

## TERRY'S CLOTH

GIL: Adelaide became an off and on member of the church. I cross the street when I see one.

*Lights up on Jackson's Funeral Home that has been lurk-
ing in the recesses of the prologue. GIL is staring into
nothingness. Terry smiles longingly at GIL.*

TERRY: No church. I understand.

*Silence.*

TERRY: Would you like a cup of coffee?

*GIL is staring into nothingness.*

TERRY: Cream and sugar okay?

GIL: You don't have Blue Agave Sweetener?

TERRY: Uh, I don't know what that is.

GIL: Black.

*TERRY goes offstage. He enters with coffee.*

*Silence.*

*Silence.*

*Silence.*

*TERRY takes a pen out and begins to fill out a form.*

TERRY: I need to fill out this form so that we can get "the body"
from the morgue.

GIL: *(dry)* "The body."

TERRY: Are you the next of kin?

GIL: *(sarcastically)* Yes.

TERRY: We at Jackson's Funeral Home take the worry out of
laying a soul to rest! We take care of everything! First thing
we will take care of—

GIL: —is "The body."

TERRY: And then we will take care of marching on down to
the vital statistics office to obtain the death certificate!
You won't be able to handle any of your mother's
finances, property, insurance claims or anything without
it.

GIL: Unh hunh.

TERRY: Would you want a private viewing for up to fifty people
here at Jackson's Funeral Home?

GIL: Hunh.

TERRY: Okay. Okay. Let's start with the casket?

*TERRY pages back the red curtain to reveal the funeral
home with caskets.*

WILD WITH HAPPY

TERRY: Well, to start with, we have your basic pine box. Affordable. Sort of like an Ikea bookshelf.

GIL: Ikea?

TERRY: Not the best, but reliable! But I am sure you don't want to deal with that right? Only the best for your mother!

GIL: The best on a budget!

TERRY: Your mother deserves our very best! Like our oak veneer. Glossy finish. Simple but classic, like a Chanel suit, only $4995.

GIL: How about Liz Claiborne?

TERRY: Brazilian cedar veneer! Cream interior. The Lexus of caskets only $9995!

GIL: I could put a down payment on a real Lexus for that!

> *GIL checks his iPhone.*

TERRY: African pad oak inlay. Ebony Fashion Fair veneer! Gold plated luxury! Cushioned in silk! Top of the line! It's like checking into a Four Seasons.

GIL: Only you don't check out! BAM!!!

TERRY: That's funny.

GIL: *(dead pan)* You funny!

> *GIL just stares deadpan at TERRY.*

TERRY: Internment! Or the better name for it, "The final resting place!" We can place her anywhere you'd like. Evergreen, Northwood, Woodlawn or the very best, Fernwood!

> *GIL checks his iPhone.*

TERRY: *(He smiles)* "Closer to God," they say! The best views are from the top of the mountain!

GIL: What's she gonna see?

TERRY: *Shall we talk about Flowers? We can put you in touch with our florist Mrs. Beletha Carvel-Jackson.

GILS: *Beletha?

TERRY: She can start you off with a few arrangements starting at around $1500 . . .

GIL: I need to have sex right now.

TERRY: Excuse me?

GIL: I NEED TO HAVE SEX RIGHT NOW!

TERRY: I think that is a little inappropriate.

GIL: I think you trying to sell me the most expensive casket is inappropriate.

*Colman Domingo*

TERRY: I am just trying to be of comfort to you at this time.

GIL: A comfort? You wanna be a comfort to me? Make me feel like I am not about to evaporate!

TERRY: I didn't mean to . . .

GIL: You didn't mean to? I am telling you my tale of woe and you pulling out an abacus! Smilin'. Flirtin'!

TERRY: Flirtin'?

GIL: Seducin'!

TERRY: I'm not trying to seduce you!

GIL: THIS some SHIT out of a DAVID LYNCH film!

TERRY: I was just trying to calm your nerves!

GIL: I AM CALM! Geez Louise! I don't got time for this. I gotta see a man about a dog.

> *GIL goes to the door.*

TERRY: Please Mr. Hawkins.

GIL: Do NOT call me Mr. Hawkins!
I just turned forty!

TERRY: Please. Please don't go.

> *Silence*

TERRY: You are the first client that I am handling on my own. This is a family business and I am doing the work that has been passed down. I'm a little rough around the edges. I'm Terry.

> *He holds a chair out for GIL:*

TERRY: Please. Let's start over. Where are you from?

GIL: Don't let the couture fool you. I'm from around here. Why?

TERRY: You don't hear "Geez Louise" that often.

TERRY smiles. GIL is still as deadpan as ever.  Silence

GIL: My "urban" is a little worn off. I went to Yale.

> *GIL checks his cell phone again. Silence. He just stares at his phone.*

> *Silence.*

TERRY: Wow. That's great. Yale.

GIL: *(mumbles)* Yale, yeah, whatever.

> *Silence.*

TERRY: I am so sorry about your mother.

*GIL'S phone rings.*

GIL: Could I have another cup of that coffee?

TERRY: Sure. Of course. No problem. I'll make a fresh pot.

*TERRY exits.*

*GIL looks at his phone. We hear the opening sound of Natalie Cole's song "Peaceful Living." GIL is staring at his phone that starts to ring.*

## PEACEFUL LIVING

*We enter GIL'S memory. ADELAIDE is on a chaise lounge that floats in. She has a princess phone up to her ear. ADELAIDE holds a huge bottle of Lubriderm lotion. She is in her slip. There is a dress with white beading lying on the chaise.*

GIL: Hello?

ADELAIDE: Hello?

GIL: Hello?

ADELAIDE: *(suspiciously)* Hello?

GIL: Hi Mom. What's wrong?

ADELAIDE: Why? What did you hear?

GIL: Nothing, you just don't sound like yourself.

ADELAIDE: A girlfriend of mine—you remember Ms. Lavinia?

GIL: No.

ADELAIDE: Yes you do. Ms. Lavinia? Got a big laugh?

GIL: No, I don't remember her.

ADELAIDE: Yes you do! Real big thick ankles?

GIL: *(lying)* O.K. Yeah, I remember her. Big laugh. Cankles.

ADELAIDE: *(tickled)* I did not say cankles. That's not nice.

GIL: Anyway, Adelaide, what?

ADELAIDE: Well, she brought a friend over for my bi-monthly ladies lunch! Now, You know, I don't like strangers in my house! Well, this woman, I think her name was Shavon or something, I think she put a curse on me!

GIL: What?

ADELAIDE: I almost died yesterday.

GIL: What?

ADELAIDE: A curse!

GIL: I don't understand. Are you okay?

ADELAIDE: I simply asked her to take off her shoes when she came in the door. You know I don't like people tracking their lives in my house. She looked at me kind of funny. Then I made the mistake of asking her to use a coaster for her pineapple spritzer and she looked at me kinda sideways! And when she got up to use the bathroom, I simply told her I laid out hand towels, chile, you woulda thought I told her that Ike Turner was in there waiting for her! And then, during our ladies lunch she proceeded to contradict everything I said. If I said the sky was blue-she said that she wasn't so sure. For the life of me, I don't know why Lavinia would bring someone like that to my elegant home. Well, I found out when Shavon, Sherelle or whatever her name was, was in the bathroom that Lavinia was her host. This woman was at least sixty and from Haiti.

GIL: Haiti?

ADELAIDE: Mmm hmm, she was staying with Lavinia for free in exchange for light housekeeping duties. Now, Ms. Lavinia may be a big-ole thick woman who laughs like a man who's got some unfortunate cankles, but she is SMART! Chevron just kept staring at me in a funny way and muttering something under her breath.

GIL: What do you think it was?

ADELAIDE: Witchcraft or something!

ADELAIDE AND GIL: I get feelings about these things!

ADELAIDE: Ooohh girl, you should have seen her. She was just as evil as sin. She was wearing this tight brown dress cutting off all her circulation and those men's work boots?

GIL: Timberlands?

ADELAIDE: Yes, Timberlands.

GIL: I'm getting off the phone!

ADELAIDE: What sixty-something year old woman wears Timberlands? And I am GIVING her sixty-something because she looked as old as Methuselah! She was wearing Timberlands and I was suspect! She had the thinnest hair I've ever seen on a grown woman. Her hair was real thin and was pulled to the back in a couple of plats. I guess she

WILD WITH HAPPY

was fussing with it in the bathroom cause when she came out it was everywhere. Honey, it look like she had a head full of baby hair! She was evil. You know women who can't grow no hair are evil. I am sure she took one look at my thick Indian hair and reached for her spells and potions. The moment she and Ms. Lavinia left I started getting sick. I told you she was Haitian, didn't I?

GIL: Unfortunately.

ADELAIDE: SHE PUT A CURSE ON ME! My face got all swolle up, I started throwing up and I had a fever. I felt sick as a dog and my hair itched. *(pause)* If the UPS man didn't show up with my Limited Edition Genuine Porcelain Cinderella Doll from the QVC, I would be speaking to you from beyond the grave right now. Hello. Hello? GIL? GIL?

GIL: *I don't know what to say to that.

ADELAIDE: *Well, say something! You haven't called me in a month of Sundays. I want to catch up on you!

GIL: *I ain't got nothing to catch up on.

ADELAIDE: Catch up on dreams!

GIL: *Dreams are childish.

ADELAIDE: *So cynical.

GIL: Hard not to be. I live in New York. Terrorists and street meat!

ADELAIDE: I had a dream.

GIL: What, you Martin Luther King?

ADELAIDE: No, but he was in it!

GIL: Okay?!!

ADELAIDE: Martin Luther King Jr. and Natalie Cole! Hmph, with all that curse, I tossed and turned all night! We were all shopping for doorknobs. Isn't that strange? Doorknobs! Martin Luther King wanted to buy a big red one and Natalie, hmph, was being very picky.

> *TERRY brings GIL some more coffee and pulls out two packets of Splenda. Adelaide crosses to exit. It is a cross-fade of sorts from present to past.*

ADELAIDE: She finally found a tiny little lavender doorknob and she turned to me and started to sing that song "Peaceful Living." You remember that—?

GIL: *(dryly)*—This isn't Blue Agave Sweetener! *(beat)* Thank you.

*GIL sits and stares into his coffee.*

   *Silence.*

GIL: My best friend was supposed to join me to make these decisions. I have to get this all taken care of and get back to New York.

TERRY: I know a lot about loss.

GIL: Oh really?

TERRY: If you let me, I'd like to try and help.

GIL: What? You got a magic wand around here that's gonna bring my mother back to life?

TERRY: No. No I don't.

   *Silence.*

TERRY: Gil is that short for . . . ?

GIL: Nothing. Just Gil. Like Cher.

   *Silence*

TERRY: Would you mind if I tried something with you?

GIL: *(skeptical)*"??!!"

   *He gets up slowly and rolls up his sleeves.*

   What are you doing?

TERRY: I promise I won't bite.

   *GIL stares at TERRY.*

GIL: Okay…this better not have a price tag on it.

TERRY: This is on me! Just close your eyes it won't hurt.

GIL: That's what they all say.

TERRY: You're funny.

GIL: Hilarious.

TERRY: Shhhh.

GIL: No-shushing! I have a dead mother.

TERRY: Please. Close your eyes. Please.

   *TERRY smiles and reassures GIL He begins a series of breaths behind GIL'S head and then he moves his hands around his neck and then heart.*

TERRY: Inhale with me.

GIL: "!???!??!"

TERRY: Inhale.

   *Terry inhales. GIL bursts into laughter.*

GIL: I don't know what you are doing, I need to—

TERRY: I know that this may seem a little unorthodox given the environment.

GIL: Coffins and whatnot.

TERRY: But I think this will help you.

> *They inhale. TERRY performs a combination of breath, Chakra, energy, and Reiki. Gil is in disbelief. Terry really works at this. Gil goes from amazement, not being interested to finally succumbing.*

TERRY: "Prana" is breath or vital energy in the body. "Prana" represents the pranic energy responsible for life, and "ayama" means control. Turn up the corners of the mouth and breathe. What we are doing is a little "Pranayama." It is control of breath. We have got to get the life force flowing especially during this vulnerable time. From the top of your head down to your feet. This is a little energy work that I have been studying. I take classes part time at Nature's Body Works downtown. This work has healing qualities if you let it work on you. It can help focus your energy. This can connect you to the flow. You walked in with so much darkness. But in darkness there is light. We can work to guide you to the soft light.

GIL: Uh, no thank you.

> *TERRY puts his hands on GIL'S shoulders and slowly moves them down his arms and raises them and pulls up to release his shoulders. GIL lets out sounds of pain and then finally ecstasy.*

TERRY: The path to healing. This will place you on firm ground and you will know, truly, that you are here. This is an eastern practice.

> *He moves his hands around GIL'S arms, chest and lower stomach.*

GIL: This seems a little southern to me!

TERRY: You talk a lot.

GIL: Look—

TERRY: Breathe. Clear your mind so that you can see. This is a time of transition for your mother and for you.

GIL: Mmm hmmm.

TERRY: But first you have to quiet your mind and BREATHE. Deep breaths. Thats it. I'm gonna be right back—I got something that's gonna touch your spirit. Keep breathing.

*(Pause)* I see you. I see through all that anger and darkness. You're a dreamer. You're a romantic. You are beautiful. Strange but beautiful.

> *ADELAIDE crosses back in as TERRY crosses out. Back in GIL'S memory.*

ADELAIDE: It was strange but beautiful. Natalie finally found a tiny little lavender doorknob and she turned to me and started to sing that song "Peaceful Living." You remember that?

GIL: Mmm hmmm. Making me stand on your feet when I was little and forcing me to sing it over and over.

ADELAIDE: I asked you to sing it once! You were the one who kept on singing. Natalie was singing it to me and she placed my hand on hers and told me to turn the knob. I didn't want to turn it. Martin Luther King said that it was okay. So I turned it and I woke up.

GIL: You have some strange dreams.

ADELAIDE: Just like you. You are just like me. Probably more me, than me!

GIL: You alright?

ADELAIDE: I gotta new dress. It's sharp! It's white with beading around the neckline. You know, for the past year I can't keep no weight on . . . Gil, it would be nice if you drove down from the Big Shiny Apple to see Ms. Adelaide and accompany me to church.

GIL: Adelaide, I told you already . . .

ADELAIDE * I know, I know, you are scared of church!

GIL: *I ain't scared of church, just the people!

ADELAIDE: *Maybe they can baptize me.

GIL * We just gonna walk in and they gonna to baptize you?

ADELAIDE: *I gotta do something to get this completely off of me.

GIL: *Don't you need an appointment or something?

ADELAIDE: *I don't know. Maybe they can throw some holy water on me or something!

GIL: *You can't just walk up into a church and get holy water thrown on you like it's "The Exorcist!"

ADELAIDE: This is an Exorcism! This woman put a curse on me!

GIL: I have an audition on Monday.

ADELAIDE: What's it for?

GIL: Nothing.

ADELAIDE: TV?

GIL: No.

ADELAIDE: A Movie?

GIL: No.

ADELAIDE: A Broadway play?

GIL: No.

ADELAIDE: Vegas?

GIL: NO!

ADELAIDE: What then?

GIL: *(under his breath)* A Craisin.

ADELAIDE: A who?

GIL: *(inaudible)* A Craisin.

ADELAIDE: A what?

GIL: *(even more inaudible)* A Craisin.

ADELAIDE: A RAISIN? *A Raisin in the Sun*?

GIL: No, a CRAISIN! A National commercial to play a Craisin. A dried cranberry that you snack on like raisins!!!

    *Silence*

ADELAIDE: It's healthy, right?

GIL: Can we talk about something else other than my fledgling career? Or my lack of a fledgling career!

ADELAIDE: Oh, honey. You have a degree in English Literature from Yale. You can read.

GIL: *I don't need an English Literature degree to be a nightshift proof reader and a C-list commercial actor.

ADELAIDE: *I told you, you can do anything that your heart desires. As long as you are happy. You want me to write Oprah?

GIL: *No. No. No.

ADELAIDE: I wrote her six times already.

GIL: What she gonna do?

ADELAIDE: *She's gonna come through.

GIL: *She don't care nothing about me.

ADELAIDE: *We can pray for Oprah to grant your wish. I still haven't heard anything from her yet but you gotta play the game to win right?

GIL: Right!!!

ADELAIDE:* Have you been calling in to Power 99 FM like I told you? Remember that free trip to Disney last year!

*Colman Domingo*

You could be a winner! Now look, you've had a lot of roles, albeit with no lines, on all those Law and Order shows. But you just have to believe more in your dreams.

GIL:* No. I don't have time to call in to radio stations. *(pause)* I don't want to talk about dreams! They don't come true.

*She squeezes a bottle of Lubriderm lotion and it makes a fart sound, she slaps her hands together and rubs it with a forceful motion and rubs the lotion on her elbows.*

GIL: Ugh! I hate that sound why must you do that?

ADELAIDE: I do it because I want to know that it's working. *(squirts more lotion)*

GIL: It works without all of that squirting and slapping.

ADELAIDE: *(in regard to the lotion)* It's an event! I'm telling you, you gotta take care of yourself! I got some new herbs from the herbalist a couple of days ago for my new treatment. I got me some herbs and I'm getting prayed up! Now you know I don't want to get into it on the phone but you gotta pray on your situations. You need to be open to love in your life. I know that boy broke your heart, but that's what they do.

GIL: *Adelaide, I don't want to talk about him.

ADELAIDE: What DO you want to talk about?

GIL: Nothing! You called me!

ADELAIDE: Men ain't shit and then they die! You gotta get up, brush your knees off, shake your wig, and start all over again.

*Silence*

GIL: I don't think you realize that you just made me sound like a hooker.

ADELAIDE: So what, things don't work out as planned. So what?! You gotta let go and open up to something new. Magic. It baffles me why you don't have anybody. You are a prize. You gotta pray on your "love" situation.

GIL: There is no need to pray on my "love" situation. I live in New York. I can get a "situation" anytime!

ADELAIDE: That's your problem! Too many "situations" and not enough love!

GIL: Bye.

ADELAIDE: Maybe it was my fault! I could never keep a good

man around for you to look up too!

GIL: Bye.

ADELAIDE: I haven't given you the greatest inspiration for healthy relationships have I?

GIL: Bye.

ADELAIDE: No real father figures for almost forty years. Maybe that's why you are gay.

GIL: Bye.

ADELAIDE: Everyone should be able to have love. Especially "The Gays!"

*Silence*

GIL: Adelaide, look, I've stopped putting my faith in "the Gays" or in my silly little dreams.

ADELAIDE: Your heart has really turned to stone.

GIL: No, Cast Iron! And there ain't no magic potion that is going to fix it! I'mma take my magic wand on down to the post office and like Aunt Glo says, "Get a real job!"

ADELAIDE: I thought you told me that being an actor is a real job!

GIL: I lied! It's make believe.

ADELAIDE: I taught you to believe in make believe!

GIL: *I live on Earth! With its toxins and its poisons and its fumes. I'm an enchanted middle-aged grown man, who still has $80,000 of student loans, an illegal sublet in Spanish Harlem, and I'm still reeling from being left by "my gay" a year ago. There is no make believe.

ADELAIDE: *Don't say that.

GIL: *Oprah ain't NEVER gonna answer your letters, princes don't come back, and there ain't a lotion or potion or tale to keep a person from . . .

*Silence. GIL looks at his cell phone.*

ADELAIDE: Ok. I will try to get you next Sunday. Ladies First Sunday! Maybe you can stay over and we can go down to the bank. I wanna get your name on my papers and show you my deposit box and I want to talk to you about the life insurance policy.

GIL: Okay. Okay.

*We hear the sound of gongs from ADELAIDE'S Cinderella clock.*

---

ADELAIDE: *(beat)* Oh, that old clock. "Old killjoy." I gotta go get my dress taken in. Your Aunt Glo talked me into buying the wrong size. You know she is always trying to run things. Talking about, I don't know my size! I gotta go.

GIL: Bye.

ADELAIDE: Gil?

GIL: Adelaide?

ADELAIDE: *(Sings)* Have you been to the very top, of the highest hill

ADELAIDE AND GIL: *(Sings)* Where the air is fresh and sweet and the sky is so clear

ADELAIDE: I love you.

> *TERRY enters with a Reiki wand, incense, bells etc.*

GIL: I—

> *GIL stands up abruptly. Lights snap the memory of ADELAIDE into darkness.*

GIL: I'm sorry I can't! I just can't have you touching my spirit right now. I have too much to do!

TERRY: It's ok. You are grieving. This behavior is normal.

GIL: No! No coffee. No casket. No flowers. No touching my spirit! Cremation please.

TERRY: Wow. Okay. Would you like to view "the body" first?

GIL: It's just "The Body" right?

> *ADELAIDE exits.*

GIL: I don't have any money and she had very little insurance. Cremation please.

TERRY: Well, Mr. Hawkins—

GIL: Mr. Jackson of Jackson's Funeral Home, I would like cremation.

TERRY: Gil, would you like to confer with your family?

GIL: No.

> *TERRY goes to his portfolio and pulls out a sheet of paper and hands it to GIL. GIL points to a package on the sheet of paper.*

GIL: That's what I want!

> *Silence*

WILD WITH HAPPY

TERRY: *(with concern that opens into a gentle smile)* If that's what you want? That's what you want!

> *The lights flicker. TERRY and the funeral home fade away. We still see ADELAIDE'S chaise with the white dress with beading lying on it. We hear the faint sound of Natalie Cole's Peaceful Living. Dreamlike. GIL lies down and holds the dress close to him. An armoire full of clothes floats in.*

## AUNT GLO GLOWS

> *We hear the sounds of a disgruntled woman. She is "fit to be tied."*

AUNT GLO: Cremation??? I can't believe you did that? We don't do that! Oh lord! God help him!

> *This is AUNT GLO: She is played by the same actress that plays ADELAIDE: She is a disheveled mess. She has on a "Suzette Charles" collection short and sassy wig. She wears a velour track suit and has a fanny pack around her waist. She has a pill bottle in one hand and a glass of water in the other. GIL trys to get a word in at times but it is just not possible.*

AUNT GLO: You're supposed to come together as a family and plan! That is what family is for! Oh lord! You got to call on the family. You can't make decisions by yourself in this state! It's grief! Grief! My number is in the little black book on your mother's nightstand. Under the letter G for Glo! Lawd ham mercy! I was supposed to go with you! To make arrangements! When I talked to you last night about your mother's sudden passing, I told you to call me when you got in and I would go with you to the funeral home! View the body! Oh Lord! My fingers were itchin'! I knew something wasn't right! I was worried! I have been pounding on that door for hours. I had to climb up on the fire escape. Five floors Gil! Five Floors! Neighbors looking at me, about to call the po-lice! I'm having to explain who I am, while scaling the walls like I'm Spiderman! Had to pull the dang screen off the window. Luckily that window hadn't been fixed in years and I know how to jimmy it open with my car key! This is not the time for layin' around. Get up! No time to be Rip Van Winklin' or Sleeping Beauties! THERE ARE THINGS TO DO! WHAT ARE YOU GOING TO DO WITH HER THANGS? YOU KNOW WHERE HER PAPERS ARE? HER ACCOUNTS? YOU KNOW WHERE THE SKELETONS ARE KEPT?

*GIL shoots AUNT GLO a look.*

AUNT GLO: I just wanted to make sure that you were listening to me? And why are you lying around with a dead woman's dress??? GET UP! THERE ARE THINGS THAT MUST BE DONE BEFORE YOU CAN LAY DOWN!

*AUNT GLO is going through an armoire full of clothes, hats, gloves, and shoes.*

AUNT GLO: We got calls to make. Plan the repast. Put that fancy little English "lititure" degree of yours to use! Write the eulogy! Hire a photographer.

GIL: For what?

AUNT GLO: To take pictures.

GIL: I don't want pictures of a funeral!

AUNT GLO: It's not about you!

GIL: So it's about you?

AUNT GLO: We will hire a photographer!

GIL: I DON'T WANT TO REMEMBER THIS!

*Silence*

*AUNT GLO pops a pill. Drinks down a full glass of water.*

AUNT GLO: It's so hot today. Got my pressure up! Wooo. Mmm mmm mmp. Did you know, she had just decided to start going to church again? It was like she was GETTING READY!!! She was a good woman.

*Referring to a dress.*

AUNT GLO: This is awfully . . . Latin. My sister loved her colors. *(Wails, then)* Praise the Lord. Mmm mmm mph. Have you reached out to your father?

GIL: He forgot about us years ago. No need.

AUNT GLO: He should at least know. Out of respect.

WILD WITH HAPPY

GIL: Out of respect, he should stay away.

AUNT GLO: You're in GRIEF! GRIEF!!!! I saw that on that Dr. Medical something. That woman wrote about it. Lizabeth . . . Cuba . . . Gooding! The stages of grief! You got, stage one and two! Denial mixed in with a little anger. Mmm mmm mmph. It's something. People must know when it's their time. They start to GET READY!!! *(indicates to a box on the shelf)* What's that? QVC?

GIL: Let me see that.

*He gets up and retrieves a box. He opens it.*

AUNT GLO: Making decisions to burn bodies. Our people just don't do that. I'm not one to judge but that is going to be between you and your God. It just ain't right. Y'all both have always been so funny in your thinking. You know what she told me the day before she died? She told me that she thought some woman who wore Timberlands put a curse on her a few months ago. Do you know anything about that? Of course not because you hadn't spoken to her in weeks.

GIL: *Well, actually, the "Curse" was—

AUNT GLO: *Now these are nice! She loved her shoes. A little high in the heel for me but she would want me to have these. *(Wails)*

*AUNT GLO is piling up the clothes, hats, baubles, shoes, tchotchkes, keepsakes and heirlooms. GIL reveals the Limited Edition Genuine Porcelain Cinderella Doll.*

GIL: Adelaide believed in curses and magic and fairytales. I'm keeping this.

AUNT GLO: Stage three?! BARGAINING! That ain't gonna bring her back! The only thing you need to believe in is our SAVIOR. *(To herself)* Is that Cinderella? She usta have a whole collection of those thangs. Now, do I got room in my trunk or should I make two trips?

*GIL laughs in a sort of quiet maniacal way where you cannot distinguish whether he is laughing or crying.*

GIL: Strange you laughing like that.

I feel like I am having an out of body experience.

AUNT GLO: Mmm hmm. I don't know what stage that is? You and my sister, god rest her soul, are very special. Special.

*(beat)* Well, I made a few cakes and thangs so that we don't get talked about after the reception. Ms. Divers died and there wasn't a wang to be found or a glass of Kool-Aid to wet peoples mourning mouths and her people got talked about all day and all night! Adelaide deserves the best. My onliest sister. *(an excessive wail)* Help me father. Just so sudden! Now did you call the church for the services?

GIL: Aunt Glo . . .

AUNT GLO: Cause you supposed to call them as so they can get the body.

GIL: Aunt Glo . . .

AUNT GLO: But since there is no BODY to get—

GIL: Aunt Glo . . .

AUNT GLO: But you know, I am not trying to get all up in your business although that is/was, praise God, my onliest sister!

GIL: AUNT GLODINE!

    *Silence*

AUNT GLO: Yes, GILBERT?!??!

GIL: I am not having the services at a church.

AUNT GLO: Then where? The TGI Fridays?

GIL: Aunt Glo.

AUNT GLO: The Dave and Buster's? Tony Roma's . . . a place for Rib's? Fuddrucker's?

GIL: I don't think a church is right.

AUNT GLO: "You don't think a church is right?"

GIL: I don't subscribe to organized religion!

AUNT GLO: Organize? Subscribe?

GIL: It's not happening in a church!

AUNT GLO: But that's what you supposed to do. It's what everybody wants. What do you mean subscribe? We gonna have people, COLORED PEOPLE, coming from Alabama, North Carolina, Chicago, Rochester, Lord help us—DETROIT! You cannot NOT have a church service!

GIL: Aunt Glodine. Adelaide—

AUNT GLO: Hold the phone! Hang up and dial again! I know that you and you mother were a bit more "modrin'" but please refrain from calling my sister, "Adelaide" around me.

GIL: ADELAIDE—

AUNT GLO: Help me Father.

GIL:—just started going to ANOTHER church a minute ago! We don't know those people.

AUNT GLO: Those people are church people.

GIL: When's the last time you've been in a church?

AUNT GLO: This is not about me! I think that that is what your MOTHER would have wanted. And a MOTHER should be called MOTHER. I don't know why she let you call her that!

GIL: Because that was her name!

AUNT GLO: It's not respectful. But look. I ain't trying to get all up into that. You cremated your mother! That is the craziest thing I ever heard of. Our people just don't do that! Black people don't do that! You don't do that unless a person was burned or mutilated or to fat to fit in a coffin!!! (*Pause*) Gil, I know that you are in grief right now. So am I! But please try to make some sense out of all of this. Not non-sense.

GIL: AUNT GLO: I'm taking care of Adelaide's services. I'm her son.

*Silence.*

*AUNT GLO pops in another pill. Silence.*

AUNT GLO: Do you still have a problem with meat?

GIL: I don't have a problem with meat. I just don't eat it!

AUNT GLO: Well, we normal people will want meat. Lots of MEAT at a Repast! It's what people do!

*AUNT GLO has piled hats, clothes and everything, all over her body. She looks absolutely ridiculous. GIL starts to leave.*

GIL: Got Enough?

AUNT GLO: Maybe could? Maybe could not!

*Radio silence. Gil has no idea what she has just said as she butchers the English language. He turns to exit.*

AUNT GLO: Where you goin'?

GIL: To see if my friend checked into the hotel.

AUNT GLO: What "friend?"

GIL: You don't know him.

*GIL starts to leave.*

AUNT GLO: When you get back I'll help you figure out who gets what. You know how people are, when a person dies everybody wanna come in an want to pick over everything like crows on a carcass!

*GIL starts to leave yet again.*

AUNT GLO: I'll try to make my greens with turkey instead of pork. Is that alright?

GIL: "??!!" *(beat)* But that's . . . That's fine AUNT GLO: That's fine.

*We hear the base note of "Nice and Nasty" by the Salsoul Orchestra. GIL exits. Lights fade on AUNT GLO as lights come up on MO.*


# THE GREAT ESCAPE

*Rittenhouse Square Park in Philadelphia.*

*The entrance of Mo comes complete with the Salsoul Orchestra's song "Nice and Nasty." MO is sitting on a park bench. He is dressed in fabulous New York hairdresser attire. Hightop colorful sneakers, drop crotch pants, a tank top that exposes his nipples, and motorcycle jacket or something with fringe. He has a haircut with bangs.*

MO: *(to an unseen bicyclist)* NICE BIKE!!!! Hola Papi Como Estas! Ohh Philly is CUTE! Damn they grow em thick up in around here!

*GIL enters.*

MO: *Hey Boo! My cell phone is out of service.

GIL: *Mo, your cell phone is out of service.

MO: Fucking Sprint. They just cut a bitch off with no warning! Damn! How did you know I was over here?

GIL: The consierge at the hotel told me that you were over here scaring the locals.

MO: Oh, so he's been keeping an eye on me. Hmm.

GIL: What took you so long? You are supposed to be here yesterday!

MO: I got a Zipcar instead of taking that Chinese bus. All them smells! Colored people and Chinese food. Did you go to the funeral home? I'm sorry I couldn't get my nerve up to meet you there. I don't like dead bodies.

GIL: You said that you would be here for me.

MO: I'm sorry. I am here for you now. What you need—Oh shit look at that fine ass muthafucka! Why all the brothas in Philly got beards? Mustafa's and shit! Bean pies!

*Silence*

MO: Ok. Done. Death does something to my endorphins. Do you like my bangs?

GIL: Just 48 hours ago you and I were laughing at Lady Vulva's Tranny Bingo Brunch and today I'm trying to slay a witch.

MO: A witch?

GIL: My Aunt Glo.

MO: Oh Lord. Is she the one that rocks the velour sweatsuit?

GIL: Since 1985.

MO: And getting on your last dry nerve?

GIL: She and I don't agree on services or cremation.

MO: Cremation?

GIL: I decided on cremation before I had sex with the funeral director.

MO: Sex with a funeral director?!?!

GIL: I told him that I wanted cremation, he said "If that's what you want!" and then I . . .

*TERRY enters disheveled in a pool of light. Shirt open, pants almost falling off. Post-coital exhaustion. In a pool of light on a bench with MO, GIL speaks to TERRY.*

TERRY: Oh my God!

GIL: Oh my God!

MO: Oh my god!!

TERRY: It's ok. I am glad I could be here for you! Man, I feel like all the lights are turned on! Shit! All the lights are turned on! Is that the door? My father! Go out through the side door.

*TERRY runs out.*

MO: Go out through the side door!? What the? Oh-unh uh! NOW, I HAVE HEARD EVERYTHING! A Funeral Director? A Director of Funerals? Dead Mother?

GIL: You talkin'?

*Colman Domingo*

MO: Check mate!

GIL: And I left a shoe.

MO: A good one?

GIL: Kenneth Cole.

MO: Let it go.

GIL: And now, Glodine wants me to have a church memorial.

MO: As long as it's not like my cousin, Feet Manses

GIL: Feet Manses?

MO: He had BIG-ASS feet! Hmmm. Anyway. *(realizing)* He had BIG-ASS feet? No, that is not what I was talking about. Ooooh, churl! It was a hot steaming mess. My cousin was unfortunately fallen due to being a statistic among many of our young men.

GIL: He was a drug dealer.

MO: I was trying to elevate his chosen profession. He was a drug dealer. He got beaten up over some money and left to die in an alley. They even took his sneakers. His funeral was such a mess. This deaconess sang "The Lord's Prayer" so slow that halfway through, I swear she was singing it in reverse! There were all these teenagers in there looking more angry than sad. They looked like they were ready to fuck up everything and everybody! Just hostile! Like a pack of wolves! The grown folks were trying to keep order over the proceedings. Some fool who looked like a more unattractive Biggie Smalls went up to the casket and put Cazelle Sunglasses on Feet Manses face! My Aunt Punchy, a handsome looking woman, went up to retrieve them. Now, nobody fucks with Aunt Punchy! She looks like she could cut you with her face! *(notices cyclist returning)* THAT IS A NICE BIKE! I WOULD SURE LIKE TO BE THAT SEAT!

GIL: You see? I don't want all that wailing and theatrics.

MO: What actor doesn't like wailing and theatrics?

GIL: I haven't ACTED in years!

MO: True.

GIL: Churches! Filled with judgment! Powdered wigs and gavels. There is something about people wailing and wringing their hands to the heavens, that just dries up everything inside of me! It's just all too much. I'm having her cremated and that's the end of the story.

MO: Oh. OK. I am so sorry—

GIL: DON'T.  I have too much to do. I've get all this settled and to get back to New York and move on!

MO: You know you can't get all of this settled in one day?

GIL: Oh yes I can! I can get all of this settled and get back to New York before these people make me lose my mind! "Up in here, up in here!"

*The sounds of the park engulf the space.*


## WHY NOT?

*We snap back into ADELAIDE'S almost empty apartment.*

GIL: Hello? Aunt Glo? Left the door open! This won't take long. The boxes in there are going with me back to New York.

MO: *(taken aback)* This is your dead mother's apartment!

GIL: Yes, this is what a dead mother's apartment looks like.

MO: I'm here for you. I'm here!

*MO refers to the white dress and the Cinderella doll on the chaise.*

MO: Are these things going?

GIL: Yes.

MO: Your mother loved her fairytales. Silver linings and Happy Endings.

GIL: Would you put that in a box for me. There are boxes in the bedroom.

*MO begins to go into the other room. He stops for a moment and looks at the Cinderella doll and at GIL. AUNT GLO enters. She now wears an oversized t-shirt that says on the front "Drew Carey pick me, to fly for free." on the back is says "or send me home in an SUV." The lettering is iron-on letters.*

AUNT GLO: Whatchu doing in here doin' talking to yourself for, chile?

GIL: *(simultaneously)* Geez Louise!

MO: *(simultaneously)* Oh my God!

AUNT GLO: What's that?

*Colman Domingo*

GIL: Aunt Glo this is Mo.

AUNT GLO: Figures.

GIL: He's helping me.

AUNT GLO: Your "friend."

GIL: You can lose the euphemism.

AUNT GLO: Euphom—

MO: I'm gonna go find a box! *(beat)* I LOVE your sweatsuit.

> *MO exits.*

AUNT GLO: *(enters)* I been looking for them pearls. Have you seen the pearls?

GIL: "????!!"

AUNT GLO: Those pearls that your father gave her. That was the onliest thing that man was good for. Pearls. We had them appraised a thousand years ago after he left ya'll for that Puerto Rican woman. Mmm mm mph! She never got over that. I think that's why she held you so close. Too close for my blood! A boy has to be a boy. And well, you know. Anyway I ain't getting all up in your business but . . . are we at least settled on the church?

GIL: Aunt Glo, I told you, there will be no church!

AUNT GLO: No Church?

GIL: No Church.

AUNT GLO: I don't got time for this "no church" business.

GIL: There will be no church and services cost money.

AUNT GLO: What about her insurance?

GIL: $5,000 is nothing!

> *MO comes out from the bedroom and lingers upstage.*

AUNT GLO: How much money you got?

GIL: I live paycheck to paycheck.

You look like you got money.

AUNT GLO: Pure fiction!

We can take up a collection.

GIL: No. I'm taking care of it.

AUNT GLO: We gon' take up a collection!

GIL: *(Suddenly out of control)* I HAVE TO GET BACK TO NEW YORK! *(recovers)* I ordered the simple cremation package and we will find another time to grieve and wail and cuss each other out. And, actually, there shouldn't be a service per se. A "celebration" is what we should have!

AUNT GLO: GILBERT!!! There is something called tradition. I don't know where it comes from but that is something that we must honor.

GIL: Why?

AUNT GLO: Who knows why! All I know is that it goes all the way back to Africa! Traditions! What they teach you at those schools?

GIL: English Literature!

AUNT GLO: You already spoke English! *(beat)* All those student loans spent on stuff that Black people can't afford. Poems . . . Poetry . . . Acting.

GIL: Glodine, We just have to be as efficient—

AUNT GLO: Efficiency is laying out a body properly! And that takes time. Our ancestors were from the motherland and all the way back to "Lucy" they had procedure.

GIL: Procedure?

AUNT GLO: Rituals!

GIL: So we should cut a hole in the side of the house and push her out through it, feet first?

AUNT GLO: *What? What are you talk about? You talking crazy!

GIL: *No no no no no! I'm talking AFRICAN! LUCY! DEATH RITUALS! TRADITIONS! THORNS AND STICKS! ANIMAL SACRIFICE! SACRIFICING AN OX! LET'S SACRIFICE AN OX! Turn the pictures to face the wall! Cover up the mirrors! Prop her dead body on her bed and sit vigil next to her 'til morning and bury her before sunrise before the witches and sorcerers wake up to try and take over Adelaide's corpse!!

AUNT GLO: Witches and Sorcerers? I don't know what brand of African they taught you at school but—

GIL: *Why don't WE just shave off all our hair and wear black. For a year!

AUNT GLO: *Your just supposed to do things right!

GIL: *That's African!

AUNT GLO: *That was my onliest sister.

GIL: And that was my onliest mother.

AUNT GLO: Well then, ACTOR, then you should have ACTED like it! Acted like that was the onliest mother you had! Always out of reach and could never take a moment to come down and take your mother to a doctors appointment. She said that you couldn't handle it! Hunh, SHE couldn't handle it! Stories and Cinderella doll's. Everybody living in a fairytale!

GIL: You don't know anything about me!

AUNT GLO: I don't have to. What I do know is that I. WAS. HERE. and YOU. WEREN'T!

GIL: Aunt Glo—

AUNT GLO: For the past few months you have been MISSING in ACTING!

*Silence*

*AUNT GLO pops a pill in her mouth and regroups and sits on the chaise.*

AUNT GLO: *(sincerely)* We are not like the Jews! Shovin' a body in the ground five seconds after they die! You hear me? You are just doing things too fast! It must be the Internets or something!

*Silence*

AUNT GLO: Gil, you didn't even have people over the day after your mother's passing! That just… *(unspoken; "breaks my heart")*. You are supposed to have people over and just sit. That's all. Sit. Let people get a chance to catch their breath. Give everyone a chance to just come together. Just sit.

*Silence*

*AUNT GLO picks up the Cinderella doll looks at GIL, looks at MO, shakes her head and puts the doll down. She exits.*

THAT'S WHAT I WANT.

*7am. Terry's Funeral Home. TERRY enters in a lab coat, safety googles, gloves and a mask. He has a tube of lipstick in his hand.*

GIL: Hello??? *(He sees TERRY)* I don't know what you're thinking, but I am soooo not into that.

TERRY: Oh I'm sorry, I was in the middle of putting some finishing touches on a client.

GIL: I'm here to pick up my mother.

*There is an awkward silence.*

TERRY: Ok. I will get your mother for you. Just have a seat.

GIL: I'll stand, thank you.

TERRY: Whatever you'd like.

GIL: For now I would really like for you to take that mask off, it's really freaking me out.

TERRY: Oh, I'm so sorry. Mask. Off. *(smiles)*

*Another awkward silence.*

TERRY: Okay! I will get your mother for you.

*TERRY goes off stage to retrieve "the body." TERRY returns with the urn. He holds it out for Gil. But GIL does not take it. GIL bursts into laughter.*

GIL: Oh. Um. Oh. Oh my God.

TERRY: I did what you wanted. Right?

GIL: Is she all in there?

TERRY: Yes.

GIL: A whole body can fit in there?

TERRY: Yes.

*Silence*

GIL: *(to the audience just like the prologue opening)* I had a Saint Bernard. When I was five. A Big Dog! My father bought it for me. On one of his passes through my childhood. We lived in a tiny row home with the tiniest backyard. Adelaide was pissed. I called him King Henry the Eighth. He was big and fat and ate like a horse. Two hundred and fifty pounds and I was five and I loved him. He died. Poisoned. By our next door neighbors. Crazy right? Who poisons a dog? Our next door neighbors! I had put him outside the night before because it was hot and the night breeze was better to cool down that big old body. I awoke on a drizzly Saturday morning and went out to bring King Henry the Eighth inside. I called for King Henry the Eighth. I called again. And again. And again. He was in the corner of the yard, sopping wet with white foam around his mouth. I shook him. I tried to open his eyes. There was no life. There was nothing. I held that 250 pound body in my arms until the SPCA came and pulled him away. This is better.

*MO enters*

MO: Gil, this big old dyke of a meter maid is trying to let me have it for being double parked on a one way street *(to*

*offstage meter-maid)* I AIN'T SCARED OF THE PO PO!
CALL THE PO-PO!! CHECK MY RECORDS. I AIN'T
SCARED OFF THE PO-PO! TELL THEM TO GET THE
JAILS READY! WHAT!? WHAT!!? Hello! What y'all
doing?

GIL: Car!

MO: But I was just . . .

GIL: Car!

MO: Nice to meet you!

> *MO exits*

> *GIL stares at the urn.*

TERRY: About the other day… That was probably just something that you needed to get out of your-our system. Grief
does strange things to people. I'm not sure if I'm cut out
for this work. I mean, I had sex with you in my families
funeral home. *(laughs)* I'm sorry, you have your mother's
ashes in your hands. What is wrong with me? I am flooded
with guilt. This is a funeral home!

GIL: You just realized that. Didn't the coffins tip you off?

TERRY: You just probably needed touch! I'm a healer.

> *GIL shoots him a look.*

TERRY: NOT in THAT way. In a healing way.

GIL: I apologize for attacking you.

> *They laugh into silence. GIL sobers up. He stares at the
> urn. TERRY takes this in.*

TERRY: Grief is a low chakra and it feels endless when you are
looking at it from the outside.

> *Silence*

TERRY: When you are standing on the edge, waiting to jump
into it, you think you can't but when you're in it it doesn't
matter because it's real and its true and it just becomes part
of you and it never goes away it just becomes part of the
fabric of who you are. Your grief is as unique as you are.
King Henry the Eighth and all.

> *TERRY leans in and kisses GIL: It is a long but sweet kiss.
> GIL softens for a moment and then turns cold.*

GIL: Could I have my shoe? My shoe. I left it here yesterday.

TERRY: I haven't seen a shoe around here.

GIL: Oh well.

TERRY: Is there anything you need?

GIL: Thank you for the . . . everything.

> *GIL exits.*

TERRY: *(under his breath)* Can I call you?


# JUST SIT!

*Seconds later. Terry's Funeral Home. There is a pounding on a door. AUNT GLO is breathing heavy and sweating profusely. She makes her way in and barely looks at Terry. She rummages through her bag searching for a checkbook. He bag is filled with things that only AUNT GLO would have in her purse: A ball of yarn, half roll of toilet paper, a bottle of Kaopectate, panties, Mad Libs, Cheap Chinese slippers, etc.*

AUNT GLO: Terry! Terry! TERRY!

TERRY: Hello?

AUNT GLO: Who are you?

TERRY: Terry.

AUNT GLO: Terry? Terry two or three?

TERRY: Four actually.

AUNT GLO: When did I get so old? Your people been putting my people in the ground for a long time. Glo Hawkins! Y'all take great care of everybody. Everybody. Your business is the only business that thrives. Thrives you hear me? How old are you? Cain't be no more than, what? Twenty-something odd years? What, you running this funeral home now? Ain't you a little young?

TERRY: With all due respect I am thirty and I have my Masters in Business Management from the Keller Graduate School of Management.

> *Pause*

AUNT GLO: *(dry)* That don't mean nothing!

TERRY: Is there something I can help you with?

AUNT GLO: I tried to call over here but I almost lost my mind with that automated instruction. What y'all doing over her that you can't get to a phone? I gotta go online to make an appointment now?

TERRY: Actually, I am trying to get us to have more of a social media presence.

AUNT GLO: Social Media? Mmm hmm! "Internets."

TERRY: May I help you?

AUNT GLO: Actually, yes! My nephew has seemed to have misplaced his natural born mind. He asked you to burn the body!

TERRY: I am so sorry Mrs.—

AUNT GLO: Ms—

TERRY: Ms. Hawkins.

*TERRY grabs a chair and brings it over for AUNT GLO.*

AUNT GLO: The community is supposed to come together: To plan! To support! To grieve! Don't nobody need anybody anymore? Now everybody is grieving on their own. I think the "internets" are the problem. Can I please have a glass of water? *(TERRY goes to get the water)* First there was dial up but then apparently that was too slow! Everybody telling me I gotta get that DSL cable. Why? I got HBO and Showtime! But they said I would be able to surf and get online and chat and things like that. *(TERRY returns with the water)* MICROWAVE OVENS! Thank you. Good looks run in the family. You look just like all the other Terrys! Good looks get the grieving widows to spend all of they insurance money on the funeral services hunh? Mmm hmmm. Anyway. Everybody just stays online and stays to themselves. No real relationships. The "internets" are keeping families apart. Adelaide, my sister, god rest her soul, even had one of them SPACEBOOK accounts set up by Gil so that she could keep up with him. If I gotta find out what going on with you on a page over the "internets"-there is a problem. What, nobody know how to pick up a phone anymore??? No, because there is texting and "twitching" going on. You know, Gil told me that, that is the way he let's folks know what is happening moment to moment. No one needs to know what is going on with you moment to moment unless they are THERE! You ain't there then somebody will TELL you about it. Go over their house and tell 'em about it. Have a piece of pie and talk. Or not talk just be together.

That is called communication! I am so sorry do you have a dead body to burn or anything right now.

TERRY: No ma'am. I don't burn bodies.

AUNT GLO: It ain't right, it ain't right!

TERRY: Everyone has their own personal right to choose!

AUNT GLO: Oh really? Is that right?

> *She pulls out a checkbook.*

AUNT GLO: I don't got time for all this! You take checks?

TERRY: Uh, Yes.

AUNT GLO: Is your father here?

TERRY: No, he isn't here Ms. Hawkins.

AUNT GLO: Can I have my sister please?

TERRY: Your nephew already picked her up.

AUNT GLO: Where did he take her?

TERRY: I'm not sure.

AUNT GLO: I don't have time for all this nonsense! When an elder asks you a question, you answer! What is wrong with your generation? Where did he take her?

TERRY: He didn't say where he was going.

AUNT GLO: Too fast, too fast! The "INTERNETS!!!"

TERRY: Can I get you a cup of coffee?

AUNT GLO: It's as hot as Satan's toilet out there! I don't want no coffee! I need to talk to Terry! *(she yells)* TERRY!!!

TERRY: I am Terry!

AUNT GLO: Terry! Terry two or three! Big Terry! Grand Terry!!! Oh Lord! Oh! Oh my God.

> *AUNT GLO gets dizzy and is about to pass out. The following dialogue happens at a frenetic pace.*

AUNT GLO: *I can't breathe. Oh my-Pills-my purse-I have to catch my-I'm hot-

TERRY: *Sit. Sit. Please sit down! Take it easy. Deep breath! Get control of you breath. Inhale with me! Exhale! Once more.

> *They inhale and exhale together.*

AUNT GLO: MY PILLS!

> *He hands AUNT GLO her purse. She takes out a pill bottle and takes two pills. She drinks some water. She opens another bottle and takes two more pills. She pops in an Altoid.*

*Colman Domingo*

TERRY: Do you need me to call a doctor?

AUNT GLO: For what?

*She rummages through her purse for a cell phone. Pulling out all sorts of things. Everything but the cell phone. Think "Monty Python."*

TERRY: Well, I just thought . . .

AUNT GLO: Everything is just moving too fast! I'mma get with the program. My phone! My new phone that my Mexican co-worker unlocked! Show me how to use it! It's got that CP-PS on it. I can track Gil.

TERRY: You mean GPS.

AUNT GLO: I mean CP-PS. Colored People's Positioning Systems.

TERRY: How is that possible?

AUNT GLO: Mexicans! I just told you my Mexican unlocked it for me! I put a tracking device on that Cinderella doll just in case something like this happened! Talking about Africans, witches and sorcerers! It's linked up to my phone! The Mexicans can do anything!

*We hear the sound of the CP-PS on AUNT GLO'S phone. It's in Spanish.*

TERRY: Do you speak Spanish?

AUNT GLO: What kind of question is that?

TERRY: Do you think he's gone far?

AUNT GLO: Burnt his mother up and running around with something called Mo?

TERRY: I'm worried about him.

AUNT GLO: What's that glint in your eye?

TERRY: Nothing. I'm going with you!

AUNT GLO: We drivin! Follow that Doll!


# HITTING I-95

*MO at the wheel of a convertible. He wears a lovely scarf on his head like Sophia Loren and cat eye glasses. GIL has the Cinderella doll in one hand and the urn in the other.*

MO: *(speaking to himself)* The last time I was up and around

WILD WITH HAPPY

here, I spent time with my baby cousin Khanundrum.Yes, Khanundrum, the "h" is silent! I was reading her a story about Winnie the Poo and low and behold the story just kept revealing to me, that Winnie the Poo-Poo was a BIG OLD PIGGY BOTTOM! Seriously! What bear runs around with no pants on? Always running into the woods with his "friends" in search of honey? Horrifying!!! So, I started to read all of the children's books that was in the nursery to Khanundrum! Snow White and the Seven Dwarves! All about some evil queen that is angry that someone is fairer than you.

*GIL'S phone rings. MO looks down at it.*

MO: Speak of the Evil Queen and she appears!

*MO silences GIL'S phone.*

MO: And OFF! Hmph! Little Red Riding Hood. A little White girl trying to deliver a pie to grandma and finds a wolf in drag instead. And some big strappin' lumberjack comes to her rescue. Goldilocks and the Three Bears! Just breaking and entering! Those bears should have wore that ass out for eating up there shit, breaking their chair and sleeping in their beds! And the fairytale queen herself! Cinderella! Another story about a white woman in distress! But what? Her foot is the only foot that fits that glass Jimmy Choo and what? BAM! She is a princess and gets to marry the hot-ass prince charming! Hmph! But that only happens to White princesses. Tiana has to work her ass off. Trying to open another Cajun restaurant in the South! Making beniet's and turning into a frog and whatnot.

*GIL wakes.*

GIL: What the hell are you talking about?

*GIL notices the exit sign.*

THE NEXT FIVE EXITS THE DISTRICT OF COLUM-BIA!!!??
MO: SURPRISE!!

# AUNT GLO'S 1987
# OLDSMOBILE CUTLASS SUPREME

*AUNT GLO and TERRY, driving in AUNT GLO'S 1987
Oldsmobile Cutlass Supreme. AUNT GLO is at the wheel.
TERRY is looking out the window and preoccupied with
his cell phone.*

AUNT GLO: I WANTED TO BE A SOLID GOLD DANCER!
What was that child's name? Darcel! Mmm mm mph. Had
that long flowy hair, all the way down her back.

*TERRY'S phone rings. He fumbles with the phone.*

AUNT GLO: I wanted to be a dancer but when you are the
oldest you can't always get what you want! Like the good
Lord says, "Honor they mother and thoust father and they
days will be long upon da earth!"

TERRY: I'm all about my mom and dad but I also have to honor
myself. I think holistic work is where I belong, not in the
funeral home. There I said it! I said it. YES!!!

AUNT GLO: I'm not gonna have to put you out of this car will
I? I got enough crazy going on.

TERRY: Have you always honored your parents wishes over
your own?

AUNT GLO: Honored my parents wishes? When I was coming
up my parents were dirt poor. I grew up on a boot and
a shoe! I had to get a job. Couldn't even finish high
school. Adelaide was coming up when thangs got a little
better for us. Adelaide always had her own mind and
freedom to do what she wanted to do. She had to get
married. Pregnant at nineteen! Had to drop out of a good
school for nursing. Spent her life catching up. Having
a baby with man that didn't want her, days work and
trying to be some singer. I have been a seamstress over
at the Quartermasters for 31 years. Do you know what
I'm saying? "Go on out there and get you a job with
benefits!" I have a stack of benefits and I am looking
retirement square in the chin. I didn't get to do what I
wanted to do but I've got security. I wanted to be a Solid
Gold dancer! So look, you can't always get what you
want but you can make due. Can you see me?

TERRY: Yes.

AUNT GLO: Cause I'm still here!

TERRY: "You are unique, and if that is not fulfilled, then something has been lost."

AUNT GLO: Excuse me?

TERRY: Martha Graham.

AUNT GLO: I don't know who that is.

*TERRY'S phone rings.*

AUNT GLO: You just gonna keep ignoring that call?

TERRY: *(picks up)* Hi Daddy. I stepped out, I had the calls forwarded to my cell. Yes Daddy. I'm not feeling well. Hold on for a second *(To Aunt Glo)* Would you excuse me for a moment? *(whispers)* Daddy, I need you to go in, I'm not feeling well. Unh hunh. I made the right side of her face match the left. Ms. Tiny's family will be very happy.

AUNT GLO: Tiny Green?

TERRY: *(into the phone)* I'm sorry?

AUNT GLO: Tiny Green?

TERRY: *(into the phone)* Yes. Her family brought her make-up, dentures and a blue wig.

AUNT GLO: Not the blue wig!

TERRY: *(into the phone)* When Cousin Ronnie comes back with the death certificates we can do that.

AUNT GLO: *(simultaneously)* Blue. Oldsmobile blue! Her family aught to be ashamed of themselves! I don't know why nobody ever told that colored blind woman that she bought a wig that was a shade of blue. Mmm mm mph. A blue wig.

TERRY: *(simultaneously into the phone)* But Daddy, we have to hire someone more stable, he just got out! Do you know that I've been missing my Past Life Regression Therapy class? It's just as important! Well, that's what I want to do. You're not listening. That's what I want! We can't have this conversation right now. *(Hangs up)*

AUNT GLO: Everything alright? You still my ride-or-die?

TERRY: Everything's alright. I can't believe we are on an old school car chase! FOLLOW THAT CAR!!!

AUNT GLO: We still trackin' him? We been on I-95 for hours.

TERRY: He is in Richmond, Virginia!

AUNT GLO: Richmond? Why on earth is he going to the seat of the Confederacy???

TERRY: I can't believe we're doing this.

AUNT GLO: Believe it! I got a little bit of a lead foot if you haven't noticed. I like a fast car! I'mma just pull into this rest stop. *(BAM!!!! She backs into a parked car.)* Well, we gonna have to switch off. I ain't blind, but at night, I can't tell an off-ramp from an elevator. Yes lord, WE DRIVIN'! I don't fly and the train makes me tho up, and I do NOT get the bus. Especially after that Oriental man decapitated that White boy in Canada a few years ago on a Greyhound bus. I do NOT get the bus! And since you burned the body, we are following that car! Shoot, I've been through Nixon, Reagan and both Bushes. We'll be fine. We have Jesus in the drivers seat. We're just passengers. What else do we need? WE DRIVIN'

*MO is driving. GIL holds the Cinderella doll and urn.*

GIL: WHY ARE WE IN GEORGIA?

MO: Trust me!

GIL: That is exactly what a person who is not to be trusted says!

MO: Just a little detour.

GIL: I don't have time for your antics Mo! I've got to get what's left of my life in order!

MO: A little detour, that's all.

GIL: What I need is a sledgehammer!

MO: For what?

GIL: To knock you OUT! PULL OVER. I'm done!

MO: What did I tell tell you back in 200 B.C? When you first arrived in New York?

GIL: What? What the hell are you talkin' about?

MO: When you sat down in my makeup chair and you had a little hangover from being out at "The Club" the night before? You just moved to New York as a bubbly, fresh, ingenue . . .

GIL: I ain't never been bubbly, fresh or an ingenue . . . .

MO: You sat up in my make up chair.

GIL: PULL. OVER.

MO: The first time I beat your face!

GIL: PULL. OVER.

MO: The first time I beat your face to DEATH on that awful set of—

GIL: *(laughs)* "Jumpin' and Jackin'!"

MO: *(laughs)* They tried so hard to give Gary Coleman another series!

GIL: *(laughs)* Nobody wanted that!

MO: What did I say?

GIL: *(laughs)* You said that no matter how early in the morning it is . . .

MO: *(laughs)* No matter how much you drank last night . . .

GIL: *(laughs)* No matter if your cat just died . . .

MO and GIL: *(laughs)* Or your man bust you in the eye, I got enough MAKE-UP, to cover it up!

MO: *(laughs)* I cover it UP! That's my motto! I cover it up! I've covered it up! *(suddenly very serious)* I don't want you to do that! I've done it for years and looking at how you have been handling all of this, I think that you are on a collision course.

GIL: Mo—

MO: Listen, I lost my mother when I was twelve and I spent years wishing I could do something for her but I was powerless!

GIL: Mo—

MO: *(fierce)* Two years of hospitals and "Mommy is tired" and "Mommy hurts" and Mommy is shopping for wigs and missing baseball games and then one day a kiss and be a good boy and "mind your grandmother" and then gone!

GIL: Mo—

MO: We have got to deal with this! *(full on Oprah as Sophia in the Color Purple)* "DON'T CHANGE PLACES WITH ME MISS CELIE!!!"

## WHEN IN ROME

*TERRY is driving. AUNT GLO now sits in the passenger seat with a "To Go" container on her lap. She rifles through her bag and pulls out a bottle of Kaopectate.*

AUNT GLO: If I prepared to drive a thousand hours, I would have fried up a chicken or two! That "Country Buffett" got too much to choose from! Twenty-two styles of pork! I don't trust places with too many selections. You can't get

*Colman Domingo*

everything right! But when in Rome! *(beat)* You sure are handlin' my "Betsy!"

TERRY: I haven't heard anyone call a car "Betsy" in a coon's age!

AUNT GLO: Chile, I call everything something!

TERRY: You're funny!

AUNT GLO: *(dry)* You funny.

> Silence

AUNT GLO: So, do you lie to your father often?

TERRY: Lie?

AUNT GLO: Telling Big Terry you weren't feeling well.

TERRY: Did you overhear…?

AUNT GLO: Black people don't know how to whisper!

TERRY: He doesn't like to hear the truth.

AUNT GLO: The truth shall set you free!

TERRY: Do you always speak in proverbs?

> Silence. She thinks.

AUNT GLO: YES! *(pause)* I speak God and Truth! GOD AND TRUTH.

TERRY: God and Truth! People talk so much about God and Truth. But do people really want the truth?

AUNT GLO: I do!

TERRY: No, no . . . Most people want a truth that is comfortable. For instance, you and your nephew. What is the issue of him following his truth just as you follow your truth? What about the need for a person to do what's in their hearts? I think people act out because of their fear of being alone, especially around death! Fighting their loneliness with sex, drinking, drugs, but some of the most sensitive ones with a quiet, intensely personal search. Everybody is just searching, trying to figure it out. Everything doesn't have to be a battle!


## BILL COLLECTORS AT MY DOOR

*GIL and MO are at a gas station in the middle-of-nowhere U.S.A.*

GIL: NO!

MO: Come on! Get in the car!

GIL: You are out of your fucking mind!

MO: Maybe! But get in the car! These rednecks are starting to look at us.

GIL: *(pulls out cell phone)* I don't care! I'm gonna get a livery cab to get me to the nearest airport back to New York. open the trunk so I can get my shit.

MO: NO!

GIL: No service! WHERE THE FUCK AM I??? Open this trunk or I'm gonna light this bitch up!

MO: Gil, listen to me!

GIL: I'm not in the mood for listening to someone who gets some sick enjoyment out of kidnapping someone and his dead mother's ashes.

> *GIL picks up the Cinderella doll and reaches for the urn. MO intercepts the urn.*

GIL: Put my mother down!

MO: She wants you to go with me!

GIL: You hearing voices? Gimme my mother!

MO: Your mother wants you to go with me!

GIL: I'm gonna kill you! I swear fo' God! Right here in the middle of Dixie!

MO: YALE ALUM . . . That redneck attendant is looking at us!

GIL: *(to an unseen redneck)* Mind your business Jethro!

MO: I need you to trust me on this!

GIL: I don't trust anyone!

MO: Let me do this!

GIL: Let you take me somewhere I don't know? Have we met?

MO: You have to get in this car, on the road and not control every moment!

GIL: You can't even keep your cell phone on and I am supposed to surrender to you?

MO: *(He thinks, pause)* Yes!

GIL: *(to unseen redneck)* JETHRO CALL ME A CAB!!!!

MO: LOOK! Watching the way you deal with all of this, I realize that I have spent my life covering  things up that I can't deal with and I really don't think that that has made me the picture of perfect mental health!

GIL: Your point?

MO: My point is. I feel like ever since I lost my Mom I've had a hundred pound weight placed on my chest . . . and have been trying to catch my breath for a . . . WOOOOOOOO! *(He does something completly off color to change his mood from distraught to recovered)* Okay. Done! MAKEUP!!!!!!

    *GIL begins to walk away.*

MO: LOOK, GIL, YOU ARE GOING TO GET IN THIS CAR AND STRAP YOURSELF IN WITH YOUR MOTHER BECAUSE SOMETIMES WHEN YOU DON'T KNOW WHERE YOU ARE GOING YOU HAVE TO LET SOMEONE ELSE TAKE THE WHEEL! YOU CAN'T CONTROL EVERYTHING!

GIL: *(screaming like a little girl)* FUCK YOU I'M LEAVING!

MO: *(screaming like a bigger little girl)* FUCK YOU! WE'RE GOING TO DISNEYWORLD!!!

    *We shift to AUNT GLO and TERRY'S Car.*

AUNT GLO: ORLANDO, FLORIDA?

TERRY: That's what the CP-PS says?

AUNT GLO: Why on God's green Earth would he be stopped in Orlando, Florida?

TERRY: Maybe he wanted to take his mother's remains to Orlando, Florida?

AUNT GLO: She ain't never been to no Orlando, Florida. The onliest place in Florida that she ever went to was . . . .*(beat)* . . . HAS HE LOST HIS MIND?

    *She dials GIL'S number on her cell phone. GIL and MO get out of the car. We see amusement park lights on their faces.*

AUNT GLO: PULL OVER!!!

GIL'S VOICEMAIL: *(Voicemail)* Hi! Thank you for giving me a call today. I must be out living my life like its golden. You know what to do! Like "Nike" says "Just do it." Leave me a message and I will try to get back to you as soon as I can. If this is of an important urgent business matter please feel free to call my manager, Stacey Rose at (212).445.7329 or my agent Charlie Shafir at (212).854.5077. You can also friend me on facebook or tweet at the real Gil Hawkins. Do not dwell in the past. Do not dream of the future, concentrate the mind on the present moment. Bye!

*AUNT GLO is now out of the car on the side of the road.*

AUNT GLO: YOU HAVE LOST YOUR MIND! You can't have no funeral services in DISNEY WORLD! I don't know what has been filling your head, excuse my French, LIVING LA VIDA LOCA, but when a person dies, Praise Jesus, there are supposed to be funeral services. A church, a choir, a program, flowers, a casket, help me father, A CASKET! NOT AN URN! What kind of word is that anyway? URNNNNN!!! A wreathe of flowers on the door! You need a wreathe of flowers on the door!!! And a HURST! A HURST!!! Limos for the family with big orange stickers that said funeral on 'em! So other cars know that they shouldn't break the line of cars during the processional. THE PROCESSIONAL!!! What is wrong with you boy? People need a processional! People need to wear black and veils! And WEEP!!! You gotta let people come and weep! FALL OUT and LAY over the casket weep! If they don't weep there, then they could do it at the CEMETERY, where they toss FLOWERS on the CASKET. THE CASKET, not the URN! You don't toss flowers on an URN! Toss flowers on the CASKET AND REACH THEIR GRIEF STRICKEN ARTHRITIC FINGERS TO THE BOWELS OF THE EARTH AS THEIR LOVED ONE IS TAKEN ON AN ELEVATOR TO THEIR FINAL RESTING PLACE SIX FEET UNDER. YOU CAN'T HAVE A FUNERAL SERVICE IN ORLANDO, FLORIDA!!!! YOU CAN'T WEAR BLACK IN FLORIDA!!!

*BLACK OUT! MUSIC! FANFARE! DRAMA!*

*AT MICKEY'S PEARLY GATES*

*MO and GIL arrive at Disneyworld. As they drag through, MO twirls a baton. They are a little worn down from the sixteen hour trip. Mo twirls a baton.*

MO: VIPs coming through! VIPs! We have passes! Yes we do! Passes. Excuse us! Excuse us! (He does a high kick) Give 'em a kick! Uh! Let em know that you still got it. Like in high school! Don't you typical American families have manners and know that it is not polite to stare?

*He turns to GIL is checking his voicemail messages.*

MO: GIL??!!!

CALLER #1: *(VOICE OVER)* Hey Gil, I am so sorry to hear about…

    *He deletes*

CALLER #2: *(VOICE OVER)* Gil I just found out….

    *He deletes*

CALLER #3: *(VOICE OVER)* Oh my God…Wow…

    *He deletes*

CALLER #4, #5, #6, #7, #8:, *(VOICE OVER)* I am so sorry, I'm so sorry, I'm so sorry, can I borrow five dollars, I'm sorry.

    *He deletes them all.*

AUNT GLO: *(VOICE OVER)* YOU HAVE LOST YOUR MIND! YOU can't have no funeral services in Dis—

    *He deletes*

COMMERCIAL AGENT: *(VOICE OVER)* Gil. Joan Spangler's assistant. Hope you got the flowers. They took you off of hold for the Craisin spot. The Ad Agency really liked you but they went with Flavor Flave. Maybe you should try rappin'! It could get you more legit work. You are released.

    *He deletes*

TERRY: *(whispered)* *(VOICE OVER)* Gil, Hi. It's Terry. I just wanted to uh . . . tell you that uh . . . I am on the road headed to Disney . . . I thought you would need some help with your . . .

AUNT GLO: *(VOICE OVER)* They don't believe in clean bathrooms in Florida do they?

TERRY: *(VOICE OVER)* Um, I'll call you back.

    *He deletes. He and MO think.*

GIL AND MO: I don't want to think about it.


## O.P.U.L.E.N.C.E. OPULENCE!

*The curtains open to reveal a suite fit for Cinderella. It is beyond, BEYOND the actual Cinderella suite at Disneyworld. The actor that plays Aunt Glo / Adelaide is now dressed to*

*the nines in a Cinderella ball gown. She breezes around the
room so gracefully as enchanting music plays. She reveals
her glass slipper and blows a kiss to the audience. Before
she drifts away through the balcony doors she puts a finger
up to her mouth. "Sssshhh!" And she is gone.*

*Mo and Gil enter the suite.*

MO: Bam! What?! GET INTO IT! The Cinderella Suite!
Yaaaaassssss! Yaaaaaaasssssssss!

*(Gil places the Cinderella doll and the urn on the desk.)*

MO: When you have worked in the service industry like I have for
a billion years, you know a friend, who knows a friend, who's
got a friend, who can help a bitch out! But note, my liege, we
have to vacate by 6 A.M., under the cloak of night.

*(Mo picks up a remote control and aims it at the mirror
that transforms into a ninety-six-inch flatscreen television. This is something that only Mo and Gil can see
offstage.)*

MO: This friend of a friend has a limit to his hook-up! Oooh,
look at that monstrous flat-screen TV! It's HUGE! BAM!
*(Gasps.)* CINDERELLA!!! *(Suddenly we hear the intro to
a Disneyesque song. Sung sweetly. Birds chirp and the song
reeks of dreams, make believe, and love. Gil grabs the remote
and turns it off. Silence. Silence. Silence. Sincerely.)* Okay.
Okay. This is crazy. I'm sorry. I just get ideas. *(Refers to his
hair.)* Like these bangs. Sometimes an idea should be just that!
An idea! I just thought this was something that you needed.
You know? A little magic. I thought that's why you wanted
me to be here for you! A fairy to sprinkle some fairy dust!

GIL: I don't need any fairy dust.

MO: You can't just cremate your mother and move on.

GIL: Oh, so I need the Cinderella Suite?

MO: You need something to bring you back to life. Didn't you
tell me that you and your mother came here about a year
ago and you had the time of your life?

GIL: I was being sarcastic! SHE had the time of her life, I had
just broken up with Clewby!

MO: Why would you go out with someone named Clewby in
the first place?

GIL: Anyway—

---

419

MO: Think about it. Your mother is now in the place where she had the time of her life!

GIL: Adelaide lived in a fantasy and didn't realize that all of this living in a fantasy costs! Spent everything for the promise of a fairy tale ending!

MO: Everybody wants a fairy tale ending.

GIL: Spent her last dime on a Limited Edition Genuine Porcelain Cinderella Doll from the QVC.

MO: Gil—

GIL: Buying into dreams and faith. There is evil lurking around every corner and frogs ain't Prince Charming. This is all just commerce and hoodwinks!

MO: Well, I don't know about all that, but Gil, can't you just imagine the spirit of your mother being here? In a Cinderella ball gown twirling for the Gods!

GIL: Why don't I just imagine Santa Claus and the Tooth Fairy and Antonio Sabato, Jr. and a check for a million dollars and—

*(A cuckoo clock announces eleven coo-coo's 11:00 p.m.)*

MO: Your mother believed in happily-ever-afters.

*(There is now a light glowing from within the Cinderella doll. Mo is in awe.)*

GIL: Mothers are dead in fairytales.

*(Suddenly we hear the sound of wind and chimes, the flatscreen television that we imagine comes on. Magic! Gil and Mo see Adelaide as Cinderella twirling gently on the air. We hear the lyrics of a sweet and gentle song about having faith in dreams. The song is so sweet that it is heartbreaking. They listen for a full two minutes in stillness and silence. Mo and Gil's eyes well with emotion. Suddenly there is a pounding on the door.)*

AUNT GLO: GIL?! Open this door! I know you're in there! Open this door!

TERRY. There is a tracking device in the Cinderella Doll!

MO: WHAT?!

GIL: DOLL?!

TERRY. YUP!

AUNT GLO: MEXICANS!

WILD WITH HAPPY

*(Mo opens the door. Aunt Glo enters. She is loaded down with Disneyworld paraphernalia. She wears an oversized Mickey Mouse hand.)*

AUNT GLO: One day I just woke up and found myself chasing down my dead sister's urn, and somehow I ended up in Disneyworld! Oh my God, This is beautiful!

GIL: AUNT GLO: I can explain.

MO: No, Gil, I can explain. I did this.

AUNT GLO: Your mother, my sister, God rest her soul, must be turning in her grave, or turning in that urn, to think that she hasn't been given a proper service and burial. Where is that urn? *(Gil holds it out to her. She retrieves it with care.)* I don't understand you. Is this your idea of laying a person down? Is this your idea of ritual? I don't understand you or any of this. Is that crystal? That is beautiful! GIL? Answer me. Is that crystal?

GIL: What?

*(Aunt Glo shifts into Adelaide as the lights shift.)*

ADELAIDE: Is that real crystal?

*(Adelaide is wearing a princess tiara and holds a brochure of the Cinderella Suite at Disneyworld. Subtle Disneyesque music plays.)*

## EPILOGUE The Caged Bird Cuckoo's

GIL: Wow. As a matter of fact, the last time I was in Disneyworld, thanks to Adelaide being the ninth caller on Power 99 FM, Adelaide kept bugging me about seeing the Cinderella Suite. She was looking through the brochure and was so inquisitive on whether or not the chandelier in the suite was real crystal.

ADELAIDE: Is that real crystal? *(Lights shift into the same tone as the prologue. Subtle Disneyesque music plays.)*

GIL: I'm not sure.

ADELAIDE: Real or not real, it is fabulous! Look at this! Everyone is happy! Look at all this random joy on the street! People doing the hula-hoop.

GIL:  Children and grown-ass people gorging themselves on sweets.

ADELAIDE:  Minnie and Mickey performing at 12, 2, 4—

GIL AND ADELAIDE: And 6!

ADELAIDE:  In the middle of the Magic Kingdom! Parades on the hour! For no reason but to be happy…just joy! Why can't real life be like this? Wouldn't you love to just get up and grab some glitter and put on a Pocahontas outfit on a Tuesday morning just to go to the post office?

*(Gil is about to respond, his body language feys out.)*

ADELAIDE:  Forget I asked. *(We see words either projected or on a placard. Reads a placard/projection.)* "Hope is the greatest of the gifts we'll receive." I like that one. "Everyone needs someone, he must need someone too." That's for you. *(Reads a placard/projection.)* "My soul is there beside you, let this candle guide you." *(Reads a placard/projection.)* "Love is a song that never ends."

GIL AND ADELAIDE:  "Love is a song that never ends"

ADELAIDE:  Here come the fireworks!

*(They watch the globe open and explode with light. We see the light on their faces.)*

ADELAIDE:  I believe.

GIL:  *(For Adelaide's benefit.)*  I believe.

ADELAIDE: Good…Good…Funny how all this light can take away all your troubles. The trouble with…my heart……the weight loss…the kidney failure…it's Lupus. *(Gil slowly begins to move away from ADELAIDE: The present becomes a memory again. Gil watches the memory of the conversation.)* That's what the doctor said. *(Silence.)* I'm sorry. I just found out. I'm okay though. I'm fine. I'm fine. People live with it all the time. Took awhile to diagnose. *(Silence.)* I didn't know when to tell you. *(Silence.)* Lupus. She's like a sixty-year-old woman with Timberland boots. Trying to upset and destroy. But she don't know me, I got a little of my sister in me, I don't go down without a fight. *(Silence.)* Maybe this wasn't the right moment. Fireworks and whatnot. *(Silence. The fireworks illuminated on their faces change colors.)* We gotta believe in something. 'Til the very end. I know I must sound like a stupid little girl but we have to sprinkle fairy dust and keep on believing.

GIL:  We stuff ourselves with hope. A meal too expensive and we could never afford.

ADELAIDE:  Where do you see that?

GIL:  But lacking the appetite for what has been served. A new table with horns of plenty awaits in spring. Summer is hot and blows gales of heat but wait for spring.

ADELAIDE:  I don't see that one.

GIL:  They say "Time heals." It stitches the deep red purple heart of love. Love is elusive. Not fully comprehended nor exceptionally near our grasp. It cuts like a waning moon touched by the hand of God.

ADELAIDE:  Where is that?

GIL: I just made that up.

> *(Gil returns back inside of the memory. He stands next to ADELAIDE: Gil is distraught.)*

ADELAIDE:  "It cuts like a waning moon touched by the hand of God!" *(She thinks.)* He lives here in the Magic Kingdom, you know.

GIL:  Who?

ADELAIDE: God! Walt told us so. All over his kingdom! "Hope is the greatest of gifts we'll receive," and so on. *(She takes in the reverie.)* Look at all of this magic. Fireworks and magic. Everybody is just happy. Just wild with happy. *(The fireworks intensifies.)* GIL...(Adelaide sings a few bars of a song. Sweet, soulful and hopeful.)

GIL: We should head back to the hotel. *(Adelaide sings a little more.)* Adelaide people are starting to look at us! *(Adelaide sings a little louder.)* You just don't give up, do you? *(Adelaide sings full out! She nudges Gil to finish the song with her. He sorrowfully obliges. Gil and Adelaide stumble over the last lyrics with mmm hmm da da da's and resolve. Gil stands alone. Lights bring us back into the suite.)*

GIL:  I couldn't even look at her, my own mother, because I thought all my seams would fall apart. She made up stories to let me know how she was doing and I couldn't let myself hear them. For years I have been trying to just keep my head above water and this was just all too much! The woman with the Timberland boots. Aunt Glo, I don't have the key to my heart or my mind, I just know that I stopped. Right here in the middle of the Magic Kingdom. I just stopped.

---

*Colman Domingo*

And all this time I wasn't there. Right when she needed me the most. I have been missing in acting.

AUNT GLO: You know what? Life is not a box of cherries. It's not a bowl of chocolates. It's a long trip down a winding road where you can't even see where you are going. You are going to drive and set off with a map and you may lose your way at times. You're gonna have accidents and want to drive over the next cliff. But Gil, I'm telling you, not because I am as old as the sun, but I'm telling you that I know because I have lost many a person in my life including my sweet sister. Death is a thief. That thief called death offers us an opportunity to grow into this life a little more.

GIL: I've been standing still and covering it all up.

AUNT GLO: You gotta move forward.

GIL: I've been so broken.

AUNT GLO: *(Reassuring.)* Let your heart be broken open.

GIL: I wasn't there.

AUNT GLO: (Reassuring.) But, you are here now!

> *(The clock begins to strike twelve! Suddenly we see the most fascinating fireworks display outside of the balcony! These fireworks begin to engulf the entire theater, house and all. Silence. We see the silhouette of our company captivated by the light.)*

GIL: Let's send her off.

AUNT GLO: What do you mean?

GIL: A Ritual. Procedure. Tradition.

AUNT GLO: Lucy?

GIL: Mickey.

AUNT GLO: Mickey?

GIL: And Minnie.

AUNT GLO: You Goofy?

GIL: Fireworks and magic! *(Silence.)* Your souvenirs! *(Gil grabs the souvenir bag.)*

GIL: How about these? *(He hands Mo and Terry souvenir horns.)*

GIL: When the time is right, announce my mother's return to God's loving arms. My mother found God here in the Magic Kingdom. Let's give her some magic. That would be the best ritual for my onliest mother. Your onliest sister. Who believed. Let's sprinkle some fairy dust.

*(Silence. Gil smiles at Aunt Glo. Aunt Glo smiles at Gil for the first time. She nods in agreement. GIL picks up the urn.)*

AUNT GLO: Ashes to ashes.

GIL: And dust to dust. *(Gil pours some of the ashes from the urn into Aunt Glo's hands and then some into his own. They move to the balcony. The horns blow! They toss the ashes off the balcony. The fairy dust/ashes SPARKLES and GLITTERS! Tower bells ring! We hear an orchestrated version of a Disneyesque song. The fireworks burst! Eventually the fireworks and music build and gradually take over the entire theater. Silence. Silence. Silence. They all stand in the reverie of the fireworks. Silence. Silence. Silence. The fireworks end. Silence. They turn around. Wide-eyed, bright, exhilarated and moved to tears. A Disneyesque music plays softly. Silence.)*

GIL: Maybe we can spread her ashes in some other places. *(Silence.)* She always wanted to go to sing in a cabaret in Paris.

AUNT GLO: Then we'll spread some near that *(Butchers pronunciation.)* Champs Elysees.

*(Silence.)*

GIL: She would always say that she wanted to have a dress designed by Bob Mackie. Something Diahann Carroll would wear in Hollywood when I would be accepting my Oscar.

AUNT GLO: Then we'll spread some at the foot of that Golden Gate Bridge.

GIL: But that's in San...

AUNT GLO: We will spread some anywhere you'd like.

GIL: Anywhere we'd like.

AUNT GLO: I got a stack of money coming to me, GIL: I have my pension, IRA's, C.D.'s, money market, U.S. savings bonds and retirement funds. Maybe it's time to do something different. I could get used to this traveling.

GIL: For now, AUNT GLO: I would like to just sit. That's all. Sit. Give everyone a chance to catch their breath. Just sit.

*(Aunt Glo sits next to Gil and puts her hand in his. They just sit. That's all. Sit. Silence. Silence. Silence. Mo's phone rings. The ringtone is COMPLETELY inappropriate for this sensitive moment.)*

*Colman Domingo*

MO: Thank you Jesus! It's back on! A Bitch is back in business! Yaaaaasssss! Yaaaaasssss! *(Silences the phone.)* Oh, I am SO sorry. *(Mo readjusts to sit in silence. Silence. Suddenly, Terry pulls out Gil's Kenneth Cole shoe.)*

TERRY: Hey. GIL. I've been meaning to tell you. I found your shoe!

*(Gil smiles. His eyes well with tears. He is beginning to feel everything! Gil takes everyone in as if for the first time. Lights flicker like angels taking flight. We see a hologram of Adelaide on the balcony in the Cinderella ball gown spinning around with sparkles and glitter falling from the sky. As lights fade we hear the sound of pixie dust and the faint echoing sweet sound of Adelaide.)*

ADELAIDE: *(Voiceover.)*

Love is a song that never ends.

Love is a song that never ends.

Love is a song that never ends.

Love is a song that never ends.

*(The theatrical curtain slowly closes and we hear the Disneyesque ending music complete with the lettering THE END being written across the curtain.)*

*END OF PLAY*

# RIGHTS & PERMISSIONS